A Lifetime of Dissent

A Lifetime of Dissent

Corliss Lamont

A LIFETIME OF DISSENT. Copyright © 1988 by Corliss Lamont. All rights reserved. Printed in the United States of America. No part of this book may be reproduced in any manner whatsoever without written permission, except in the case of brief quotations embodied in critical articles and reviews. Inquiries should be addressed to Prometheus Books, 700 East Amherst Street, Buffalo, New York 14215.

91 90 89 88   4 3 2 1

Library of Congress Cataloging-in Publication Data

Lamont, Corliss, 1902–
   A lifetime of dissent.

   1. United States—Politics and government—1945–
2. Civil rights—United States. 3. United States—
Foreign relations—1946–   . 4. Humanism. 5. Lamont,
Corliss, 1902–   . I. Title.
E743.L37   1988   973.92   88-15100
ISBN 0-87975-463-X

Contents

Preface 7

1	Equivocation on Religious Issues (1934)	9
2	Are We Being Talked into War? (1952)	21
3	The Civil Liberties Crisis (1954)	33
4	The Humanist Tradition (1952)	53
5	Dangers of American Foreign Policy (1952)	59
6	Back to the Bill of Rights (1951)	73
7	The Myth of Soviet Aggression (1952)	85
8	Challenge to McCarthy (1954)	93
9	The Congressional Inquisition (1954)	107
10	The Assault on Academic Freedom (1955)	123
11	The Right to Travel (1957)	141
12	To End Nuclear Bomb Tests (*with Margaret I. Lamont*) (1958)	157
13	A Peace Program for the U.S.A. (1959)	181
14	My Trip Around the World (1960)	191
15	The Crime Against Cuba (1961)	211
16	My First Sixty Years (1962)	227
17	The Enduring Impact of George Santayana (1964)	251
18	The Tragedy of Vietnam: Where Do We Go from Here? *(by Helen B. Lamb)* (1964)	263
19	Vietnam: Corliss Lamont *vs.* Ambassador Lodge (1967)	287
20	The Meaning of Vietnam and Cambodia (*with Helen Lamb Lamont*) (1975)	303
21	Trip to Communist China: An Informal Report (1976)	319
22	Adventures in Civil Liberties (1977)	331
23	The Myth of Immortality (1979)	341
24	Militant Activist at 84 (1986)	357
25	The American People's Right to Know (1987)	373
26	Jesus as a Free Speech Victim (*by Clifford J. Durr*) (1987)	387
27	The Assurance of Free Choice (1987)	397

Preface

In the early 1930s I added to my general writing by occasionally publishing a brief pamphlet on some controversial issue. The best of these initial pamphlets was, I think, *Equivocation On Religious Issues* (1934). Hence I have placed this essay first in this volume as an appropriate introduction to the Basic Pamphlet Series, on which the book is primarily based.

I started with *Are We Being Talked Into War?* 36 years ago in 1952 and since that time have published a Basic Pamphlet every few years, making a total of 27. Two pamphlets I have merely edited. The series has covered many aspects of public affairs, with emphasis on civil liberties, Humanism, international relations and world peace.

My first wife, Margaret Irish Lamont, collaborated with me on *To End Nuclear Bomb Tests* (1958); while my second wife, Helen Lamb Lamont, wrote the best-selling *The Tragedy of Vietnam* (1964) and collaborated with me on *The Meaning of Vietnam and Cambodia* (1975).

I believe that the Basic Pamphlet Series, expressing in general a dissident viewpoint, has contributed to American understanding of fundamental issues in the fast-changing, violent and revolutionary world of the 20th century. I feel that I have carried on in the tradition of Tom Paine and the Haldeman-Julius pamphlets.

Corliss Lamont, 1988

1
Equivocation on Religious Issues
(1934)

Everyone knows Professor John Dewey's oft-quoted statement that, "Philosophy recovers itself when it ceases to be a device for dealing with the problems of philosophers and becomes a method cultivated by philosophers, for dealing with the problems of men." This statement has been interpreted and misinterpreted in various ways, and perhaps I may be forgiven for one more attempt to say what it means or ought to mean. Professor Dewey was thinking particularly of the artificial problems of epistemology which have received so much emphasis in modern philosophy. I do not think he meant that philosophers are unjustified in concerning themselves with certain highly technical and abstruse problems which are beyond the grasp of most men, but which have an important bearing on those wider problems which *do* confront most men. Hence the statement means for me, first, that those technical problems should be real and significant and, second, that philosophers have an obligation to go beyond those special problems, to show their bearing on the broader problems which face mankind, and to attempt solutions of these broader problems in terms which the average person can understand. This implies frankness and clarity of treatment, and a definite effort toward using non-technical terms.

Now, it is my firm conviction that among these broader problems those of religious belief still remain exceedingly important among men or at least among a sufficient number of men to make it the duty of philosophy to deal specifically with them. Most important of all among questions of religious belief I consider those of the existence of God and the existence of immortality. And by God I mean a personal God and by immortality

I mean personal immortality, survival of the individual after death. I do not claim that these two problems are important in the sense that they are constantly on men's minds; it is rather that until they are settled definitely one way or another they come back again to plague us. And philosophy is obligated to deal with them, not only because men in general need guidance, but also for its own philosophical sake. I do not see how any metaphysics can be considered complete or satisfactory that does not reach some conclusion on the problem of God; or how any ethics can be worked out without reference to the problem of immortality as well as to the problem of God. While it may be said that philosophy in the past has tended somewhat to overemphasize such problems, philosophy has certainly done right in concerning itself seriously with them. The real trouble has been that philosophy has tended to turn into a mere apology, open or disguised, for such leading religious conceptions as God and immortality.

It is the primary purpose of this essay to consider the attitude of contemporary thought and philosophy toward these two conceptions. It is possible to make a classification of four different groups. Firstly, there are those, still powerful in strength and number, who affirm the existence of God and immortality. Secondly, there is a lesser group which is sincerely agnostic on these questions. Thirdly, we have a steadily increasing class of persons who clearly and openly deny the existence of God and immortality. They frankly acknowledge their atheism, since that term most accurately describes their position. Then, fourthly, there is that rather large number who in various ways avoid the issue. The greater proportion of these do not actually believe in God or immortality in any ordinary sense of those terms. Most of them, I feel, belong by rights to the third group and ought to be supporting the group. It is this fourth and last class that I wish particularly to analyze. The first three divisions for the most part know what they think and say what they think about God and immortality. But I am tempted to believe that the members of the fourth division are somewhat muddled, and at least there can be no doubt that they muddle others.

The easiest and most frequent way of equivocating on the issue and qualifying for the fourth group is by indulging in the gentle art of redefinition. This procedure has recently assumed large proportions and is practiced by some of our best-known thinkers. Let us look first at a few representative redefinitions of the idea of God. We can do no better than to start with Professor Whitehead. "God," he says, "is not concrete, but He is the ground for concrete actuality. . . . He is the principle of concretion." Very apt is Mr. Walter Lippmann's comment on this to the effect that "a conception of God, which is incomprehensible to all who are not highly trained logicians, is a possible God for logicians alone." I might add, however, that there are even some highly trained logicians to whom Dr. Whitehead's God does not mean much. It is also interesting to note that, while Professor Whitehead has discarded a great many traditional philosophical terms and has invented a whole new vocabulary to escape misunderstanding, he has seen fit to confuse his readers with perhaps the most equivocal word of all, namely, God. Dr. Kirsopp Lake repudiates anthropomorphism, but retains a God who is the sum of all ideal values. He appeals to a tradition that reaches back at least as far as Origen and claims that it was this same redefinition of the word "God" which "made Christianity possible for the educated man of the third century." Professor Alexander asserts that "God as actually possessing deity does not exist, but is an ideal tending towards deity which does exist. . . . As an actual existent God is the infinite world with its nisus towards deity." "For any level of existence," he explains, "Deity is the next higher empirical quality."

Mr. Julian Huxley writes:

> I wish you here to agree to my giving the name of God to the sum of the forces acting in the cosmos as perceived and grasped by the human mind. We can therefore now say that God is one, but that though one, has several aspects.

A few years later Mr. Huxley gives a most enlightening comment on his own definition when he admits that, "God, in any but a purely philosophical, and, one is tempted to say, a Pickwickian sense, turns out to be a product of the human mind." Professor Durant Drake, becoming very Pickwickian indeed, tells us:

> I will say that in a very real sense I believe in God, both transcendent and immanent. God as transcendent is an essence, the ideal Good, bearing much the same relation to specific goods as philosophy does to the sciences. God as immanent is the Power which is visibly in the world making for righteousness and all Good. God is the universal self in each of us, our good will and idealism and intelligence which binds us together and drives us on by inner compulsion toward that ideal life for which in our better moments we strive.

Dr. Jesse H. Holmes describes God as that unifying element within which moves men to unity in a brotherly world. Dr. Henry Nelson Wieman, who produces a new definition of God every time he puts pen to paper, says—I select at random—"God is that interaction between individuals, groups, and ages which generates and promotes the greatest possible mutuality of good." Professor John H. Randall, Jr. writes in *Religion and the Modern World* that "There is no room for God save in the aspirations and imagination of men"; but later in the same book suggests that "We take the word 'God' as the symbol of man's supreme allegiance." Then "faith in God may mean faith in the possibility of sharing ever more fully this vision of the highest perfection." And faith in Divinity will be "the hope that men may see more clearly the ideal possibilities of human life, and, seeing, reweave the tangled fabric of their lives." In an article in the *Christian Century* Professor Randall defines God, in much the same way, as "the totality of that which has the power to evoke" the vision of "the idealized possibilities of value and associated human living." And he talks mystically of the divine as the "order of splendor."

It would be possible, of course, to go on citing indefinitely instances of a similar nature. I shall call a halt at this point, however, except to mention in passing the remarkable ideas of God current among some scientists, such as Eddington and Jeans, Millikan and Conklin. These men have set forth their views on many different occasions. Perhaps the best place in which to find out what they and their ilk are thinking about religion and God and immortality is a symposium called *Has Science Discovered God?* (New York, 1931). There you are able to find almost any kind of God you want, depending only on your predisposition to identify Him with electricity, love, spherical trigonometry, the quantum theory, or the music of the spheres.

I suppose that the first and fairest question to ask our redefiners is, What is the purpose and value of this complex and bewildering game? I imagine that their chief answer is that they do not wish to cut themselves off from the great and beautiful tradition that goes under the name of Christianity. The loss of intellectual precision that results from these many different conceptions of God is more than compensated, they think, by the preservation of a community of feeling. They wish to work within the tradition or within the church and win people over gradually to a new and more acceptable idea of God; to evolve a religion relevant to modern conditions while retaining the hallowed and well-loved words of old. All this would become impossible if they acknowledged themselves as atheists. Such an acknowledgment would turn the religious element against them in wrath, would wound the sensibilities of many worthy and pious citizens, and stir up bitter and fruitless controversy. There is the additional consideration that the term atheist has certain undesirable connotations apart from its primary meaning as simply a denial of theism. It has frequently been associated with enemies of society and narrow-minded dogmatists. Herein Professor Morris Cohen makes a pertinent comment. He says,

> I confess that I have never been able to understand any theism that was not anthropomorphic. . . . (But) . . . . I do not like to call myself an atheist, because those who apply that term to themselves seem as a rule singularly blind to the limitations of our knowledge and to the infinite possibilities beyond us.

The attitude of the redefinitionists perhaps comes most appropriately under the heading of what is sometimes called "strategy." Direct, frontal attacks on the old ideas do not, we are told, result in progress. They stiffen the defense mechanisms of the faithful and handicap the critic by making him appear a crank and a radical. In relation to the term atheism this argument is closely analogous to the one put forward by persons who admit privately that they are Socialists but who refuse to make public acknowledgment of this fact. They say that it would "destroy their usefulness" to be classed as Socialists. Some of them, akin to those who aim to reform the church from within, plan to win subtly the Republicans and Democrats to socialism, though always being careful to call it something else. What these strategists in the field of both religion and of politics seem to forget is that if they frankly stated their positions without mincing words, the weight of their names and their numbers would soon cancel the opprobrium attached to the terms which they fear to use. They could add honor and significance to these terms. Professor Cohen, for instance, who fears that atheism has the connotation of dogmatism, could show that this connection is not a necessary one. Since science itself today rests ultimately on probabilities, it would be in order for Professor Cohen to state that he is not absolutely certain of the non-existence of God, but that the probabilities of that non-existence seem so overwhelming that he must disbelieve in such a Being and classify himself as an atheist.

I am aware, of course, that the present is not the only time in which there have been redefinitions of God and other religious terms. But I venture to suggest that in the past also, especially during the periods of church terror and censorship, redefinition was often a matter of strategy and indeed outright fear. It enabled a man to keep his intellectual conscience without losing his physical head. Today, however, there is far less justification for what seems to me a kind of playing politics with God. In commenting on Dr. Lake, Mr. Walter Lippmann remarks "that the notion of adopting a policy about God somehow shocks" him "as intruding a rather worldly consideration which would seem to be wholly out of place." I wonder what God, if there turns out to be one after all, would think about these people who damn Him with faint praise. Would not He, too, be shocked? And I wonder if He would not be justified in punishing these redefiners for breaking the third commandment, that is, for taking His name in vain.

Let us turn now briefly to the matter of hurting people's feelings. Sir Arthur Keith, former president of the British Association for the Advancement of Science, presents what I have discovered to be a widespread state of mind. He writes,

> Deep in my heart I find a strange reluctance to set down my innermost beliefs concerning God, man, and the universe. My Presbyterian upbringing,

the fact that I am sixty-four, and have acquired some degree of worldly wisdom, may have something to do with it. The real explanation, however, lies deeper: it is fear—cowardice, if you will. . . . We cannot discuss our innermost beliefs openly and candidly without commiting an assault on persons whose comradeship we desire to retain. Hence most of us choose to be silent; wrangling is painful, and the paths of peace pleasant.

This presents to us a truly remarkable picture. Here is one of the most intelligent and eminent scientists of the age who, though he has made public acknowledgment of his unorthodox views on religion, confesses that he dreads to come out with his opinions because he will offend the ignorant. But why should not the ignorant blush for their ignorance rather than the learned blush for their learning? And as far as philosophy is concerned, is it not one of its prime functions to offend, to hurt, to upset, to pry and pull people loose from vain and fanciful opinions? The history of intellectual progress reveals nothing more clearly than that every new truth must deeply wound the feelings of those with vested emotional, ideological, or economic interests in outworn ideas. It is for this reason that, as Professor Cohen puts it, "the mission of philosophy is to bring a sword as well as peace."

My most serious objection, however, to the kind of redefinitions that we have considered is that they engender intellectual confusion and disingenuousness. In the first place, there is the probability that, no matter how clearly the definition may be set down, old meanings and associations will come crowding in upon such a blessed and hypnotic word as "God." Indeed, the fact that it does possess such deep emotional overtones is one of the reasons why men hate to drop the term even when its new meaning is as different from its old as black is from white. In science, it is true, a number of terms are continually being redefined, but hardly ones around which have been built up great religions and mass emotional response. In the second place, and more importantly, as Dr. Sidney Hook has put it, "The first duty a philosopher owes to the community is a sense for the ethics of words." I think that most of our redefiners violate this duty. I do not demand that they should define God exactly as I do. But surely a line must be drawn somewhere beyond which a word cannot legitimately be used. There ought to be a minimum definition of God. Perhaps we could set up as this minimum standard Matthew Arnold's "a power not ourselves that makes for righteousness,"—with power understood not merely as the magnetic quality of ideas and ideals, but as an active force working for the good totally independent of mankind. If this were done, practically all the redefinitions I have cited would have to be discarded and their makers classified as atheists, which is in fact what they are. I am fully aware that this suggestion would include, for example, Spinoza and his God and also the many persons, such as Albert Einstein, who have adopted

Spinoza's God as their own. But such a step would constitute a great gain for clarification and for truth. It would directly clarify in an ethical as well as in a religious and metaphysical sense. For if our highest aim is, for instance, to actualize on this earth the ideal possibilities of human life, then we shall make far more progress by stating our goal as exactly that than by mixing people up by calling it God.

The above remarks find an excellent illustration in the book, *Is There a God? A Conversation,* the contents of which were first published as a series of articles in the *Christian Century.* This book consists of a three-cornered debate among Douglas Clyde Macintosh, a theist, Max Carl Otto, an atheist, and Henry Nelson Wieman, whose status seems to be uncertain both to himself and everyone else. Dr. Wieman defines God alternatively as that which "generates and promotes the greatest mutuality of good," as "that which rightly demands the supreme devotion of all humans living," and as "a total system of patterns constituting supreme good and including the highest possibilities of glory and blessedness that may (or may not) ever visit this universe." Professor Macintosh and Professor Otto, the theist and the atheist, are finally forced in the interests of truth to take a stand together against the *hic-et-ubique* redefinitionist. What they say about Dr. Wieman is worth noting. Professor Otto sums up for both by stating that "an easy way to prove the existence of God to the satisfaction of everyone is to reduce the definition of the term until it means no more than everyone, even the confessed atheist, will have to admit. Thus the definition of God virtually proves his existence. . . . The word God is made to stand for so much that it loses all distinctive meaning." Professor Otto goes on to explain that,

> Belief bought at this price costs too much. It not only impoverishes the religious life . . . . but it tends to dissipate the mental discipline so laboriously and slowly achieved by men. . . . The one thing needful is not that we should find blanket terms under which we seem to agree, but that we should drag out our disagreement into the clearest possible light, and so find out what we are talking about. Not only our language, but our intelligence, suffers from preferring vague unity to distinct differentiation.

These comments apply with aptness to all the redefinitions and redefiners we have mentioned. And they apply particularly, we may add, to philosophers, one of whose acknowledged and most important aims is to achieve for themselves and others a precise and unequivocal terminology.

That Professor Macintosh should join with Professor Otto in trying to preserve the integrity of religious terminology indicates that too much redefinition is as obnoxious to a genuine theist as to a sincere atheist. The redefiners mutilate a time-hallowed and well-loved vocabulary, yet provide very little in return for this questionable procedure. For their God concepts have precious little religious value. Their gods cannot be worshipped or prayed to; they do not govern the universe or the earth, or watch over mankind; they do not do anything, nor do they possess personality or mind or consciousness. I cannot imagine any large group of men becoming emotionally aroused over such gods. And these gods are so distant in meaning from the traditional God of Christianity that I doubt whether a continuity that resides merely in the use of the same word is worth bothering about.

Redefinitions of "immortality" and "resurrection" take place with the same purpose and the same result. It is often difficult to tell whether a believer in immortality means survival of the personality after death, the attainment here and now of a certain "eternal" quality of life and thought, the permanence of every man's influence, the biological transference of the germ-plasm from generation to generation, or the indestructibility of the material particles of the human body. This matter is particularly confusing because almost everyone would admit the existence of the three last named types of immortality. The real issue is and always has been whether there is personal immortality, that is, a life beyond the grave for the individual human consciousness with its memory and awareness of self-identity essentially intact. But this issue is only too frequently avoided, slurred over, or lost in vague generalities. Clarification here would seem very definitely to demand that types of immortality other than that of personal survival be acknowledged as secondary and be described with a proper qualifying adjective, such as "influential," "biological," "material," and so forth.

Sophisticated moderns are prone to take the attitude that it is a waste of time, and even vulgar, to pay serious attention to the question of a future life. And they are likely to quote from Spinoza that, "A free man thinks of nothing less than of death, and his wisdom is not a meditation upon death but upon life." But Spinoza, be it remembered, had already concluded that there was no personal immortality. For him the most significant problem connected with death was settled. It was comparatively easy for him, therefore, to lean back in his chair with the satisfying consciousness that he was a free man. And it seems probable that most of those who cite him as above have already made up their minds concerning this same issue. For them further inquiry may indeed seem useless. If they and Spinoza are free men in the sense of the lines quoted, it is because they have finally come to understand the meaning and place of death. The necessary prelude to such understanding, however, must be for everyone long and careful reflection. And however emancipated a twentieth-century philosopher may himself be, it is yet his duty to provide guidance and enlightenment on the matter of immortality, which today as in the past constitutes perhaps the most vital of all religious problems to most men.

I might mention in passing that the current redefinitions of religion seem to me especially pernicious and befuddling, since they bring under the heading of religion such very different and in some cases positively irreligious phenomena as nationalism, communism, and even atheism. Some of these redefinitions would by implication assign the name of religion to any socially organized enterprise that succeeds in winning the devotion and emotions of men. On this basis football, trade unions, and poetry societies are all forms of religion. Here again, if we are to maintain sanity, a minimum definition is necessary. And I would suggest that it is illegitimate to call any human activity a religion unless there is involved in it at some point or other appeal to, reliance on, or faith in supernatural elements, powers, or states of being. Incidentally, the widespread redefinitions of religion, as of God and immortality, indicate clearly to me the growing weakness of Christianity, especially Protestant Christianity, with its apologists everywhere trying desperately to hold the allegiance of intelligent men by the most far-fetched interpretations of traditional ideas.

Redefinition is not the only way of avoiding the issues of God and immortality. The position may be taken that those issues are unimportant or irrelevant. In an article in the *Journal of Philosophy* entitled "Religion and the Philosophical Imagination," Professor Irwin Edman writes as follows:

> The business of an emancipated philosopher, emancipated, that is, from literalness in both religion and philosophy, would appear to be something different from arguing a case for or against what religion says, and saying rather what it is or does. . . . Philosophy must cease to treat as formulas what is really a high and consequential form of art. It must cease to criticize on the ground of truth and falsity what is rather estimable and appreciable as a metaphor. . . . It would display a singularly illiberal lack of understanding to condemn religious doctrine for literal falsity. . . . The error of religion and of critics of religion has been to estimate ideal constructions by criteria of facts. In other words to take metaphors as dogmas.

I gather that Professor Edman would consider my approach to religion as old-fashioned and behind the times by reason of my laying too much stress on intellect and ideology and too little on emotion and imagination. He would feel that I have forgotten the heart of man with its ineradicable needs and yearnings and convictions, that I have neglected the happy poetic process, to quote him again, "by which that heart has fulfilled those of its longings which nature or current society denied."

On the contrary, I am only too well aware of those longings; but well aware also that the heart has frequently fulfilled them in ways most fanciful, dangerous, and defeatistic. Hearts and emotions do not function *in vacuo;* they associate their expressions with definite beliefs. While it is true that religion is much more than a system of beliefs it is also true that a definite set of beliefs is necessary to any religion. This is true even of the new religion that Mr. Edman hopes will develop. It would be pleasant, very pleasant indeed, if all religious persons today adopted the attitude of Mr. Edman, Mr. Santayana, and their school that traditional concepts of God and immortality are to be taken as metaphors and poetry rather than as truth. But the fact is, whether we consider the past or the present of religion, that unless what Mr. Edman calls poetic symbols are taken quite literally by the great masses of men, those symbols have little real and moving efficacy. Herein lies a dilemma: the Gods are believable only. as myths, but as myths they are no longer Gods.

I grant that it is both legitimate and fruitful to interpret religion as poetry on the grand scale, providing that interpretation is not made central or exclusive. I am not therefore taking religious ideas simply in a literal sense. What I am taking literally is the literalness of the belief in those ideas. Sheer evidence compels me to do that. In dealing with the literal-minded we must for the nonce be literal-minded ourselves. The only way to win Fundamentalists, for example, to Mr. Edman's own theory of religion is to show that their age-old doctrines are false and absurd in fact. And the only way to do that is to demonstrate to them specifically why their ideas of God, immortality, and so on are unreasonable. Not otherwise will they ever attach their hearts to the new symbols or to the new meanings of the old symbols belonging to the new religion about which Professor Edman talks.

In another and later essay, "Poetic Insight and Religious Truth," Mr. Edman acknowledges that, "The effectiveness of religion to the believer rather than the student has lain not in its poetic appositeness and beauty but in its literal truth." He neglects to state, however, that this is still the case in the world today for the vast majority of both Christians and non-Christians. He still seems to expect that a modern religion deserving and receiving the allegiance of modern men can be constructed on the basis of the same old symbols and formulae purged of their intellectual absurdities and moral crudities through the blessed art of redefinition. And he still thinks that it is far more important and appropriate for a truly emancipated mind to analyze the moral and poetic significance of religious beliefs than to show that all emancipated minds must deny the pretensions of these beliefs to truth.

My own conception of the function of philosophy in this field is somewhat different. I think that its first duty is to point out the falsity of outworn religious ideas, however estimable they may be as metaphor. As a matter of fact, there is no reason why philosophy should not demonstrate the falsity to those who need enlightenment, and the metaphor to those few sophisticates who can appreciate it. These two approaches are not inconsistent and they are both necessary. We cannot act as if all religion were poetry while the greater part of it is still functioning in its traditional guise of illicit science and backward morals; we cannot act as if all religion were metaphor when the most powerful sections of it are still teaching the metaphor as dogma; we cannot nonchalantly assume that supernaturalism is a dead issue when it is still one of the predominant influences in this country and throughout the world.

Another way of treating these issues as unimportant and irrelevant is to say that, after all, intellectual analysis is not a very effective method in any case. What will undermine and is undermining traditional religion, we are told, is the "intrusion of more and more secular interests upon the mind and time of man. The unknown and presumably devout Dutchman who invented golf at the close of the Middle Ages, pious Henry Ford, who made motoring cheap and popular, the reverent Gutenberg whose printing created the Sunday newspaper, and Lee DeForest who made possible the radio—these men have been more effective and deadly in their contribution to the destruction of supernatural religion" than all the Lucretiuses, Huxleys, and Ingersolls since the beginning of history. I am willing to grant a certain amount of truth to this argument; but even so, it does not relieve philosophers from the obligation, in those spheres where they are influential, of taking a clear and determined stand on issues of religious belief.

In his little book on religion, *A Common Faith* (1934), Professor John Dewey starts out by showing that intelligence must reject all supernaturalist interpretations of the origin, control and destiny of the universe and man. But in the second chapter he introduces considerable confusion by suggesting his own definition of God. He states:

> We are in the presence neither of ideals that are completely embodied in existence nor yet of ideals that are mere rootless ideals, fantasies, utopias. There are forces in nature that generate and support the ideals. They are further unified by the action that gives them the coherence and solidarity. It is this *active* relation between ideal and actual to which I would give the name *God*. And would not insist that the name *must* be given.

Dr. Dewey then adds: "There are those who hold that the associations of the term with the supernatural are so numerous and close that any use of the word *God* is sure to give rise to misconception and be taken as a concession to traditional ideas."

Dewey's qualms were abundantly justified. No sooner had *A Common Faith* been published than a flood of misconceptions and misinterpretations swept philosophic and religious circles. Each reviser and commentator gave his own opinion of what Dewey meant by the word God, and naturally there was widespread disagreement. Ministers and theologians tended to welcome Dewey as a new convert to theism and the well-known religious journal, *The Christian Century*, ran a whole symposium entitled, "Is John Dewey a Theist?"

Finally, in May 1935 I initiated a correspondence with Dr. Dewey that revealed more explicitly the significance of his redefinition. On August 16 he wrote me: ". . . The meaning in my mind was essentially: if the word *God* is used, this is what it *should* stand for; I didn't have a recommendation in mind beyond the proper use of the word."

Regarding the subject matter of this essay, I expect that equivocation on religious issues, which has gone on for many centuries, will in all probability continue unabated into the future. This is in the nature of philosophy, of religion and of the basic conflict between clarity and confusion, between truth and illusion.

2
Are We Being Talked into War?
(1952)

1

The American people as a whole today, as throughout the history of this nation, are fundamentally in favor of international peace. Yet there is in our midst a rash and blustering minority that month after month and year after year gives voice, especially in American newspapers and magazines, to aggressive, provocative and well-publicized war talk. As a teacher of philosophy and a worker for world peace, I have become increasingly concerned over this constant sabre-rattling, which is of course directed primarily against the Soviet Union. To show for the record how dangerous this propaganda is, I think it may be worthwhile to summarize some of the more drastic proposals printed in the press for bombing the Soviet Republic from border to border, slaughtering its population by the millions and laying waste its economy.

The journalistic peak of incitements to war against Soviet Russia occurred, in my opinion, with *Collier's* special edition of October 27, 1951, entitled: "Russia's Defeat and Occupation, 1952-1960, Preview of the War We Do Not Want." The editors of *Collier's* devoted this entire issue, including profuse and lurid illustrations, to a melodramatic account of a third world war. They printed and sold 500,000 extra copies.

In a foreword *Collier's* stated: "Our over-all conception of this issue was confirmed in study and consultation with top political, military and economic thinkers—including high-level Washington officials and foreign-affairs experts, both here and abroad." This gave the number a quasi-official standing which was certain to be noted in diplomatic circles throughout the globe. A United States Senator, Margaret Chase Smith of Maine, was one of the twenty-one prominent individuals who wrote a special article for the edition. Others who in like manner contributed to this remarkable enterprise were Hanson W. Baldwin of *The New York Times;* Stuart Chase, economist; Allan Nevins, Professor of History at Columbia University; Walter Reuther, president of the United Automobile Workers of America; Robert Sherwood, dramatist; and Walter Winchell, newspaper columnist and radio commentator.

According to the *Collier's* fantasy, the Soviet Government initiated the Third World War in May, 1952, by sending to Belgrade two secret agents to assassinate Marshal Tito (the attempt failed); and then ordering the Albanian, Bulgarian, Hungarian and Rumanian armies, backed by fifteen Soviet divisions, to attack Yugoslavia. But as I read through the various articles by big-name writers, all suddenly become "experts" on the U.S.S.R., the issue took on more and more the aspect of a streamlined psychological scheme for justifying war against Soviet Russia. And there can be no question that it provided a carefully worked out blueprint for the conquest of the Soviets. Even the bitterly anti-Soviet *New Leader* stated: "While *Collier's* editorially disclaims the theory of preventive war, its special number can be construed, not inaccurately, as a plea for preventive war."

The cover of this edition had a map showing U.N. and U.S. forces in occupation of Moscow, the whole of the Ukraine and all the so-called satellites. And the contents tried to allay the American people's natural apprehension over a war with Soviet Russia by picturing the defeat of the Communists as "inevitable." In *Collier's* simple victory program, the American-led coalition knocked out the Russians in three and a half years, with Communist China conveniently deserting the Soviet Union after a little more than a year of conflict and with the Soviet people opportunely rising in revolt against Stalin at the right moment. According to the piece by Marguerite Higgins of the *New York Herald Tribune,* the U.S.S.R. lost 32,000,000 dead during the war.

Russians who saw the *Collier's* preview of World War III must have been simply appalled. We can sense their reaction by imagining our own feelings if a prominent Soviet magazine gave over a whole issue to describing Soviet Russia's conquest of the United States, occupation of its key regions and the sovietization of its economy. In fact, a French magazine, *L'Observateur* satirized *Collier's* idea by precisely reversing it, printing a cover with a Russian soldier standing guard over America and the red flag flying over the city of Washington. The effect of the *Collier's* coup was far-reaching in Western Europe. Asserted Alexander Werth in *The Nation:* "*Collier's* has managed not only to make the United States odious in the eyes of millions of Europeans—as years of Communist propaganda have not done—but also to make it rather ridiculous."

During the very same week of *Collier's* sensational issue, *The Saturday Evening Post* published an article by a retired British general, J. F. C. Fuller, calling for the immediate adoption by the Western Powers of a plan completely and permanently to dismember the U.S.S.R. "This means," General Fuller said, "that the Soviet Empire must be dealt with as was the Turkish—that is, split up into its component parts, each part becoming an independent country." In this mad scheme the General would have the Western Powers cooperate with an organization known as the Anti-Bolshevik Block of Nations, the A.B.N. *The New Leader* describes this organization of reactionary emigrés as a "fascist band of separatist sects."

2

Such open incitements against the Soviet Union have been going on for years; they predated the post-war tensions between the United States and Soviet Russia and were widespread long before the Second World War ended. They had, in truth, already reached a danger point shortly after the great Soviet victory at Stalingrad in February, 1943, when the diehard anti-Soviet elements in America and Europe became horrified at Soviet socialism's immense strength and commenced to refurbish the thesis that Russia was the real enemy. At that time the notion of a war with the Soviets was so much discussed that Maurice Hindus, in his *Mother Russia* published in the spring of 1943, felt obliged to include a whole chapter called, "Will We Have To Fight Russia?" Mr. Hindus, a well-known writer on the U.S.S.R., answered in the negative.

In September of 1944, almost a year before the final triumph over the Axis Powers, William C. Bullitt, embittered ex-Ambassador to Soviet Russia and France, played up the idea of a third world war in an article in *Life* entitled "The World from Rome." According to Mr. Bullitt, Western civilization was being threatened "by hordes of invaders from the East." Talking about what he claimed was the prevailing viewpoint of the Italians, he wrote: "A sad joke going the rounds in Rome gives the spirit of their hope: What is an optimist? A man who believes that the Third World War will begin in about fifteen years between the Soviet Union and Western Europe, backed by Great Britain and the U.S. What is a pessimist? A man who believes that Western Europe, Great Britain and the U.S. will not dare to fight."

In 1945, subsequent to President Roosevelt's death and the surrender of the Nazis, the American Government became so concerned over the rising tide of war talk against the U.S.S.R. that it took specific action. Thus on May 28, 1945, over a nation-wide broadcast sponsored officially by the U.S. State Department, Archibald MacLeish, then Assistant Secretary of State, lashed out at the suggestions of an inevitable Armageddon between the United States and Soviet Russia: "There is no necessary reason in the logic of geography, or in the logic of economics, or in the logic of national objectives, why the U.S.A. and the Soviet Union ever should find themselves in conflict with each other, let alone in the kind of conflict reckless and irresponsible men have begun now to suggest."

In 1947 Paul H. Griffith, National Commander of the American Legion, and later Assistant Secretary of Defense, urged President Truman to order an atomic bomb dropped "some place over there" in order to demonstrate American support of "the people of the world who wanted to remain free." Mr. Griffith himself revealed this fact in a radio interview at Washington, D.C., on June 6, 1950. Reported *The New York Times,* "Presumably Mr. Griffith meant that a bomb be dropped on the Soviet Union, but this could not be confirmed. . . . Mr. Griffith declined to comment on the meaning of 'some place.' " However, Mr. Griffith's coyness ought not to deceive anybody as to what country he had in mind.

Also in 1947 George H. Earle, Democratic ex-Governor of Pennsylvania and former American Minister to Bulgaria and Austria, advocated on the radio an attack on the Soviet Union as soon as possible and without a formal declaration of war. "One nice little bomb dropped on the Kremlin," Earle boasted, "and the Russian people of 165,000,000 would fly to pieces with centrifugal force." Previously Earle had ranted against the Russians over the Town Meeting of the Air and had demolished the straw-man of a Soviet atom-bomb assault on the United States with the violent assertion: "We can and will wipe out every city, town and village in Russia."

During 1948 there took place a mounting crescendo of American war incitements against the Soviet Union. In February, in a letter to *The New York Times,* Mr. Maxwell Anderson, the dramatist, lamented the fact that Russia "tries to give us no provocation that might lead to war" and demanded that the United States force "a showdown of military strength with Russia before Russia's military strength has caught up with ours." Speaking with incredible recklessness, Mr. Anderson concluded: "I don't know how to bring on a crisis, but there are professional diplomats who might know how if our nation were sufficiently aware and had the will to do it."

In March former Major General Claire Chennault of the U.S. Air Force told the House Foreign Affairs Committee, as *P.M.* correspondent Alexander H. Uhl reported it, "that air bases in Western China were superior to those in North Africa for bombing the industrialized areas of Russia in the Ural Mountains. The whole Committee watched with fascination as he pointed out the 'target objectives,' as he called them, on an illuminated globe."

In May *Newsweek* ran a featured article discussing a recent speech by General George C. Kenney, Commander of the U.S. Strategic Air Command. The General, starting with the pretense that the Soviets might soon assault the United States, outlined plans to carry death and destruction by means of air power to the very vitals of the Soviet Republic. Expanding on the implications of this thesis, *Newsweek* explained that "American strategy called for securing bases around the perimeter of Russia and then striking back from the air. . . ." Planes loaded with atom bombs "would go out from England in very small groups—perhaps in twos and threes. Flying at more than 35,000 feet they would seek to slip into Russia unnoticed. Their targets: first, Moscow—Moscow above all. Then the other large cities of European Russia—Kiev, Leningrad, Kharkov, Odessa. . . . American strategists are thinking . . . in terms of closing the circle of air bases around Russia, making it smaller and smaller, tighter and tighter, until the Russians are throttled. This means getting bases through combined air, sea and ground operations ever closer to Russia's heartland, then using the bases for sustained bombing and guided-missile attacks."

On June 9, 1948, the Soviet Government vigorously protested to the American Government against the *Newsweek* article, stating that it violated a United Nations resolution against war propaganda. This resolution in part reads: "The General Assembly condemns all forms of propaganda in whatever country conducted, which is either designed or likely to provoke or encourage any threat to the peace, breach of the peace or act of aggression." The American Government took no action regarding the Soviet protest.

In its issue of Sunday, May 30, 1948, *The New York Times Magazine* published "What Air Power Can—and Cannot—Do," by Hanson W. Baldwin, well-known military expert of the *Times*. Mr. Baldwin, who is one of America's more moderate commentators, discussed frankly some of the chief difficulties in the way of successfully bombing Soviet Russia from the air and thought that ordinary strafing in the daytime would be too dangerous for American planes. "Night bombing," he asserted, "or bombing from high above the clouds would, therefore, be preferable." Yet, added Mr. Baldwin, "and this is perhaps the greatest disadvantage the offense would suffer in bombing attacks upon Russia, we have no really satisfactory maps of most of the Russian interior." It was this article to which Andrei Vishinsky, then a Deputy Foreign Minister of the Soviet Union, called attention in an address before the United Nations Assembly at Paris on September 25, 1948, as an instance of the open instigation "of war against the U.S.S.R. and the new democracies."

Not to be outdone, *Look* magazine, on June 22, the precise anniversary of the Nazi invasion of Soviet Russia, ran as its lead article, "Air Force Plans for Bombing Russia," as the title was announced on the front cover. The author, Ben Kocivar, declared that he had "recently talked about the problem with a number of top Air Force and Navy officials," one of whom at least favored a so-called preventive war against the Soviet Union. The *Look* analysis pointed out that "the only long-range planes we have in operation ready to go are our World War II B-29s with an operating radius of some 2,000 miles. 'Draw a couple of thousand-mile circles around the industrial heart of Russia,' a general told me [Mr. Kocivar] 'and you will see why we must have operating bases outside this country.' The two-thousand-mile ring, as the map shows, borders Greenland, Iceland, England, France, Italy, Greece, Egypt, Saudi Arabia and India. We need these bases not only for offensive operations, but to prevent the Russians from using them against us."

In August, Henry Luce's *Life,* taking up the refrain, printed a detailed description by General Carl Spaatz, retired Chief of Staff of the U.S. Air Force, on how the United States could bomb the Soviet Union into submission. General Spaatz said that "air bases have the same significance that naval bases had in the last century" and that, comparable to the British Empire in its heyday, America must at once secure a global framework of bases for the development of air power. "Space is no longer an effective shield," asserted the General. "Now an attacker would not have to plod laboriously and bloodily along the Minsk-Smolensk-Moscow road to strike at the Russian vitals. The air offers a direct, operationally feasible route for a determined attacker to knock out the industries that it has cost the Russians so much to create."

In September *The Saturday Evening Post,* determined to keep up with its rivals, made its own blood-curdling contribution to the master plan of smashing the U.S.S.R. In an article entitled "If War Comes—," Joseph and Stewart Alsop, using the well-worn pretext of a Soviet attack on America, predicted: "From Baku north to Leningrad, from Smolensk east to Novosibirsk, the vitals of the Soviet state will be scorched and destroyed with the terrible fire of the atomic bomb." Then the authors listed the many places where the United States must have air bases, beyond its own borders, in Europe, the Near East and the Far East.

For 1949 I find in my files a clipping from *The New York World-Telegram* of March 14, with the dateline of Washington, D.C., and reading as follows: "About seventy strategic targets in Russia have been marked by military planners as possible objectives for attack in event of a war, it was learned today. The Air Force has given the Joint Chiefs of Staff documented assurances that the B-36 superbomber could strike every one of these, flying out of bases on this continent and returning without refueling. The targets have been marked off on top-secret maps at the national defense establishment. Reliable military authorities said they include major Soviet industrial centers. All would be within a 4,000-mile radius of air bases in Alaska and Labrador."

In August, 1950, Francis P. Matthews, Secretary of the Navy, told an audience in Boston that the United States should be willing to pay "even the price of instituting a war to compel cooperation for peace." This recommendation of a preventive war against the Soviet Union caused such a scandal in official circles that the next day the U.S. State Department issued a special statement: "Secretary Matthews' speech was not cleared with the Department of State and his views do not represent United States policy. The United States does not favor instituting a war of any kind." President Truman, however, permitted Mr. Matthews to continue as Secretary of the Navy.

In March, 1951, Lieutenant General Norstad, Commander of the United States Air Force in Europe, declared at Frankfurt, Germany: "There is no target in the Soviet Union that cannot be attacked by United States bombers." In April Charles E. Wilson, Director of Defense Mobilization, said at Washington that if Stalin "could see the new bombs, which are far more devastating than anything we knew in the last war, he'd realize that these new bombs will make fine 'calling cards' from the United States for Russia." Mr. Wilson added the usual disclaimer: "I hope we never use these bombs—that we never have to—but it is comforting to know that they will be on hand if needed."

In May *Look,* one of the most persistent offenders in outlining sensational attacks on the Soviet Union, published an article called "Can Our A-Bombers Get Through?", with a map showing the chief centers to be bombed in the U.S.S.R. and their exact distance from American air bases. Reported *Look:* "We have ringed Russia with a multitude of airfields, scores of them. Even if by some military miracle all these bases in Germany, England, Spain and North Africa should be denied to us, the U.S. Air Force still could deliver the A-bomb on Russia from air bases in the continental United States. . . . Ten planes, B-50s and B-36s, would cross the frontiers of Russia at approximately the same time from ten different directions. Each would be carrying an atomic bomb, and each would have a target or choice of targets. From the Air Force point of view it would be ideal if the weather were extremely murky. . . . Attacking planes would be scheduled over targets at night. They would bomb by radar sighting, which is reasonably accurate." There can be no doubt about it—*Look* has the plans worked out in meticulous detail.

In November, 1951, Senator J. Allen Frear, Jr., a Delaware Democrat, declared that the United States should drop an A-bomb on the Kremlin. The Senator said: "The one place to use the atomic bomb is at the source of the Korean war. That source is the Soviet. I think the Soviet has given us provocation." The Very Reverend J. Brooke Mosley, Dean of the Cathedral Church of St. John in Wilmington, promptly sent to Senator Frear a telegram of protest, reading: "This is suggesting that we immediately destroy 100,000 civilian men, women and children in an act of murderous aggression. I believe that such an amazing recommendation should be labeled for what it plainly is: A morally irresponsible, vicious and bloody suggestion, unworthy of this country and certainly unworthy of Christian people."

Morally on the same plane as American threats of war against the U.S.S.R. have been the various suggestions made in the United States to assassinate Premier Joseph Stalin. The worst example I have seen of this outright incitement to murder appeared in *The American Magazine* of February, 1951, under the title "Why Doesn't Somebody Kill Stalin?" The article was featured on the cover. Its author was Ellsworth Raymond, who served for six years as a political analyst and translator for the American Embassy in Moscow and who during World War II was stationed in Washington as Chief of the U.S.S.R. Economic Section, Military Intelligence, U.S. Army General Staff.

Mr. Raymond started his article as follows: "'Wouldn't it be a wonderful thing if somebody killed Stalin?' This is a question I've heard over and over since the cold war turned hot. Many people today blame the world's troubles on this one man, who has held Russia in his iron grip for twenty-five years. They believe his death would bring peace to mankind." The author goes on to show that unfortunately Stalin is very well protected against assassins and outlines the many precautions the Soviet leader has taken. In the middle of the piece there is a picture of Premier Stalin with the reproduction of a target and its concentric circles superimposed over his face. the obvious intent is to suggest that someone should shoot for the bull's-eye.

In August, 1951, the publishing house of Farrar, Straus and Young brought out a new novel by Sterling Noel called *I Killed Stalin.* The story is told in the first person and the advertisements played up the quotation: "The date was 1959 when the most dangerous manhunt in the world was ended." This registers the fact that the "hero" of the book finally tracked down Stalin and shot him to death. Once again to reverse the situation, imagine the reaction of Americans in every walk of life if a leading Soviet magazine ran an article called "Why Doesn't Somebody Kill Truman?" and a Soviet publisher followed this up a few months later by issuing a book with the title *I Killed Truman!*

3

We must not blink the fact that terrorism in foreign lands is a method that now definitely figures in the minds of American officials. In September, 1951, the American Congress passed a Mutual Security Act, signed by President Truman, which sets aside the handsome total of $100,000,000 to finance the activities of "selected persons who are residing in or escapees" from Soviet Russia or any of the countries allied with it. An amendment incorporated in the new law reads that this sum is to be used "either to form such persons into elements of the military forces supporting the North Atlantic Treaty Organization or for other purposes." It is the vague clause "for other purposes" which carries the most sinister connotation.

In October, 1951, Congressman Charles J. Kersten, Wisconsin Republican and sponsor of the amendment in question, publicly protested that a new United Nations code under consideration would conflict with the American legislation. He was referring to Section 5 of "Offenses against the Peace and Security of Mankind," prepared by the U.N. International Law Commission. This section outlaws "the undertaking or encouragement by the authorities of a state, of terrorist activities in another state, or the toleration by the authorities of a state, of organized activities calculated to carry out terrorist acts in another state."

In a letter to Warren R. Austin, chief United States delegate to the United Nations, Mr. Kersten said that the enactment of the proposed U.N. code "might prevent groups in this country, as well as our Government, from assisting in the liberation of the peoples of Eastern European countries and other countries enslaved by the Communist tyranny." He added that "one of the main objectives of a real liberation movement is to strike terror into the hearts of the Communist tyrants. . . . Liberation will not be achieved merely by propaganda and parliamentary maneuvers." Mr. Austin replied to the frank and undiplomatic Representative from Wisconsin that "the attempt to restore a people's freedom does not seem to merit the characterization of 'terrorist.' "

The Soviet Government, however, felt that Mr. Kersten knew what his amendment was meant to accomplish better than Mr. Austin; and in November, 1951, protested officially to the U.S. Government that the Mutual Security Act violated the Roosevelt-Litvinov agreements made in 1933 at the time of American recognition of the Soviet Union. The Soviet note charged that the Act "constitutes crass intervention of the United States in the internal affairs of other countries. At the same time it represents unparalleled violation of the standards of international law and is incompatible with the normal relations between countries and respect for state sovereignty. The adoption of such a law cannot be regarded as other than an aggressive act aimed at further complicating relations between the United States and the Soviet Union. . . . The law envisages financing persons and armed groups in the territory of the Soviet Union and a number of other states for carrying out subversive activity and sabotage within the above states." We must grant that the Soviet Government presents a very strong case.

This matter of the Mutual Security Act ties in closely with the general war propaganda against Soviet Russia and the whole hysterical atmosphere prevailing in America. The United States Government has done little to discourage this state of mind. President Truman could have vetoed the Mutual Security Act; and from 1948 to 1952 he or his Cabinet officers could have administered some effective rebuke to the American *provocateurs* of war. Instead, a high Government official, the Secretary of the Navy, joined, as we have seen, in the hate-Russia, hit-Russia chorus. In fact, it must be admitted that the war incitements aid and abet the Truman-Acheson foreign policy by conditioning the people of the United States to the idea of American-Soviet hostilities and by creating a psychology favorable to colossal armaments.

4

In this pamphlet I have included only the highlights in provocative statements carried by the American press calling for or describing war with or subjugation of the Soviet Union. Because I listen to the radio so infrequently, I have undoubtedly missed many similar utterances over the air which were not reproduced in the newspapers. And in any case I do not pretend that my coverage of the press has been thorough. But the quotations I have given, a number of them from officials or ex-officials of the U.S. Government or armed forces, are representative of an influential group in the United States. Although this group is a minority one at present, it is conceivable that a swing in the political pendulum could bring it into power.

Here we have one set of reasons why the Soviet leaders and the Soviet people harbor some doubts as to the peaceful intentions of America. They naturally wonder, having been the victims of ruinous aggression during the First and Second World Wars, whether the enemies of the U.S.S.R. are going to make a third attempt to put an end to the first socialist commonwealth. Nor is it only people in Soviet Russia or other Communist lands who are apprehensive about where the United States is heading. Mr. Frank Owen, editor of the conservative *London Daily Mail,* recently remarked that American war hysteria was "not only terrific but terrifying." A leading Republican, John Cowles, President of *The Minneapolis Star and Tribune,* wrote in *Look* in October, 1951: "Many highly intelligent Europeans and Asians, individuals who loathe Russian totalitarianism and believe completely in the democratic ideal, fear that through ineptness the United States is going to blunder into war with Russia, or that we will become so provoked at Russia's exasperating conduct that we will ourselves precipitate war."

Actions are of course more important than words. Yet in the tense situation that has developed since the Second World War, widely publicized statements that threaten the Soviets with armed violence, bombing, military conquest and dismemberment can hardly be said to help the cause of international peace. Such fulminations, furthermore, can be interpreted as a conscious effort to counteract the American people's traditional longing for peace. Yet some of those who indulge in this bombastic talk evidently do not themselves realize fully the implications of what they are saying. And their attitude is typical of the immaturity which many keen observers see as a widespread trait of American political life.

While Soviet writers, speakers and government officials currently use harsh and vituperative language only too often in reference to foreign countries, their public pronouncements do not threaten war, aggression or any incendiary act on the part of the Soviet armed forces. There is to be found in the Soviet press not a single statement by anyone concerning war that is comparable to the shocking, clenched-fist abuse which pours forth year after year from the United States. The fundamental attitude of the Russians is well represented, I venture to suggest, in the Act passed by the Supreme Soviet in 1951 outlawing war propaganda throughout the U.S.S.R. and imposing penalties of up to twenty-five years in jail for violation of this new law.

As for America, I believe it is time for our people, through the power of public opinion, to deal more seriously with the reckless war cries which continue in this country and which constitute an offense against both reason and public morality. It would be the height of folly to let ourselves be talked or shouted into war. Eternal vigilance is not only the price of freedom, but also a necessity for peace.

3
The Civil Liberties Crisis
(1954)

America's Bill of Rights, the greatest state document on civil liberties in the history of mankind, is today being violated in so many different and far-reaching ways that it is in effect being repealed. The present threat to constitutional freedom is much worse than that following the First World War. In fact, never before in the history of this country have American liberties been curtailed or negated on so wide a scale. No American dissenter in any field can speak out against prevailing orthodoxies or join the organizations of his choice without running the risk of having his constitutional rights abridged, his public reputation damaged, his livelihood threatened or his freedom suspended through a jail sentence.

This civil liberties crisis is all the more serious and difficult to cope with because the greater part of the drive against freedom is carried on under the guise of legality. Thus the Federal Government is disregarding the Bill of Rights in unprecedented administrative orders and rulings; Congress has recently passed bill after bill clearly violative of the Constitution; Congressional committees utilize their official power to ride roughshod over the constitutional liberties of witnesses; and private business enterprises everywhere use their legal right to hire and fire as a means of discriminating against unorthodox or controversial individuals.

I find that I cannot adequately review the current civil liberties situation in the United States without referring to at least 25 points. They are as follows:

1. *Congressional inquiries.* During the past two decades and especially since the Second World War, House and Senate committees of investigation

have gone far beyond their legitimate scope of gathering facts pertinent to legislation. They have disregarded numerous constitutional guaranties by questioning witnesses about their personal beliefs and political associations. And they have transformed their hearings into actual "trials," thus usurping the functions of the Judiciary and violating the three-way separation of powers in the American Constitution, whereby the Executive, Judicial and Legislative branches of the Government are all assigned definite responsibilities. These committees, surreptitiously fed names by the Federal Bureau of Investigation, constantly by-pass the law in arrogating to themselves the triple role of, in effect, prosecuting, finding guilty and punishing victims who have committed no illegal acts but whose opinions or associations are deemed dangerous. The four worst committees have set up a veritable Congressional Inquisitions.

(1) Oldest of these is the House Committee on Un-American Activities, of which Representative Harold H. Velde, Republican, of Illinois, is at present chairman. It was founded in 1938 and early set the pattern for hounding liberals, radicals and dissenters in general. The resolution establishing the Un-American Committee directs it to investigate "subversive and un-American propaganda" and is, therefore, unconstitutional on its face. For "propaganda" means precisely the diffusion of certain ideas; and for Congress to inquire into ideas of any variety, as distinct from activities, is a violation of the First Amendment guaranty of freedom of speech. Yet the Un-American Committee has functioned for more than 15 years with little interference, attempting to intimidate individuals and organizations throughout the country and hounding many courageous witnesses to jail on the charge of criminal contempt.

(2) In 1950 a number of Senators decided that the House Un-American Activities Committee should not get all the publicity and headlines for chasing the Reds, and established a special Senate Committee on subversion. This was the Senate Subcommittee on Internal Security, first headed by Senator Pat McCarran,* Democrat, of Nevada, and now chaired by Senator William E. Jenner, Republican, of Indiana. The Jenner Committee has likewise made an outstanding record for persecution and demagogy. Its worst offense was its investigation in 1952 and 1953 of allegedly subversive Americans employed by the United Nations. This inquiry violated both the U.S. Constitution and the U.N. Charter, caused disruption and demoralization of the U.N. staff, and led directly to the suicide of Mr. Abraham H. Feller, an American citizen and General Counsel for the United Nations.

(3) The Senate Permanent Subcommittee on Investigations, with Senator Joseph McCarthy, Republican, of Wisconsin, as Chairman, has been of course the most flagrant of all the committees in flouting the Con-

---

*Senator McCarran died suddenly on September 28, 1954.

stitution, brow-beating and smearing witnesses, and making distortion and dishonesty a fundamental method of operation. The activities of the McCarthy Committee have dramatically brought out the principle that *civil liberties are indivisible.* Having violated with impunity the rights of liberals, radicals, trade unionists and teachers, and having usurped Judicial powers in doing so, McCarthy finally turned the same sort of inquisitorial techniques against the United States Army. Soon he was bullying and insulting Army personnel, including General Ralph W. Zwicker and Secretary of the Army Stevens. In September 1954 the Senate Select Committee that reviewed charges against McCarthy reported that his treatment of General Zwicker "was reprehensible, and that for this conduct he should be censured by the Senate."

During the Army-McCarthy hearings in the spring of 1954, it became clear that individuals in various departments of the U.S. Government were leaking information to the Senator about Federal employees who were supposedly "subversive." Although the existence of such a spy network reporting secretly to an individual Senator is contrary to security regulations and in violation of the law, dictator McCarthy proudly announced that nobody was going to prevent him and his Committee from having the practice continued. Both Attorney General Brownell and President Eisenhower denounced McCarthy for trespassing on Executive powers and substituting government by an individual for government by law. But the time to have stopped McCarthy was at the start of his abuse of the right of Congressional inquiry, before his inquisition had gathered such momentum and before he had built up so much personal power and prestige.

Many witnesses during the past few years have invoked the Fifth Amendment provision against compulsory self-incrimination in refusing to answer the improper questions of Congressional committees. However, recently a number of witnesses have tried another approach by relying on the First Amendment and the governmental separation of powers. Among these have been author Harvey O'Connor, Leo Huberman, co-editor of *The Monthly Review,* and myself.* All of us defied the McCarthy Committee on the constitutional grounds just cited, feeling that it was our duty as citizens not to cooperate with any official who was trampling upon the Constitution. O'Connor and I have both been cited for contempt by the Senate and indicted by a grand jury. But our respective trials may not take place until the Supreme Court hands down a decision in the case of Julius Emspak, a trade union leader who partly relied on the First Amendment in declining to answer questions before the House Un-American Activities Committee in 1949.

(4) The House Special Committee to Investigate Tax-Exempt Founda-

---

*Both the Lamont and O'Connor cases were dropped by the U.S. government.

tions, headed by Representative B. Caroll Reece, Republican, of Tennessee, has during the past year become one of the chief Congressional menaces to freedom of opinion. In 1952 this Committee, of which the late Representative Eugene E. Cox, Democrat, of Georgia, was chairman, investigated some 1,500 American foundations for possible subversion and uncovered little that even Congressional extremists could call "un-American." In 1954, however, Mr. Reece and some of his colleagues, feeling they had been cheated of their share of the headlines, decided to open up the inquiry again.

This time the Committee concentrated on a few of the larger foundations, such as the Carnegie, Ford and Rockefeller Foundations. The Committee rendered a verdict before hearing the evidence by announcing prior to this second investigation that American foundations had taken part in a vast plot to swing the United States to the Left through radical teaching in the colleges and universities. The Committee paraded a group of venomous witnesses who testified to this effect in public hearings and who depicted the leading foundations as honeycombed with Red conspirators. Then, just as the foundations were about to testify in reply, Chairman Reece called off the public hearings and told the foundations that they could rebut by mail. The Carnegie Foundation, undoubtedly expressing the sentiments of the other foundations under attack, issued a statement protesting this procedure and accusing the Committee of making "completely unfounded charges" based on a "shocking combination of innuendo and implication."

2. *Congressional legislation that violates the letter or spirit of the Bill of Rights.* The reactionaries today are far more subtle than after the First World War when they resorted to crude illegalities and brute force to suppress radicals and progressives. Now they pass unconstitutional laws which do the job far more effectively. In 1954 the Eisenhower Administration and Congress made an all-time record by pushing through no fewer than eight anti-subversive bills that violate the Constitution. These measures enact much of McCarthy's program; they are McCarthyism sweetened by the appearance of legality.

The basic premise of the anti-subversive program is that the Government stands in mortal danger of being violently overthrown by a terrible Communist conspiracy. This is sheer nonsense. But Congress, behind the smokescreen of this ranting demagogy, is legislating America steadily in the direction of fascism. We must remember that Hitler's accession to power in 1933 was achieved legally. I cite eight of the worst laws now on the statute books:

(1) *The Communist Control (Brownell-Butler) Act of 1954.* This piece of legislation outlaws the Communist Party and is one of the most vicious of the measures making a mockery of the Bill of Rights. It deprives the Communist Party of "any of the rights, privileges and immunities attendant upon legal bodies," thus making it impossible for the Party to collect dues, have bank accounts, sue in the courts or run candidates for political office.

The Act, amending the Internal Security Law of 1950, also sets up a new classification, that of the "Communist-infiltrated organization," which is defined as an organization the effective management of which is conducted by one or more individuals who are agents of the Communist movement or who are engaged in giving aid or support to it. All trade unions or employers found to be Communist-infiltrated will lose their rights under the National Labor Relations Act and so will be fatally crippled in their functioning. Of course it is trade unions which will feel the chief impact of this provision.

The Communist Control Act was passed in August of 1954 during the last hectic days of the 83rd Congress, and "was promoted," to quote *The New York Times,* "as a political coup by so-called Democratic 'liberals' " in the Senate. These Democratic Senators wished to pose, in an election year, as more anti-Communist than the Republicans, particularly because McCarthy had been accusing the Democratic Party of "twenty years of treason." So, for the paltry purposes of partisan political advantage, there was enacted a bill which the anti-Communist *New York Post* describes as "a wretched repudiation of democratic principles" and "an outrageous affront to free society." The Act sets a precedent whereby conceivably the Republican Party might outlaw the Democratic Party because of its "treasonous" activities. This law is so extreme, so confused and so obviously contrary to the Bill of Rights that there is genuine hope that the U.S. Supreme Court will declare it unconstitutional.

(2) *The Immunity Act of 1954.* This measure passed by a suppression-loving Congress goes a long way in nullifying the Fifth Amendment, which guarantees every American against compulsory self-incrimination. The pretext for this law is that so many witnesses before Congressional committees have invoked the Fifth Amendment in refusing to answer questions.

The Immunity Act provides that a Federal court judge may grant a witness immunity from prosecution when testifying on matters of national security or defense before a Congressional committee, a grand jury or a Federal court. If a witness under these circumstances still refuses to answer questions, then he can be sent to jail for contempt. If he lies, he will face perjury charges. There is doubt, however, whether the grant of immunity will protect an individual against prosecution by a State or municipality; and it certainly will not protect him against being dismissed from employment, the denial of a passport, social ostracism or other extra-legal penalties that may flow from his forced testimony.

The over-riding reason behind the passage of the Immunity Act was to give Congressional committees more scope for violating freedom of opinion and association. The minority report of the House Judiciary Committee was firmly against the measure and asserted that it would "turn men of conscience into informers." "What legislative lack does the reported bill fill?" this dissenting statement asked. "It is not the function of Congress to expose private personal guilt. It is not the function of Congress to prepare cases for prosecution. It is not the function of Congress to relieve the Executive branch of the Government of its constitutional responsibility of law enforcement. When a committee of the Congress investigates, it does so to gather evidence for its own purposes, that of legislating wisely and adequately. The investigations of Pearl Harbor, Teapot Dome, the work of the Truman Defense Committee and the LaFollette Civil Liberties Committee did not suffer for lack of Congressional power to immunize witnesses."

(3) *The Smith Act*. This Congressional Act of ill fame makes it a crime, with severe penalties in fines and imprisonment, to advocate or conspire to advocate the overthrow of the Government of the United States by force and violence. Thus it annuls one of the chief principles expressed in the American Declaration of Independence and cancels out our great tradition of free speech, which has held that mere opinion and advocacy, even of revolution, is permissible in our democracy; and that only concrete actions or direct incitements are to be classed as criminal.

Under the Smith Act the U.S. Government has already indicted 120 Communist leaders of whom 81 have been convicted. All of these persons were accused, not of actually advocating revolution, but of conspiring to teach and advocate it at some indefinite future time. In June 1951, the Supreme Court upheld the constitutionality of the obviously unconstitutional Smith Act, with Justices Douglas and Black maintaining in forceful dissents that it ran directly counter to the First Amendment guaranteeing freedom of speech.

(4) *The Internal Security Act of 1950 (McCarran Act)*. This atrocious piece of legislation was passed by Congress over the veto of President Truman, who called it "an omnibus bill . . . which would put the Government of the United States into the thought-control business." Among other things, this measure provides that all organizations finally adjudged by the Subversive Activities Control Board as "Communist-action" or "Communist-front" groups must register with the Attorney General and send him complete annual financial reports, including the source of all monies received; and must stamp all publications sent through the mails, together with their envelopes and wrappers, "disseminated by a Communist organization." It is a crime for any member of such an organization to apply for or receive an American passport. All members of a Communist-action group, such as the Communist Party, must have their names registered with the U.S. Attorney General.

The Internal Security Act also makes provision for concentration camps in case of invasion of U.S. territory, a declaration of war by Congress or an insurrection in aid of a foreign enemy. In such an event the Attorney

General is authorized to arrest "each person as to whom there is reasonable ground to believe that such person probably will engage in, or probably will conspire with others to engage in, acts of espionage or sabotage." This means that thousands of Americans could be thrown into detention camps merely on suspicion. They would be imprisoned first; only later would they have an opportunity to prove their innocence.

After the Communist Party was officially declared to be a Communist-action group by the Subversive Activities Board in April 1953, it took the decision to the courts on constitutional grounds. It will undoubtedly carry its appeal in due course to the United States Supreme Court. Meanwhile, Congress has included in the Communist Control Act of 1954 important sections of the Internal Security Act and has amended the latter so that the Subversive Activities Control Board henceforth has the duty to determine whether an organization is "Communist-infiltrated."

(5) *Walter-McCarran Immigration Act.* In 1953 the late Senator McCarran, the Joe McCarthy of the Democrats, was again the moving spirit in putting through an anti-freedom measure. For many years the American Government has treated aliens in an unjust and arbitrary fashion; the new Immigration Act insists that they be regarded as a species of criminal to be arrested and deported wholesale on the flimsiest pretexts of having "subversive" opinions or associations. Fourteen million foreign-born Americans, citizens and non-citizens, are threatened by this law.

This Act provides not only that aliens in the United States be hounded from pillar to post, but also sets up formidable obstacles to further immigration from abroad and to the granting of even temporary visas to visiting foreigners. Distinguished scholars and scientists are frequently refused admission to this country on the grounds that they once supported a suspect committee for peace or civil liberties; and sometimes even persons officially engaged in United Nations business are barred from entering the United States. Scientific associations are finding it increasingly difficult to hold international conferences in America because the Immigration Act prevents so many foreign experts from attending.

The effect of all this is that the autocrats and bureaucrats in Washington have reversed America's traditional role of being a democratic refuge for oppressed individuals fleeing from dictatorial governments or stifling economic systems abroad.

(6) *The Welker Act of 1954.* This is another repressive piece of Congressional legislation that requires all Communist and "Communist-front" organizations in the United States to register under the Internal Security Act full information regarding whatever printing presses and duplicating equipment they use, down to the last mimeographing machine. This bill, which constitutes an amendment to the Internal Security Act, was passed unanimously by both the Senate and House of Representatives.

(7) *The Expatriation Act.* This vindictive and malicious law was first proposed by President Eisenhower in his message to Congress in January of 1954. It deprives of citizenship any person, even though native-born, who is convicted of knowingly and actively participating in a conspiracy to overthrow the Government by force and violence. An individual so convicted loses the right to vote, to run for political office, to serve on a jury or to obtain a passport. He will also be subject to constant Government surveillance. The measure is directed primarily at Communists who, already unjustly sent to jail under the Smith Act, are liable to receive this additional punishment for what they did not do.

(8) *The Taft-Hartley Act.* I discuss this law under point 12, "The troubles of trade unions," on page 45.

3. *State and municipal violations of the Constitution.* States and cities have not lagged far behind the Federal Government in putting into effect the whole paraphernalia of the up-to-date witch-hunt against alleged subversives. There has been a flurry of "run-them-out-of-town" statutes. Several State legislatures have passed "Little McCarran" Acts. In California the Senate committee investigating subversive activities has aped all the worst practices of the House Committee on Un-American Activities. In New Hampshire the State Attorney General has been conducting his own inquisition in violation of the Bill of Rights. One of his chief victims has been Paul Sweezy, co-editor of *The Monthly Review,* who relied upon the First Amendment in declining to answer questions obviously outside the scope of the inquiry, including ones about a lecture he gave on socialism at the University of New Hampshire. Mr. Sweezy has been declared in contempt of court and intends to fight his case up to the U.S. Supreme Court.

Long a scandal has been the disregard for the Bill of Rights by the police in American cities. This includes illegal search and seizure, and various types of police brutality such as solitary confinement or beatings in order to obtain evidence. Needed corrections are better trained police, fullest publicity on abuses, and civil suits against policemen for lawless conduct.

4. *The loyalty purge of the Federal Government.* The search for alleged subversives in the U.S. Government has been going on ever since 1947 when President Harry S. Truman issued his first Executive Order on the subject. The more than 3,000,000 Federal employees are constantly subject to investigation, and all prospective employees must run the gauntlet. In 1951 President Truman made the situation measurably worse by calling for the discharge of a Government employee if there was "reasonable doubt" as to his loyalty. This vague criterion supplanted the previous—and slightly more concrete—standard of "reasonable grounds" for believing an employee disloyal.

The loyalty investigations in general, as Professor Henry Steele Commager of Columbia University points out, "do not deal with acts for the very good reason that there are already laws on the statute books that take care of all conceivable subversive acts. They deal, instead, with imponderable things like intentions, thoughts, principles, and associations, with that shadowy realm which has ever been the happy hunting ground of tyrants." Professor Commager's remarks apply to both the Government's loyalty program and its "security" program, in which employees, even though considered loyal, are dismissed as security risks if they are judged to be, for instance, irresponsible or indiscreet. In 1954 the noted scientist Dr. J. Robert Oppenheimer, who had played a leading part in America's original production of the atomic bomb, was dismissed from the Atomic Energy Commission on security grounds.

5. *The U.S. Attorney General's list of alleged Communist, fascist and subversive organizations.* This blacklist, now consisting of no less than 256 groups, was originally drawn up and made public as a part of President Truman's loyalty order, but soon became on its own account a serious threat to American civil liberties. The Attorney General promulgated this list without giving any of the organizations mentioned a hearing or a chance to refute the charges against them. This official declaration of subversion by decree wrought havoc with the organizations concerned, since people became afraid of joining them, since those with tax exemption for contributors quickly lost this status—purely through political malice—and since the owners of halls and hotels used the blacklist to deny meeting facilities to the groups in question.

In April of 1951 the Supreme Court of the United States ruled that the Attorney General must present in court adequate reasons for placing on his list three organizations which had brought suit against him to contest the listing: the Joint Anti-Fascist Refugee Committee, the International Workers Order and the National Council of American-Soviet Friendship. But this ruling did not question the constitutionality of an official Government blacklist. And the Attorney General dodged the decision so successfully that the cases were still in litigation in 1954, seven years after the original listing, when a Federal court decided that the issue was moot because the Subversive Activities Control Board had taken over the duty of branding these particular organizations as subversive. The decision has been appealed.

It is significant to note that the original Supreme Court decision came approximately three and a half years after the Attorney General's list was originally announced; and that the cases were still in the courts three years later. This brings out the fact that governmental rulings and legislation violative of the Bill of Rights can be on the books for years before the Supreme Court passes judgment on them. Meanwhile individuals and organizations must suffer legal harassment, defense costs and public disrepute.

In 1952 Congress took the extreme and fantastic step of adding to the Federal Housing Act the Gwinn Amendment, which requires from all tenants in residential units constructed under the Act a statement that they do not belong to any organization designated as subversive by the Attorney General. The constitutionality of this law is at present being challenged in the courts.

6. *The U.S. State Department's denial of passports.* In its undemocratic policy of building up an Iron Curtain, the American Government is refusing to let people out of the country as well as to let people in. During the past decade the State Department has cancelled or denied passports in the cases of thousands of progressives, radicals, even slightly unorthodox scholars and others. The passport authorities are very evasive about the reasons and usually repeat only the vague formula: "Your travel abroad at this time would be contrary to the best interests of the United States."

It is perfectly clear, however, that the State Department takes this position because the applicants in question dissent from some of the foreign or domestic policies of the U.S. Government. Such discrimination on political grounds is clearly contrary to the spirit of the Bill of Rights. In the summer of 1951 I myself was refused a passport on the customary pretext and later appealed, in vain, to President Truman to intervene on my behalf.* Since that time the State Department, due to a Supreme Court decision, has been forced to set up a Passport Appeals Board. Several cases are now pending in the courts challenging on constitutional grounds the arbitrary denial of passports.

7. *The new doctrine of guilt by association.* The time-honored American legal doctrine is that guilt is always personal. However, in most of the Congressional inquiries, Federal laws and governmental actions that I have discussed, this theory has been thrown overboard. Instead, individuals are judged guilty because they belong to some unpopular organization or because they have "undesirable" friends and relatives.

The Federal Government's loyalty purge, starting in 1947 and depending to a large extent on the Attorney General's blacklist of organizations, initiated this new trend. Today, only seven years later, the theory of guilt by association has been enshrined as a major concept in American law and government rulings. No doctrine is better suited to the purposes of a tyrannical government.

8. *Illegal and extra-legal activities on the part of Government agents.* Government agents, especially those employed by the Federal Bureau of Investigation, have increasingly been violating the law by unauthorized tapping of telephone conversations. In recent trials judges have repeatedly thrown out evidence brought forward by the Department of Justice when the defendant showed that it was secured by means of illegal wire-tapping. Yet everyone knows that the F.B.I. continues to carry on this contemptible

---

*Owing to a favorable ruling of the U.S. Supreme Court, I regained my passport in 1958. See "The Right to Travel," p. 141.

form of spying on a wide scale. Attorney General Brownell hoped that during its last session Congress would make the lawless behavior of his Department perfectly legal by passing a bill to authorize wire-tapping, but the measure fortunately did not go through.

F.B.I. snooping in general has gone to extreme and outrageous lengths and frequently has had the effect of intimidation. A favorite device of the F.B.I. is to send agents around to question the elevator man or other employees in an apartment house about the "subversive" views and associations of someone residing in the building. J. Edgar Hoover's men often call on unsuspecting persons suspected of having the wrong friends, relatives or associations and scare them half to death. The average American does not know that he is under no legal obligation to answer the questions of F.B.I. agents. During the past two years F.B.I. agents have questioned many of my friends about my beliefs and activities and have apparently been making a desperate effort to obtain information that could be used against me.

There is now mounting evidence that Government agents are opening and reading the mail of suspects in post offices and are listing the magazines and newspapers that such persons receive. This tampering with the mails is a monstrous violation of the law. The F.B.I. records in its dossiers all the "information" it can gather in these various ways. It keeps files on the incredible total of more than 70,000,000 Americans and has a staff of more than 1,000 persons working in the file section alone. Here we have developing fast the basis for a police state in the U.S.A.

9. *The utilization of perjury and frame-up against "subversives."* There can be no doubt that in trials and loyalty investigations involving Communists, radicals, liberals and others suspected of "subversion," perjured testimony has repeatedly played a role. Embittered ex-Communists, cringing ex-spies, Government agents and miscellaneous informers have sworn under oath to statements that are obviously untrue. All such persons constantly face the temptation of cooking up new and sensational evidence so that they will continue to be paid $25 to $50 a day by the Government for testifying.

I am of the opinion that false testimony was a weighty factor in the recent prosecution of Harry Bridges, West Coast trade union leader, for alleged perjury. In 1953 the U.S. Supreme Court finally threw out the Bridges case. The perjury indictments of Prof. Owen Lattimore of Johns Hopkins University—the latest handed down in October 1954—are a complete political frame-up. In 1951 Charles E. Davis publicly confessed that, while in the employ of Senator McCarthy, he had tried to frame John Carter Vincent, American envoy to Switzerland, as a dangerous Red. He falsely signed the name of a Swiss Communist to a faked telegram to Vincent, hoping to trick the latter into an indiscreet reply.

In 1954 the Department of Justice announced that it was dropping a perjury indictment against Val R. Lorwin, who had been "Case 54" in Senator McCarthy's original list of "subversives" in the U.S. State Department. At the same time the Attorney General dismissed the public prosecutor who obtained Lorwin's indictment because he had knowingly made false statements to the grand jury which considered the case. As to professional informers, the situation had become so scandalous that in 1954 the Department of Justice dropped from its payroll as unreliable three perennial Government witnesses: Paul Crouch, Manning Johnson and Harvey M. Matusow. The last-named told Methodist Bishop G. Bromley Oxnam: "I have lied again and again in my statements to these committees and in my reports, and I want to go to each individual about whom I have falsified and ask his forgiveness."

I was the victim of a little frame-up myself in 1951 when the Senate Internal Security Committee tried to give the impression that I had been responsible for a memorandum concerning the Institute of Pacific Relations headed "To E.C.C. from C.L." It was only after a vigorous public protest on my part that the Committee acknowledged that the initials "C.L." were those of Mr. Clayton Lane, a former officer of the Institute.

10. *Pressures against lawyers who defend dissenters and Communists.* During the past few years such heavy pressures have developed against lawyers who take on the defense of radicals that it has become most difficult for Communists and others to find adequate legal counsel. In 1950 after the trial of the first eleven Communist leaders under the Smith Act, Judge Harold R. Medina ruled that all five of the defense lawyers were guilty of contempt and took the unusual course of sentencing them to jail for terms ranging from three to five months. This extreme and vindictive action naturally caused alarm among lawyers throughout the country.

Another important factor in the situation is that competent lawyers hesitate to defend radicals because they think it will lose them good clients and react against their business in general. I know several attorneys who have personally wanted to step into radical cases, but whose partners have vetoed the idea on the grounds that it would ruin the firm.

11. *Restrictions on the right of assembly.* Organizations critical of prevailing patterns of thought have found increasing obstacles in the way of hiring meeting halls or staging street demonstrations. This is partly due to the widespread use of the U.S. Attorney General's blacklist of organizations by the owners of halls and hotels to ban meetings. Local municipal ordinances have also been growing more and more repressive. For instance, in 1951 the New York City Board of Education barred all organizations believed to be Communist, totalitarian, subversive or fascist from holding meetings in public schools.

The classic case on street meetings occurred during the First World

War when a Socialist stood on a street corner in the Bronx and started to read aloud the Declaration of Independence. Just after he had read, "Whenever any Form of Government becomes destructive of these ends, it is the right of the people to alter or abolish it," a policeman arrested him. The Socialist protested: "But I didn't say that. Thomas Jefferson said it." "Where's that guy?" demanded the cop. "We'll get him too!"

12. *The troubles of trade unions.* Under the enlightened Administration of President Franklin D. Roosevelt, the democratic rights of trade unions, so frequently and extensively violated in the United States, were recognized and backed by the Government. But since Roosevelt's death the rights of trade unions and their members have again become seriously jeopardized, particularly since the adoption in 1947 of the Taft-Hartley Act. This bill was passed by Congress over President Truman's veto and supersedes to a large extent the liberal National Labor Relations (Wagner) Act of 1935.

Among the provisions violating the Bill of Rights and the Constitution is that requiring a non-Communist affidavit of all union officials as a condition of access to the National Labor Relations Board; and that prohibiting trade unions from contributing, either in cash or in the form of publicity, to the campaigns of candidates for Federal office. The Act also considerably broadens the scope of court injunctions for the prevention of strikes. All trade union organizations, including the conservative American Federation of Labor, advocate repeal of the Taft-Hartley Act.

As we have seen, Congress imposed further restrictions on the functioning of trade unions in the Communist Control Act of 1954, which puts "Communist-infiltrated" unions beyond the pale. The criteria for determining what is a "Communist-infiltrated" organization are so vague and broad that the Government could probably make the charge stand against almost any union in the land which it wanted to get. Hence, this new law basically threatens the whole trade union movement in the United States.

13. *The decline of academic freedom.* Few schools, colleges or universities in America have been, even in the best of times, 100 percent faithful to the principles of academic freedom. Since World War II the situation has grown much worse. During the 1948 presidential campaign several college teachers lost their jobs merely because they supported Henry Wallace and the Progressive Party. In 1953 an especially outrageous case was that of W. Lou Tandy, Professor of Economics and Sociology at the Kansas State Teachers College, who was dismissed for exercising his constitutional right of signing a petition to President Eisenhower asking that he pardon the 11 Communist leaders sent to jail as a result of the first Smith Act trial.

At the same time more and more State legislatures have been putting through measures requiring teachers to sign special loyalty oaths and ordering the dismissal of any teacher associated with an organization on the Attorney General's blacklist. Typical is New York's Feinberg Law along these lines.

Teachers in general in the United States are now being treated as a species of second-class citizens whose loyalty is so questionable that strict control of their ideas must be maintained and special legislation passed to guard the community against them.

In addition to these various woes, teachers recently have had to endure the high-handed investigations of Congressional committees. When teachers have exercised their constitutional prerogatives and refused to answer, on the grounds of the First or Fifth Amendment, questions put by the Jenner, McCarthy or Velde Committees, they have usually been summarily dismissed by the college or university employing them. Only a few educational institutions, such as Harvard, Columbia and Sarah Lawrence, have stood firm for the rights of their employees.

In a special study of 72 colleges and universities throughout the United State, *The New York Times* reported in May 1951: "A subtle, creeping paralysis of freedom of thought and speech is attacking college campuses in many parts of the country, limiting both students and faculty in the area traditionally reserved for the free exploration of knowledge and truth." Both teachers and students fear that Government agents are planted in courses to take note of any unorthodox ideas advanced. When in 1943 I taught in Cornell's Contemporary Study of Russian Civilization, the staff discovered that two Government agents were enrolled as students and sending regular reports to Washington on what was said in lectures and discussion periods.

In April 1953, Dean Carl W. Ackerman of the Columbia School of Journalism issued a strong public protest against the snooping of Government agents in which he said in part: "The practical problem which confronts deans, professors, school teachers and students today is political freedom to discuss public affairs in classrooms or at lunch or at a 'bull' session without fear that someone may make a record which may be investigated secretly, upon which he may be tried secretly and also convicted secretly, either by a governmental official or a prospective employer."

14. *Loyalty oaths in general.* The imposition of loyalty oaths is now being extended beyond the teaching profession to other categories of employment. In California, Maryland, Pennsylvania and New Hampshire there are now laws requiring all public employees and office holders to sign a loyalty oath. The California Levering Act rules in addition that the governing boards of any organization having tax exemption must take the loyalty oath. This includes churches and other religious bodies. Several Protestant churches have refused to sign the oath and are planning to carry the issue to the courts on the grounds that it violates the First Amendment provision establishing separation between church and state.

15. *Purges and censorship in the motion picture industry.* When in 1947 the House Committee on Un-American Activities first investigated

the movies for "subversive" tendencies, the big Hollywood producers surrendered and put into effect a general purge against Communists and "fellow-travelers." Of course they started off by firing the Hollywood Ten, who had courageously refused to answer the Un-American Committee's questions violating the First Amendment and who consequently went to jail for a year for contempt of Congress. The atmosphere in Hollywood is well illustrated by the case of the studio which in 1950 planned to do a movie of Hiawatha, but shelved the project because it was felt that to depict this Indian chieftain's efforts at peacemaking among the warring tribes of his day might be construed as Communist propaganda.

When motion picture directors, producers and writers are not censoring themselves, other people are doing it for them. Recently attempts have been made—successful in some localities—to ban "Lost Boundaries," "Pinky," "The Bicycle Thief," "The Miracle," "Oliver Twist," and "Salt of the Earth." Catholic groups were able to get "The Miracle" suppressed as sacrilegious in New York State, although the U.S. Supreme Court later ruled that this action by the State Censor Board was illegal. Communist groups boycotted "Oliver Twist" on the grounds that it was anti-Semitic. We must object to self-appointed censors, whether Catholic, Communist, American Legion or anything else.

16. *Purges and censorship in radio and television.* The notorious book *Red Channels, the Report of Communist Influence in Radio and Television,* published by a group of ex-F.B.I. agents, is used by most radio-television companies as a blacklist against the actors and actresses therein accused of "subversive" activities or associations. These days any performer on radio or television who has become "controversial" is usually eased out of his job. In the realm of commentary and discussion on public affairs, there is hardly a liberal commentator left on the air. Liberals and radicals find it almost impossible to obtain broadcasting facilities even if they or their sponsors agree to pay for time. When McCarthy's friend, Robert E. Lee, was appointed in 1953 to the Federal Communications Commission, which oversees the radio and television industry, the various companies in this field became even more nervous about letting any dissenter on a program.

17. *Purges and censorship in publishing.* During the past few years book publishers have become more and more reluctant to issue titles of a left or liberal nature. New volumes that do not utterly condemn Soviet Russia and Marxism have practically disappeared. Fearful of investigation by some Congressional committee, publishers have begun to cleanse themselves. In 1952 Little, Brown & Company of Boston forced the resignation of its editor-in-chief, Mr. Angus Cameron, who had been responsible for building up a list that included a number of progressives and some radicals.

When in the summer of 1951 a New York publisher issued a book by an author noted for his dissents, the landlord told the publisher that he must vacate the premises because of putting out such a work. The publisher told the landlord that the eviction would be illegal, that he would fight it right up to the Supreme Court and make a big civil liberties issue out of it. After this the landlord dropped the matter. This incident demonstrates how important behind-the-scenes economic pressures can be in the sphere of freedom of opinion.

18. *The banning of books and magazines.* Throughout much of American history narrow-minded citizens haunted by fear have made efforts to suppress books by dissenters, radicals and realistic novelists. Tremendous furor has been stirred up over novels that treat sex relations frankly. In recent years attempts have been made to ban James T. Farrell's *Studs Lonigan* trilogy, William Faulkner's *Sanctuary* and Erskine Caldwell's *God's Little Acre*. And Jewish groups have tried to have removed from public schools both Shakespeare's *Merchant of Venice* and Dickens' *Oliver Twist,* on the grounds that these classics are anti-Semitic.

Other groups have sought to have basic textbooks, such as those by Professors David S. Muzzey and Harold Rugg of Columbia University, banned from educational institutions. Also a serious problem are the censorship activities of the U.S. Post Office, which often refuses to mail books or magazines that it considers obscene or subversive and sometimes brings a criminal action against a publisher. Public libraries here and there have thrown out magazines regarded as subversive, such as *The Nation, The New Republic, Negro Digest* and *Soviet Russia Today*. The public schools of New York City also have dropped *The Nation* because it printed Paul Blanshard's informative articles critical of Catholicism (later issued in book form).

In 1953 an even more sinister development occurred when, under the pressure of Senator McCarthy and his investigating committee, the U.S. State Department removed hundreds of alleged subversive volumes from its numerous overseas libraries. In some cases the books were literally burned. This "book-burning" movement quickly spread and two of my own works, *The Peoples of the Soviet Union* and *Soviet Civilization,* were burned in the streets of Chicago by a mob which broke up a meeting on behalf of American-Soviet understanding and cooperation. The grand climax of tragic absurdity occurred in November of 1953 when Mrs. Thomas J. White, a member of the Indiana Textbook Commission, demanded that the story of Robin Hood be removed from school textbooks because it promoted the Communist line of rob-the-rich-to-pay-the-poor. Mrs. White also stated that references to Quakers should be eliminated from books because "Quakers don't believe in fighting wars."

19. *Political discrimination in private employment.* America's armaments program, laws against Communists working in defense plants and increasing hysteria over "the Red menace" have led to more and more

political discrimination in private employment. Such discrimination has gone far beyond industries producing for defense to private enterprise in general, particularly in education and the entertainment industry; it has extended beyond the firing of Communists to the firing of liberals, dissenters and civil libertarians who uphold their constitutional rights before Congressional committees. One of the most significant measures of the gravity of the present civil liberties crisis is the fact that the penalization of political dissent has come so generally to include depriving men of the right to work and make a living.

20. *Misuse of the jury system.* In the English-speaking countries the jury system developed as a protection for defendants against malicious prosecutions by the government and prejudiced decisions by the judiciary. In the United States today, however, juries are frequently picked from groups and classes who may be expected in general to be opposed to political dissenters and racial minorities. Negroes and manual laborers are more than often excluded from jury panels and juries, depending on local conditions.

A major problem is that many of the most important trials are held in Washington, D.C., where juries are preponderantly composed of U.S. Government employees. There is a great deal of psychological pressure on such jurymen to hand down verdicts which conform to what the Government, as represented by the Department of Justice, hopes to achieve in the way of sending political dissenters to jail.

21. *The activities of private vigilante groups.* Private educational and pressure organizations play an active and usually beneficial role in American political and cultural life. A number of them, however, are fundamentally opposed to the Bill of Rights and democracy; and carry on virulent crusades against individuals and groups that dissent from orthodoxy. Such organizations represent non-governmental McCarthyism. Outstanding in its repressive tendencies and record is the American Legion, with the Catholic War Veterans, the Daughters of the American Revolution and the Minute Women of the U.S.A. not far behind.

Today there are a thousand and one groups, some functioning nationally, some locally, whose purpose is to fight the menace of communism, expose Communists, tell off the fellow-travelers and disrupt "subversive" meetings. A number of these organizations are very suspicious of "internationalists" and so have as pet hates the United Nations, the American Association for the United Nations and the United World Federalists. The number of *individual* vigilantes on the prowl has greatly increased since Director J. Edgar Hoover of the F.B.I., in a recent public pronouncement, invited all Americans to send in reports to his organization on any persons showing signs of being "subversive."

22. *Attempts to break down the separation between Church and State.* Article I of the Bill of Rights starts off with the statement: "Congress shall

make no law respecting an establishment of religion, or prohibiting the free exercise thereof." Our Founding Fathers were determined that the United States should not have an official State religion functioning in an interlocking directorate with the Government. President George Washington asserted that "the Government of the United States is not in any sense founded upon the Christian religion." For the American Government to give any one religious group in the community a special official status is to violate the Constitution.

The traditional separation between Church and State extends to the field of public education. Yet in recent decades religious groups, particularly the Catholic Church, have been making strenuous efforts to smuggle religious teaching into the public schools of this country. In 1947 a courageous American mother, Mrs. Vashti McCollum, won her fight in the U.S. Supreme Court against religious instruction in the schools of her city, Champaign, Illinois. But practices contrary to this decision still go on in many localities. The religious zealots have also thought up the idea of "released time," in which children are freed from regular classes one hour each week in order to receive religious instruction in institutions of their faith apart from public school property. In 1952 the Supreme Court declared this innovation constitutional.

In 1954 the movement to make religion official from the governmental viewpoint gained ground when Congress amended the Pledge to the Flag by inserting the words "under God." Thus the last part of the Pledge now reads: "one nation *under God,* indivisible, with liberty and justice for all." (Italics mine—C.L.) In the same year the first U.S. postage stamps, in 3-cent and 8-cent denominations, appeared bearing the motto "In God We Trust."

23. *Discrimination on grounds of religion or philosophy.* The Bill of Rights clearly implies that all Americans, regardless of their religious beliefs or associations, should live on terms of mutual equality and justice. But discrimination against certain religious groups prevails today in many parts of the United States. Small dissenting sects like Jehovah's Witnesses have a hard time; and even members of so powerful a group as the Catholic Church have suffered greatly from religious prejudice in those communities where they constitute a minority.

Freedom of religion under the American Constitution implies freedom *from* religion. As Justice Jackson of the U.S. Supreme Court stated in a recent dissent, "The day this country ceases to be free for irreligion, it will cease to be free for religion, except for the sect that can win political power." Yet serious prejudice and discrimination persist in this country against those who believe in no religion or who give allegiance to an antisupernaturalist philosophy such as Humanism, with its stress on the happiness of mankind upon this earth. Also in a number of States legal discriminations still exist against acknowledged atheists.

THE CIVIL LIBERTIES CRISIS   51

These discriminations extend even to the sphere of military service. In dealing with conscientious objectors who oppose war on the grounds of religious training and belief, the Selective Service Act of 1948 limited draft exemptions to those who have faith in a Supreme Being. This excludes members of Humanist or Ethical religious groups who reject belief in God and the supernatural. Thus the new law clearly violates the conscience of the individual.

24. *The poll tax.* Several Southern States still make voting in political elections dependent on the payment of a poll tax. This restricts voting not only on the part of the Negro population, but also on the part of many of the poorer Whites in the South. All anti-poll tax laws proposed in Congress have failed to pass so far due to filibusters by Southern diehards in the Senate. The filibuster technique as developed recently in Congress is itself a grave violation of democratic government.

25. *Racial prejudice and discrimination.* Violations of the American Constitution and of American democracy in this category are everyday matters in practically every part of the country. This prejudice and discrimination are inflicted in varying degrees on all racial minorities in the United States: French Canadians in the North, Mexicans in the Southwest, Indians in the Rocky Mountain area, Orientals in the Far West, Jews and Negroes wherever they live. The segregation that goes hand in hand with undemocratic and unethical practices extends to education, employment, housing, hospitals, hotels, restaurants, theaters, traveling facilities, bathing beaches, sports in general and even burial in cemeteries.

Since our 17,000,000 Negroes constitute by far the largest racial minority in the United States, their problems loom largest in the present situation. Despite all sorts of promises by both the Democratic and Republican Parties, Congress has failed to set up a permanent F.E.P.C. (Fair Employment Practices Commission). Nor has it enacted a Federal Anti-Lynching Bill, which would enable United States authorities to take prompt and direct action against the wanton murderers of Negroes.

Yet all in all since World War II prejudice and discrimination against the Negroes have lessened. And in 1954 the Negro people gained one of their greatest victories when the U.S. Supreme Court outlawed separate public schools for Negroes and Whites throughout America. Of course the impact of this decision will be felt primarily in the South.

* * *

In this summary of the present civil liberties situation in the United States I have been as brief as I could. Obviously it would be possible to elaborate extensively on each of the 25 points I have discussed and to bring in additional ones. However, I hope I have made clear the depth and breadth of civil liberties violations and why an atmosphere of fear and conformity is so pervasive in this country today. This atmosphere prevails even at private dinner parties and in respectable clubs where people are more and more reluctant to put themselves on record, even informally, concerning controversial issues.

As the English philosopher, Bertrand Russell, expressed it not long ago: "America, which imagines itself the land of free enterprise, will not permit free enterprise in the world of ideas." The most virulent kind of censorship—self-censorship—has taken over. The majority of the people do not *need* to be censored anymore; they just remain silent, excusing themselves on the basis of the old adage, "Discretion is the better part of valor."

There is an obligation and necessity today for believers in American democracy to do their utmost to bring about a reversal of current trends. This is a task for principled conservatives as well as for liberals and radicals, since the institution of free speech is of priceless value to all members of the American community.

Although I have given the dark side of the picture, I am sure there is plenty of democratic fighting spirit left in the American people. This is evidenced in a growing resistance to repression throughout the country; and in the fine work of recently formed organizations such as the Citizens Committee to Preserve American Freedoms of Los Angeles and the Emergency Civil Liberties Committee of New York City. The general decline in the influence and prestige of Senator McCarthy is another favorable sign. And we certainly cannot give up the hope that the United States Supreme Court, in ruling on repressive legislation and civil liberties cases yet to come before it, will hand down decisions in support of freedom.

America's great battle for the Bill of Rights is only now beginning. Our own Resistance movement is just getting under way.

4
The Humanist Tradition
(1952)

Twentieth-century Humanism is a philosophy which rejects all belief in the supernatural and which sets up as its supreme aim the happiness, freedom and progress of all humanity in this one and only life. The Humanist viewpoint also includes Freedom of Choice for all human beings. No less important than the goals of Humanism are its *methods;* and it insists that in solving their problems men should rely upon the methods of reason, science and democracy.

It is sometimes thought that modern Humanism is a new and radical viewpoint which has no roots in the past of Western civilization. This is not true. For in the West there have been outstanding Humanist thinkers and writers in every era. And the Humanist tradition goes back at least as far as the Golden Age of Greek culture from the sixth through the fourth centuries B.C. In this tradition there are five main strands which Humanism tries to weave into an integrated whole. I shall describe them very briefly.

First, there is the contribution of philosophy as such. Here the two philosophies closely allied in thought with Humanism—Naturalism and Materialism—both stem from ancient Greece. Aristotle, who believed that Nature constitutes the totality of things, was the first great Naturalist and had no faith in either immortality or God as properly defined. In seventeeth-century Holland Spinoza revived the Naturalism of Aristotle in a rigorously worked out system based on the newly established facts and laws of fast developing modern science. Like Aristotle, Spinoza brought in highly abstruse and redefined concepts of God and immortality, but they bore no similarity to the personal God and personal immortality of Christian theology.

We must remember that philosophers throughout history have constantly indulged in a drastic and frequently misleading redefinition of basic terms. Some thinkers have done this because they sincerely considered it intellectually justified; others clearly because they could avoid social, religious or political pressures, and perhaps even preserve their lives, by the strategy of using some of the time-honored words. I am convinced that one of the keys to Western thought is the well-known dictum: "All wise men have the same religion, but wise men never tell." The basic idea behind this saying is, of course, to be applied to all controversial fields, whether religion, philosophy, biology, economics, politics or anything else. And we know that today in America "wise men" are becoming more discreet than ever in giving public utterance to what they really believe.

In the twentieth century John Dewey has brought Naturalism up to date and developed it in precise and scientific terms. He is the great contemporary philosopher of scientific method and actually knows more about the fundamental assumptions and implications of science in general than do most specialized scientists. Dewey has an enthusiastic and influential following among younger philosophers in the United States, although in Europe the tendency is to neglect or misunderstand him.

The general philosophy of Materialism, stressing the fact that the foundation stuff of the universe is matter in motion, was also first formulated in ancient Greece. There the brilliant Democritus, the so-called laughing philosopher, propounded the theory that the ultimate constituents of existence are tiny atoms whirling through the void and interacting according to a definite causal sequence. As we know, science verified this general theory some 2300 years later. Epicurus, another Greek thinker, further developed the materialistic viewpoint, especially in an ethical sense; and Lucretius, the versatile philosopher-poet of ancient Rome, gave, in his *On the Nature of Things,* the greatest philosophical poem ever written, a detailed and fully rounded version of Materialism.

The materialistic philosophers of the French Enlightenment, such as Diderot and Holbach, were too mechanical in their approach; but their errors were corrected by the dynamic or evolutionary Materialism characteristic of nineteenth-century Germany and represented by Feuerbach and Marx. Marx, of course, called his philosophy Dialectical Materialism. In its general attitude toward the universe and the destiny of man, it is close to Naturalism and Humanism; but Marxist Materialism departs from these two philosophies in the radical economic and political views associated with it, as well as its strict determinism and militant anti-religious position.

The second strand in the Humanist tradition comes from the great religions of mankind. Humanism is anti-theological and anti-supernatural, but it incorporates in its philosophy many of the ethical teachings of outstanding religious leaders like Jesus, Confucius and William Penn. Any humane philosophy must include such New Testament ideals as the brotherhood of man, peace on earth and the abundant life. There is much ethical wisdom, too, in the Old Testament and its Ten Commandments. Without accepting any ethical principle as a dogmatic dictum never to be questioned, the Humanist certainly adheres in general to a Biblical commandment such as, "Thou shalt not bear false witness against thy neighbor."

In the modern evolution of Christianity the Unitarians have come closest to the Humanist viewpoint and in twentieth-century America have given considerable stimulus to the Humanist cause. Many Unitarian ministers and churches in the United States definitely support Humanism. Like a number of other Humanists, these Unitarian Humanists call Humanism a *religion* rather than a philosophy. Another important religious group Humanist in outlook is the American Ethical Union, with separate Ethical Societies in New York, Brooklyn, St. Louis and other cities.

A third and most significant strand in Humanism is the scientific. The Humanist insists that his inclusive philosophy must be consistent throughout with the established facts and laws of science. Modern astronomy has of course blasted the old theory that man and his earth were the focal point of the universe in space and time. We know that our entire solar system represents only a tiny splotch of light in a great spiral nebula or galaxy containing some thirty billion stars; and that throughout the infinitely vast cosmos there are billions of other such flaming galaxies. Nature, it seems, has no particular regard for man and is neutral toward his welfare and what he considers the good.

Modern physics has demonstrated that matter, far from being an inert and base substance as the ancients thought, is a thing of the most tremendous dynamism, complexity and potentiality. We need no supernatural intervention in terms of Divine creation and guidance to explain why such remarkable stuff has flowered into whirling suns and planets and life itself, including the human species. Modern biology comes to complete the story and to chart convincingly man's long evolution upward from lower forms of life and according to natural law. Death, instead of being man's greatest enemy, is seen in this picture to be as necessary a part of natural processes as birth; an essential factor in the evolution which produced the human race; and a basic condition for continuing progress and for giving future generations their full chance to enjoy the sweetness of life.

Humanism believes that death marks the end of the conscious human individual and that therefore there is no personal immortality. The sciences of biology, psychology and medicine all lend support to this viewpoint by showing the intimate and inseparable relation between the human body and the human personality, which includes mind and memory. Body and personality are born together; they grow together; and they die together.

The human being is an interfunctioning oneness of body, mind and spirit which must attain its happiness and fulfillment in this world and not in some mythical realm beyond the grave or crematory.

More important for Humanism, however, than any scientific fact or series of facts is the modern scientific *method* of experimentation and verification. The Humanist claims that scientific method represents reason or intelligence at its most precise; and that men should rely upon it as the best way of solving their individual, social and international problems. This method judges whether an idea is true or not in terms of its *consequences;* and applies to the sphere of ethical decision as well as to all other fields of human conduct. True scientific method foreswears dogmatism and always leaves the door open for new facts and sounder reasoning to prove that some currently accepted view is wrong.

It is scientific method, too, which has brought about the invention of the machine and the enormous development of modern technology. This machine technology in industry, agriculture and the arts of communication has made possible the attainment of the Humanist aim of an abundant life, both material and cultural, for all people in every nation. But the achievement of this goal may be immeasurably set back by world-wide atomic war and ruin caused by the failure of statesmen and governments to carry over into international affairs the cool and objective procedures of reason and science.

Enriching the Humanist tradition, fourth, are the contributions of literature and art. Again, we start with ancient Greece and note that the leading dramatists—Aeschylus, Aristophanes, Euripides and Sophocles—wrote in a distinctly Humanist spirit. From the Bible, viewed as literature, we take two great Humanist documents, *The Song of Solomon,* with its superb love passages, and *Ecclesiastes,* with its central theme of enjoying life to the full while one is able, even though all human happiness and achievement seem transient.

Passing quickly to modern times, we find much of a Humanist nature in the work of the bold, witty, all-encompassing Voltaire in eighteenth-century France. In England of the nineteenth century the militant genius of Shelley denounced in verse the evils of religious supernaturalism and gave us a magnificent Humanist poem in *Prometheus Unbound.* Shelley, too, together with Keats, Byron and Wordsworth, constituted a school of English Nature poets outstanding in the history of literature. These poets all stressed the beauty and splendor of the external world—a motif most important in the Humanist philosophy. In nineteenth-century America Bryant and Whitman also wrote memorable Nature poetry, while today Robert Frost is the foremost figure in this field.

In his *Earth Is Enough* the American poet, Edwin Markham, put into simple language the key ideas of Humanism. Thus the poem starts:

> *We men of Earth have here the stuff*
> *Of Paradise—we have enough!*
> *We need no other stones to build*
> *The Temple of the Unfulfilled—*
> *No other ivory for the doors—*
> *No other marble for the floors—*
> *No other cedar for the beam*
> *And dome of man's immortal dream.*

There have been many novelists who in general have supported a Humanist position in their writings. In England this was true of George Eliot, Thomas Hardy, John Galsworthy and H. G. Wells; in America of Theodore Dreiser and Sinclair Lewis. In France after the middle of the nineteenth century the names of Gustave Flaubert, Émile Zola, Alphonse Daudet, Guy de Maupassant and Anatole France stand out as preeminently Humanist. The great German novelist, Thomas Mann, has repeatedly affirmed his Humanist beliefs.

In the sphere of music Beethoven's Fifth Symphony, portraying the triumph of man over fate, and his Ninth Symphony, assertive of the brotherhood of man, are Humanist in spirit. And Wagner treats of a central Humanist conception in his series of operas, "The Ring of the Nibelung," which tells the story of disintegrating godhead and humanity supplanting it. The final opera of the tetralogy, "The Twilight of the Gods," brings this theme to a dramatic culmination as Valhalla crashes down in flames. In sculpture the stirring statuary of the Frenchman, Auguste Rodin, perhaps brings out best the Humanist affirmation of the radiant actualities of life on earth. In painting the most effective expression of the Humanist attitude is to be found, I believe, in the incomparable murals of the Mexican painters, Orozco, Siqueiros and Rivera. They have done some of their best work in the United States.

The fifth strand in the Humanist tradition, and absolutely essential to it, is the idea of democracy and democratic procedures as developed down the ages. Here again we start with ancient Greece, where Athenian democracy, even though it was severely limited in scope, laid down some of the main patterns. After the downfall of the Greek city states the idea and practice of democracy fell pretty much into disuse until the modern era. Following the American Revolution of 1776 and the French Revolution of 1789, democracy again came into its own, particularly in the new American Republic. In the American Bill of Rights the Humanist sees the greatest state document on free speech and civil liberties in history.

The Humanist insistence on democracy necessarily follows from its stress on the use of reason and scientific method. For reason and science cannot reach their full flower unless they are able to develop in a democratic atmosphere where it is understood disagreements will be settled through the competition of ideas in the market place and through resort to the ballot box instead of violence. The scientific method constantly encourages the trying out of new ideas and the questioning of the most basic assumptions in every field. It therefore demands a completely democratic society where all thinkers can feel free to dissent without fear of reprisals from fellow-citizens, the government or private organizations.

Humanism's supreme goal of the welfare of all mankind requires democratic institutions and attitudes, not only in one's own country, but also throughout the world. In this progressive age the Humanist concept of democracy includes not only *political* democracy, but likewise *radical* democracy, and equality for women everywhere. Humanists are militantly opposed to discrimination or prejudice on the grounds of race, color or physiognomy. Such discrimination and prejudice, often leading to horrible persecution and outright slaughter, are among the vilest attributes of the fascist state.

I have tried to give a compact summary of the chief elements that make up the long and illustrious Humanist tradition in philosophy. Naturally I have been able to mention only the highlights in this venerable tradition. Humanism is frankly eclectic and incorporates in its over-all viewpoint whatever relevant truths it can discover in other philosophies or in any realm whatsoever of human thought and cultural achievement. Most of the persons mentioned in my summary were not complete and consistent Humanists in my sense of the word; nor did they use the term *Humanist* to describe their position. Nonetheless, because of what they actually thought and wrote, they can legitimately be placed in the Humanist tradition. By the very nature of their beliefs, Humanists feel not only a sympathetic association and intellectual bond with millions of their fellowmen today, but also with many of the eminent thinkers and common people of the past.

In my judgment Humanism, presenting an inclusive, consistent and scientifically based view of man and the universe, is a philosophy peculiarly appropriate to the mature and inquiring modern mind. Although neither now nor at any future time can there be any finality in the Humanist synthesis, it will always remain, I believe, a philosophy that appeals to intelligent and socially minded persons and that tends to bring unity among the nationalities and races of mankind.

5
Dangers of American Foreign Policy (1952)

1

In his speech of November, 1945, Under Secretary of State Dean Acheson, referring to American-Russian relations, said: "For nearly a century and a half we have gotten along well—remarkably well when you consider that our forms of government, our economic systems and our special habits have never been similar. . . . Never, in the past, has there been any place on the globe where the vital interests of the American and Russian people have clashed or even been antagonistic—and there is no objective reason to suppose that there should, now or in the future, ever be such a place. There is an obvious reason for this. We are both continental peoples with adequate living space—interested in developing and enjoying the living space we have. Our ambition is to achieve the highest possible standards of living among our own peoples, and we have the wherewithal to achieve high standards of living without conquest, through peaceful development and trade. We have that opportunity, moreover, only to the extent that we can create conditions of peace and prevent war. Thus the paramount interest, the only conceivable hope of both nations, lies in the cooperative enterprise of peace."

Mr. Acheson's words are as applicable today as in 1945. But Mr. Acheson as Secretary of State has, I submit, followed policies inconsistent with his earlier opinions. As the member of President Truman's Cabinet primarily responsible for the foreign policy of the United States, he has taken the lead in curtly turning down the repeated proposals of the Soviet Government over the past few years for a top-level conference between the U.S.A. and the U.S.S.R. for the purpose of coming to an over-all settlement. Mr. Acheson and Mr. Truman have fallen into the bad habit of stigmatizing all such offers as mere propaganda on the part of the Soviet Union. The trouble is, of course, that the American Government cannot admit the sincerity of Soviet peace campaigns without undermining its favorite thesis that Soviet aggression is the great menace facing the United States and the world at large. The underlying premise of the Truman Doctrine, the cold war, the North Atlantic Pact and the stupendous American armaments program is that Soviet armies will invade and overrun Western Europe if they have the opportunity.

Undoubtedly many high-ranking officials of the U.S. Government, as well as members of Congress and party leaders in the country at large, do not themselves really take stock in the fearful Soviet military threat which they keep talking about. But the originators of our bi-partisan foreign policy have succeeded in creating a situation in the United States in which loud cries about Soviet aggression and Communist conspiracy have become fundamental to orthodox political ritual both during and between elections. The high priests of the Democratic and Republican Parties have become the prisoners of their own myth-making and must maintain the pretense of absolute Soviet wickedness lest the foundations of their ideology melt away in the light of the simple truth.

A lamentable consequence of all this is that a powerful public opinion has grown up in America which regards as appeasement any attempts to work out a peaceful accord with the Soviets. So it is that in various quarters the whole notion of peace has become suspect; and peace committees, peace meetings, peace addresses, peace articles are all regarded as most likely originating in a Soviet plot to undermine the strength of the United States and its allies. In 1950 a Hollywood studio went so far as to suppress a movie on the story of Hiawatha, because it was felt that the Indian chief's constant smoking of the Peace-Pipe and general opposition to war might be interpreted as un-American. The continuing Red hunt on the part of such agencies as the House Committee on Un-American Activities and the Senate Committee on Internal Security, and by such demagogues as Senators Joseph McCarthy and Pat McCarran, has made most members of Congress and most citizens afraid to agree publicly with any part of the Soviet peace program, lest they then be smeared as Communists.

Today most Americans tend to reject almost automatically any idea, in the controversial realms of economics, politics and international relations, which originated in Soviet Russia or is generally approved there. In fact, this trend has gone so far that the relatively few dissenters who do express agreement with some Soviet doctrines may be indicted or jailed as foreign agents on the grounds of "parallelism" between their views and those of the Soviet Government. Yet if Americans for one reason or another feel unable ever to agree with Soviet opinions, then the Soviets are actually controlling them in reverse by forcing them always to support contrary conclusions. The truly independent mind cannot permit itself to be placed in such a senseless position.

2

I wonder how many millions of Americans, during the steady deterioration of American-Soviet relations since the end of World War II, have asked themselves the question I have so often put to myself: Would the present American-Soviet impasse have developed if President Franklin D. Roosevelt had lived out his last term of office through 1948? My answer has always been that while these post-war years would have been difficult in any case, President Roosevelt, with his wide experience in foreign affairs, his political sagacity, his liberalism and wisdom, would have been able to lay the basis for continuing American-Soviet cooperation. Assuredly he would have had the moral strength and the basic statesmanship to resist Winston Churchill's suggestion in his famous Fulton, Missouri, speech of March, 1946, for an Anglo-American military alliance against the Soviet Union.

President Truman, however, never noted for his forcefulness of personality or independence of mind, fell in readily with Churchill's anti-Soviet rhetoric and apologia for a cold war. Moreover, being unsure of himself on international issues, Mr. Truman has consistently leaned on others in the formulation of American foreign policy rather than assuming leadership himself. And he has often taken very bad advice, as in accepting the "containment" thesis put forward in the magazine *Foreign Affairs* in 1947 by Mr. X, now universally recognized as Mr. George Kennan, present Ambassador to the Soviet Union. Also President Truman, despite his dismissal of General MacArthur for sabotaging American policy in Korea, has on the whole relied heavily upon the military mind.

Writing in the *New York Herald Tribune* about the powers of the National Security Council, composed chiefly of military men and defense secretaries, Mr. Sumner Welles, former Under Secretary of State, asserts: "No President since General Grant has had such childlike faith in the omniscience of the high brass as the present occupant of the White House. It is no surprise to learn that President Truman invariably approves every decision of the Council. . . . The Council passes on all important questions in this country's international relations and decides the policy to be adopted. It has now been given authority by the President to determine our political objectives in every part of the world. . . . But no emergency can justify the control of this country's foreign policy by a Council which reaches its decisions from a military standpoint."

Generals and admirals, secretaries of war and navy and air, have traditionally been in favor of continued expansion of the services in which they function. Such expansion increases their power, prestige and sense of mission. Furthermore, they tend to look for the solution of international tensions in terms of war rather than of diplomacy. These are some of the reasons why civilian control over the U.S. defense departments is of such great importance. But there are many indications that the White House in general bows to the Pentagon. And one unhappy sign of this is President Truman's willingness to spur on a dangerous armaments race, to foist Universal Military Training on America and to encourage wild war scares as the occasion demands. Even an anti-Soviet stalwart like Congressman Joseph W. Martin, Jr., leader of the Republican minority in the House of Representatives, has stated: "Down through the years the high officials of this Government uttered time and again the direst warnings of bloodshed when a particular piece of legislation they wanted was before Congress."

In September, 1951, as reported in *The New York Times,* President Truman signed a "measure authorizing a $5,864,301,178 global military construction program, including a ring of secret overseas bases close enough to the Soviet Union so that the Air Force could retaliate against attack and neutralize the enemy's war potential. It was the largest amount ever voted for military construction during peacetime." Although the stated reason for this vast appropriation was that it was essential for defense, it is obvious that the air bases alluded to could also be used for a sudden A-bomb onslaught against the U.S.S.R. The acknowledged U.S. policy of building a round-the-world network of air bases, now several hundreds in number, as near as possible to the frontiers of Soviet Russia and its allies, makes the Soviets understandably nervous.

There are grounds for believing that Harry Truman hopes to go down in history as one of America's greatest Presidents because of his militant crusade against communism. Be that as it may, he will certainly be remembered as the Chief Executive who engineered through Congress the largest peacetime budgets of almost 71 billion dollars, with 49.7 billions earmarked for military purposes, exclusive of payments to veterans. For the fiscal year of 1953, running from July 1, 1952 to July 1, 1953, the President demanded, shortly after new Soviet peace overtures, a budget of over 85 billions.

Of this budget, which the *Wall Street Journal* terms "so monstrous as to defy reasoned comment," approximately 76 percent or 65.1 billions are for national security, including 52.4 billions for the armed forces and 10.5 billions for international security (aid to U.S. allies). This does not include 4.2 billions for veterans and 6.2 billions for interest, chiefly on loans which financed past wars. Fourteen billions of the new budget are to go to the building of airplanes, while 1.7 billions are for speeding up the stockpiling of atom bombs as part of a 5- to 6-billion dollar program over the next few years for mass production of America's "fantastic new weapons." The 1952 Soviet budget allocates to defense 24 percent or 113.8 billion rubles, equal to 28.4 billion dollars at the official exchange rate. (The Soviet budget, however, covers a much larger proportion of the national economy than the American.)

The astronomical U.S. totals mean that President Truman is asking the United States to spend approximately 180 million dollars a day on defense, which is about 3.7 times the entire 48-million budget of the United Nations for 1952. Let that sink in: in a single day the U.S. is to expend for military purposes over three and a half times what the U.N. can devote to international peace during a full year. Or, to make another comparison, the U.S. is to pour into defense every day more than twice as much as the total endowment of Columbia University, America's fourth largest educational institution. These colossal armament figures seem alarming not only to the Russians, but also to some of America's own allies.

The skyrocketing U.S. armaments outlays of the past few years have kept the American economy booming and headed off the depression that many competent economists think would have otherwise taken place. A brink-of-war economy, with government spending on a huge scale stimulating business and bringing enormous profits, is one way of temporarily overcoming fundamental economic difficulties in a capitalist economy. Government expenditure on weapons of war is the favorite form of public works for capitalist businessmen, since it results in very profitable contracts and since the end product is something that does not compete, like public hydroelectric developments or public housing, with private capitalist enterprise.

As a larger and larger proportion of American business becomes geared to the manufacture of arms and the servicing of armies, it grows harder and harder to turn back from a brink-of-war economy to a peace economy. It is for the time being more expedient, especially from a political viewpoint, to accelerate the armaments boom than to put the brakes on it. And the terrible Communist blunder in Korea played directly into the hands of those powerful groups in America which had been agitating for an expanded armaments program.

That program has become so prodigiously enlarged over the past few years, and so interwoven with the basic fabric of the economy, that government officials, private businessmen and even trade union leaders are anxious lest the general cold war and the little hot war be concluded too quickly and peace break out. Typical was the reaction to talk of peace in Korea as reported in the *Wall Street Journal* of May 16, 1951: "Stock prices experienced the sharpest decline since March 13. Brokers ascribed the break to widespread peace rumors. . . . Traders are fearful that the end of hostilities might also halt rearmament and catch leading companies with swollen inventories unbalanced for peacetime production."

As Mr. Norman Thomas, an outspoken anti-Soviet crusader, has said: "Millions of Americans, despite their best hopes, have acquired a vested interest in the economic waste of the arms race. Its sudden end would be greeted with an outpouring of joy, but it would be followed by economic panic—unless we were ready with constructive plans for a cooperative war on hunger, illiteracy and disease." Such plans the powers-that-be do not have, although vastly extended government spending for great economic projects at home and Point 4 abroad, assigned only $600,000,000 in the 85-billion Truman budget, could obviously be just as much of a business stimulus as shoveling unending billions of dollars into the maw of Mars.

Resilient as it is, even the American economy will not be able to stand indefinitely the strain of such enormous arms budgets and staggering government deficits as those imposed by the Truman Administration. And if the people as a whole finally start to offer serious objection to the armaments burden, reckless political leaders may be tempted to overcome popular opposition by actually plunging America into a world war. When war preparations seem to the rulers of a country the easiest way to maintain prosperity and full employment, the danger is that they will choose the path of international conflict in preference to facing an immediate economic crisis and running the risk of becoming discredited.

The disturbing distension of armaments has already inflicted on the American people a spiral of inflation, with rising prices and rising taxes cutting drastically into the consumer's income. As ex-President Herbert Hoover stated in his address of January 27, 1952: "The outstanding phenomenon in the United States is the dangerous overstraining of our economy by our gigantic expenditures. The American people have not yet felt the full impact of the gigantic increase in government spending and taxes. Yet we already suffer from the blight of inflation and confiscatory taxes. We are actually in a war economy except for world-wide shooting. We are diverting more and more civilian production to war materials. . . .

"Since the end of the Second World War the purchasing power of our money, measured in wholesale price indexes, has decreased 40 percent. . . . It is the average family who pays the bulk of taxes, both income and hidden. Among them are corporation taxes. These are ultimately passed on to their customers or the corporation would quickly go bankrupt. . . . These huge taxes are also overstraining our economy." In addition, President Truman's reckless program is using up America's limited natural resources, such as iron ore and oil, at such a furious rate that coming generations, under whatever form of economy, will be seriously handicapped. The Washington spendthrifts are robbing future Americans of their birthright for a wasteful mess of bombs and battleships, guns, tanks and warplanes.

3

The burgeoning American armaments economy has brought the United States to a condition, as described by Walter Lippmann, "of gigantic, almost explosive, industrial expansion which draws tremendously and competitively on the available supplies." America's accelerating need for raw materials, scrap metal and finished goods to meet the insatiable demands of a defense policy run wild has made it increasingly difficult for Britain, France, Italy and the Benelux countries to find the necessary imports for their own needs; to pay the inflated prices asked, most frequently by American manufacturers; and to put across their vast rearmament programs, in conformance with American foreign policy, without more and more depressing their own standards of living through domestic inflation, crushing taxation and a sheer lack of consumers' goods.

Mr. Aneurin Bevan commented most persuasively on the situation in his speech of April 23, 1951, when he resigned in protest as Minister of Labor in the British Labor Government: "It is now perfectly clear to anyone who examines the matter objectively—the lurchings of the American economy, the extravagance and unpredictable behavior of the production machine, the failure of the American Government to inject the arms program into the economy slowly enough has already caused a vast inflation of prices all over the world. It has disturbed the economy of the Western World to such an extent that if it goes on more damage will be done by this unrestrained behavior than by the behavior of the nation the arms are intended to restrain. . . .

"I say, therefore, with full solemnity of the seriousness of what I am saying, that the £4,700,000,000 arms program is already dead. It cannot be achieved without irreparable damage to the economy of Great Britain and the world. . . . The fact is that the Western World has embarked upon a campaign of arms production and upon a scale of arms production so quickly and of such extent that the foundations of political liberty and parliamentary democracy will not be able to sustain the shock." (In his challenging book, *In Place of Fear,* published in the spring of 1952, Mr. Bevan expands this thesis in detail.)

In December, 1951, Winston Churchill, soon after he became Prime Minister for the second time, declared frankly in the House of Commons that Britain would be unable to complete on schedule its three-year $13-billion rearmament program. He said that he was giving Aneurin Bevan "honorable mention" for having, "it appears by accident—perhaps not from the best of motives—happened to be right." Early in 1952 Churchill's Conservative Government launched a new *austerity* program "to avert national bankruptcy." Measures included a drastic curtailment of the social services, cuts in the civil service staff, a sharp reduction in manufactured goods for the home market and a record low European travel allowance of approximately $70 per year for each Englishman.

The remarks of Bevan and Churchill raise the portentous question of whether the long-range effect of American policy will not be to force Western Europe farther and farther to the left instead of rescuing it from the Communists. A most significant report issued in March, 1952, by the ultra-conservative U.S. Chamber of Commerce puts the issue squarely: "There is little surplus fat in Western Europe to permit the luxury of large armies. It will take decades fully to repair the destruction of the recent war. . . . Further sacrifices would inevitably drive many into the already large Communist and Socialist Parties. It would seem the part of wisdom, given these trends, not to overlook the political and economic problems of Europe. Heavy emphasis upon the military may well backfire."

The only sound way, of course, to prevent the spread of Communist regimes is to institute far-reaching social and economic reforms which will do away with poverty, unemployment, depression, currency crises and the other ills which have afflicted Europe over the past few decades. But the heavy-handed Truman Administration, insisting everywhere on the *warfare* state in place of the *welfare* state, has offered no effective plan for permanent economic well-being and is, on the contrary, depressing living standards in the nations it purports to be aiding.

The careening American economic juggernaut has affected for the worse not only England, France and Western Europe in general, but the entire world. Wholesale price increases since the start of the Korean war amounted, as of July, 1951, to more than 30 percent in Mexico, more than 33 percent in Brazil, more than 42 percent in Finland and more than 51 percent in Japan. If President Truman would study his own reports more carefully, he would be more conscious of the unhappy consequences of his policies. For example, his Mid-Year Economic Report of 1951 stated: "The enormous price increases which have occurred constitute in some countries a danger to political and social stability, and to the security program of the free world. . . . Because the economies of these countries have been under great strain and because in some of them the political and social situation is tense, inflation raises not only the question of equitable distribution of the economic burden of defense; it also raises the grave question of the ability of their governments to carry through the needed defense programs and maintain economic stability."

With the economic situation steadily deteriorating in the very nations the American Government proclaims it is saving from the Soviet menace, the Truman Administration has all along insisted that its allies follow its own policy of curtailing trade with members of the Soviet-led bloc for the purpose of weakening Communist military potential. This has meant a severe decline in commerce between Western and Eastern Europe and the cutting off of Japan from China, which has traditionally been both its best customer and its main source of raw materials. The lack of normal trade relations with Western Europe has indeed been some handicap to the Soviet Union and the smaller Eastern European countries in their postwar economic reconstruction; but it has been considerably more of a handicap to the Western European economies.

This is because Soviet Russia and its allies, with their far-reaching economic planning, have been better able to adjust to the falling off of trade than the West. Furthermore, the American-imposed barriers against economic relations with the East have forced the North Atlantic Pact countries to attempt to fill the vacuum through trade with the U.S. This endeavor is impossible of fulfillment because European exports run into the barrier of America's high tariffs and because European imports must be paid for in dollars. These difficulties have combined to create a critical and continuing dollar deficit. The U.S. "get-tough" policy towards the U.S.S.R. is toughest of all on the peoples of Western Europe.

In July, 1951, the American Government took the extreme step of breaking off its formal trade and commercial agreements with Soviet Russia and its allies in Eastern Europe, despite the fact that these nations have been most desirous of maintaining trade relations with the West. American business of course loses out economically from this short-sighted policy. The total value of exports from the U.S. to the U.S.S.R. fell from $149,504,000 (including $50,540,000 in aid and relief) in 1947 to $27,879,000 in 1948, to $6,617,000 in 1949, to a trickle of $621,407 in 1950 and an estimated $70,000 in 1951.

Walter Lippmann makes some pertinent and penetrating remarks about the all too successful American campaign to cripple international trade. "A dominating part of Congress," he writes, "which Mr. Truman and Mr. Acheson have felt it necessary to appease, is demanding a virtual embargo and blockade of the whole Communist orbit. The reasoning of these Congressmen is that an embargo and blockade of this kind would hurt the Communists more than it hurts the United States. That, considering our immense self-sufficiency and enormous financial power, is no doubt true. But from this truth they have jumped to the quite unwarranted conclusion that the embargo hurts the Communists more than it hurts our weak and stricken allies. That is not true, and we shall be learning more and more, but in the hard way, how untrue it is."

Mr. Lippmann analyzes the situation further: "The great problem looming on the horizon is how to keep the large, congested, industrial populations of Britain, West Germany and Japan at work and at a standard of living which they will accept as reasonable for themselves. To deal with this problem we are compelled—as things stand now—to replace the markets and sources of supply which they have lost by finding markets and sources of supply within the world which is dependably in the Western political orbit. This is perhaps the most radical reconstruction and rerouting of the trade of the world which men have ever dreamed of trying to bring about." Although Mr. Lippmann does not say it, the chances are slim that this drastic and unnatural alteration in long-established trade patterns will succeed.

The reference by Mr. Lippmann to appeasement on the part of the Truman Administration brings out the extent to which American foreign policy is being formulated, not for the benefit of the American people or the world, but to enable the Democratic Party to stay in power by outdoing the Republican Party in anti-Soviet and anti-Communist declarations and deeds. President Truman's announced determination to "contain" communism has been far more successful in containing the Republicans than in its original goal. And the Russians cannot help wondering whether this perpetual merry-go-around of American political maneuvering might not lead one party or the other to precipitate a world war as the culmination of the great contest in denouncing, hating and combating the alleged Communist menace.

Furthermore, current in Administration and congressional circles is a strong feeling that an armed conflict with the Soviet Union is inevitable. Mr. Demaree Bess corroborates this fact in *The Saturday Evening Post:* "A fatalistic feeling has pervaded both major political parties that we can solve our own and the world's problems only by overthrowing the expanding Soviet Empire by force of arms. This fatalism has spread so widely that we no longer pay much attention to the most belligerent statements by our representatives in Washington."

One of the most disturbing—and threatening—features of American foreign policy is that the U.S. has lined up as allies an incredible assortment of fascist or semi-fascist governments dedicated to violence, terror and tyranny. The so-called "free world," supposedly banded together to extend the blessings of intellectual liberty and political democracy, includes sixteen Latin American dictatorships or quasi-dictatorships (I exclude here Cuba, Guatemala, Mexico and Uruguay); the royal fascist regime of Greece; the cruel police state of Turkey; the Formosan remnants of Chiang Kai-shek's bloody and primitive fascism; the Union of South Africa with its horrible racist laws; Franco's Falangist Spain, established with the help of Hitler and Mussolini and perpetuated in their image; the Nazi-tending republic of Western Germany; and still semi-feudal Japan with its thin veneer of democracy. This roll call obviously shows that "the free world" is a propaganda myth.

Mrs. Vera M. Dean of the moderate Foreign Policy Association makes clear in the weekly *Bulletin* of that organization the strange double standard characteristic of American policy: "In Eastern Europe Washington has urged free and unfettered elections and has denounced the establishment of dictatorial governments dominated by Communists. Yet at the Bogotá conference of 1948 the United States proposed recognition of governments in Latin America without inquiry into their character and without the requirement of prior elections. In the opinion of many observers, this doctrine has encouraged seizure of power by military juntas in Peru, Venezuela and El Salvador at the expense of the kind of middle-of-the-road regimes we have urged for Eastern Europe and the Balkans."

The efficient manner in which the United States Government has enlisted in its coalition well-nigh every reactionary force and gangster government throughout the world indicates the possible use of such elements in the unscrupulous rough-and-tumble of aggressive warfare. Certainly the make-up of the American-led bloc must in itself awaken grave apprehensions in the Soviet mind. And when in addition the Truman Administration insists on the provocative rearmament of Western Germany and Japan, both the Russians and all other peace-loving peoples have a right to be anxious. Let us remember that already coming to the fore in post-war Western Germany and Japan are the same sort of economic and political groupings which so ruthlessly unleashed the Second World War.

The Japanese Peace Treaty, forced upon the world by the United States at San Francisco in September, 1951, summarily violated the 1943 Cairo Agreement, which promised the return of Formosa to China; and also the 1945 Potsdam Declaration, which guaranteed that there should be no revival of Japanese militarism. The Treaty provided for continuing American military occupation of Japan and for numerous U.S. bases for land, sea and air forces. With India and Burma refusing to attend the San Francisco conference because of their opposition to the Treaty and with the Chinese Republic deliberately excluded, representatives of two-thirds of the people of Asia took no part in this settlement directly affecting that half of the earth's population living in the Orient.

Closely related to the Truman Administration's collaboration with the support of reactionary regimes is its reversal of America's traditional attitude of sympathy towards the aspirations of colonial peoples for self-determination and independence. Americans are themselves a proud and freedom-loving people who threw off the yoke of empire through revolution. But today the United States has become the great champion of Western imperialism, resorting to dollar diplomacy, political intimidation and military violence in taking over the suppressive functions of faltering empires.

4

The effects of American foreign policy, then, since Mr. Truman took over the White House, have been such as to cause deepest misgivings throughout the globe. The apparent readiness of leaders in the United States Government to risk blowing civilization to smithereens for the sake of political advantage, the bellicose attitude of many American journalists, radio commentators and other prominent citizens, the stratospheric sums spent on atom bombs and other weapons, the expanding global ring of U.S. air and military bases, America's alliance with outright fascists or old-fashioned military dictatorships, the rearming of Western Germany and Japan—all these things raise the question whether American policy is not directed towards war rather than peace through preparedness. Even the conservative *London Economist* states: "In large measure the present American program is designed for fighting Russia, not for staying at peace by deterring a Russian aggression." And some of the missteps that Soviet Russia and other members of the Communist bloc have taken in foreign policy are attributable in no small degree to fear of American intentions and a sharp defensive reaction to them.

Most of these deplorable developments flow from a policy that has been worked out and put through as the answer to the danger of "Soviet aggression." Returning to this theme for a moment, let us cite a man who, in the American community, is as respectable as the Washington Monument and who was denouncing the Soviet Union and all its works for years before Harry Truman even became a Senator. I refer to Mr. Herbert Hoover, who, in his speech of January, 1952, noted that Western Europe, in its judgment as to the risk of a Communist invasion, takes a view "profoundly different from the attitude of Washington."

"There is in Europe today," asserted Mr. Hoover, "no such public alarm as has been fanned up in the United States. None of those nations has declared emergencies or taken measures comparable with ours. They do not propagandize war fears or war psychosis such as we get out of Washington. Not one European country conducts such exercises in protection from bombs as we have had in New York." Mr. Hoover then cited eight major reasons why public opinion in Western Europe estimates the "risk of invasion as so much less than does Washington." "I cannot say," he added, "whether these eight assumptions are correct or not. But they do contribute to Western Europe's lack of hysteria and their calculation of low risk and, therefore, their lack of hurry to arm. In any event this whole European situation requires that the United States recalculate our own risks and reconsider the possible alternatives."

I have quoted ex-President Hoover at some length, not only because of the intrinsic soundness of the statements cited, but also in order to show that conservative defenders of the capitalist system, opponents of socialism and enemies of the Soviet Union are also critical of American foreign policy and agree on important international issues with liberals and radicals. The point is that the U.S. drift toward war and a garrison state is likely to prove catastrophic for the well-being of all Americans, regardless of their political and economic viewpoints.

Another conservative gravely troubled by the international situation is Pope Pius XII. In a Christmas message broadcast to the world on December 23, 1950, the Supreme Pontiff of the Roman Catholic Church appealed to Soviet Russia and the Western Powers to enter into direct negotiations before their deepening cleavage degenerated into war. "How earnestly," he pleaded, "the Church desires to smooth the way for these friendly relations between peoples! For her, East and West do not represent opposite ideals, but share a common heritage to which both have generously contributed and to which both are called to contribute in the future also."

Now it is precisely "direct negotiations," especially with the United States, that the Soviet Government has been suggesting over the past few years and to which the Truman Administration has turned a cold—very cold—shoulder. The U.S. Government argues that diplomatic negotiations for the settlement of the cold war and the easing of American-Soviet tensions should take place within the framework of the United Nations. Yet the United States has itself by-passed the U.N. whenever it seemed convenient, as in the drawing up and effectuation of the Truman Doctrine regarding Greece and Turkey, the institution of the North Atlantic Treaty and the N.A.T.O., and the rearming of Western Germany and Japan.

Certainly the founders of the United Nations never intended that its establishment was to rule out special conversations and confidential negotiations between two or more of its members. Indeed, the first Article in the U.N. Charter's Chapter on the Pacific Settlement of Disputes reads: "The parties to any dispute, the continuance of which is likely to endanger the maintenance of international peace and security, shall, first of all, seek a solution by negotiation, enquiry, mediation, conciliation, arbitration, judicial settlement, resort to regional agencies or arrangements, *or other peaceful means of their own choice.*" [Italics mine—C.L.]

The negative American attitude towards Soviet overtures has brought forth from the conservative David Lawrence, writing in the conservative *New York Herald Tribune,* the following comment: "The biggest barrier to world peace today has been erected by persons inside and outside Washington who have closed their minds to any further discussion with the Russians. This school of thought says conferences are no good, that Russians can't be trusted, that sooner or later there will be war and that America must stay on a war footing every day and night, borrow unearned billions from tomorrow's generations and even perhaps fight a 'preventive war,' striking before the enemy can. The exponents of that doctrine have nothing to offer but physical force and threats."

Soviet foreign policy does not and cannot function within a vacuum; to be realistic it must take into consideration the fundamental forces operating in international affairs, including the actions and policies of the United States, world capitalism's acknowledged leader. Hence the Soviet Government shapes and re-shapes its own policies with the particular attitude of America always in mind. As we have seen, you do not have to be a Soviet diplomat to feel that the effects of current American policy are not conducive to world peace and economic stability. If I am correct in my analysis, then the economic, trade, armament and cold war policies of the Truman Administration, while certainly not helpful to the Soviet-led coalition, will not in the long run be helpful, either, to U.S. capitalism and democracy. And these policies may well prove fatal for Western Europe.

The all-out anti-Soviet atmosphere in the United States so stifles objective thinking that there is a tendency here among many leaders in government, business and public opinion to discard summarily as bad any move that would be good for the Soviet Union or the other Communist countries. Now indubitably international peace, disarmament and a normal exchange of goods on the world market would be beneficial for the Communist nations. But to reject these aims on this account is to negate the processes of reason. For plainly the fulfilment of such goals would also be immensely beneficial to America and the rest of the non-Communist World. *Mutual self-interest is the key to ending the present American-Soviet impasse.*

There is much in Soviet international proposals that is valid not only for the U.S.S.R., but also for the U.S.A. A sound American peace policy is bound to have a number of basic points in common with Soviet policies. During the war against the Axis Soviet Russia and the United States drew up and faithfully carried out many joint military agreements which were to the obvious interest of both countries. In those years high officials in the Roosevelt or Truman Administrations did not turn down suggestions merely because they were initiated or advocated by the Soviets. It is not sensible to do so today.

War and violence have always been the worst ways to deal with problems between countries. There is a far, far better method for the solution of current dilemmas—for nations, for peoples, for governments, for capitalists, for Communists, for conservatives, for radicals, for politicians, for businessmen, for this alliance and that bloc, for East and West. That is the method of reason, understanding, negotiation and compromise. I believe that this method now demands that the American Government give more serious and reasonable consideration to Soviet proposals for disarmament, international control of atomic energy, the re-establishment of East-West trade, the unification of Germany and a Five-Power Peace Pact.

Above all, it is time for Washington to accept the invitation of the Soviet Government to have highest ranking officials from each side sit down and talk things over calmly, with the aim in mind of coming to a general agreement on peaceful co-existence and settling the chief issues in dispute on terms advantageous to both the U.S.A. and the U.S.S.R.

6
Back to the Bill of Rights (1951)
Foreword to the Fourth Printing (1961)

Since this pamphlet was first published early in 1951, violations of the Bill of Rights have steadily increased. There has been a serious decline in academic and cultural freedom; and more and more political dissenters have lost their jobs—in government, in education and in private business, especially the entertainment industry. The Congressional Inquisition has become a monstrous cancer in the body politic; Congress has passed a new crop of repressive measures; and the courts uphold flagrantly unconstitutional legislation.

Four of the worst laws recently passed by Congress gravely infringing upon civil liberties are: the McCarran-Walter Immigration Act of 1952, which bears down heavily on aliens and foreign-born American citizens; the Communist Control Act of 1954, which outlaws the Communist Party; the Immunity Act of 1954, which goes far in nullifying the Fifth Amendment guaranteeing every American against compulsory self-incrimination; and the Welker Act of 1954, which requires all so-called subversive organizations to register with the Government whatever printing presses and duplicating equipment they use.

However, because this pamphlet pays particular attention to the Smith Act, passed by Congress in 1940, I shall try to bring that discussion up to date.

On June 4, 1951, the Supreme Court of the United States, by a 6-2 decision, affirmed the constitutionality of the Smith Act and the conviction of the first eleven Communist Party leaders prosecuted under it for conspiring to advocate and teach the forceful overthrow of the American Government. Thus the Supreme Court scrapped the First Amendment to the Constitution as a poor security risk which it is too hazardous for this country to retain in these critical days.

The Supreme Court decision has in effect outlawed the teaching or advocacy by any group or organization of the very doctrine embodied in our Declaration of Independence. This revered document states that when the American people have suffered under some system of government a long train of abuses, usurpations and other evils, "it is their right, it is their duty, to throw off such government, and to provide new guards for their future security." Like the overwhelming majority of Americans, I believe that we possess adequate democratic means for peaceful changes, even of a drastic nature, in the social structure. But we surrender this nation's birthright and denigrate its origin when we deny citizens, however misguided, the liberty to say that violent revolution is justified.

The American people can no more afford to accept as final this 1951 ruling of the Supreme Court than they accepted as final the Dred Scott decision of 1857 broadening the scope of slavery in the United States. What the noted historian Burton J. Hendrick said about that decision in his book, *Bulwark of the Republic: A Biography of the Constitution,* is surprisingly relevant to the current Communist case: "The main incentive actuating the judges' minds was political. It is a startling conclusion, but it rests upon definite evidence. The majority judges clearly abandoned, for the moment, the unbiased interpretation of the Constitution and sought to step into a new arena and solve the great political question of the time."

I have included as a special appendix Mr. Justice Black's dissent from the Smith Act decision as the best brief comment on the unsound reasoning of the Supreme Court majority. Curiously enough, the late Justice Jackson, whom I quote to advantage several times in my paper, was a member of this majority. But his separate concurring opinion, and also that of Mr. Justice Frankfurter, indicate that they agreed most reluctantly.

After the Supreme Court decision had given the go-ahead signal, the U.S. Department of Justice, from 1951 through 1954, indicted and arrested on conspiracy charges 119 more Communist officials, of whom 68 have been tried and convicted and three acquitted. Since the Court refused in 1952 to hear the appeals of six Baltimore defendants and early in 1955 of thirteen "second-string" Communist leaders in New York City, there is little likelihood of any of the other convictions being reversed. However, a new trial was granted two of the New York Communists, Alexander Trachtenberg and George Blake Charney, after the professional informer, Harvey Matusow, had confessed in a sworn affidavit and in his book, *False Witness,* that he had testified falsely against these men at their trial.

In 1954 the Department of Justice, which in previous prosecutions of Communists had chosen to rely on the anticonspiracy provision of the Smith Act, started to use the clause in this statute making mere membership in certain organizations a crime. Thus it indicted three Communists on the charge that as members of the Communist Party they knowingly belonged to an organization advocating the overthrow of the U.S. Government by force and violence, and that they themselves intended to bring about such overthrow.

The first Communist to be tried under this new type of indictment was Claude M. Lightfoot, executive secretary of the Illinois Communist Party. He was found guilty by a jury in Chicago in January 1955 and received the stiff sentence of five years in jail and a $5,000 fine. The weakest link in the Government's claim that membership in the Communist Party is in itself criminal is that the Internal Security (McCarran) Act of 1950 specifically states that "neither the holding of office nor membership in any Communist organization by any person" shall constitute per se a violation of the Act "or of any other criminal statute." If the Supreme Court upholds the Lightfoot conviction, the way will be open for the Department of Justice to proceed in the same manner against thousands of rank-and-file Communists throughout the country.

In 1948 when the Department of Justice brought to trial the eleven "first-string" Communists, it indicted them under both the conspiracy and membership provisions of the Smith Act. The defendants, however, obtained a severance of these indictments, and the Government prosecutors never pressed the one based on membership in the Communist Party. But when five of these originally convicted Communists came out of jail in March of 1955, the Department of Justice immediately had them re-arrested under the old membership clause indictment. It is difficult to see how this new prosecution can succeed in the face of the Fifth Amendment guarantee against any person being "twice put in jeopardy" for the same offense.

Yet again and again during the past few years the Department of Justice and the courts have disregarded the Bill of Rights and the Constitution in the heat and hysteria of the wildest witch-hunt that America has ever seen. This nullification of our civil liberties has taken place for the most part under the cloak of specious legality. While there are signs now that the tide may be turning once more in the direction of freedom, the American people have a long, tough battle ahead to fully re-establish the Bill of Rights.

April, 1955.   C.L.

Back to the Bill of Rights

(A paper read December 28, 1950, at a meeting of the American Political Science Association at Washington, D.C., on the subject of "Has a totalitarian political party any rights, moral or legal, under democratic government?")

I believe that a totalitarian political party ought to have full legal rights under democratic government, but that the moral rights of such a party must differ according to the specific program that it supports. For the purposes of this discussion I shall concentrate on Fascist and Communist Parties and shall not attempt to argue over the vague and doubtful meaning of the word *totalitarian*.

The important question which this symposium raises relates to democratic governments throughout the world and to countries of varying social and economic development. I am of the opinion that totalitarian parties in any true democracy should possess the same legal rights as any other party to organize, publish periodicals, distribute literature, elect candidates to political office, hold meetings, put on radio programs and undertake any other activities characteristic of a political party. Totalitarian parties as organizations and their members as individuals are of course properly subject to the ordinary laws of the nation in which they function. If, for instance, a Fascist or a Communist Party, or an individual Fascist or Communist, or any other person, violates a statute against treason, espionage, sabotage, murder, inciting to riot, failure to register as an agent of a foreign power or conspiracy to overthrow the government, then a democratic state has not only the right but the duty to prosecute the offender to the limit of the law.

But if a democratic government prosecutes a Fascist or Communist Party, or individual members of these parties, because of the expression of unpopular or extreme opinions—or goes to the length of suppressing the parties altogether—then it is violating the long-established principles of free political association and undermining the very democracy it is pledged to uphold. While admittedly there are always difficult borderline cases, I think that the correct line to draw is in general the traditional one between words, ideas or opinions, on the one hand, and overt acts on the other hand. Words, however, can sometimes become a constituent part of an illegal action, as when Davis says to Jones: "I will give you $1,000 if you kill Brown." Davis can then be indicted for a conspiracy to commit murder, but not for the crime of uttering certain words.

It is my contention that every democratic government, including that of the United States today, can adequately protect itself against extremists of whatever variety by vigilantly exercising the established police powers of the state and taking legal measures against political groups, or individuals associated with them, when words issue in overt illegal action. As Mr. Justice Jackson of the United States Supreme Court stated in his opinion of May 8, 1950, in the case of the *American Communications Association versus Douds:* "Only in the darkest periods of human history has any Western government concerned itself with mere belief, however eccentric or mischievous, when it has not matured into overt action; and if that practice survives anywhere, it is in the Communist countries whose philosophies we loathe."

The general philosophy that lies behind the ideal of complete civil liberties is well known. We might all agree that in certain situations the suppression of free speech could result in some limited social gain. But the long-run dangers of such suppression, in destroying the public's faith in democratic institutions and fatally rupturing the fabric of democracy, far outweigh the temporary advantages of dictatorial expediency. As the framers of the American Constitution and Bill of Rights made clear, unabridged freedom of speech—with its associated freedoms—is a transcendent social and political value upon which rests, to a very considerable degree, the collective welfare, wisdom, order and progress of the democratic community. There is and can be no more significant value in a democracy than freedom of speech and opinion. To curtail, mutilate or negate this freedom is to strike at the heart of the democratic process.

In times of emergency, freedom of speech, freedom of the press and freedom of assembly are, if anything, even more essential to the health of the democratic state. For in such times a nation needs more than ever an alert and critical public opinion that will help to guide the country through crisis. If, however, a disastrous flood, a great earthquake or an armed invasion results in a declaration of martial law, some abridgment of civil liberties is justified. For then the machinery of democratic government may well have broken down to such an extent that some of the established rules of democracy may become temporarily irrelevant. Of course at all times in relation to free speech there are legitimate *non-political* qualifications as embodied, for example, in the laws against libel, obscenity and false advertising.

In this turbulent era the greatest hope of the American people and of all mankind is that the voice of reason will prevail. Reason, intelligence in its most precise and successful form, is nothing more nor less than the modern scientific method of experimentation and verification; and perhaps the most pressing task of the present is to carry over that method more effectively from the natural sciences into the realm of politics, economics and international relations. But scientific method in public affairs can play its proper role only in the atmosphere of democratic institutions and free speech. New ideas, even ideas that are considered ludicrous, dangerous or hateful, must be given a hearing. The crackpot may turn out to be the trail-blazer; the genius is likely to start his career by being a minority of one. It is dissenting minorities which throughout history have usually shown the way to human progress. In a free society minorities must be scrupulously protected and guaranteed the democratic opportunity of evolving into majorities. "We must not forget," asserted Justice Jackson, then Attorney General of the U.S., in an address made in 1940, "that it was not so long ago that both the term 'Republican' and the term 'Democrat' were epithets with sinister meaning to denote persons of radical tendencies that were 'subversive' of the order of things then dominant."

The life of reason, the appeal to the supreme court of the mind, implies in its very essence peaceful persuasion through the free exchange and competition of ideas in the open marketplace of thought. This social procedure, this combination of democratic and scientific methodology, is, I suggest, much more important for the future of the nation and the world than any other single discovery or achievement made hitherto in the history of the race. It is a procedure which, as long as mankind endures, will enable societies to make fundamental changes in their structure in a peaceful and orderly manner.

Implicit in the method of science and democracy is the rejection of a dogmatic attitude and the encouragement of constant questioning—questioning even of the most basic assumptions. Hence persons and groups in a truly democratic community have the legal and moral right to argue, if they so choose, that the nation should substitute for intelligence the dictates of some revealed, authoritarian religion or for democracy some form of authoritarian, political dictatorship. They have a right to attempt to win over, if they can, a majority of the electorate to one or the other of these erroneous anti-democratic theses. Democratic self-government does indeed imply, among other things, that the people may make mistakes and, in fact, terrible mistakes. This is a risk we have to take in order to remain free. As Justice Oliver Wendell Holmes put it twenty-five years ago in his dissenting opinion in the Gitlow case: "If, in the long run, the beliefs expressed in proletarian dictatorship are destined to be accepted by the dominant forces of the community, the only meaning of free speech is that they should be given their chance and have their way."

But can democratic government logically permit totalitarian parties to advocate the violent overthrow of the state? I am convinced that the answer is "Yes" and that the right to advocate revolution is a basic constitutional liberty in a democracy. No doubt all but a handful of Americans would agree with me that there exists in the United States the necessary political machinery for peaceful and democratic change in a conservative or a radical direction. But we could be wrong; and as democrats we cannot legitimately outlaw either legally or morally those who challenge our position on this issue. In the field of politics there are no impregnable absolutes. As professional or amateur observers of the political scene, we surely would not wish to claim that America has attained such a high state of democratic development that from now till the end of time no advocacy of revolution, or actual revolution, could be warranted. To quote Justice Jackson again in the Douds case: "We cannot ignore the fact that our own government originated in revolution and is legitimate only if overthrow by force may sometimes be justified. That circumstances sometimes justify it is not Communist doctrine but an old American belief."

The leaders and supporters of a democratic government will presumably utilize all available techniques of education and communication to offset the propaganda of totalitarian groups. But I repeat that the point at which a democratic government has the right and obligation to take punitive legal steps against revolutionists is when they concretely plan and conspire to seize control of the government by force or when through specific, overt action they violate some law. If a democratic government arrests, jails, suppresses or executes totalitarians or anyone else for mere propaganda and opinions, no matter how repugnant they may seem to established mores, it then and there ceases to be a truly democratic government.

Certain practical considerations support the principles which I have been outlining. A democratic government will find it easier to keep track of and protect itself against totalitarians and their parties if it does not drive them underground. It is far better for extremists to rant in public than to plot in private. Equally important is the fact that when one leftist or rightist group is deprived of its constitutional liberties, many other groups in the democratic community are endangered. If the state takes away freedom of speech and association from, for example, all acknowledged members of the Communist Party, then a further witch-hunt is sure to begin in order to ferret out the *secret* Communists and the so-called fellow-travelers. This is certain to include an inquisition into the beliefs of liberals, progressives and well-nigh all dissenters in the community.

Justice Jackson has well described the situation in his opinion of September 25, 1950, ordering that the bail of the eleven Communist leaders, convicted in the lower courts under the Smith Act, be continued. He states: "The right of every American to equal treatment before the law is wrapped up in the same constitutional bundle with those of these Communists. If in anger or disgust with these defendants we throw out the bundle, we also cast aside protection for the liberties of more worthy critics who may be in opposition to the government of some future day." Scientists, teachers, intellectuals, liberals of every variety should make no mistake about it: When the bell of suppression tolls, it tolls for thee!

Another consideration to keep in mind is that the chief domestic danger that the American republic has been facing in this era is that of espionage.

In this connection what the self-confessed spy, Harry Gold, stated at his trial is significant: "I was told by my first Soviet superior to stay away from it [the Communist Party], never to read *The Daily Worker* and never to read liberal literature or express liberal thoughts." The way to catch spies, then, is apparently not to follow the common practice of hounding the Communist Party and banning liberal magazines like *The Nation*.

I have thus far referred to Fascist and Communist Parties without differentiating between them. But at this point I wish to assert that in my judgment there is a great moral difference between them. Whatever similarities exist in the *means* used by Fascist and Communist Parties to win and maintain state power, their *ends* are quite dissimilar. Morally Communist Parties are on an obviously higher plane than Fascist Parties in that they have such aims as (1) complete racial democracy and non-discrimination; (2) full equality between the sexes; (3) educational and cultural opportunity for everyone; (4) a planned socialist economy of abundance on behalf of all the people; (5) the attainment of political democracy when the transitional need for dictatorship has passed; (6) the teaching of an inclusive and integrated philosophy of life; and (7) the achievement of international peace. In spite of the colossal blunder and act of international immorality on the part of the Communist-controlled North Koreans in committing aggression against South Korea, I am convinced that Communist Parties are on the whole desirous of seeing world peace established.

In the above seven points I have not tried to cover all the basic differences between the Communists and Fascists; but my summary indicates the relevance of the remark once made by Mr. John Strachey, Minister of War in the British Labor Government, namely, that Communism and Fascism are like two express trains going in opposite directions. The notion that Communism and Fascism are fundamentally the same is a dangerous untruth. It is my view, then, that Communist Parties do possess moral rights under a democratic government, but that Fascist Parties, best symbolized by Hitler's Nazis, possess hardly any. Frankly, however, I regard most of the arguments to deprive totalitarian parties of political rights on the grounds of their lacking moral rights, or of being absolutely incorrigible, as fancy rationalizations of a desire to suppress those whom we do not like.

Turning now to the current condition of democracy in the United States, I find that our country since the close of World War II has been continuously violating the principles which I have enunciated in this paper. The unrestrained behavior of the House Committee on Un-American Activities and of certain Senatorial Committees, the loyalty purge of the Federal Government, the Attorney General's listing of alleged subversive organizations, the unconstitutional Smith Act, the legislative monstrosity of the McCarran Act with its concentration camp provisions, the extensive drive against aliens, the widespread establishment of loyalty oaths for teachers, scores of state and municipal laws and ordinances penalizing non-conformity, restrictions on freedom of expression in the fields of journalism, publishing, the radio and the motion picture, hesitation to discuss confidential matters or controversial political issues over the telephone because of the extensive and illegal wiretapping by government agents, the severe pressures against lawyers who take on the duty of defending Communists or other radicals, pervasive fear among professional people and the population at large of registering dissent from prevailing patterns of thought—all these things testify to the dangerous inroads that have been made upon the American Constitution, the Bill of Rights and the spirit of democracy.

The present trend in America is to whittle away more and more of the Bill of Rights in the name of an anti-Communist and anti-Soviet crusade which has substituted invective, prejudice and hysteria for objective thinking on public affairs. Government bodies, courts of justice, bar associations and lip-service civil libertarians are all engaged in re-writing the First Amendment to read: "Congress shall make no law . . . abridging the freedom of speech, except for the Communist Party, its members and its sympathizers." In this drive against left-wing groups and individuals the new and remarkable concept of "guilt by association" is increasingly taking the place of the time-honored American legal doctrine that guilt is always personal. And "guilt by accusation" is replacing the long-accepted presumption that a man is to be considered innocent until proved guilty.

Another new and dubious doctrine that has recently been running wild is the "clear and present danger" rule. As laid down by Justice Holmes in the Schenck case in 1919, "The question in every case is whether the words used are used in such circumstances and are of such a nature as to create a clear and present danger that they will bring about the substantive evils that Congress has a right to prevent. It is a question of proximity and degree." In 1927 Justice Brandeis, in his opinion in the Whitney case, attempted to clarify the matter: "To courageous, self-reliant men, with confidence in the power of free and fearless reasoning applied through the processes of popular government, no danger flowing from speech can be deemed clear and present, unless the incidence of the evil apprehended is so imminent that it may befall before there is opportunity for free discussion."

Professor Alexander Meiklejohn, in his little book, *Free Speech and Its Relation to Self-Government,* brilliantly argues that despite the great contribution of Justice Holmes to a liberal jurisprudence, his origination of the "clear and present danger" test was a mistake. I think Professor Meiklejohn may be right; but what is altogether certain is that recent applications of the Holmes doctrine are wrong. Thus Judge Learned Hand of the U.S. Court of Appeals, in an opinion handed down in 1950, affirming the conviction of the eleven Communist leaders under the Smith Act, transformed the idea of a clear and *imminent* danger into that of a clear and *probable* one at some future time that might be even a hundred years hence. The lesson is that if we start making restrictions on freedom of speech, we open the door to congressional and judicial interpretations that patently thwart the First Amendment.

So far as violent revolution is concerned, we can state that there is a present and imminent danger of it only when a conspiracy is under way and actual preparations are being made for carrying it into effect. But in such circumstances the United States Government can move at once on the basis of Section 6 of the Criminal Code which forbids conspiracies to overthrow the government and conspiracies to resist or obstruct the execution of *any* federal law. The Communist leaders have been prosecuted, however, not for a conspiracy to commit a crime of conduct, but for an alleged conspiracy to commit an alleged crime of *speech*. And there is no conclusive evidence, in my judgment, that they ever advocated, or planned to advocate, the forceful overthrow of our Government. The prosecution and conviction of these men run directly counter to the great American tradition of freedom of opinion.

Looking at the history of American democracy during the first half of this century, we must admit repeated failure in the field of political and civil liberties. The two worst periods in this respect have been those immediately following the First World War and the Second World War. We are correct, of course, in placing a large share of the blame on those members of Congress and government officials who, although they are sworn to uphold the Constitution, so often become leaders in subverting it. But I must confess my dark suspicion that a large proportion of the American people themselves, I fear even the majority, give only lip service to the Bill of Rights.

Without trying to assess all the causes, economic and otherwise, for this lamentable situation, we can at least assert that America requires far more education concerning civil liberties. Organizations such as the American Civil Liberties Union are important in this field; yet we need to pay more attention to the subject at the school and college level. At the Yale Law School, Professor Thomas I. Emerson teaches a half-year course on "Political and Civil Rights" which is almost unique in American education. But this course for graduate students comes a little late in their lives. I suggest that every college should present such a course; and that considerably more emphasis should be given to this subject matter in high schools and secondary schools. It ought to be plain that if we do not educate our youth in the fundamentals of democracy, we shall not get democracy.

In conclusion, let me state that Karl Marx and his followers have all along contended that capitalist democracy is insincere about civil liberties and will throw them overboard in times of stress and strain. Although in America today resistance to the trends I have been emphasizing is still very strong and although we have made significant gains in combating racial discrimination, the fact remains that much is taking place in this country which gives comfort and corroboration to Communist theory. The triumphs of the reactionary demagogues paradoxically become the triumphs of the Communist prophets. There is a simple remedy for all this. That is for the people, the press, the courts, the Congress and the Government of the United States to return to uncompromising support of the Bill of Rights and the Constitution.

Appendix: Justice Black's Dissent Regarding the Smith Act

Dissenting Opinion of Mr. Justice Black, June 4, 1951, in the Case of the Eleven Communist Leaders Indicted and Convicted under the Smith Act

Here again, as in *Breard v. Alexandria,* decided this day, my basic disagreement with the Court is not as to how we should explain or reconcile what was said in prior decisions but springs from a fundamental difference in constitutional approach. Consequently, it would serve no useful purpose to state my position at length.

At the outset I want to emphasize what the crime involved in this case is, and what it is not. These petitioners were not charged with an attempt to overthrow the Government. They were not charged with non-verbal acts of any kind designed to overthrow the Government. They were not even charged with saying anything or writing anything designed to overthrow the Government. The charge was that they agreed to assemble and to talk and publish certain ideas at a later date: The indictment is that they conspired to organize the Communist Party and to use speech or newspapers and other publications in the future to teach and advocate the forcible overthrow of the Government. No matter how it is worded, this is a virulent form of prior censorship of speech and press, which I believe the First Amendment forbids. I would hold Section 3 of the Smith Act authorizing this prior restraint unconstitutional on its face and as applied.

But let us assume, contrary to all constitutional ideas of fair criminal procedure, that petitioners, although not indicted for the crime of actual advocacy, may be punished for it. Even on this radical assumption, the only way to affirm these convictions, as the dissent of Mr. Justice Douglas shows, is to qualify drastically or wholly repudiate the established "clear and present danger" rule. This the Court does in a way which greatly restricts the protections afforded by the First Amendment. The opinions for affirmance show that the chief reason for jettisoning the rule is the expressed fear that advocacy of Communist doctrine endangers the safety of the

Republic. Undoubtedly, a governmental policy of unfettered communication of ideas does entail dangers. To the Founders of this Nation, however, the benefits derived from free expression were worth the risk. They embodied this philosophy in the First Amendment's command that Congress "shall make no law abridging . . . the freedom of speech, or of the press . . . ." I have always believed that the First Amendment is the key-stone of our Government, that the freedoms it guarantees provide the best insurance against destruction of all freedom. At least as to speech in the realm of public matters, I believe that the "clear and present danger" test does not "mark the furthermost constitutional boundaries of protected expression" but does "no more than recognize a minimum compulsion of the Bill of Rights." (*Bridges v. California,* 314 U.S. 252, 263.)

So long as this Court exercises the power of judicial review of legislation, I cannot agree that the First Amendment permits us to sustain laws suppressing freedom of speech and press on the basis of Congress' or our own notions of mere "reasonableness." Such a doctrine waters down the First Amendment so that it amounts to little more than an admonition to Congress. The Amendment as so construed is not likely to protect any but those "safe" or orthodox views which rarely need its protection. I must also express my objection to the holding because, as Mr. Justice Douglas' dissent shows, it sanctions the determination of a crucial issue of fact by the judge rather than by the jury. Nor can I let this opportunity pass without expressing my objection to the severely limited grant of *certiorari* in this case which precluded consideration here of at least two other reasons for reversing these convictions: (1) the record shows a discriminatory selection of the jury panel which prevented trial before a representative cross-section of the community; (2) the record shows that one member of the trial jury was violently hostile to petitioners before and during the trial.

Public opinion being what it now is, few will protest the conviction of these Communist petitioners. There is hope, however, that in calmer times, when present pressures, passions and fears subside, this or some later Court will restore the First Amendment liberties to the high preferred place where they belong in a free society.

7
The Myth of Soviet Aggression (1952)

In April, 1951, the conservative *Wall Street Journal* declared: "Unfortunately, the tactic of the manufactured crisis has been used so often that neither the Congress nor the people know what they can believe." The fact is, of course, that both the Truman and Eisenhower Administrations, in order to push their enormous armaments programs through Congress and to justify the continuation of the cold war, have felt compelled to resort to the device of keeping the American people in a state of alarm over some alleged menace of Soviet or Communist origin.

The manufactured crisis depends on the manufactured myth. And of all the myths conjured up by the anti-Soviet forces of the United States and the Western World, the most far-fetched and far-reaching is that the Soviet Union is bent on military aggression. The underlying premise of the North Atlantic Pact is that Soviet armies will invade and over-run Western Europe if they get the opportunity. The same premise lies behind the colossal expenditures on armaments by the American Government year after year.

Building up the bogey of Soviet aggression has been a remarkably convenient and successful means of producing in America an atmosphere of hysteria and fear. I am convinced that this anti-Soviet propaganda is false and dangerous, and as harmful to the establishment of world peace as to the maintenance of American democracy. Assuming the Soviet Government realizes that a third world war would in all probability follow if it attacked any country anywhere, I see at least twenty reasons why Soviet military aggression is most unlikely, either now or in the future:

First, the Soviet Russians, remembering poignantly their terrible losses in property and human life during the First and Second World Wars, and especially in Hitler's cruel and destructive invasion, are utterly opposed, from the viewpoint of simple self-preservation and national well-being, to undergoing a third and perhaps even worse ordeal in an international conflict involving the use of atom and hydrogen bombs.

Second, the Soviet Russians, having almost completed the reconstruction of their devastated areas, wish above all to go on with the building of socialism and the transition to communism. They have no desire to see this program set back for years through an all-out war.

Repeated and reliable reports from Soviet Russia during the period of the post-war Five-Year Plans indicate that the Soviet people are in fact preoccupied with tremendous projects of peaceful economic construction and that their minds are not dwelling upon dreams of military conquest. The Fourth Five-Year Plan completed in 1950 attained most of its main social and economic goals. Instead of a serious inflation due to disproportionate armaments production, as in the United States, the Soviet Union has put through six general price reductions of a sweeping nature since the close of the Second World War. And the Fifth Five-Year Plan, 1951-55, places a greatly increased emphasis on the production of consumer goods.

Third, the Soviet Union, stretching over two continents and larger than all North America, possesses within its vast domains practically all the raw materials necessary for its economy. It needs no new territories to provide it with natural resources. The U.S.S.R., however, is glad to supplement its own basic wealth through doing business with other countries, as I explain under point nine.

Fourth, the huge size of Soviet Russia, together with its material riches and continuing economic development, guarantees plenty of room for the expanding population. Over-population, which has often been used to justify military conquest, is not a problem in the Soviet Union.

Fifth, the public ownership of the main means of production and distribution in the U.S.S.R. prevents private individuals and groups from profiting financially from armaments or any other war activity.

Sixth, although in the current disordered and threatening state of the world the Soviet Republic must maintain an army and armaments for defense, it stands as always for disarmament agreements between the different nations and has repeatedly made concrete proposals towards this end, both in the United Nations and elsewhere. The Soviet people regard armaments as a necessary evil during the transition to enduring peace; and they do not in the slightest require them as a stimulus to economic prosperity.

Seventh, the Soviet plan calling for the destruction of all atom bombs everywhere and for effective international supervision of atomic energy, with adequate U.N. inspection of atomic facilities in each country, demonstrates its own wish and intention to use its atomic resources for peaceful purposes and the further economic upbuilding of the nation.

Eighth, Soviet Russia's economic system of socialist planning, having overcome the great economic depressions, famines and periods of mass unemployment so characteristic of the past, makes altogether needless and irrelevant the classic method of military adventure as a way of temporarily submerging internal crises and sidetracking the revolutionary discontent of the population. Furthermore, since the Soviet people always have the purchasing power to buy back the goods which they produce, there is no overwhelming pressure to acquire foreign markets and spheres of influence for getting rid of surplus products. In brief, what I am suggesting here is that the Soviet Russians have eliminated, so far as their own country is concerned, the chief economic roots of war-making and war-mongering.

Ninth, the Soviet Union, despite its relative self-sufficiency in an economic sense, desires normal international trade with the other nations of the earth. It has ever sought to establish good business relations with the United States and Western Europe, exchanging raw materials for machinery and finished goods. The Soviet Russians infinitely prefer peaceful and mutually advantageous commerce with the West to war.

Tenth, the Soviet Government has repeatedly stressed the feasibility of the capitalist and Communist nations of the earth peacefully co-existing and cooperating on limited but important international ends. The Soviet Russians remain militantly opposed to the capitalist economic system and militantly in favor of their own; but they believe that war between the capitalist and Communist systems, especially in this era of atom bombs and other weapons of fearful destructiveness, may well prove ruinous to both. Although some Marxist and Soviet theoreticians have occasionally talked loosely and grandiloquently about the "inevitability" of armed conflict between the capitalist and Communist worlds, Soviet foreign policy has long rejected this idea.

Eleventh, while the Soviet Russians clearly wish to see world socialism established, they do not favor trying to extend Communist principles to other lands through the means of armed invasion. The Soviets support the thesis that "Revolution cannot be exported," but must be the outcome of indigenous radical movements in whatever country is concerned. They gave moral encouragement, to be sure, to the successful Communist revolution in China, but no military aid. Marxist theory claims that capitalism will eventually collapse in every nation through its own inner contradictions and the pressure of the working class. The Soviet Russians take this theory very seriously. And it would be sheer madness for them to undergo the terrific burdens and dangers of war in order to spread socialism when they are convinced that this new system is bound to come in due course anyway.

Twelfth, the idea of military aggression and international war, except in legitimate self-defense, is contrary to the mainstream of Marxist and Soviet doctrine, from Karl Marx down to the present time. In the tense days of 1939, when the Second World War had already broken out, the Soviet Union went to war against Finland in order to re-adjust the frontier, especially near the key city of Leningrad, for better defense against the Nazi menace. I think this was a mistake, but at least it was understandable in view of the critical European situation. And only two years later Hitler and the Finns together did invade the U.S.S.R.

Even on the assumption that the North Koreans were guilty of aggression against the South Koreans in the summer of 1950, it still remains true that it was North Korea which launched the attack and not Soviet Russia. Furthermore, foreign intervention on behalf of the North Koreans in the fall of 1950 came from Communist China, which felt menaced by the U.S.-U.N. advance towards the Manchurian border. The complex and explosive Korean situation brings out the point that it is not objective to claim that Moscow is responsible for all the trouble in the world and especially for the indigenous and often violent revolutionary, nationalist or independence movements which are boiling over or have swept into power in the long-oppressed colonial and semi-colonial countries of Asia, the Middle East and Africa.

Thirteenth, despite the fact that the Soviet Union possesses mighty armies and air fleets, no responsible leader in its governmental, military, economic, journalistic or cultural affairs has once made the suggestion during the troubled years since World War II that it should initiate a preventive war or bomb a foreign country. This record contrasts very favorably with the statements by many leading public figures in the United States, some of them government officials, that America should launch an atom-bomb assault on Soviet Russia; and with the frequent publication in the American press of detailed blueprints for such an attack, pointing out on maps the precise cities and industrial areas in the U.S.S.R. which are to be knocked out.

Fourteenth, indicating the basic Soviet attitude toward war, the Supreme Soviet of the U.S.S.R., corresponding in its political functions to the United States Congress, passed in March, 1951, a law making any kind of war propaganda illegal in the Soviet Republic. The maximum penalty under this new law is twenty-five years in jail.

Fifteenth, the Soviet regime has at no time deteriorated into a military dictatorship, as did the great French Revolution of 1789 when Napoleon Bonaparte finally seized control and proceeded to march armies all over Europe. Since the Second World War civilian authority has continued to reign supreme in the Soviet Union. As Dorothy Thompson said in 1951, "Soviet generals are very much in the background. No hint comes out of Russia that they have anything to do with making political policy. American generals are all over the place, and patently do influence political policy."

One of them was elected President of the United States in 1952.

Sixteenth, the Soviet Government has made no concrete military moves in any part of the world indicating aggressive intentions against any country. On the other hand, the Soviet Union carried out extensive demobilization of its armies during 1945, 1946 and 1947. The continual rumors of threatening Soviet troop movements have never turned out to have a basis in fact. Of course, regular army maneuvers take place from time to time in the U.S.S.R., as in other nations.

Seventeenth, if the Soviet Government were really plotting military aggression against, for example, Western Europe, it would presumably have started the war before the rearmament of the Atlantic Powers had made such headway and at a time, such as the fall of 1950, when the American military forces were preoccupied in the Far East.

Eighteenth, if we review the history of Soviet foreign policy from the birth of the Soviet Republic in 1917 down to the outbreak of World War II, we find a continuous and consistent record on behalf of international peace and understanding. In the early years Lenin as Premier of the Soviet state did his best to achieve peaceful relations with the other countries of the earth, a number of which attempted to bring about the downfall of the Communist regime through armed intervention. In the later period the Soviet Union, under the leadership of Joseph Stalin and with Maxim Litvinov as its able Foreign Minister, joined the League of Nations and tried unceasingly to build an effective system of collective security with the Western democracies against Fascist aggression. Clearly, it was not Soviet Russia's fault that the League failed to follow out the commitments of its own Covenant and thus stop Hitler and Mussolini.

Nineteenth, during the years following the triumph of the allied nations over the Axis Powers, Soviet Russia, in accord with its past record, has steadfastly striven for international peace and reasonable agreements with the United States. Since 1945 the Soviet Union has made its own share of serious mistakes in foreign policy, chiefly of a tactical nature, and has at times acted in an arbitrary, brusque and obdurate manner. But on the whole it has shown a willingness to compromise for the sake of world amity and a desire to make the United Nations a successfully functioning organization. Soviet leaders have given voice again and again to the theme of peaceful co-existence between the Communist and capitalist blocs; and have repeatedly urged a conference between highest officials on either side to the end of seeking a way out of the continuing international impasse.

Twentieth, while the government headed by Premier Stalin definitely pursued the path of peace, the new Soviet regime led by Premier Georgi M. Malenkov has become relatively more conciliatory and has effected a considerable relaxation in both domestic and foreign policies. For the first time the Soviet Government has been granting exit permissions to the Russian wives of American newspaper correspondents; it has reached an agreement with Turkey for joint use of the waters controlled by an important dam in Soviet territory; it has substantially reduced Soviet controls in the Soviet-occupied sector of Austria; it has been consistently cooperative in the effectuation and carrying out of the Korean truce; and it has reiterated its desire to reach a settlement of the German problem with the Western Powers and to participate in a Five-Power Conference, including China, for the purpose of lessening tension in international relations. These and many other Soviet actions since the death of Stalin lead me to believe that the Soviet Union more than ever is sincerely on the side of peace.

In March, 1953, in one of his first addresses as Premier, Mr. Malenkov stated: "At the present time there is not one disputed or undecided question that cannot be decided on the basis of the mutual understanding of interested countries. This is our attitude towards all states, among them the United States of America."

The viewpoint that the U.S.S.R. is not plotting aggression has gained wider and wider acceptance. In the *New York Herald Tribune* of November 3, 1953, the always lucid Walter Lippmann wrote: "Reduced to its simplest elements the governing assumption of American policy is still that of 1950—that Western Europe is threatened by a Soviet military aggression, and that all policies must be directed, must be pinpointed, to the objective of resisting that aggression. . . . This assumption is, however, no longer that of any West European government, including the British, or of any important section of opinion in Europe." In other words, the idea of a Soviet Russia poised for attack still seems to obsess the United States Government; but the Europeans, who are infinitely more vulnerable to such aggression than the Americans, do not harbor such a delusion. And we must seriously raise the question whether the highest officials of the American Government really believe in the talk about Soviet aggression or whether they promote this fantasy for propaganda purposes.

As for the top-level conference which the Soviet Union has kept requesting and America has kept rejecting, even Prime Minister Churchill is on record as favoring it. On May 11, 1953, he told the House of Commons: "I believe that a conference on the highest level should take place between the leading Powers without long delay." The next day Pope Pius XII endorsed the idea in a speech at the Vatican. In October Churchill repeated that his government "still believes that we should persevere in seeking such a meeting between the heads of Governments." Sir Winston was still pressing for the proposed parley when he, President Eisenhower and Premier Laniel of France met at the Bermuda Conference in December, 1953.

I am convinced that a Big Two or Big Four or Big Five high-level conference would be eminently worthwhile and could reach broad agreements mutually advantageous to the nations taking part. Whether or not such a meeting occurs in the near future, however, the Soviet insistence on talking things over and trying to reach an intelligent international settlement hardly indicates a warlike spirit.

In the twenty points outlined in this pamphlet I have sought, without attempting to cover the whole subject in detail, to summarize the main reasons why I think there is no real danger of Soviet military aggression. The United States cannot work out a sound and successful foreign policy if it relies on a distorted picture of the world we live in and continues to give credence to the myth of Soviet aggression.

8
Challenge to McCarthy
(1954)

Every American who wishes to see the democratic institutions of this country maintained and strengthened must be alarmed over the declining state of our civil liberties. In the general onslaught on the Bill of Rights Congressional committees of investigation have been playing a more and more sinister role. The House Committee on Un-American Activities, established in 1939 and now under the chairmanship of Representative Velde, the Senate Subcommittee on Internal Security,* set up in 1950 and now headed by Senator Jenner, and the Senate Permanent Subcommittee on Investigations† with Senator McCarthy as chairman, have vied with one another in lurid inquiries that make the newspaper headlines and at the same time flagrantly violate traditional American freedoms.

All three of these committees ride roughshod over the Bill of Rights by asking unconstitutional questions about political beliefs, associational activities and personal or private affairs. They attempt to destroy careers and reputations through public smears and innuendos, and through the new and abhorrent doctrines of guilt by association, guilt by accusation and guilt by gossip or rumor. Thus these committees throw overboard the time-honored legal concepts that guilt is always personal and that a man is deemed to be innocent until he is proved guilty.

These Congressional committees of inquisition have usurped the powers of the judiciary by holding trials of individuals, finding them guilty and

---

*This is a subcommittee of the larger Judiciary Committee.
†This is a subcommittee of the larger Committee on Government Operations, of which McCarthy is also chairman.

bringing about their punishment, while denying the witness most of the legal safeguards long established in the administration of justice in English-speaking countries. The committees do not ordinarily inflict punishment directly; but witnesses who are questioned suffer severe penalties, through the wide publicity given to charges against them and through frequently losing their jobs and being put on a blacklist that makes future employment most difficult. Many teachers and government employees have been summarily dismissed from their positions either because of unproved accusations which put them under a cloud of suspicion or because, standing on the Fifth Amendment to the Constitution, they refused to answer questions which were calculated to make them witnesses against themselves.

This well-recognized guaranty against compulsory self-incrimination has recently received a great deal of emphasis and publicity. But it is only one of five provisions in the Fifth Amendment; and actually is not so important as the provision which states that no individual shall "be deprived of life, liberty or property without due process of law." This principle was repeated in the Fourteenth Amendment as applying to the States. What the Congressional committees are constantly doing is precisely to neglect or negate "due process of law" which is so fundamental to the whole American system of justice.

These Congressional committees purport to be exposing and counteracting far-reaching Communist plots for wrecking the American Republic. But in fact they are engaged in a witch-hunt against all ideas and associations that do not conform to right-wing orthodoxy. The investigations in general, as Professor Henry Steele Commager of Columbia University points out, "do not deal with acts for the very good reason that there are already laws on the statute books that take care of all conceivable subversive acts. They deal, instead, with imponderable things like intentions, thoughts, principles and associations, with that shadowy realm which has ever been the happy hunting ground of tyrants."

Actually the Federal Bureau of Investigation possesses long dossiers on almost all those who are called before the Congressional committees. But since these witnesses—the bulk of them radicals, liberals or dissenters of some sort—have not violated any law, the committees attempt to encompass their ruin through the extra-legal, and often illegal, methods of inquisition. Furthermore, the questions that McCarthy, Jenner and Velde ask are very infrequently of the sort that might reveal useful information, but are designed to hold the victim up to detraction and abuse or, worse, to trap him into a perjury indictment.

We must all agree that the investigative function of Congress can be helpful and important in its authorized purpose of preparing the way for new legislation. But it is obvious that over the past decade Congressional committees have constantly roamed far beyond their proper authority and have arrogated to themselves powers never delegated to them by the United States Constitution or by any federal law. It is high time to put an end to the tyrannical conduct of these committees and to see that they operate according to the rules of democracy and decency.

The present Congressional witch-hunts come under the telling description of McCarthyism that ex-president Truman gave in his television address in 1953: "It is the corruption of truth, the abandonment of our historical devotion to fair play. It is the abandonment of 'due process of law.' It is the use of the big lie and the unfounded accusation against any citizen in the name of Americanism or security. It is the rise to power of the demagogue who lives on untruth; it is the spread of fear and the destruction of faith in every level of our society. This is not a partisan matter. This horrible cancer is eating at the vitals of America and it can destroy the great edifice of freedom."

The most menacing figure in the movement called McCarthyism is of course Joseph R. McCarthy himself, junior Senator from Wisconsin. And the most reckless and dangerous of the Congressional committees in the field today is the Senate subcommittee which he heads. In the fall of 1953, through no choice of mine, I had a head-on collision with this committee and learned a good deal about it through personal experience. I feel that it may be worthwhile to tell others, some of whom may be called upon to undergo a similar ordeal, exactly what happened. So here is my story.

On Tuesday, September 22, 1953, I was in my study near Columbia University writing the first chapter of a long-planned book on civil liberties when, at five minutes to twelve, the apartment phone rang and an unknown person announced that he had a subpoena for me from Senator McCarthy's investigating committee. I told him to wait and immediately called my lawyer, who said that I might as well accept it.

So I went down to the front hall of the apartment house and accepted service of the subpoena. It summoned me to appear before the committee the next day at 2:30 P.M. at the United States Courthouse in New York City. I was disturbed to realize that I had only a little more than twenty-four hours to prepare myself for the ordeal. A witness should be given at least three or four days between the serving of the subpoena and his appearance at a Congressional hearing. It is typical of McCarthy's unscrupulous tactics to try to catch his victims off guard and to allow them no adequate opportunity to prepare.

I had known of course that one of the Congressional investigating committees would probably tap me eventually, and had been thinking off and on about possible courses of action. I had been especially impressed by an article in *The Nation* in May of 1953 entitled "How to Stop the Demagogues," by Philip Wittenberg, the attorney, and had talked briefly with him about the new approach he recommended. He had informally agreed to take my case if I were called by a Congressional committee.

Fortunately for me Philip Wittenberg was in town and was able to advise me. I arrived at his office at 12:30 on Tuesday and had three long conferences with him before my Wednesday deadline. We settled the general principles on which I would stand, and rehearsed a number of probable questions and the type of answer or refusal to answer I should make to them.

The events leading up to my subpoena from McCarthy are enlightening. The Senator had recently discovered that the Military Intelligence Section of the United States General Staff published in 1953 a pamphlet under the title of *Psychological and Cultural Traits of Soviet Siberia.* Without my knowledge this Army manual listed in its bibliography my book *The Peoples of the Soviet Union,* a study of Soviet national and racial minorities, published by Harcourt, Brace in 1946. On the basis of this mere listing McCarthy widely asserted that the Army document "quoted heavily" from me, although in fact it used no quotation whatsoever from my work.

On September 9 Senator McCarthy gave the press excerpts from the Army pamphlet and made the absurd claim that it was Communist propaganda. On September 11 the Army disclosed that McCarthy had failed to release passages hostile to the Soviet Union and to reveal that the purpose of the pamphlet was to develop among the United States armed forces "an understanding of the Soviet people which will be militarily useful in case of war." The Army stated that only 100 copies of the manual had been printed, with some 40 distributed to high Army officials; and that since the document had a secrecy classification as "restricted," McCarthy's unauthorized release of much of it constituted a violation of the espionage law. The Army then proceeded to declassify the pamphlet from its restricted status "as a result of prior disclosures" on the part of McCarthy.

With these facts in mind, Mr. Wittenberg and I appeared before the McCarthy committee at the United States Courthouse early Wednesday afternoon, September 23. Senator McCarthy was of course presiding as chairman and was the only member of the committee present. He had announced this hearing as a closed executive session, which is supposed to be strictly private. Hence I was surprised to see about a dozen spectators, men and women, sitting in one corner of the room. In another part, by himself, sat the ever loquacious and pliant witness Louis Budenz, whom I recognized from his newspaper photographs. He was present, I felt sure, for the primary purpose of intimidating me.

McCarthy did all the questioning himself, constantly pacing back and forth at the end of a long table. Throughout the hearing he was neither abusive nor impolite but asked his outrageous questions in a quietly persistent manner. His personal behavior was far more restrained and dignified than that of the shouting, table-pounding members of the House Un-American

Activities Committee—particularly Representatives John E. Rankin and J. Parnell Thomas—who had questioned me in Washington in 1946.

I took my most decisive step at the very start when I asked permission to read a prepared statement objecting to the jurisdiction of the committee. Since an objection to jurisdiction is absolutely basic and takes precedence over everything else, McCarthy had to allow my statement to be put into the record. In this three-page document, which had been drawn up by Mr. Wittenberg in precise legal terminology rather than in eloquent language about the Bill of Rights, I challenged the legal and constitutional power of the McCarthy committee to inquire into my political beliefs, my religious convictions, my associational activities, or any other personal and private affairs. I advanced three main grounds for this position.

In the first place, I cited the protections of the First Amendment and quoted the concurring opinion of Justice Douglas in the 1953 United States Supreme Court decision supporting the refusal of Edward Rumely, executive secretary of the right-wing Committee for Constitutional Government, to give testimony and produce materials before a committee of the House of Representatives. "The power of investigation," wrote Justice Douglas, "is also limited. Inquiry into personal and private affairs is precluded." In addition, I emphasized the First Amendment's guaranty of freedom of the press and urged that since Congress could not pass laws interfering with freedom of the press and since a Congressional committee can only make inquiries relevant to constitutional legislation, McCarthy had no right to ask me questions about the origin, content and purposes of my writings. Several of the Senator's questions were designed to disclose my sources of research as a scholar and the precise persons with whom I had discussed problems pertaining to my book. Such inquiries constitute attempted interference with freedom of research and of scholarship.

In the second place, I relied heavily on the three-way separation of powers in the American government by which the legislative, judicial and executive branches possess definite and limited functions. Thus I claimed that McCarthy's committee would be trespassing upon the powers of the judiciary—from the Department of Justice through the courts and down to grand juries and trial juries—by inquiring into my personal beliefs and affairs. When in 1952 the Truman Administration instead of Congress decreed the government seizure of certain steel companies, the United States Supreme Court declared the action unconstitutional precisely because it violated the tripartite separation of powers. It did this although the Korean emergency was still acute.

In November, 1953, ex-President Truman, in his letter refusing to testify before the House Committee on Un-American Activities regarding the Harry Dexter White case, maintained that the committee was invading the rights of the executive branch of the government by subpoenaing him. In thus taking his stand on the doctrine of the separation of powers, Mr. Truman rendered valuable aid to the campaign to curb Congressional committees through the enforcement of this same general constitutional principle.

In the third place, I claimed that the statutes authorizing the appointment of the Senate Committee on Government Operations precluded an investigation of me on the basis of my written works, since I was a private citizen not in the employ of the Federal Government and was not even consulted about the listing of my book in an Army publication.

Also in my opening statement* I volunteered the information that I was not and never had been a member of the Communist Party. This I did in order to throw McCarthy off balance and to forestall his customary allegations in the press.

After receiving my statement in silence McCarthy launched into a long series of questions. I answered a few concerning recorded facts. Yes, I had published a book about the peoples of Soviet Russia, had written a chapter for *U.S.S.R., a Concise Handbook,* and had sent a letter to *The New York Times* criticizing the decision of the United States Supreme Court in holding the Smith Act constitutional.

But most of McCarthy's inquiries I refused to answer, giving as my reason each time the objections expressed in my initial challenge to the jurisdiction of the committee. Almost every question the Senator asked was loaded: as, for example, "Did you know that Mr. A, who wrote a chapter in this book used by the United States Army, was a member of the Communist Party?" "Did you know that Mr. B was a member of the Communist conspiracy?" and "Do you know any member of the Communist Party who to your knowledge engaged in either espionage or sabotage?" Instead of declining to answer, I should have preferred to say "No" to all such questions; but that would have undermined my legal position. And there was always the possibility, too, that McCarthy was trying to trick me into a response that, revealing some slip of memory, would lay the basis for a perjury indictment.

Chairman McCarthy continued with his grilling for about an hour and then brought the hearing to a close. He said that I could not obtain a copy of the record because this session was "strictly executive." At the same time he ordered me to appear at a public hearing the following Monday, September 28, in Washington. At this point McCarthy, having taken the position all along that my Wednesday hearing was an executive session and therefore "closed," suddenly announced that he was going to give a résumé to the press.

Accordingly, he called the reporters in and talked to them for some thirty minutes, informing them that I was guilty of contempt on at least

---

*For my complete statement see Appendix I, pp. 102–104.

two dozen counts. As McCarthy had made public his version of the hearing, I gave out to the newspapermen copies of my statement objecting to the jurisdiction of the committee, and discussed briefly the reasons for my stand. The press gave me excellent coverage; but usually McCarthy's tricky new device of giving publicity to *his* version of a so-called private hearing from which reporters are barred is most disadvantageous to the witness. As Telford Taylor, reserve brigadier general and chief prosecutor at the trial of the Nazi war criminals, has said: "It is an outrageous procedure, obviously designed for the sole purpose of publicity."

On Friday afternoon, September 25, a telegram came to my home from Senator McCarthy stating that my Monday hearing had been postponed. The wire added, "However, you are under continuing subpoena and both you and your counsel will be notified when your appearance is required." McCarthy went ahead with his public session Monday morning and examined other witnesses. To my astonishment the transcript of this hearing showed that at the very beginning the Honorable Senator had asserted: "Mr. Lamont has not been subpoenaed. He was notified that he could come today and purge himself of the contempt of failure to answer last week. Is Mr. Lamont here?" "There was no answer," the transcript recorded.

Of course McCarthy had sent me no such message and had said in his own telegram that I was still under subpoena. Apparently he thought that the cancellation of my hearing might be interpreted as a retreat on his part and felt obliged to give the false impression that the responsibility for my not appearing rested with me.

At the same time the Senator used his two misstatements and the calling of my name as an excuse to make public the complete minutes of the "private" executive session at which I was examined on September 23. I immediately protested to Senator McCarthy against this whole procedure. On October 24 Mr. Francis B. Carr, Executive Director of the subcommittee and former head of the F.B.I. in New York City, wrote me to say that the passages to which I had objected had been deleted from the record. This correction, however, did not offset the erroneous impression given originally to the press and the public by McCarthy's unprincipled conduct.

Each person summoned by a Congressional committee must make his own decision, taking into consideration all the particular circumstances in his case, as to the policy he will pursue. I believe, for instance, that reliance on the Fifth Amendment may be fully justified and that we must defend the right of witnesses to use it without any penalties being imposed upon them by either public or private authorities. However, in seeking a court test to halt the excesses of Congressional committees we cannot utilize the Fifth Amendment. We must stand upon the First Amendment and the separation of powers in the American governmental system.

The course I followed before the McCarthy committee was the same in principle as that taken by two well-known writers, Leo Huberman and Harvey O'Connor, in July, 1953. These two courageous men led the way in this new type of challenge to the Congressional witch-hunt. Mr. O'Connor was promptly cited for contempt by the Senate and later indicted by a grand jury in Washington, D.C. His trial has been postponed until after the United States Supreme Court hands down a decision in the case of Julius Emspak, Secretary and Treasurer of the United Electrical, Radio and Machine Workers. Mr. Emspak's principled refusal to answer the questions of the House Committee on Un-American Activities in December, 1949, has led to the Supreme Court's taking for the first time a First Amendment case dealing with Congressional investigations. The Emspak case was argued before the Supreme Court on January 12, 1954.

On December 16, 1953, Mr. Albert Shadowitz, an engineer called before the McCarthy committee, invoked the First Amendment in refusing to answer a number of questions. Mr. Shadowitz stated: "I am going to follow completely the course of action advised by Dr. Albert Einstein both to everyone in general* and by personal consultation to me in particular." If Mr. Shadowitz is cited and indicted for contempt, we shall have yet another First Amendment case for decision in the courts.

What I and the other witnesses I have mentioned are trying to do through our respective cases is not to cripple the power of Congressional investigations, but to have them reasonably and specifically limited in scope and methods, according to the principles of the Constitution.

Since McCarthy dragged me into the picture in connection with alleged subversion in the United States Army, it is relevant to note that his investigations of the Army have been a complete farce up to date. With much fanfare McCarthy announced that he was going to reveal dangerous sabotage and espionage in the Army Signal Corps Laboratories at Fort Monmouth, N.J. His charges were never sustained. Instead, wrote Walter Millis in the *New York Herald Tribune* of December 8, 1953, "this really vital and sensitive military installation has been wrecked—more thoroughly than any Soviet saboteur could have dreamed of doing it—by the kind of anti-Communism of which Senator McCarthy has made himself the leader and champion. The Fort Monmouth situation is truly scandalous."

It is significant that my challenge to the McCarthy committee has received wide support from conservative as well as liberal and radical sources. I have, for instance, talked with a number of Republicans who are bitterly opposed to McCarthy and who are firmly backing me in my present battle with him. This includes many of my fellow-alumni of Harvard College, who have become strongly anti-McCarthy because of the Senator's unfair and intemperate attacks on Harvard and its new President, Dr. Nathan M. Pusey.

---

*See Dr. Einstein's letter of May 16, 1953, Appendix II, p. 104.

Editorial comment on my case has also been most encouraging. *The New York Times* stated on September 25: "The action of Corliss Lamont in defying the McCarthy committee on the ground that the latter is unconstitutionally violating the personal rights of private citizens raises again the interesting and important question of how far Congressional committees can properly go. . . . Many citizens who have no use for communism are disturbed over the degree to which these committees are threatening an incursion into the domain of private rights and constitutional guaranties. . . . The ultimate disposition of this case may help define the area in which privacy of the individual is still protected. "

On September 29 *The Washington Post* said in an editorial that I had "challenged the jurisdiction of Senator McCarthy's Government Operations Committee on substantial and significant grounds. . . . The basic issue, of course, is whether the courts, which have been understandably reluctant to impose broad, general checks upon the power of Congress to investigate, will be more willing to impose checks upon individual committees attempting to exercise powers which Congress has not conferred upon them." On the same day a *St. Louis Post-Dispatch* editorial asserted that, "If the Senate should vote a contempt citation against Mr. Lamont, it would undoubtedly produce a test case that would go all the way to the United States Supreme Court where demagogues fare less well than they do in Congress. . . . Many Americans will applaud Corliss Lamont for having, in effect, spoken up for them and their right to be secure in their thoughts and their personal lives."

Seven other newspapers—as far west as Iowa and as far south as Texas—and also *The Nation* and the *New Republic* printed favorable editorial comments on my case. The Jersey City *Journal* sounded an optimistic note: "On this one don't bet on McCarthy. He looks as though he had got himself trapped off first base." The editorial reaction in general indicated that editors and journalists throughout the country are becoming more conscious of the menace of Congressional committees run wild.

The militant Emergency Civil Liberties Committee quickly gave me full support against McCarthy and helped to rally public opinion by sending copies of the *Times* editorial to a large number of educators. Then in January, 1954, the American Civil Liberties Union issued a statement backing my case on the First Amendment issues which I had raised.

After Congress had reconvened for its new session early in January, 1954, Senator McCarthy followed up his previous threat by asking the full Committee on Government Operations to approve his request that the Senate cite me for contempt. I immediately sent a memorandum outlining the constitutional grounds for my position to all thirteen members of the Committee. In an unprecedented action this Committee, instead of approving McCarthy's proposal, voted on January 11 to submit my case to the U.S. Department of Justice for an advisory opinion. It decided on the same procedure in regard to Albert Shadowitz, to whom I have already referred, and Abraham Unger, a lawyer. These decisions were a serious setback for McCarthy and show that the larger Committee had reservations as to whether contempt citations were justified in the three cases under consideration.

At the present writing there is no indication as to what the recommendation of the Justice Department will be. But I remain convinced that my position is sound both legally and morally. If the Senate finally cites me for contempt and I am then indicted, I shall certainly carry my case up to the Supreme Court of the United States should the lower courts decide against me. If I eventually lose, the penalty of from one to twelve months in prison is a small price to pay for the satisfaction of having upheld the cause of civil liberties against McCarthy and for the privilege of fighting in the ranks of freedom.

Joseph McCarthy, the most dangerous demagogue in America's history, is engaged in burning not only books, but the Bill of Rights itself. It is a great responsibility to find oneself suddenly in the front lines of the continuing battle of McCarthy versus the American people. And as a teacher, philosopher, scholar and writer, I naturally take my stand with all others who are striving to uphold the great American tradition of dissent and independent thinking against thought control and the ugly procedures of would-be dictators.

Postscript

The U.S. Senate cited me for contempt of Congress and the Department of Justice pushed through an indictment. But my case never came to trial because a Federal District Judge, Edward Weinfeld, dismissed the indictment in 1955 on the grounds that McCarthy's Subcommittee of Investigation had never been legally or officially established by its parent Committee on Government Operations. A Federal Appeals Court unanimously approved this decision in 1956. And so it turned out that the witch-hunting McCarthy Committee had no constitutional right to investigate anyone.

Appendix I

Statement made by Corliss Lamont on September 23, 1953, before the Senate Permanent Subcommittee on Investigations, Senator Joseph R. McCarthy, Chairman.

1. I, Corliss Lamont, residing at 450 Riverside Drive, in the borough of Manhattan, City of New York, having been subpoenaed before this

committee by subpoena dated the 21st day of September, 1953, and signed by Joseph R. McCarthy, as Chairman, do hereby respectfully object to the power and jurisdiction of this committee to inquire into:

(a) My political beliefs
(b) Any other personal and private affairs
(c) My religious beliefs
(d) My associational activities.

2. Let it be understood that I am a private citizen of the United States, that I hold no office of public honor or trust and I am not employed in any government department.

3. To dispose of a question causing current apprehension I am a loyal American; and I am not now and never have been a member of the Communist Party.

4. The grounds of my objection are:

(a) As stated in *United States vs. Rumely,* 97 L. Ed. 494, a case involving a refusal to give testimony before a committee of the House of Representatives, the Supreme Court of the United States said, in a concurring opinion by Mr. Justice Douglas:

> The power of investigation is also limited. Inquiry into personal and private affairs is precluded.

(b) The Supreme Court of the United States has said in *Jones vs. Securities and Exchange Commission,* 298 U.S. 1, through Mr. Justice Sutherland:

> The citizen when interrogated about his private affairs has a right before answering to know why the inquiry is made; and if the purpose disclosed is not a legitimate one he is not required to answer.

(c) Under the First Amendment to the Constitution the power of investigation by Congress into matters involving freedom of speech and freedom of the press cannot be used in the absence of legislative intent or power. The Congress of the United States has no constitutional right to legislate with regard to prior restraint on utterance in either form; and as to any books already written or statements made, no *ex post facto* law can be passed determining innocence or criminality, and therefore any investigations into my writings is beyond the power of this committee.

5. Under our Constitution our Government is a government of limited powers, tripartite in form, consisting of the legislative, the judicial and the executive, and any inquiry into personal conduct, personal beliefs, associational activity lies within the jurisdiction of the Judicial Department, and the exercise of this power by the legislature is an unconstitutional invasion of the power of the judiciary.

The Supreme Court has held that this separation of powers is fundamental to the existence of our democracy and that not even an emergency warrants an invasion of the powers of one department by the other, *Youngstown Sheet & Tube Co. v. Sawyer,* 343 U.S. 579.

6. The jurisdiction of this committee is further limited by the statutes which constitute and set forth its function and sphere of authority. Under the rules of the Senate and the statutes organizing the appointment of this standing committee, this committee has no authority to examine into the personal and private affairs of private citizens. Any action with regard to my books by officials of the Government was done without my prior knowledge or consultation with me. I took no part in any proceedings involving any governmental authority and therefore this committee is without power to examine me under the rules and statute governing it.

7. This committee is not a competent tribunal. The resignation from this committee of all members belonging to one of the major parties, i.e., the Democratic Party, has deprived this committee of its competency to act until it has been properly constituted.

Appendix II

Letter of May 16, 1953, from Dr. Albert Einstein to Mr. William Frauenglass, teacher of English at the James Madison High School, New York City. Mr. Frauenglass, standing on the Fifth Amendment, had refused to answer questions as to political affiliations put to him by the Senate Internal Security Committee.

Dear Mr. Frauenglass:

The problem with which the intellectuals of this country are confronted is very serious. The reactionary politicians have managed to instill suspicion of all intellectual efforts into the public by dangling before their eyes a danger from without. Having succeeded so far they are now proceeding to suppress the freedom of teaching and to deprive of their positions all those who do not prove submissive, i.e., to starve them.

What ought the minority of intellectuals to do against evil? Frankly, I can see only the revolutionary way of non-cooperation in the sense of

Gandhi's. Every intellectual who is called before one of the committees ought to refuse to testify, i.e., he must be prepared for jail and economic ruin, in short, for the sacrifice of his personal welfare in the interest of the cultural welfare of his country.

However, this refusal to testify must not be based on the well-known subterfuge of invoking the Fifth Amendment against possible self-incrimination, but on the assertion that it is shameful for a blameless citizen to submit to such an inquisition and that this kind of inquisition violates the spirit of the Constitution.

If enough people are ready to take this grave step they will be successful. If not, then the intellectuals of this country deserve nothing better than the slavery which is intended for them.

Sincerely yours,
A. Einstein

9
The Congressional Inquisition (1954)

Public opinion in America recently became aroused as never before over the uncontrolled behavior of Congressional investigating committees when the Senate Permanent Subcommittee on Investigations,* headed by Joseph McCarthy, turned its inquisitorial techniques against the United States Army.

McCarthy's onslaught against the Army reached its height in February of 1954 when the Senator from Wisconsin went to shameful extremes in his questioning of Brigadier General Ralph W. Zwicker concerning the honorable discharge of Major Irving Peress, a dentist in his command, whom McCarthy had branded as "a Fifth Amendment Communist." When General Zwicker refused to divulge detailed information about this matter on the grounds that Army regulations prevented him from doing so, McCarthy became most abusive and repeatedly insulted the General. After this testimony was released a wave of indignation swept over Washington and indeed the whole nation.

Although Secretary of the Army Robert T. Stevens compromised at first regarding the Zwicker affair, the Army struck back hard two weeks later. At that time it made public that Senator McCarthy and Roy M. Cohn, the Chief Counsel of his Committee, had exercised heavy pressures, including threats of "wrecking" the Army and harassing it through investigations, in order to obtain preferential Army treatment for Private G. David Schine, formerly special staff consultant to the Committee. This scandal and the ensuing investigation into it considerably diminished

---

*This is a subcommittee of the larger Committee on Government Operations, of which Senator McCarthy is also Chairman.

McCarthy's influence and prestige.

Senator McCarthy's assault on the Army brought his Committee's investigations full circle and convincingly demonstrated that the democratic rights guaranteed under the American Constitution are indivisible. For McCarthy's callous violation of the civil liberties of Communists or alleged Communists, of so-called fellow-travelers, of trade unionists and of progressives finally led, as his inquisition gathered momentum, to the hounding of anti-Communist liberals, State Department officials and Army personnel with long records of heroism. He started by usurping Judicial powers and ended up by invading the Executive function through interfering with established Army procedures and trying to order around military officers as if he were the Commander-in-Chief.

Despite the growing antagonism to Grand Inquisitor McCarthy throughout the country, and in Republican as well as in other political circles, there is no assurance that either his Committee or the other Congressional investigating committees will henceforth cease their outrageous practices and conduct inquiries within constitutional limits.

While the McCarthy Committee has gone furthest in flouting the American Constitution and trampling upon the rights of witnesses, other committees have not lagged far behind. I refer especially to the House Committee on Un-American Activities, established in 1939 with Representative Martin Dies, Democrat, of Texas, as Chairman and now headed by Representative Harold H. Velde, Republican, of Illinois; and to the Senate Subcommittee on Internal Security,* first set up in 1950 with Senator Pat McCarran, Democrat, of Nevada, as Chairman and now headed by Senator William E. Jenner, Republican, of Indiana.

The House Un-American Activities Committee established in its early years the basic patterns for unconstitutional investigations and has served as the prototype for other Congressional committees and for similar State committees. Although the very resolution bringing this House committee into being is violative of the American Constitution, it has functioned almost without let or hindrance for more than 15 years, riding roughshod over the civil liberties of countless individuals and organizations in the United States, and giving encouragement to every reactionary force in the country.

In its brief existence the Internal Security Committee of the Senate has also made an outstanding record for the persecution of liberals, progressives, trade unionists, radicals, teachers, United Nations employees and intellectuals in general. During 1952 and 1953 its investigation of allegedly subversive Americans employed by the United Nations violated both the United States Constitution and the United Nations Charter. This particular witch-hunt created disruption and demoralization on the U.N. staff.

---

*This is a subcommitte of the larger Judiciary Committee.

It led directly to the suicide, in November, 1952, of Mr. Abraham H. Feller, an American citizen and General Counsel for the U.N., who plunged to his death from his 12th floor apartment in New York City. Mr. Feller had become terribly disturbed over the injustice being done to many persons by the Committee and was fearful lest he himself eventually fall victim to its reckless charges.

It would be possible to write an entire book giving the shocking details of the investigations carried on, particularly during the past few years, by the McCarthy, Jenner and Velde committees. In this pamphlet, however, it is my aim to present a brief, over-all view of the unconstitutional actions, anti-democratic practices and other evils perpetrated or brought about by the chief Congressional investigating committees. The following 25 points endeavor to sum up the situation:

1. These congressional committees violate the First Amendment to the Constitution, particularly its provisions guaranteeing freedom of speech and freedom of the press, by inquiring into ideas, beliefs and associations.

The enabling resolution bringing into being the House Committee on Un-American Activities plainly shows that the Committee's mandate is on its face unconstitutional. In the first place, the resolution's directive to investigate "un-American propaganda activities" is an invitation to negate the First Amendment's guaranty that Congress shall make no law "abridging the freedom of speech." For the word "propaganda" means precisely the diffusion of certain *ideas;* and for Congress to investigate ideas of whatever variety is a threat to free discussion and to the unhampered controversy and propaganda of all sorts which are the lifeblood of a democracy.

In the second place, another part of the resolution directs the Committee to inquire into "subversive and un-American propaganda that is instigated from foreign countries or of a domestic origin and attacks the principle of the form of government as guaranteed by our Constitution." Here the phrase "subversive and un-American" is so vague and ambiguous that it easily functions as a device for encroachments on ordinary free speech. For the Un-American Committee naturally considers as "subversive" and "un-American" those opinions with which its members fundamentally disagree. And so it is that the Committee has all along concentrated on investigating persons and organizations that support ideas of which it disapproves.

In the third place, as to investigating propaganda that attacks "the principle" of our form of government, that necessarily means an inquiry into ideas. For to attack a political principle is to conduct a controversy in the realm of opinion. To make such a controversy subject to Congressional investigation runs counter to the First Amendment because it interferes with and discourages freedom of speech, on the part of both the political scientist and the average citizen.

Not only the Un-American Committee, but also the McCarthy and

Jenner committees have spent most of their time asking witnesses about their ideas in the fields of politics, economics or culture. A number of courageous and principled witnesses have been cited by Congress for contempt, tried and found guilty because of their refusal to answer such questions on the ground that they violate the First Amendment. The Supreme Court of the United States has not yet given a ruling in a case of this kind. But a new crop of witnesses, including author Harvey O'Connor and myself, challenged the McCarthy Committee in 1953 on the basis of the First Amendment.* And there is good reason to believe that the Supreme Court will eventually take on appeal at least one of the more recent cases. This Court is also expected shortly to render a decision in the case of trade union leader Julius Emspak, who in 1949 relied upon the First Amendment as well as the Fifth in defying the Un-American Committee.

The McCarthy Committee, especially, has recklessly disregarded freedom of the press as guaranteed in the First Amendment by carrying on an inquisition regarding "subversive" books in the U.S. State Department's overseas libraries or used by some other branch of the government. McCarthy's vicious attacks on such books and their authors in 1953 resulted in a widespread "book-burning" movement. He subpoenaed both Mr. O'Connor and me to testify before his Committee because the United States Government had utilized our books in some manner.

The American Civil Liberties Union clarified this freedom of the press issue in its public statement opposing my citation for contempt by the United States Senate: "The naked question in this case is whether the Government can investigate any author of any book. We say that this broad question is involved for the reason that every book published in the United States occupies a place in the Library of Congress; almost every newspaper is purchased by one or another government agency. All these are used by government personnel at some time or other for some purpose. Therefore, if inquiries into associations of those who write books is possible in Mr. Lamont's case, it is possible in the case of every author, of the editor of every newspaper."

The House Committee on Un-American Activities has extended Congressional contempt for the First Amendment by brushing aside the guaranty of freedom of religion. Although still treading lightly in its threatened full-dress investigation of religion in America, this Committee has already called before it several clergymen and has unconstitutionally questioned them about their religious associations and activities.

2. *The Congressional committees violate the Fourth Amendment which ensures "The right of the people to be secure in their persons, houses, papers and effects against unreasonable searches and seizures."*

---

*O'Connor and I both won our cases without reading the First Amendment.

In 1946, for instance, the Un-American committee demanded by subpoena all the financial records and correspondence of the National Council of American-Soviet Friendship, including the records of all contributions. It made the same demand on the Joint Anti-Fascist Refugee Committee and the National Federation for Constitutional Liberties. These were illegitimate attempts on the part of the Un-American Activities Committee to carry through "unreasonable searches and seizures" and conduct "fishing expeditions" of the sort American courts have in the past condemned in no uncertain terms. And one of the aims was to obtain, through the long lists of contributors to these three organizations, the names of persons the Committee could harass and persecute as "subversives."

The three organizations in question refused to deliver up their records and correspondence to the House Committee. As a consequence the officers responsible in each organization were cited for contempt, indicted, found guilty and jailed. These defendants relied legally on the First Amendment as well as the Fourth, but the United States Supreme Court refused to review their cases when appealed.

3. The Congressional committees violate the most important provision of the Fifth Amendment by denying "due process of law" to the witnesses whom they summon. They in effect hold trials of witnesses, find them guilty and bring about their punishment. But at the same time they do not give the "defendants" the right to enjoy the legal safeguards long established in the administration of justice.

4. The committees violate the intent of the Fifth Amendment provision against self-incrimination by attributing guilt to those who invoke it and by effecting their punishment. It has long been an accepted doctrine under our legal system that there is no presumption of guilt if a witness declines to answer a question on the grounds that by doing so he might tend to incriminate himself. Yet the Congressional investigating committees, asking such questions as "Are you a member of the Communist party?" or "Have you ever been a part of the Communist conspiracy?" almost invariably brand the witness as "a Fifth Amendment Communist" if he refuses to answer for fear of self-incrimination. It is not generally realized that if in this sort of situation the witness answers even *one* question, then he may waive his right to invoke the Fifth Amendment in regard to all further questions on the same subject.

Nine times out of ten, witnesses who rely on the constitutional guaranty against self-incrimination lose their jobs, either because the committees bring pressure on the employer or because the employer—be it a business enterprise, an educational institution or a government department—wishes to cooperate with the committee and is determined to get rid of all "controversial" characters. Just as the mediaeval Inquisition of the Christian Church found heretics guilty and then handed them over to the secular authorities for punishment, so the Congressional Inquisition finds the heretics of today guilty and turns them over to their employers for punishment. Of course our forefathers who put the provision against self-incrimination in the Bill of Rights never intended that those who relied upon it should be penalized.

5. *The committees violate the spirit of the Sixth Amendment by not permitting witnesses to cross-examine their accusers and to have witnesses in their own defense.* This is another violation of due process. At the hearings professional informers and perjurers-for-profit have full freedom to slander, invent, misrepresent and insinuate. But the witness is not allowed to answer back or to ask questions or in general to defend himself adequately.

6. *The committees violate the Tenth Amendment, which limits the power of the Federal authorities, by trespassing upon the functions of local self-government.* Both the House Un-American Activities Committee and the Senate Internal Security Committee have repeatedly made gratuitous investigations of teachers in public schools and colleges in such cities as Boston, New York and Philadelphia. Public schools and municipal educational institutions have always been regarded in America as a distinctively local responsibility. Congressional committees have no more business interfering with local education than with the local police department or fire department.

7. *The committees disregard the three-way separation of powers in the American system of government by constantly usurping the functions of the Judiciary, from the Department of Justice through the courts and down to grand juries and trial juries.* One of the provisions of the Fifth Amendment is that "No person shall be held to answer for a capital or otherwise infamous crime, unless on a presentment or indictment of a Grand Jury." The Congressional committees, however, nullify this guaranty and take over the work of grand juries by asking witnesses detailed questions about their alleged crimes and trying to build up a case against them. The committees then proceed illegitimately to assume the powers of courts and hold "trials" of individuals and organizations. They act as if they were prosecutor, judge and jury all combined.

As Senator Wayne Morse of Oregon stated in a speech in February, 1954: "We have reached such a point in the conducting of Senate investigations which go into the question of the innocence or guilt of persons under investigation that it is a legal fiction to argue that, in fact, such persons are not standing trial." In my own refusal to answer questions before the McCarthy Committee in September, 1953, I relied heavily on this contention and asserted: "Under our Constitution our Government is a government of limited powers, tripartite in form, consisting of the Legislative, the Judicial and the Executive; and any inquiry into personal conduct, personal beliefs, associational activity lies within the jurisdiction of the Judicial Department, and the exercise of this power by the legislature is an unconstitutional invasion of the power of the Judiciary."

8. *The committees violate, in effect, that section of the Constitution which forbids Congress to pass bills of attainder.* The United States Supreme Court defines a bill of attainder as "a legislative Act which inflicts punishment without a judicial trial." And in a recent case the Court held: "When our Constitution and Bill of Rights were written, our ancestors had ample reason to know that legislative trials and punishments were too dangerous to liberty to exist in the nation of free men they envisaged."

As I have shown in Point 7, the Congressional committees continually conduct trials. And as made clear in Points 4 and 18, they are able to inflict serious punishment on witnesses, apart from initiating contempt action against them.

9. *The committees violate the separation of powers, again, by usurping the prerogatives of the Executive and trespassing upon the functions of various Departments of the Federal Government.* The most flagrant example of this unconstitutional conduct occurred when the McCarthy Committee tried to force General Zwicker to disregard Army regulations by revealing confidential information and censured him for carrying out orders, of which McCarthy disapproved, from his superiors in command.

As *The New York Times* explained in a lead editorial, there is a serious invasion of the Executive power "when the Legislative branch attempts to interfere with the legal and proper actions of subordinate executive officers carrying out their assigned functions. If there are objections to the way they do their duty, there is just one person in each agency who is responsible, and that is the head of the agency." President Eisenhower commented on the episode by stating: "The ultimate responsibility for the conduct of all parts of the government rests with the President of the United States. That responsibility cannot be delegated to another branch of government."

10. *The committees violate, in effect, that provision in the Constitution which bans* ex post facto *laws.* The United States Supreme Court describes an *ex post facto* law as "one which renders an act punishable in a manner in which it was not punishable when it was committed." The investigating committees make guilt retroactive in this sense by bringing about the punishment of persons because 10 or 15 years ago they joined in good faith an organization which is now declared or reputed to be "subversive." This practice also assumes as valid the unacceptable doctrine of guilt by association.

11. *The Senators and Representatives who are members of the Congressional investigating committees repeatedly violate their solemn oath as public officials to support the American Constitution by trampling it under foot, especially the Bill of Rights, in the ways already described.* It is a curious paradox that so many members of Congress—individuals who ought to take leadership in preserving and protecting the Constitution—are leaders in the anti-democratic movement to destroy America's constitutional liberties. It would be difficult indeed for any witness to be

as subversive as the Congressional committees which have done so much to undermine the Bill of Rights.

12. *These committees violate the rules of Congress by asking questions beyond the limited scope of investigations and not pertinent to legislation.* Congressional committees most emphatically do have the right to look into certain specified fields such as railroads, banking and currency, foreign relations, campaign expenditures and so on. However, the McCarthy, Jenner and Velde committees recognize no limits whatsoever for their inquiries; they investigate whomever and whatever they please, ever concentrating on what they consider "dangerous thoughts." Furthermore, their questions are rarely of the sort that might reveal information useful for new legislation, but are designed to hold the witness up to detraction and abuse, or worse, to trap him into a perjury indictment.

13. *The committees abuse Congressional powers by permitting their chairmen or other members to operate as irresponsible one-man committees touring the country, summoning witnesses and staging hearings at will.* This practice concentrates too much authority in the hands of one Senator or Representative, who might be restrained to some degree were other members of the committee present. Senator McCarthy provides the outstanding example of this trend towards personal dictatorship.

This practice may well be illegal. As Dean Erwin N. Griswold of the Harvard Law School has recently said: "There is nothing about the nature of membership in the Senate or House of Representatives which should give each member a general commission to go through the length and breadth of the land, far from his own state or district, far from the seat of the general government, making inquiry about any subject, even on formal delegation to him from his house or one of its committees. Committees I am willing to accept. Sub-committees of one give me pause." It is to be noted that the new law which went into effect in New York State in May, 1954, establishing a fair procedure code for legislative investigations, rules out one-man committees and requires two committee members to be present at any hearing where testimony is taken.

14. *The Congressional committees have continually relied in their investigations on a motley assortment of professional informers, cringing ex-Communists and confessed ex-spies, all receiving from $25.00 to $50.00 a day for testimony of dubious honesty and value.* Again and again in these inquiries there has appeared the same troupe of wandering performers, whose continued pay depends upon their being able constantly to present new and sensational evidence. Persons who have in the past made a career out of lying and betraying their country are suddenly elevated by these committees into heroes and heroines whose every word is taken as sacred; and whose miraculously stimulated memories of events occurring many years previously are considered sufficient to condemn teachers, writers,

clergymen, government employees and others who have long records of honorable and distinguished service. Moreover, these raconteurs from the underworld of politics have complete immunity from suits for libel or slander while telling their lurid tales at a Congressional hearing.

In February, 1954, a group of 19 leading churchmen in New England and New York, including five bishops, wrote to the Senate Judiciary Committee urging that its Subcommittee on Civil Rights investigate the present role of informers in the United States. The letter stated in part: "The informer is a public accuser. When functioning under government protection or privilege the informer accuses with immunity. Up to now, informers who have been profuse in accusations against fellow citizens have not been cited for or charged with perjury in a court of law. Yet we have strong reason to believe that some informers who have traduced large numbers of citizens have not spoken the truth. Sworn admissions by some of them, conflicting statements at different times, and the testimony of ministers of the Christian Church and others as to the untruthfulness of these various professional witnesses should be the subject matter of investigation by the Subcommittee on Civil Rights."

15. *The committees gravely injure the reputations and careers of witnesses and others through public smears and innuendos based on unproved and unevaluated charges.* Such charges are often made in public hearings by the professional informers just discussed under Point 14. It is these accusations that usually receive the newspaper headlines and get the witness into serious trouble with his employer and in his social relationships.

Many teachers, government employees, actors and others have been summarily dismissed from their positions because of being put under a cloud of suspicion by melodramatic charges aired before some Congressional committee or released by it. The committees keep in their files a vast amount of unevaluated material about individuals and organizations, some in the form of newspaper clippings and much in the form of malicious "information" sent in by vigilante volunteers. According to the National Council of Churches of Christ in the U.S.A., "Sometimes persons of ill will have been able to send things in for the files, receive back the items as official releases of 'information from the files of the House Committee on Un-American Activities' and distribute them as such."

In addition, the Congressional committees have made a constant practice of "leaking" to some reporter or columnist vindictive stories about an individual they are about to subpoena. The idea is to crucify the victim in advance if possible. Favorite outlets for putting this tactic into effect have been the Hearst newspapers and especially Walter Winchell's column.

16. *The committees attempt to trap witnesses into slips of memory or careless answers to loaded questions and thus pave the way for perjury indictments.* As far back as 1950, Senator McCarthy hinted at the possible

role of perjury actions. At a hearing on U.S. foreign relations he asserted: "We find where Communists are concerned they are too clever. They work under ground too much. It is hard to get them for their criminal activities in connection with espionage, but a way has been found. We are getting them for perjury and putting some of the worst away. For that reason I hope every witness who comes here is put under oath and his testimony is gone over with a fine-tooth comb, and if we cannot convict some of them for their disloyal activities perhaps we can convict them for perjury."

One of the questions McCarthy asks most frequently at his committee hearings is: "Are you or have you ever been a member of the Communist conspiracy?" For the average witness to answer "No" to such an indefinite question, when the catch-all term "Communist conspiracy" might be interpreted to include many organizations fighting for peace or civil liberties, could place him in immediate danger of perjury charges.

The prime example of a Congressional committee setting the stage for a perjury indictment took place in 1952 when Senator Pat McCarran's Internal Security Committee put Professor Owen Lattimore of Johns Hopkins University through 12 days of gruelling hearings. Since Professor Lattimore answered fully and freely hundreds of questions put to him by the Committee about speeches, meetings, trips, engagements, associations, conversations and even thoughts which had taken place over the past 25 years, it was not surprising that occasionally he fell into minor inaccuracies and inconsistencies. The Committee insisted that he had deliberately lied and was later able, through unscrupulous political pressures, to have him indicted for perjury on seven counts. One of these impossibly vague counts was that Lattimore had falsely testified when he said that he had "never been a sympathizer or any other kind of a promoter of communism or Communist interests." A Federal judge has dismissed this count and three other counts, and cast serious doubts on the remaining three. Meanwhile, the Government is appealing its case in this most infamous perjury action in the history of American jurisprudence.

17. The committees repudiate the long-established juridical concept that guilt is always personal and substitute for it the new and abhorrent doctrine of guilt by association. If a Congressional committee can show that an individual belongs or belonged to an organization listed by the U.S. Attorney General as "subversive"—in a procedure which is itself unconstitutional—then it smears him as a Communist or fellow-traveler. And the victim is likely to lose his job or at least his standing in the community. Men have been fired because of subscribing to liberal publications like *The Nation* or *New Republic,* because they signed a public petition protesting the violation of civil liberties, or because they had friends or relatives who were thought radical.

Henry Steele Commager, Professor of History at Columbia University, has called this doctrine of guilt by association wrong in logic, wrong legally, wrong practically and wrong morally. On the logic of the matter he writes: "If all the subversives in the land asserted that two and two makes four, two and two would still make four. If a particular cause is worthy of support, it does not cease to merit support because men we disapprove support it. There is a persuasive reason why conservatives and liberals alike should subscribe to this principle, and that is a practical one. For if bad support could damage a good cause, then all that would be needed to tarnish the Declaration of Independence or destroy the Constitution would be the endorsement of these documents by the Communist Party; all that would be needed to ruin the Republican Party or the American Legion or the American Bar Association would be approval of their objectives by the *Daily Worker.*"

18. *The committees violate the time-honored legal doctrine that a man is to be considered innocent until he is proved guilty.* Their techniques bring into play guilt by accusation and guilt by rumor as well as guilt by association. As I have pointed out, the well-paid informers and others who have chosen to join the profession of denunciation have a field day at the Congressional hearings. Since the witness is given no chance to cross-examine his accusers and to refute them, it is almost impossible for him convincingly to disprove the wild, scurrilous and rambling charges that may be made against him.

The committees, furthermore, have in general taken the view that an individual who invokes the Fifth Amendment against self-incrimination thereby establishes his guilt. In essence, the committees hold that once a man is accused at one of their hearings—and the questions themselves amount to accusation—he is to be considered guilty until he proves his innocence. And then the inquisitors put every obstacle in the way of his doing this.

19. *The committees employ "third degree" methods in that they attempt to make individuals confess to or renounce unpopular beliefs and associations through threats and the infliction of mental suffering.* In 1931 the report of the President's National Commission on Law Observance and Enforcement stated: "The phrase 'third degree' as employed in this report is used to mean the employment of methods which inflict suffering, physical or mental, upon a person in order to obtain from that person information about a crime. . . . The practice is shocking in its character and extent, violative of American tradition and institutions, and not to be tolerated."

The Congressional committees today wield against all witnesses who appear before them an implicit threat that unless they are "cooperative," they will be subject to unmerciful smears, will probably lose their jobs and may have to face contempt indictments. Witnesses go into the hearings with a feeling that vast and indefinite dangers are confronting them and that the end of their effective careers may be at hand.

The committees cause great mental anguish even in persons who have not been summoned to appear before them, but who fear that they will be subpoenaed or are involved in some way in the proceedings. So it was that Abraham H. Feller of the United Nations staff committed suicide. Another such suicide was that of Raymond Kaplan, a radio engineer employed by the Voice of America, who in February of 1952 leaped to his death in front of a fast-moving truck in Cambridge, Mass. Mr. Kaplan had become very much afraid that the McCarthy Committee would call him and make some terrible accusation against him. In his suicide note he said: "You see when once the dogs are set on you, everything you have done since the beginning of time is suspect. . . . I have never done anything that I consider wrong, but I can't take the pressure on my shoulders any more."

20. The committees arrogate unto themselves the prerogative of laying down the fundamental qualifications for teaching, preaching, writing, acting and other cultural pursuits, employing the standard of ideological conformity instead of professional competency. During his investigations of members of the Harvard faculty, Senator McCarthy arrogantly told President Nathan Pusey of Harvard what type of professor should be permitted and not be permitted to teach at the University.

The official report of the Senate Internal Security Committee published in July, 1953, sets forth a whole program for American education. According to Professor Mark De Wolfe Howe of the Harvard Law School, this report urges "that our schools and colleges should turn to the investigating committees of the states and nation and work in close collaboration with them both for the dismissal of teachers 'who have demonstrated their unsuitability to teach' and for the selection of teachers whose inquiries have not led them in unfortunate political directions."

21. The committees waste the money of taxpayers to the tune of millions of dollars a year in worse than useless inquiries and force individuals and organizations to spend enormous sums in self-defense. The expenditures of the committees themselves are only a small part of the national cost involved in the current orgy of Congressional probes. For the many individuals and organizations summoned for or threatened with investigation must expend large sums in preparing for hearings, in hiring lawyers and perhaps finally defending themselves in the courts. For example, in the 1952 investigation of American foundations, it is reliably estimated that the total cost to the 1500 foundations questioned was close to $10,000,000.

22. The committees divert the attention of Congress from its proper business of considering and enacting legislation that will benefit America. During the past decade the number and scope of Congressional investigations have increased so greatly, with many of the hearings taking place in cities far distant from Washington, that Senators and Representatives who are members of the chief committees are hard pressed for time to attend to their other duties. At the same time the inquiries raise such a furor, as in McCarthy's investigations of the U.S. Army, that Congress as a whole is affected and becomes unable to concentrate on its legislative functions.

23. *The committees facilitate the rise in influence and power of dishonest demagogues who exploit the investigative functions of Congress to further personal political aggrandizement and to increase income from lecturing and writing opportunities that their notoriety brings them.* The committee chairmen, such as Representatives Dies, Thomas and Velde and Senators McCarran, McCarthy and Jenner, have all utilized their positions in an attempt to build up their political prestige through a mad pursuit of newspaper headlines and a shrill burlesque of the truth through every possible medium of communication.

In March, 1954, Senator Eastland of Mississippi staged a one-man investigation in New Orleans for the Senate Committee on Internal Security in an obvious move to obtain publicity to bolster his coming primary campaign. His main target was the Southern Conference Educational Fund, which he tried to portray as a sinister Communist-front organization. The southerners subpoenaed by Senator Eastland as officers of the Fund—Mrs. Clifford Durr, Mr. James Dombrowski, Mr. Aubrey Williams and others—all gave a good account of themselves and refused to answer a number of questions for reasons implicit in the First Amendment.

The Congressional committees answer every criticism with the specious claim that they are exposing Communists and communism. In Chicago in April, 1954, the Most Reverend Bernard J. Sheil, a bishop of the Roman Catholic Church, made a highly relevant comment on this in a speech denouncing Senator McCarthy. Bishop Sheil spoke out against "the phony anti-Communism that mocks our way of life, flouts our traditions and democratic procedures and sense of fair play. . . . It has been said that patriotism is the scoundrel's last refuge. In this day and age anti-Communism is sometimes the scoundrel's first defense. As I remember, one of the noisiest anti-Communists of recent history was a man named Adolf Hitler."

24. *The committees keep the country in an uproar, contribute mightily to the current witch-hunt and general psychology of suspicion, and deflect the attention of the people from the vital national and international problems which confront the United States.* While there are many other aspects of the civil liberties crisis in America, the Congressional Inquisition is to be rated at present as its most sinister feature. It is the spearhead of reaction. The McCarthys, the Jenners, the Veldes and their followers, by recklessly exaggerating the menace of American Communists, continue to whip up the mass hysteria that is so destructive of freedom. By publicizing false though dramatic issues through their investigations, they confuse and distract public opinion.

To quote Bishop Sheil again: "An America which has lost faith in the integrity of the Government, the Army, the schools, the churches, the labor unions, press, and most of all an America whose citizens have lost faith in each other—*such* an America would not need to bother about being anti-Communist; it would have nothing to recommend it to freedom-loving men." "Are we any safer," Bishop Sheil added, "because non-conformity has been practically identified with treason? I think not."

25. *Finally, these Congressional committees of investigation make America's professions of democracy seem a mockery in foreign lands and steadily weaken American influence abroad.* The foreign policy of the United States Government is purportedly designed to save democracy from communism throughout the world. Thoughtful foreigners cannot help but feel that there is a large element of hypocrisy in the profession of this aim when they see that civil liberties are faring worse in America than ever before in the country's history. And it is their impression that the Congressional committees have taken the lead in this assault on American democracy.

Commenting on this situation, President Henry P. Van Dusen of Union Theological Seminary stated in a letter to *The New York Times:* "The American people need to realize that in the eyes of the world the current procedures are rapidly making this aspect of their Government something of an international laughing-stock, not to say scandal." Naturally Joseph McCarthy is the most unpopular of the inquisitors abroad. Herbert Morrison, Deputy leader of the British Labor Party, declared in February, 1954, that McCarthy above all others was harming his country's reputation and asserted that "there was no difference at all between his methods and those used by Hitler."

* * *

Despite all this havoc wrought by Congressional investigating committees, despite their power and the fears they create, the counterpressures of public opinion can go far in stopping them. When in the spring of 1953 Chairman Velde of the Un-American Activities Committee announced a plan for a nation-wide investigation of Communists in the churches, the public reaction throughout the country was so overwhelmingly hostile that Representative Velde soon started to backtrack and has done little to pursue the proposed investigation.

Although individual Senators and Representatives have drafted codes for the reform of investigative procedures, none of these measures has reached the stage where there is a real chance for its becoming law. And none of them has gone beyond minor procedural improvements in investigative techniques, leaving untouched such questions as the violation of the First Amendment and the governmental separation of powers.

Hence our chief hope for basic reform here is that witnesses will continue to refuse to answer committee questions on the grounds of these fundamental constitutional issues and thus lay the basis for a legal test in a contempt case that will finally go to the U.S. Supreme Court. Mr. Harvey O'Connor has already been indicted in such a case. In my own defiance of the McCarthy Committee, I relied on these same constitutional principles, but the Senate has not yet seen fit to cite me for contempt. What those of us who have taken this position are driving at is not to cripple the important power of Congressional investigation, but to have proper limitations placed upon it according to the American Constitution.

However these cases turn out, principled Americans who believe in civil liberties for all will continue to fight against the Congressional Inquisition, regardless of the personal consequences to themselves. We can do no better than to follow the advice of Dr. Albert Einstein, who says that it is a duty to refuse "to cooperate in any undertaking that violates the constitutional rights of the individual. This holds in particular for all inquisitions that are concerned with the private life and the political affiliations of the citizens. Whoever cooperates in such a case becomes an accessory to acts of violation or invalidation of the Constitution."

In this unceasing battle for liberty it is important, too, to join in organized, cooperative efforts. This can be done by supporting organizations that are concentrating on the struggle for civil liberties, by actively participating in civic, church and trade union groups, and by working through one of the established political parties. Both individuals and organizations can also maintain constant pressure on the Eisenhower Administration, the members of Congress and the State governments.

In the long run we can restore this country's democratic traditions only by voting into power parties and candidates pledged to reverse the authoritarian tendencies of the past decade. This is a job for conservatives as well as for liberals and radicals. It is the obligation of all freedom-seeking Americans, opposing dictatorship of any kind, to help re-establish the Bill of Rights and make this Republic once more a great and continuing bastion of democracy.

10
The Assault on Academic Freedom (1955)

As the philosophers from Plato down to John Dewey have kept repeating, the most important element of all in the moulding of a people's mind is education. The anti-democratic, anti-intellectual demagogues of today also realize this. That is why they have made such mighty efforts to stimulate heresy-hunting and thought control in the schools, colleges and universities of the United States. They proceed on the sound assumption that what happens to American education will be a primary factor in what eventually happens to America.

Few schools, colleges or universities in the United States have been, even in the best of times, 100 percent faithful to the principles of academic freedom. Since World War II the situation has grown much worse. During the 1948 elections several college teachers lost their jobs because they supported the Progressive Party and its presidential candidate, former Democratic Vice-President Henry A. Wallace. In 1953 W. Lou Tandy, Professor of Economics and Sociology at the Kansas State Teachers College, was dismissed for signing a petition to President Eisenhower asking that he pardon the 11 Communist leaders jailed as a result of the first Smith Act trial. This was particularly outrageous because the First Amendment guarantees "the right of the people . . . to petition the Government for a redress of grievances."

In a special study of 72 colleges and universities throughout the United States, *The New York Times* reported in May 1951: "A subtle creeping paralysis of freedom of thought and speech is attacking college campuses in many parts of the country, limiting both students and faculty in the area traditionally reserved for the free exploration of knowledge and truth. These limitations on free inquiry take a variety of forms, but their net effect is a widening tendency toward passive acceptance of the *status quo*, conformity and a narrowing of the area of tolerance in which students, faculty and administrators feel free to speak, act and think independently. . . . Such caution, in effect, has made many college campuses barren of the free give-and-take of ideas. . . . At the same time it has posed a seemingly insoluble problem for the campus liberal, depleted his ranks and brought . . . an apathy about current problems that borders almost on their deliberate exclusion."

The *Times* survey showed that members of the college community were inhibited in discussing controversial issues and unpopular ideas because they feared social disapproval; criticism by friends, the college authorities or legislative bodies; being labeled pink or Communist; being rejected for study in graduate schools; and being investigated by Government or private business so that post-graduate employment might be adversely affected.

In June of the same year a college teacher wrote the *New York Herald Tribune* telling how he had asked his students in an English course whether they would like to publish a pamphlet on some current problem. The answers were negative: "The F.B.I. would get you"; "They would say you were un-American"; "You would lose your job if you expressed yourself"; "I am looking for security, not trying to change anything"; "Don't stick your neck out, McCarthy will investigate you."

In 1952 the *Times* reported that repression of thought in educational institutions had extended to the banning of factual information about the United Nations and U.N.E.S.C.O. "Some school systems," the *Times* article stated, "have discarded the use of teaching materials relating to the United Nations or its specialized agencies because of highly vocal minority groups. Much of the growing opposition comes from self-styled super-patriotic organizations or critical individuals. These groups and individuals charge that the United Nations or its educational branch, U.N.E.S.C.O., is subversive or tainted with atheism and communism. They maintain that U.N.E.S.C.O. is propagandizing for world government and, through revision of textbooks, is undermining nationalism."

The controversy over this matter in educational circles has been most acrimonious in Los Angeles where an ultra-conservative faction has bedeviled the community by bitterly pushing the view that U.N.E.S.C.O. is nothing more nor less than a conspiracy to put across Soviet-dominated world government. In 1953 the issue became so hot that the city's Board of Education rejected a $350,000 grant for a special teachers training program from the Ford Foundation's Fund for the Advancement of Education, because the Foundation was considered too "internationalist" in outlook.

Later in the same year Dr. O. Meredith Wilson, Executive Secretary of this same Education Fund, pointed out: "Even in the business of education the intellect has become suspect. If a man does not conform, even to stereotypes, he is branded as an egghead and a brain-truster. Businessmen and employers talk about the importance of college degrees, at the same time shying away from Phi Beta Kappa keys."

The McCarran-Walter Immigration Act of 1952 had already written current suspicion of intellectuals and higher education into law. This it did by repealing the nonquota immigrant status of foreign professors which had been in existence for more than 25 years. Under this exemption to immigration regulations, the United States admitted 2,869 professors during the years 1925-48. Ministers of religion enjoyed the same exemption; and in the same period 8,364 of them entered this country. The 1952 statute retained the special provision as relating to clergymen, but dropped it in regard to professors.

Another adverse sign of the times for those seeking a genuine education was the circulation, from 1948 to late in 1954, of a personnel pamphlet issued by the Socony-Vacuum Oil Company and entitled *So You Want a Better Job*. This pamphlet advised young people just out of college how to make good and noted: "Personal views can cause a lot of trouble. Remember, then, to keep them always conservative. The 'isms' are out. Business being what it is, it naturally looks with disfavor on the wild-eyed radical or even the moderate pink. On the other hand . . . you will find very few business organizations who will attempt to dictate the political party of their employees." Socony-Vacuum withdrew this statement after *The Daily Princetonian,* student newspaper at Princeton University, severely criticized it.

In 1954 the play-it-safe trend in educational institutions was highlighted when the authorities at West Point and Annapolis forbade cadets and midshipmen respectively to participate in intercollegiate debates on whether the United States should recognize the People's Republic of China. An Army spokesman in Washington stated: "It is Department of the Army policy not to have United States Military Academy cadets involved in debate on such a controversial subject, on which in any event national policy has already been established."

The Navy took the position that should the Annapolis team be assigned to argue in favor of U.S. recognition of Communist China, this would be tantamount to upholding "the Communist philosophy and party line." The Navy spokesman added: "The Academy's young men are being trained to be naval officers, and to argue the Communist doctrine would make them liable to misrepresentation, as well as providing the Reds a tremendous propaganda device."

At a press conference President Eisenhower made clear that he disagreed with the decisions of the superintendents at West Point and Annapolis and would have left the matter to the judgment of the students themselves.

Roanoke College in Virginia also refused to enter a team on the affirmative side of the question, "Should the United States recognize Red China?" The debate director at Roanoke gave as the reason that the College feared its students might subject themselves to investigation in later life. One of the Roanoke debaters explained he did not want to take a chance that the thing would "kick back" on him if one day he entered the Government service. In Nebraska the same debate topic was ruled out for all the State-supported colleges.

Interference with student freedom is not limited to restrictions on expressions of opinion. In 1954 the United States Department of Defense bore down heavily on college and university students by requiring all those in R.O.T.C. training courses to take a special loyalty oath. This new regulation obliges the enrollee to name any organization on the U.S. Attorney General's so-called subversive list of which he is or has been a member, whose meetings or social activities he has attended, whose literature he has distributed, or with which he has been "identified or associated . . . in some manner."

A student admitting to any such associations cannot be formally enrolled in the R.O.T.C. program, but may participate on an informal basis. This means that he is not permitted to borrow the necessary textbooks and drill equipment or to march in uniform. And he is stigmatized in the eyes of his fellow-students because he must march alone or with others similarly disqualified.

Owing to the volume of protests over the workings of the loyalty oath, the Defense Department in April 1955 retreated to some extent and announced that in the future the oath would be applicable only to Juniors and Seniors, who have reached a more advanced stage of R.O.T.C. training.

One of the more unhappy aspects of education in America at present is that both teachers and students fear—and with justification—that government agents are planted in courses to take note of any unorthodox ideas. In 1943 when I was a member of the Cornell University staff in charge of the Intensive Study of Contemporary Russian Civilization, one of the most brilliant and likable students turned out to be a Government agent who reported regularly to Washington on what was said in the lectures and discussions. The staff had been so impressed by this man that it had asked him to return as an assistant the following year.

In 1953 Dean Carl W. Ackerman of the Columbia School of Journalism strongly protested against this sort of snooping, mentioning in particular the F.B.I., the Central Intelligence Agency, the Secret Service and the Civil Service. Dean Ackerman said in part: "The practical problem which confronts deans, professors, schoolteachers and students today is political freedom to discuss public affairs in classrooms or at lunch or during a 'bull' session without fear that someone may make a record which may be investigated secretly, upon which he may be tried secretly, and also convicted secretly, either by a governmental official or a prospective employer."

Teachers in general in the United States today are being treated as a species of second-class citizens whose loyalty is considered so questionable that strict control of their ideas must be maintained and special legislation passed to guard the community against them. More and more State legislatures have been putting through laws requiring teachers to sign special loyalty oaths and ordering the dismissal of any teacher associated with an organization on the U.S. Attorney General's blacklist. Legislators, government officials and educational administrators have more and more been taking the attitude: "Beware of the teacher! He is almost sure to be a doubtful character, probably trying surreptitiously to lead your child astray with Communist propaganda and secretly spreading subversion in the classroom. Watch out for teachers and immediately report to the authorities any suspicious conduct or conversations."

One of the worst aspects of the situation is that fear-ridden fanatics or plain busybodies in many communities send in to local school principals, superintendents and boards of education a continuing mass of derogatory, anonymous and unsupported information about teachers. Sometimes this "information" comes from officials in State or Federal Governments. On the basis of such unreliable and unevaluated data, according to *The Denver Post* in its timely series of articles on "Faceless Informers in Our Schools," at least 1,000 teachers in public schools and colleges throughout the United States during 1952, 1953, and 1954 were put on suspect lists as disloyal or subversive.

The *Post* reports: "The fact that stands out above all others about the anti-subversion drive directed at the schools is this: In the vast majority of the cases, the informers or accusers have utterly refused to face the accused, or to come forward with supporting evidence or proof."

The professional informer and government witness, Harvey Matusow, revealed in his book *False Witness* that the Board of Education of New York City employed him as a consultant for ten days in 1952 for the purpose of helping to identify Communists in the city schools. The book reproduces a letter to Mr. Matusow from Superintendent of Schools William Jansen in which Mr. Jansen states: "It may be that you have some information that would be of great value to us concerning New York City teachers who are members of the Communist Party." Another letter reproduced is from Mr. Saul Moskoff, Assistant Corporation Counsel in charge of investigating communism in New York City schools. Mr. Moskoff says: "I find that Mr. Harvey M. Matusow is in possession of important information which will be of material assistance to the Board of Education." Later, in conference with Moskoff, Matusow made false allegations about the Communist associations of a number of teachers.

The use by high educational authorities in New York City of an informer like Matusow, now a self-confessed perjurer, well demonstrates the disreputable quality of the whole academic witch-hunt.

In March 1953 Richard E. Combs, Chief Counsel for the California Senate Committee on Un-American Activities, boasted before the Jenner Committee that the Committee's work had led, in the space of one year, to the removal of some 100 teachers from California college and university faculties. Mr. Combs was pleased about the cooperation of the educational authorities: "The Committee deemed it expedient to indicate to the university administrators the necessity, particularly in the larger institutions, of employing full-time people who had had a practical experience in the field of counter-Communist activities, ex-FBI agents, and ex-Navy and military intelligence men. That has been followed. On the major colleges and campuses in California such persons are working and have been for almost since last June. They maintain a liaison with our committee."

In addition to these various troubles, teachers have had to endure for a number of years the high-handed investigations of Congressional committees. When teachers have exercised their constitutional prerogatives and refused to answer, on the grounds of the First or Fifth Amendment, questions concerning political beliefs or associations put by House or Senate inquisitors,* they have usually been summarily dismissed by the school, college or university employing them. Only a few educational institutions have stood firm for the rights of their employees.

One of America's most revered teachers, Ralph Barton Perry, Professor Emeritus of Philosophy at Harvard University, has spoken out strongly against the tendency of colleges and universities to dismiss automatically members of their staffs who get into trouble with Congressional committees. "By so doing," he states, "the institutions virtually turn over to government their authority to hire and fire. A refusal to testify does not constitute grounds for dismissal, even when it constitutes sufficient evidence for the charge of contempt. The institution will take account of other considerations, and reach its own decision on educational grounds.

"There is no reason why the institution should serve as the executioner—the instrument by which to penalize those who have offended the committees, or against whom the committees have obtained what they consider to be unfavorable evidence. . . . The issue here is the autonomy of the educational

---

*This refers to the Senate Subcommittee on Internal Security, headed successively by Senators McCarran, Jenner and Eastland; the Senate Permanent Subcommittee on Investigations, headed by Senators McCarthy and McClellan; and the House Committee on Un-American Activities, headed recently by Representatives Velde and Walter.

institution as regards the employment of its staff. It has a duty to resist all 'pressures,' whether they come from Congressional committees or from public clamor or from its own alumni."

In teacher dismissals brought about by Congressional investigations it has hardly ever been charged that the victims are professionally incompetent or have violated classroom standards by trying to indoctrinate their pupils with some sort of political propaganda. And rarely has a Congressional committee disclosed anything about a teacher that shows him guilty of any crime. Instead the committees ask insulting questions that *imply* political crime, subversion or outright treason; and often the self-respecting teacher has invoked some section of the Bill of Rights and declined to answer such loaded questions.

In commenting on the prevailing psychology among teachers, Dr. Robert M. Hutchins writes in *Look* Magazine: "Whittaker Chambers and Prof. Sidney Hook of New York University, both of whom proclaim themselves devotees of academic freedom, say, 'Don't worry; only a few teachers have been fired.' What has this got to do with it? The question is not how many teachers have been fired, but how many think they might be, and for what reasons. It is even worse than that. Teachers are not merely afraid of being fired; they are afraid of getting into trouble, with resultant damage to their professional prospects and their standing in their communities. You don't have to fire many teachers to intimidate them all. The entire teaching profession of the United States is now intimidated."

Let us consider at this point, as typical of the witch-hunt in education, what happened when the House Committee on Un-American Activities held hearings in Philadelphia during 1953 and 1954. In the fall of 1953, the Committee, with the expressed purpose of investigating "subversion" in education, subpoenaed a considerable number of teachers in the Philadelphia public schools. Out of 33 who testified before the Committee in Philadelphia or Washington, 32 invoked the Fifth Amendment and one the First, in refusing to answer the questions, all of which pertained to past activities and associations from 1939 to 1950. The Philadelphia Superintendent of Schools, Mr. Louis P. Hoyer, had also asked these teachers similar questions which in general they had not answered.

Mr. Hoyer suspended 30 of the 33 who had appeared before the Un-American Committee. Later the Board of Public Education sustained the charges against 26 and dismissed them from their jobs. All of the 26, prior to their appearance before the Committee, had had "satisfactory" ratings by their individual school principals. These ratings were based on personality, preparation, instruction techniques and pupil reaction. It is obvious that the 26 were fired primarily because of their refusal to cooperate with a Congressional committee that was violating their constitutional rights.

The one victim who refused to answer the Un-American Committee's questions on the grounds of the First Amendment was Mrs. Goldie E. Watson, a Negro teacher who had taught in the Philadelphia school system for 23 years and had always been rated as competent. In her testimony before the Board of Education she told how two representatives of the Un-American Committee, a Mr. Fuoss and a Mr. McKillip, had come to interview her at her home. They informed her that everything would be all right and that the Committee would not even subpoena her if she would "cooperate." When she asked what this meant, Mr. Fuoss explained, "That you will name other people as Communists."

After this interview Mr. Fuoss called her several times on the phone and promised job security and promotion if she would only "cooperate." As Mrs. Watson told the Board: "I couldn't do it. And it would have been the lowest type of moral courage and morals for me to have permitted myself to become a stoolpigeon and informer because I had been informed on. I wouldn't do it. I could not have returned to my classroom under these circumstances. . . . Because for me to have participated in that inquisitorial inquisition . . . would have been showing that I did not believe in the Constitution."

At the same hearing before the Board of Education Superintendent Hoyer explained why suddenly after 23 years Mrs. Watson had become an unsatisfactory teacher: "On the form, the State form provided for rating teachers, there are a number of items that enter into the competency or incompetency of a teacher. And among those items are three which I have checked as being unsatisfactory.

"The first of these is the item of civic responsibility. . . . I am of the opinion that Mrs. Watson gave evidence of a very unsatisfactory concept of civic responsibility in her appearance before the Committee of the Congress. I consider it the duty of any citizen . . . and . . . especially the duty of a teacher to so cooperate with such a body of Congress. That Mrs. Watson did not do. And I therefore consider her as incompetent and unsatisfactory on the basis of civic responsibility.

"I also have considered her judgment extremely faulty. . . . This is another item which appears on this report. And that is because of the position which she took in this connection.

"I marked also the item of appreciation and ideals, particularly the ideals part of that combination, because she gave evidence of extremely unsatisfactory ideals with regard to the duties and responsibilities of American citizenship in her appearance before the Committee."

Mrs. Watson not only lost her teaching job, but was later cited for contempt of Congress by the House of Representatives and indicted for this alleged crime. She is one of the few teachers in America who has chosen to run the risk of a year in jail by standing on the First Amendment and thereby making a court test of the powers of a Congressional committee.

She intends to fight her case up to the U.S. Supreme Court.

In recent years teachers in many a city throughout the United States have had the same sort of unhappy experience as the Philadelphia schoolteachers. New York City, where I make my home and which ought to provide leadership as regards academic freedom, has done the opposite so far as teachers in public schools and public colleges are concerned. Indeed, New York's Board of Education and Board of Higher Education have actually spearheaded the nation-wide witch-hunt against teachers and driven out of the city's educational institutions, through one means or another, more than 250 teachers during the five years from 1950 through 1954.

New York's downward trend started 15 years ago, in 1940, when the College of the City of New York forced Bertrand Russell, one of England's most eminent thinkers, out of his professorship of philosophy. A censorious faction led by Episcopal Bishop William T. Manning had demanded that Russell be ousted on the grounds that he was "lecherous, salacious, libidinous, venerous, erotomaniac, aphroditous, atheistic, irreverent, narrow-minded, bigoted, and untruthful." Unhappily C.C.N.Y. and the Board of Higher Education succumbed to the strictures that religious groups, especially, brought to bear and cancelled Russell's appointment.

New York City's anti-freedom policies reached a climax in 1955. At that time the Board of Education, three years after hiring the notorious informer, Harvey Matusow, adopted 7-1 a resolution authorizing the Superintendent of Schools to "require" teachers to inform on their colleagues. Those who failed to do so would be liable to dismissal for "unbecoming conduct and insubordination." This was the first action of the kind taken by a public body in the whole United States. The American Civil Liberties Union opposed the resolution on the grounds that "questions about another teacher's views or associations are always to be considered improper because they immediately subvert that sense of freedom which is the life center of the academic process."

New York State, which during the administrations of Governors Alfred E. Smith, Franklin D. Roosevelt and Herbert H. Lehman had established a notable record for liberalism, fell to the level of New York City when in 1949 the legislature passed the Feinberg Law to bring about the exposure and expulsion of all "subversives" from the public schools. Under this blunderbuss measure a special investigative official is appointed in each of the State's 2,536 school districts, and is required to submit annually to the Board of Regents "a report in writing on each teacher or employee. Such report is required to state either that there is no evidence ... or that there is evidence of subversiveness."

Justice Douglas's dissent from the U.S. Supreme Court's decision declaring the Feinberg Law constitutional well describes the evil effects of the statute: "The very threat of such a procedure is certain to raise havoc with academic freedom. Youthful indiscretions, mistaken causes, misguided enthusiasms—all long forgotten—become the ghosts of a harrowing present. Any organization committed to a liberal cause, any group committed to revolt against an hysterical trend, any committee launched to sponsor an unpopular program becomes suspect. . . .

"The law inevitably turns the school system into a spying project. Regular loyalty reports on the teachers must be made out. The principals become detectives; the students, the parents, the community become informers. Ears are cocked for tell-tale signs of disloyalty. The prejudices of the community come into play in searching out the disloyal. This is not the usual type of supervision which checks a teacher's competency; it is a system which searches for hidden meanings in a teacher's utterances.

"What was the significance of the reference of the art teacher to socialism? Why was the history teacher so openly hostile to Franco's Spain? Who heard overtones of revolution in the English teacher's discussion of *The Grapes of Wrath?* What was behind the praise of Soviet progress in metallurgy in the chemistry class? Was it not 'subversive' for the teacher to cast doubt on the wisdom of the venture in Korea?

"What happens under this law is typical of what happens in a police state. Teachers are under constant surveillance; their pasts are combed for signs of disloyalty; their utterances are watched for clues to dangerous thoughts. A pall is cast over the classrooms. . . . Supineness and dogmatism take the place of inquiry. A 'party line'—as dangerous as the 'party line' of the Communists—lays hold. It is the 'party line' of the orthodox view, of the conventional thought, of the accepted approach. A problem can no longer be pursued with impunity to its edges. Fear stalks the classroom. The teacher is no longer a stimulus to adventurous thinking; she becomes instead a pipeline for safe and sound information."

Justice Black, concurring in Justice Douglas's dissent, asserted in part: "This is another of those rapidly multiplying legislative enactments which make it dangerous—this time for schoolteachers—to think or say anything except what a transient majority happen to approve at the moment. Basically these laws rest on the belief that government should supervise and limit the flow of ideas into the minds of men. The tendency of such governmental policy is to mould people into a common intellectual pattern. . . .

"Public officials cannot be constitutionally vested with powers to select the ideas people can think about, censor the public views they can express, or choose the persons or groups people can associate with. Public officials with such powers are not public servants; they are public masters."

State and municipal educational institutions are of course more vulnerable to political influence than private ones and are subject to the operation of suppressive legislation such as the Feinberg Law and State Acts requiring loyalty oaths of teachers or all State employees. These are major reasons for the fact that the few colleges and universities in America which have maintained a principled position in the face of mounting pressures are private educational institutions such as Columbia, Harvard, Sarah Lawrence and the University of Chicago.

As a Harvard graduate I have been proud that the authorities at my alma mater showed no disposition to yield to the demands of Senator Joseph McCarthy to dismiss two teachers, Dr. Wendell T. Furry, Associate Professor of Physics, and Leon J. Kamin, a teaching fellow, because in 1953 they refused on grounds of the Fifth Amendment to answer questions before the Senate Permanent Subcommittee on Investigations. McCarthy went into a rage over Harvard's stand; claimed that the University was "a real privileged sanctuary" for "Fifth Amendment Communists"; and told a New York teacher who had invoked the Fifth Amendment, "You can get a letter of recommendation from your Communist cell and get a job from Mr. Pusey." At the same time the Senator threatened to introduce a bill in Congress that would end gift-tax exemptions on contributions to educational institutions which employed "Fifth Amendment Communists."

When the McCarthy Committee recalled Furry and Kamin to testify again in 1954, both men invoked the First Amendment instead of the Fifth in declining to become informers by answering questions about persons other than themselves. Owing to this action, they were indicted for contempt of Congress in December 1954. Mr. Kamin had already left Harvard to take a faculty post at McGill University in Montreal; but Dr. Furry had continued in his regular position. After his indictment, President Pusey made clear in a public statement that the University would nonetheless retain Furry as a teacher.

In 1949 Harvard had already demonstrated its adherence to principle by dismissing in no uncertain terms the complaint of Mr. Frank B. Ober, a graduate of the Harvard Law School and author of Maryland's vicious Ober Act. Mr. Ober had refused to subscribe to the Law School Fund because the University continued to employ two teachers who, he claimed, were guilty of "giving aid and comfort to communism." These were Dr. John Ciardi, Assistant Professor of English, who had spoken in opposition to the Ober Act at a Progressive Party meeting in Maryland; and Dr. Harlow Shapley, Professor of Astronomy, who had been chairman of a peace conference held at the Waldorf-Astoria Hotel in New York City.

Dr. James B. Conant, President of Harvard from 1933 to 1953, answered Mr. Ober briefly, but turned the main job over to Mr. Grenville Clark, a well-known lawyer and a member of the Harvard Corporation. Mr. Clark dealt with Ober's charges in two letters, saying in part: "You want the authorities to keep a 'closer watch on what its professors are doing.' On this point you evidently want a watch kept pretty much all the time—

presumably day and night, in term and in vacation. For you say that 'most of the damage is done outside of the classroom' and that 'it is not reasonable to close one's eyes to such extra-curricular activities'. . . .

"For Harvard to take the course you recommend would be to repudiate the very essence of what Harvard stands for—the search for truth by a free and uncoerced body of students and teachers. And it would be to make a mockery of a long tradition of Harvard freedom for both its students and its faculties. . . . Harvard, like any great privately supported university, badly needs money; but Harvard will accept no gift on the condition, express or implied, that it shall compromise its tradition of freedom. . . . I affirm again that your plan implies an extensive system of detection and trial. . . . The harm done by the effort necessary to discover even a single clandestine Party member would outweigh any possible benefit."

Mr. Clark referred to and quoted from the statement on academic freedom made by the late President A. Lawrence Lowell of Harvard in his Annual Report of 1916-17. This statement, all the more notable because it was issued during the tensions of the First World War, remains a landmark in the development of academic freedom in America. I quote it at length:

"In spite of the risk of injury to the institution, the objections to restraint upon what professors may say as citizens seem to me far greater than the harm done by leaving them free. In the first place, to impose upon the teacher in a university restrictions to which the members of other professions, lawyers, physicians, engineers, and so forth, are not subjected, would produce a sense of irritation and humiliation. In accepting a chair under such conditions a man would surrender a part of his liberty; what he might say would be submitted to the censorship of a board of trustees, and he would cease to be a free citizen. The lawyer, physician, or engineer may express his views as he likes on the subject of the protective tariff; shall the professor of astronomy not be free to do the same? Such a policy would tend seriously to discourage some of the best men from taking up the scholar's life. It is not a question of academic freedom, but of personal liberty from constraint, yet it touches the dignity of the academic career.

"That is an objection to restraint on freedom of speech from the standpoint of the teacher. There is another, not less weighty, from that of the institution itself. If a university or college censors what its professors may say, if it restrains them from uttering something that it does not approve, it thereby assumes responsibility for that which it permits them to say. This is logical and inevitable, but it is a responsibility which an institution of learning would be very unwise in assuming. It is sometimes suggested that the principles are different in time of war; that the governing boards are then justified in restraining unpatriotic expressions injurious to the country. But the same problem is presented in wartime as in time of peace. If the university is right in restraining its professors, it has a duty to do so, and it is responsible for whatever it permits. There is no middle ground. Either the university assumes full responsibility for permitting its professors to express certain opinions in public, or it assumes no responsibility whatever, and leaves them to be dealt with like other citizens by the public authorities according to the laws of the land."

Even though Harvard in my opinion has the best record on academic freedom of any university in the United States, both Presidents Conant and Pusey made one important and unfortunate qualification to Harvard's stand. Both stated, when they were rebuffing inquisitorial demagogues, that they would not sanction a member of the Communist Party as a teacher at Harvard because, to quote Dr. Pusey, "He does not have the necessary independence of thought and judgment."

This position yields decisive ground to the inquisitors because it abandons the basic principle of judging teachers according to individual professional competence and substitutes for it the unacceptable standard of what varying implications can be drawn from membership in an unpopular political organization. Thereby the doctrine of guilt by association is established in academic life, and the way is opened to that general witch-hunt among teachers which Drs. Conant and Pusey deplore.

For once we accept the premise that members of the Communist Party are *ipso facto* unfit to be teachers in American educational institutions, we set in motion an unceasing inquisition which has for its purpose the ferreting out of all Communists, open or secret, in the teaching profession. This frantic enterprise then spreads to ever-widening circles and necessarily leads to the questioning of so-called fellow-travelers, of individuals who may be or may have been members of an organization blacklisted by the U.S. Attorney General, of independent progressives and radicals who have spoken their minds freely, and of anyone about whom malicious gossip is circulated. Such goings-on are bound to create an atmosphere of apprehension among teachers.

What Justice Black says about public officials in the field of education exceeding their legitimate powers also applies to the trustees, presidents and administrative authorities of private educational institutions. Academic freedom in American education means that just as Congress, under the First Amendment, "shall make no law abridging the freedom of speech," so officials in school, college and university shall adopt no rules and take no action abridging the intellectual freedom of teachers, scholars and students.

Educational authorities violate this principle of academic freedom as soon as they dismiss or subject teachers to any kind of pressure because of their political or other beliefs, or because of their organizational or personal associations. It is proper of course to drop teachers if it can be shown concretely that they lack professional competence, have used their classrooms for propaganda purposes, or have been guilty of moral turpitude or of some other grave misconduct.

But the charges brought against alleged subversives in the educational system are simply that they hold certain proscribed ideas or are, or have been, associated with certain proscribed organizations. Since, as I have pointed out, the witch-hunt gets going as soon as Communist Party members as such are barred from teaching positions, let us consider whether such action is justified.

The main argument for automatically dismissing Communists is that the American Communist Party exercises such strict discipline over its members, forcing them to follow the "party line" in all spheres of thought and activity, that they can have no real intellectual freedom and are therefore necessarily disqualified as teachers. A secondary argument is that Communist teachers are under orders to push the cause of communism whenever possible and accordingly inject Communist propaganda into their lectures and classroom instruction. These arguments do not stand up well under the analysis of reason.

In the first place, the American Communist Party does not have the power to "force" its members to do anything, as is shown by the large numbers who have withdrawn from the organization. Tens of thousands of men and women have joined and left the Communist Party since its founding in 1923. The conclusion is inescapable that, as Professor Alexander Meiklejohn has phrased it, "They do not accept Communist beliefs because they are members of the Party. They are members of the Party because they accept Communist beliefs." When they find themselves in substantial disagreement with those beliefs, they can choose to resign and do resign. This fact alone proves that Communist Party members do not inevitably lose their intellectual freedom.

In the second place and supporting this first point, the evidence indicates that people who join the Communist Party, however unwise that step proves, may even be more independent intellectually than the average person. Certainly to espouse communism in America has been a far cry from comfortable conformity to orthodoxy, and has always been a hazard from the viewpoint of social repute, occupational security and personal relations.

Hence I must agree with Professor Meiklejohn's further observation: "Why, then, do men and women of scholarly training and taste choose Party membership? Undoubtedly, some of them are, hysterically, attracted by disrepute and disaster. But, in general, the only explanation that fits the facts is that these scholars are moved by a passionate determination to follow the truth where it seems to lead, no matter what may be the cost to them and their families."

In the third place, there is a basic element of political bias and downright hypocrisy in the argument against Communist teachers that I have cited.

For every church, every civic organization, every political party imposes some measure of discipline on its members in the sense that they are expected to subscribe to the fundamental tenets of the group concerned. The Audubon Society would not tolerate as a member a man dedicated to shooting down as many birds as possible; nor the National Association for the Advancement of Colored People a man who favored racial segregation. Although Communist Party discipline is unusually severe, so is that of the Roman Catholic Church, which has an over-all philosophy as inclusive and rigorous as that of the Communists.

The fact, then, that a teacher belongs to an organization which to one degree or another requires discipline of its members is neither sufficient reason, nor indeed a reason at all for dismissing him. Actually, Communist teachers have been fired throughout America, not because of this trumped-up discipline issue, but because they hold ideas on economics and politics to which the educational authorities object. Those authorities, while loudly proclaiming their devotion to intellectual freedom, are determined to suppress such freedom if it moves in a radical direction. It is their intention not only to get rid of all Communists and "fellow-travelers," but also to make sure that teachers are in favor of the "free enterprise" system, the anti-Communist crusade and orthodoxy in general. This is "brain-washing" with a vengeance.

Who ever heard of a teacher being fired for supporting capitalism, the cold war against Soviet Russia, the Republican Party or the Catholic Church? Although leading educators have recommended the study of communism in schools and colleges, they make clear that the treatment of the subject should not be impartial, but must discredit communism by pointing out its evils. The powers-that-be in American education, then, take pains to establish, as Justice Douglas has said, their own "party line" to which the teacher is expected to conform, while at the same time they insist that anyone who follows a leftist "party line" is thereby derelict in seeking and imparting the truth.

In the fourth place, as to Communist teachers spreading leftist propaganda among their students, I know of no case involving the dismissal of a "subversive" teacher where that charge has even been made, let alone proved. Here again the argument smacks of hypocrisy. For there are no teachers anywhere, Communist or otherwise, who are able to be so completely impartial that they never bring into their teaching their personal opinions on controversial questions. Nor would such an attitude be desirable, since it would lay cramping restrictions on the teacher's intellectual freedom in lectures and discussion.

Dr. Broadus Mitchell, Professor of Economics at Rutgers University, has well summed up this situation: "The truth is that teachers, like other mortals, have intellectual and moral commitments, and perhaps arrive at them more cautiously than some others do. If we are to pillory teachers for their attachment to beliefs, philosophical, political, religious—equating these with closed minds and unworthy acceptance of authority—the waiting-line behind the stocks must be long and number some very respectable characters."

What is objectionable is a teacher's turning his classroom primarily into an echo chamber for his own views or neglecting to present objectively both sides of controversial issues. Then indeed he may be rightly accused of propagandizing. But little evidence has been adduced that Communist teachers in America do this. And, indeed, the very lack of such evidence has led to the additional accusation that Communist teachers are so diabolically clever that they instill their insidious propaganda without the innocent pupil or the vigilant school principal ever knowing about it.

Despite these various considerations about Communist teachers, the drive to oust them and other teachers with left-wing associations or views has gone on unabated. Only a few *local* teachers unions, such as the Teachers Union of New York City, the Philadelphia Teachers Union and the Los Angeles Federation of Teachers, have maintained without compromise the traditional position on academic freedom. Professional organizations of nation-wide scope that have stood firm are the American Association of University Professors, the American Philosophical Association, and the American Psychological Association.

On the other hand, the general movement undermining teachers' rights has been aided and abetted by some of the main educators' groups, such as the National Education Association, the most powerful school organization in the United States; the Association of American Universities, composed of university administrators; and the American Federation of Teachers, A.F.L., representing teachers from school to university level. Each of these bodies has voted that Communists have no place in the educational system of the United States.

The sad truth is that American educators have in general been so preoccupied by the Communist issue during the decade following the Second World War that they have neglected their primary responsibility of maintaining and developing a first-rate educational system. At a time when there is an enormous shortage of teachers in the United States, the educational authorities have considerably lessened the available supply by driving out of the profession men and women whose competence is admitted, but who have clashed with a Congressional committee or become suspect in some way as "subversive."

Both agitated legislators—through the passage of loyalty oath statutes and witch-hunt laws—and frightened educational administrators have put a premium on conformity among teachers and have drastically curtailed the exercise of academic freedom. These developments have discouraged independent thought on controversial subjects among both teachers and students; and have deterred increasing numbers of young people from entering the teaching profession, with its peculiar occupational hazards.

No profession has a finer tradition in the battle for human liberty than the teachers'. They can claim as theirs the noblest of all freedom's martyrs—the Greek teacher of philosophy, Socrates—and many another hero of the intellect in the history of the West. America's 1,500,000 teachers have the responsibility of preserving their great tradition of freedom of thought and expression. And beyond that they have the obligation of contributing their best efforts to the general struggle on behalf of the Bill of Rights. Owing to the central function of teachers in our society, their voice, their influence, their perseverance may well prove decisive in that struggle.

11
The Right to Travel
(1957)

In the year 1215 King John of England, yielding to his rebellious barons at Runnymede, signed Magna Carta and pledged therein: "It shall be lawful in future, unless in time of war, for anyone to leave and return to our kingdom safely and securely by land and water. . . ." Since this first authoritative formulation of the right to travel, there has been a growing recognition among civilized nations that all persons, except fugitives from justice, have a natural right to travel abroad.

Until very recently American citizens in general were free to leave the United States in peacetime as they chose. For approximately 150 years an American passport was considered, as it should be today, merely a certification of identity and citizenship, a letter of introduction to foreign nations for the purpose of facilitating travel. Prior to the First World War only a handful of foreign governments required visitors to have passports.

The importance with which the right to travel is regarded throughout the world is seen in the fact that the United Nations Declaration of Human Rights, signed by the United States in 1948, affirms this basic principle in no uncertain language. Article Thirteen of the Declaration states: "Everyone has the right to leave any country, including his own, and to return to his country."

In spite of subscribing to the U.N. Declaration, however, the United States Government since the end of the Second World War and the beginning of the Cold War has widely abridged the individual's freedom to travel. This it has done, not because large numbers of criminals are trying to escape the country, but because the U.S. State Department wishes to penalize

Americans who hold dissenting opinions and is concerned lest they criticize governmental policies while traveling abroad.

Since 1947 the State Department has been steadily undermining liberties which Anglo-Saxons first won 742 years ago in Magna Carta. It has thus managed in a brief ten years to set the clock back more than seven centuries.

It is generally realized today that international travel on a wide scale is one of the best ways to break down narrow nationalistic prejudices, to facilitate normal trade between the different countries of the globe and to develop the scientific and cultural interchange so essential to the building of world peace. As President Truman expressed it in 1951: "We shall never be able to remove suspicion and fear as potential causes of war until communication is permitted to flow, free and open, across international boundaries."

These more serious objectives, however, do not constitute the only reason why individuals should have the liberty to visit foreign lands. People must be free to travel for the sake of pure pleasure and recreation, for simple sightseeing, for romance or for any other purpose that strikes their fancy. The right to travel, as part of the general right of movement, is inherent to the free man's way of life.

A curious paradox in the current situation is that while our forefathers, afflicted by religious persecution in seventeenth-century England, were permitted by the monarchy to emigrate to America on the *Mayflower* and other ships, many Americans who today are suffering from political persecution and who might wish to settle permanently in England or some other land beyond the seas, cannot do so because the U.S. Government will not grant them passports. They can only go to a few countries in the Western Hemisphere, such as Mexico or Canada, where passports are not required for Americans. Thus the State Department has curtailed not only the right to travel, but also the right of expatriation, officially recognized by Act of Congress in 1868. Again, the State Department restrictions run counter to the U.N. Declaration of Human Rights which asserts in Article Fourteen: "Everyone has the right to seek and enjoy in other countries asylum from persecution."

The State Department, which by statute is assigned the power to issue passports, has based its dictatorial policies on various Executive Orders promulgated by Presidents of the United States authorizing the Secretary of State to draw up passport regulations and giving him "discretion" over the issuance and use of passports. The Department, claiming that travel is not a right but merely a "privilege," takes the position that "discretion" includes the authority to refuse passports to individuals because of their political views. The State Department further uses as a pretext for its policy the fact that the national emergency proclaimed by President Truman on December 16, 1950, has not yet been officially rescinded.

Of course we cannot object to the Secretary of State's exercising control over procedural matters—the mechanics of administration—such as the amount of the fee to be paid for a passport, the size of the photograph attached to it, and regulations concerning minors. Nor can we criticize him for refusing passports to escaped criminals or to draft dodgers. The point in such instances is that the individual's right of movement is already legally restricted for reasons that are non-political and unrelated to traveling abroad.

From the standpoint of civil liberties, however, neither the Secretary of State nor any other government official has the "discretion" to violate the Bill of Rights in carrying out his duties. But this is precisely what the Secretary of State does when he withholds passports because of the lawful political views or associations of the applicant. He violates the First Amendment because he is punishing persons who have in the past voiced certain controversial opinions or who have exercised their constitutional liberties by joining certain organizations.

At the same time, even though comparatively few Americans are directly affected, the Secretary is indirectly warning millions of others in a well-publicized way: "Unless you abrogate your First Amendment rights of association and expression, and go easy on criticizing government policies—especially in the sphere of foreign relations—you will receive no passport." In this way the State Department helps to pressure the American people into political conformity; for not many Americans want to risk losing the opportunity of going abroad.

Besides interfering with the First Amendment, the Secretary of State's passport policy also violates the Ninth Amendment, which reads: "The enumeration in the Constitution, of certain rights, shall not be construed to deny or disparage others retained by the people." One of those "others" is freedom to travel. At the same time, because of the arbitrary way with which the State Department often handles passport applicants, the Secretary is guilty of violating the Fifth Amendment guarantee that no person shall "be deprived of life, liberty or property without due process of law."

The State Department, moveover, has displayed marked capriciousness in enforcing its own regulations and waives its rules whenever it chooses. For instance, in 1955 it granted a passport to a reporter from the Communist *Daily Worker* to cover the Summit Conference in Geneva. On the other hand, in 1957 it denied a reporter from the same newspaper a passport to attend the Fortieth Anniversary Celebration of the Soviet Union in Moscow. After the State Department started the practice of stamping passports as "not valid" for certain countries, it officially stated that Americans could visit such countries without reprisal. But several years later it announced that newsmen visiting China would be penalized. In the fall of 1957 the Department adopted still another policy with respect to Albania and Bulgaria when it said Americans could travel to those nations for "compelling reasons," which means reasons that the Passport Office likes. Another caprice of the State Department has been a tendency to ignore court decisions instead of treating them as precedents to be followed in succeeding cases.

To cite President Truman again: "Under our Constitution, it is not only the citizens who are made to conform to the principles of justice but the Government itself. And the citizen has the right to enforce his rights against the Government. The rule of law is made supreme." The State Department's repeated flouting of this "rule of law" has contributed substantially, in an ever-expanding circle of cause and effect, to the general breakdown of civil liberties and of faith in the fair dealing of the U.S. Government.

During the past decade a number of prominent Americans whose passports have been revoked or denied on political grounds have fought back against the State Department, often successfully, through the courts or by other means. These include Anne Bauer, freelance writer; Leonard B. Boudin, General Counsel of the Emergency Civil Liberties Committee; J. Henry Carpenter, Presbyterian minister; William L. Clark, jurist; Jerome Davis, educator and sociologist; W. E. B. Du Bois, veteran scholar and author; Clark Foreman, Director of the Emergency Civil Liberties Committee; Stephen H. Fritchman, Unitarian minister; Albert E. Kahn, author and publisher; Rockwell Kent, one of America's most talented painters; Arthur Miller, playwright and author of the drama, *The Crucible;* Otto Nathan, teacher and economist; Linus C. Pauling, Professor of Chemistry and winner of a Nobel Prize; Paul Robeson, outstanding Negro singer; Max Schachtman, Chairman of the Independent Socialist League (Trotskyite); Donald Ogden Stewart, author of stage and screen plays; and Anna Louise Strong, author and lecturer.

The first significant curb on the lawless conduct of the State Department occurred in July 1952 when a Federal District Court ruled that the Passport authorities must give a formal hearing to Anne Bauer, whose passport had suddenly been revoked after she attacked the extreme racist policies of America's ally, the South African Government. In supporting her case, the American Civil Liberties Union asserted that the Passport Division was an "island of old-fashioned autocratic practice."

In delivering its opinion the court said that the cancellation of Miss Bauer's passport "without notice and hearing before revocation, as well as refusal to renew such a passport without an opportunity to be heard, was without authority of law. . . . This court is not willing to subscribe to the view that the executive power includes any absolute discretion which may encroach on the individual's constitutional rights, or that the Congress has power to confer such absolute discretion. We hold that, like other curtailments of personal liberty for the public good, the regulation of passports must be administered, not arbitrarily or capriciously, but fairly, applying the law equally to all citizens without discrimination, and with due process adapted to the exigencies of the situation."

As a result of the *Bauer* decision, the State Department in August

1952, announced the establishment of a special Board of Passport Appeals; and simultaneously enacted new regulations that for the first time in the history of the United States, laid down political tests for the obtaining of passports. These regulations, which are still in effect, deny passports to three classes of individuals:

> (a) Persons who are members of the Communist Party or who have recently terminated such membership under such circumstances as to warrant the conclusion—not otherwise rebutted by the evidence—that they continue to act in furtherance of the interests and under the discipline of the Communist Party;
> (b) Persons, regardless of the formal state of their affiliation with the Communist Party, who engage in activities which support the Communist movement under such circumstances as to warrant the conclusion—not otherwise rebutted by the evidence—that they have engaged in such activities as a result of direction, domination, or control exercised over them by the Communist movement;
> (c) Persons, regardless of the formal state of their affiliation with the Communist Party, as to whom there is reason to believe, on the balance of all the evidence, that they are going abroad to engage in activities which will advance the Communist movement for the purpose, knowingly and wilfully, of advancing that movement.

The regulations further state: "Consistent and prolonged adherence to the Communist Party line on a variety of issues and through shifts and changes of that line will suffice, prima facie, to support a finding under . . . (b)."

These regulations show the extent to which the State Department has adopted witch-hunt techniques; for the rules not only contravene the Bill of Rights by bringing into play the abhorrent doctrine of guilt by association, but compound this legal defect with formulations so vague that they cannot possibly meet the test of constitutionality. For example, by what standards are persons to be identified as engaging in "activities which support the Communist movement"? Many Congressmen and many Government officials would label as "Communistic" an individual who favors the abolition of nuclear bombs, the admission of Communist China to the United Nations, unqualified civil liberties or even slum clearance.

As to "the Communist Party line," that also is far too ambiguous a term to function as a legal standard. It is often beyond the wit of man to know precisely what is the policy of the Communist Party. And as Professor Horace M. Kallen of the New School for Social Research has pointed out, accusing an individual of following the Communist line is "like charging that strangers going down the same street in the same direction are going to the same destination and going together."

The passport regulations are so elastic that they can easily be used, and have been used, to hamstring the travel rights of mild liberals or of Christian clergymen who take seriously the social principles of Jesus.

These rules, moreover, go far beyond those provisions of the Internal Security Act of 1950 (a statute not yet ruled upon by the U.S. Supreme Court) which make it illegal for members of the Communist Party or officially designated Communist-front organizations to apply for or obtain passports. For under the State Department criteria *past* members of the Party are likely to be refused passports; and those who "support the Communist movement" are suspect regardless of organizational affiliation.

To return to Miss Bauer, she made repeated efforts to obtain the hearing which the Federal court had ordered, but found that the State Department had not in reality set up the Board of Passport Appeals which it had announced. Her case finally faded away when she married a Frenchman and took out French citizenship.

It was not until approximately a year and a half after the *Bauer* decision that the State Department actually established a seven-man Board of Passport Appeals. Its hand was forced then by the passport suit of Dr. Martin Kamen, a teacher of radiation physics and biochemistry. The new board heard his appeal, but decided against him in April 1954. After further litigation he won his suit and received a passport in July 1955. Since Dr. Kamen's passport had first been revoked in 1947, it had taken him eight years to re-establish his right to travel. The State Department throughout his case had deliberately used delaying tactics which have been typical in its handling of most passport cases.

Other important developments in the passport situation also took place in 1955—the year in which Miss Frances G. Knight succeeded Mrs. Ruth B. Shipley as Chief of the Passport Office.

In June of that year a United States Appeals Court handed down a decision, in the case of Max Schachtman, declaring that all citizens have an inherent right to travel abroad. The court stated: "The denial of a passport . . . causes a deprivation of liberty that a citizen otherwise would have. The right to travel, to go from place to place as the means of transportation permit, is a natural right subject to the rights of others and to reasonable regulation under law. A restraint imposed by the Government of the United States upon this liberty, therefore, must conform with the provision of the Fifth Amendment that 'No person shall be . . . deprived of . . . liberty . . . without due process of law.'"

In the same opinion the court held invalid the State Department's contention that because Mr. Schachtman was a member of an organization on the U.S. Attorney General's subversive list, he was *ipso facto* disqualified from traveling to Europe. Shortly after the decision the State Department yielded and gave Schachtman a passport.

At about the same time as the *Schachtman* decision the Federal courts cracked down on the State Department for again ignoring the *Bauer* ruling of 1952 and ordered passport hearings in the cases of Dr. Clark Foreman, a well-known civil libertarian, and Dr. Otto Nathan, the executor of Albert Einstein's estate. The State Department, apparently nervous over the possible outcome of such hearings, promptly surrendered and granted passports to both Messrs. Foreman and Nathan.

Federal District Judge Burnita S. Matthews, who insisted on the hearing for Dr. Foreman, also ruled that the original seizure of his passport by the State Department had been illegal. One day in 1951 a State Department official had phoned Foreman at his New York apartment and had asked him if a Department agent could come by and look at his passport, which still had one and a half years to run. Foreman assented to this proposal and let the agent who called look at his passport. The agent, however, promptly pocketed the document and started to leave. "I was sent to pick up your passport," he said. Foreman protested the ruse, but to no avail.

Another passport victory in 1955 was that of William L. Clark, former chief justice of the United States courts in occupied Germany. The State Department had lifted his passport because it did not like his criticisms of American foreign policy. When Judge Clark sued for the return of his passport, the U.S. Attorney in charge of the case frankly asserted that while in Germany Clark "would have the right of free speech so long as it is not in conflict with the best interests of the United States in Germany."

Curiously enough, an editorial in the right-wing *Chicago Tribune* gave the clear civil liberties answer to this statement: "This," said the *Tribune,* "is a doctrine as pernicious as dangerous. It amounts to the assertion that the State Department can limit the constitutional right of utterance merely by decreeing that what a citizen says, or what he might say, does not serve some confused policy of its own. If the rights of citizens abroad can be limited in this way, it is difficult to see why the Government cannot assume the same power at home, forcing us all to root for its foreign policy, whether we like it or not."

The State Department's most blatant interference with free speech, however, occurred in the case of Paul Robeson, who, having been blacklisted as a non-conformist throughout the United States, wished to continue with his profession and earn regular income by giving concerts in Europe. When Mr. Robeson was denied a passport, one of the chief accusations against him was that "he has been for years extremely active politically in behalf of the independence of the colonial peoples of Africa. Though this may be a highly laudable aim, the diplomatic embarrassment that could arise from the presence abroad of such a political meddler, traveling under the protection of an American passport, is easily imaginable."

The Passport Office even prevented Robeson from going to countries in the Western Hemisphere which do not require a passport from American citizens. It was only in 1957, after seven years of effort, that he was able to get this limitation rescinded. In two successive passport suits Robeson failed on technicalities, but intends to sue yet a third time to establish his right to travel.

Following the *Kamen, Foreman,* and *Nathan* decisions, the State Department suffered another setback towards the end of 1955 when Judge Luther W. Youngdahl of the Federal District Court in Washington, D.C., not only ordered a passport hearing for Leonard B. Boudin, but ruled that the Department must reveal to Boudin the sources and content of the confidential information upon which the Passport Office had rendered judgment against him. After affirming the point that travel abroad is a right and not a mere privilege, Judge Youngdahl declared:

"The right to a quasi-judicial hearing must mean more than the right to permit an applicant to testify and present evidence. It must include the right to know that the decision will be reached upon evidence of which he is aware and can refute directly. . . . When the basis of any action by any branch of the Government remains hidden from scrutiny and beyond practical review the seeds of arbitrary and irresponsible government are sown. More and more the courts have become aware of the irreparable damage which may be, has been, and is wrought by the secret informer and the faceless talebearer whose identity and testimony remains locked in confidential files."*

When the State Department appealed the Youngdahl verdict, the Appeals Court did not decide on the issue of confidential information, but sent the case back to the Department on the grounds that no formal findings had been drawn up as to why Boudin should not have a passport. The Department then reconsidered the matter and issued a passport to Boudin without holding a hearing.

It was also in the year 1955 that two especially important passport cases were initiated—those of Dr. Walter Briehl, a California psychiatrist whose professional work required him to attend international conferences on mental health, and of Rockwell Kent, one of America's most eminent artists. Both Dr. Briehl and Mr. Kent were denied passports when they refused to answer questions put by the Passport Office about their alleged Communist and Communist-front associations, on the ground that these questions were irrelevant and unconstitutional.

The Passport Office's accusations against Dr. Briehl are typical: "It is

---

*Cf. the statement by former Secretary of State Dean Acheson in his book, *A Democrat Looks at His Party* (p. 125): "The use of a secret police dossier by the state against its citizens is capable of infinite variations and subtleties. It is and always has been a source of great power. Until we imposed this system on ourselves, it was used here only for criminals."

alleged that you were a member of the Los Angeles County Communist Party; that you were a member of the Bookshop Association, St. Louis, Missouri; that you held Communist Party meetings; that in 1936 and 1941 you contributed articles to the Communist Publication 'Social Work Today'; that in 1939, 1940 and 1941 you were a sponsor to raise funds for veterans of the Abraham Lincoln Brigade in calling on the President of the United States by a petition to defend the rights of the Communist Party and its members; that you contributed to the Civil Rights Congress bail fund to be used in raising bail on behalf of convicted Communist leaders in New York City; that you were a member of the Hollywood Arts, Sciences and Professions Council and a contact of the Los Angeles Committee for Protection of Foreign Born and a contact of the 'Freedom Stage, Incorporated.' "

It is particularly to be noted that in enumerating Dr. Briehl's alleged associations the Passport Office did not mention a single activity that was illegal. This is characteristic of present passport procedures and points to the fact that the State Department is continually violating those provisions of the Constitution (Article I, Section 9) which forbid bills of attainder and retroactive penal legislation (*ex post facto* laws). When the Department deprives law-abiding Americans of the right to travel, it is itself behaving in an unlawful manner.

In denying a passport to Mr. Kent, who wished to travel in order to paint, the State Department went to the extreme of telling him that it was "not willing at this time to grant you passport facilities to travel to any countries for any purpose." One of the chief counts against Kent was the frank information provided in his autobiography, *It's Me O Lord,* that he had belonged to several "subversive" organizations. Evidently it is dangerous to write books if you want a passport.

After exhausting all administrative remedies, Briehl and Kent, backed by the Emergency Civil Liberties Committee and with Leonard B. Boudin as their counsel, sued Secretary of State Dulles for their passports. They lost in the first trial court and lost again, in June 1957, in a Circuit Court of Appeals, 5 to 3. The two cases will be heard in 1958 by the Supreme Court.

The adverse Appeals Court decision was handed down just after Rockwell Kent had been invited by the Soviet Union to attend an exhibit of his paintings in Moscow in celebration of his seventy-fifth birthday. By coincidence the Museum of Modern Art in New York in May had opened a four months' seventy-fifth birthday exhibition of the works of Pablo Picasso, Spanish-born painter who lives in France. Like Kent, Picasso was unable to be present at the exhibition of his works because, as he admittedly had had Communist associations, the State Department would not allow him a visa for the United States. *The New York Times* headlined a story about the two exhibits, "Art Surmounts Curbs on Artists."

In the meantime the passport scandal had flared up on other fronts. Early in 1956 Congressman Francis E. Walter, Chairman of the House Committee on Un-American Activities, who had become alarmed over the liberal court decisions on passports, introduced a bill to legalize the illegalities practiced by the State Department. Congressman Walter's proposed bill would give statutory authority for the denial of passports for political reasons and would invalidate the Youngdahl decision that passport applicants should have the right to confront their accusers. The bill incorporates verbatim the vague new passport regulations issued by the State Department in 1952. A somewhat less drastic bill is under consideration by the Senate.

Later in 1956, partly on the pretext of obtaining information relevant to his bill, Congressman Walter had the Un-American Activities Committee subpoena, among others, Dr. Clark Foreman and Dr. Otto Nathan. The Committee demanded that Foreman hand over his passport to its counsel. Foreman stated his willingness to do so, provided the Chairman would assure him of the document's return. Chairman Walter, however, refused to make any such guarantee, but kept insisting that Foreman surrender the passport. Foreman answered the Committee's many questions, but held out to the end against giving up his passport. The Committee cited him for contempt, but nothing ever came of it.

The Un-American Activities Committee adopted much the same tactics towards Dr. Nathan, who also declined to give up his passport. At one point Committee Counsel Arens asked Nathan whether he had told the truth when he filed an affidavit with the State Department swearing that he was not and never had been a member of the Communist Party. Nathan felt that this question impugned his honor and refused to answer it. Also on First Amendment grounds he refused to answer a number of other questions. The consequence was that he was cited and indicted for contempt of Congress. A Federal District Court acquitted him of this offense in November 1957.

All these passport suits had arisen over the alleged political opinions or affiliations of the applicant. But at the same time as the State Department was establishing precedents for denying passports to members of the Communist Party, members of alleged Communist fronts, so-called fellow-travelers and various other types of dissenters, it with facility extended its unconstitutional policy so as to bar liberal, conservative and right-wing newsmen from going to Communist China. In 1956 Secretary Dulles announced flatly that anyone who disregarded this ban would have his passport revoked. This violation of freedom of the press brought the State Department's despotic policy on travel full circle; and again proved that once the Government flouts the rights of one group in America, the precedent will eventually endanger the rights of all.

The press of the United States has been practically unanimous in condemning the State Department ban against journalists' going to the Chinese mainland. Journalists, according to our press, have a right and a duty to report the news as they see fit and to help inform the American people about what is happening in a country where one-fourth of the world's population lives. One newspaperman who protested to Secretary of State Dulles was Arthur Hays Sulzberger, publisher and Chairman of the Board of *The New York Times*. On April 23, 1957, Mr. Sulzberger wrote Secretary Dulles a long letter, which he concluded by saying: "As things now stand, I cannot escape the feeling that the Administration is abridging the freedom of the press and using the press as an instrument in its diplomacy."

Secretary Dulles replied with an even longer letter in which he made some remarkable statements: "The constitutional 'freedom of the press' relates to *publication,* and not to the gathering of news. There are, of course, many occasions and many areas where for security or other reasons, newspaper correspondents are excluded. . . . United States foreign policy inevitably involves the acceptance of certain restraints by the American people. If it were not so, foreign policy would be impotent. . . . Foreign policy and diplomacy cannot succeed unless, in fact, it channels the activities of our people, and in this respect newspapermen have also their loyalty and patriotic duty."

Newspapers throughout the country were quick to point out that true freedom of the press relates *both* to publication and news-gathering, and that the last sentence of Mr. Dulles's letter actually admitted Mr. Sulzberger's contention that the State Department was "using the press as an instrument in its diplomacy." Dulles's statement that newsmen have "their loyalty and patriotic duty" towards foreign policy can only mean that the Secretary of State expects them to treat high governmental policy as sacrosanct and to put it above their obligation to report the news accurately.

As for channeling the activities of the American people on behalf of the Government's foreign policy and diplomacy, this brings into effect a species of "total diplomacy" that places the State Department on a sacred pedestal and treats dissent from official doctrine as unpatriotic. It is helpful to have Secretary Dulles acknowledge publicly the anti-freedom principle upon which he and his associates operate.

A few Americans have openly defied the State Department's authority and have exercised their constitutional rights by visiting Communist China. In the winter of 1956-57 three American journalists—Edmund Stevens and Phillip Harrington, a reporter-photographer team for *Look* magazine, and William Worthy, correspondent for the *Baltimore Afro-American,* the *New York Post* and the Columbia Broadcasting System—went to mainland China for the purpose of reporting the news. When Mr. Worthy's passport expired on his return to the United States, the State Department punished him by turning down his application for a renewal. The American Civil Liberties

Union is supporting Mr. Worthy's case, which is now being taken to the Board of Passport Appeals.

The Chinese situation again hit the headlines in the summer of 1957 when forty-two American students attending a Youth Festival in Moscow decided to assert their independence of bureaucratic red tape and to visit China. The State Department issued a blast against them and threatened to cancel their passports when they returned home; it even went to the absurd extreme of warning the students that they might be prosecuted under the Trading with the Enemy Act, though obviously the United States was not at war with China. The American press as a whole again opposed the State Department's attitude; and in a lead editorial the conservative *New York Herald Tribune* called it a "blunder." Later the State Department softened its policy and said that the students would be able to renew their passports if they promised to abide by passport regulations in the future.

The furor over the students' trip to China apparently resulted in such heavy pressures on the State Department that it suddenly compromised on its travel policy and gave permission to twenty-four American newsmen to visit the Chinese mainland on an experimental basis for seven months. At the same time the Department re-asserted in its release its right to control travel to China and to limit drastically the number of reporters going there.

Walter Lippmann in the *New York Herald Tribune* had some harsh words to say about this official release which Secretary Dulles had approved: "Mr. Dulles is making the claim that outside the three-mile limit he may treat the press as an instrument of foreign policy, and that the American press in foreign countries is subject to the paramount control of the Secretary of State. . . .We have here the unprecedented and impertinent assertion that the right to turn off and the right to turn on the tap of news is one of the prerogatives of the Secretary of State. . . . This is, I submit, a usurpation of power which has never before been vested in the Secretary of State—the power to determine whether, when, where and under what conditions the American press may report and gather news in foreign countries."

The unfortunate State Department release also asserted that "the United States will not accord reciprocal visas to Chinese bearing passports issued by the Chinese Communist regime." This statement naturally aroused great indignation in China. And the Chinese Government announced that it would not allow the American newspapermen to enter the country unless there were reciprocity for Chinese journalists.

However this issue is resolved, it remains clear that the State Department's restrictions on travel to China are part and parcel of its general policy of limiting the right of peacetime travel. This point is not yet generally recognized. The Hearst and Scripps-Howard newspaper chains, for example, have upheld Secretary Dulles in denying passports to Communists and alleged subversives. But they have made a great to-do over their own reporters being prevented from visiting China. The average American, however, has just as much right to seek first-hand information and experience in foreign countries as newsmen. Secretary Dulles's position that our people should know only what he thinks is good for them means that they cannot obtain the facts necessary for an intelligent evaluation of American foreign policy.

The sooner the American press and American public opinion at large come to realize that the constitutional right to travel is indivisible, the better it will be for everyone—no matter what his profession or occupation—who wishes to go abroad, whether for business, for study, for art, for health, for sports or for any other lawful reason. And the right to travel grows more important year by year as the number of Americans desiring to visit distant lands steadily increases.

Besides the passport suits I have already mentioned, there is now another case in the courts, the case of *Lamont* v. *Dulles*. It began because I myself would like very much to cross the Atlantic again, to see old friends in England, to re-visit old haunts on the Continent and to acquaint myself at first-hand with economic and political developments among the peoples of Europe.

Accordingly, in the spring of 1951 I applied for a renewal of my passport. Mrs. Shipley, then head of the Passport Division,* refused my application, giving as an excuse the usual formula that "your travel abroad at this time would be contrary to the best interests of the United States."

After a further exchange of correspondence, I sent President Truman an Open Letter in October 1951, asking him to intervene on my behalf. Although this was given considerable attention in the press, the only reply that I received was another note from the Passport Division refusing me passport facilities. I was never able to find out the specific reasons for the denial of a passport or to obtain a formal hearing on the matter. However, I did get indirect but definite word from Washington that the Passport Division had relied upon a bulky dossier concerning me and all my ideological offenses over the past twenty years, and that if I were really serious about wanting to go abroad I would have to change my "whole political orientation."

For several years I did not press my passport case, both because I was no longer particularly desirous of taking a European trip and because I soon became involved in my long battle with the McCarthy Committee. After I declined, on constitutional grounds, to answer a number of questions put by the Committee at a hearing in 1953, I was cited for contempt of Congress by the Senate and then indicted by the Department of Justice. It was not until August of 1956 that I finally won my case when a United

---

*The name was changed to Passport Office in 1952.

States Appeals Court unanimously upheld the dismissal of my indictment.

In March 1957 I felt ready to do battle once more with the Republican Administration and again made formal application for a passport. However, the application forms since the middle of 1956 had included three entirely new questions:

"Are you now a member of the Communist Party? (Answer 'Yes' or 'No').

"Have you ever been a member of the Communist Party? (Answer 'Yes' or 'No').

"If ever a member, state period of membership—from . . . . to . . . ."

As I stated voluntarily under oath before the McCarthy Committee, I am not and never have been a member of the Communist Party. However, I do not believe that a citizen's political associations are any business of his government. I declined to answer the passport questions because they are unconstitutional inquiries on the part of the State Department and because every American has a natural right to travel regardless of his political or economic views. I believe that the current passport forms in effect demand an illegal loyalty oath of the more than 600,000 Americans per year who apply for passports.

Furthermore, every passport applicant must sign an oath of allegiance that states: "I do solemnly swear that I will support and defend the Constitution of the United States against all enemies, foreign and domestic; that I will bear true faith and allegiance to the same; and that I take this obligation freely, without any mental reservation or purpose of evasion." I gladly signed this oath. In my opinion, however, I would have violated the oath if I had then turned about and answered these unconstitutional questions about the Communist Party. For me the oath of allegiance means that I must defend the Constitution, including the Bill of Rights, under all circumstances and against all enemies, even if those enemies happen to be high officials of the U.S. Government.

The Passport Office refused to grant me a passport or even to give me a hearing on the grounds that my application was incomplete and therefore not duly executed. Hence on June 18, 1957 I filed suit in the United States District Court in Washington against Secretary of State Dulles in order to re-establish my right to travel. In a letter to Mr. Dulles I said: "As an American citizen deeply concerned with the freedoms guaranteed in the Bill of Rights, I must oppose on principle and in practice State Department procedures that encroach upon my civil liberties and those of the American people. I bring this suit against you, Mr. Secretary, not for myself alone, but also to help safeguard the fundamental rights of my fellow Americans against a capricious and tyrannical bureaucracy."

Although Walter Briehl and Rockwell Kent were also unresponsive to State Department queries about their Communist affiliations,* my case differs from their cases in that the questions I refused to answer were actually printed on the passport application blank. My attorneys in this suit are Leonard B. Boudin of New York and Harry I. Rand of Washington.†

Secretary Dulles himself has gone on record (news conference of May 14, 1957) as favoring a Supreme Court ruling "as to just what the functions and responsibilities of the Secretary of State are as regards passports. And whether or not it will be held that there is a right to travel everywhere which is superior to foreign policy, I don't know. If the courts so decide, naturally, I will accept such a decision."

In a number of significant decisions during 1957 the Supreme Court upheld the constitutional rights of the individual against lawless abuse by government authorities. I refer particularly to the *Konigsberg, Jencks, Sweezy,* and *Watkins* opinions. The *Konigsberg* ruling is directly applicable to the main passport cases. For there the Court stated that Konigsberg's refusal to answer questions about possible Communist Party membership and other political associations was not a sufficient reason for the State Bar of California to exclude him and thereby prevent him from practicing law.

As I have pointed out, some of the Federal District and Appeals courts have become quite restive over the travel restrictions of the State Department. In the Circuit Court of Appeals which ruled against Briehl and Kent the three dissenting judges filed vigorous opinions. Judge David L. Bazelon was clear that "the President has not delegated to the Secretary of State the power to decide which Americans may travel and which may not." Chief Judge Henry White Edgerton concurred with Judge Bazelon and declared: "We have temporized too long with the passport practices of the State Department. Iron curtains have no place in a free world."

With the American Judiciary displaying more and more of a disposition to defend the Bill of Rights against governmental encroachments and with a more tolerant atmosphere in the realm of public opinion, there has in my judgment been a genuine turning of the tide towards the re-establishment of traditional civil liberties. And it is reasonable to hope, I think, that the American people will fully recover, along with their other basic liberties, the right to travel.

---

*In November 1957, the State Department granted a passport to Donald Ogden Stewart, the playwright, after a Federal Appeals Court decided that he had complied with passport regulations by swearing he had not been a member of the Communist Party or connected with any Communist movement for fifteen years prior to 1956.
†See Postscript.

Postscript

I lost my case in a Federal District Court and at once appealed to a U.S. Circuit Court which heard my argument in May, 1958. But in June the United States Supreme Court ruled in the joint case of Kent and Briehl that American passports could not be denied on account of an applicant's beliefs or associations. This landmark decision automatically gave me victory and I finally obtained my passport in June, 1958, after a delay of eight years.

12
To End Nuclear Bomb Tests
(1958)

On New Year's Day, 1958, there were the usual private expressions and public declarations of hope and cheer. But international tension continued much as before throughout a large part of the globe; relations between the American-led bloc of nations and the Communist-led bloc showed few signs of improvement; the colossal armaments race between the United States and the Soviet Union, including further production and testing of nuclear weapons, went on unabated; and proposals for a Summit Conference among the Great Powers seemed to be resulting in little else than endless talk.

We [Corliss and Margaret Lamont] had been very much disappointed at the reaction of the United States Government and the American people to the successful launching of mankind's first earth satellite by the Soviet Union early in October. Instead of hailing Sputnik I as an epoch-making triumph for the human race and a harbinger of science's coming control of space, our government officials and public opinion took the attitude that the Soviet achievement constituted a major defeat for the United States and a dire military threat to our national security. The result was that the U.S. Government intensified the arms race.

So on January 1 the cause of peace appeared to be bogged down in fear, apathy, misunderstanding, prejudice and unceasing liturgies of hate. In this depressing atmosphere, we started our own New Year by discussing what we might do to advance the cause of world peace. And our minds naturally turned to the terrible menace to all humanity in the continuing

---

Co-authored by Margaret I. Lamont.

development of atomic and hydrogen weapons by the United States, Soviet Russia and Great Britain. Among other things, we had been greatly impressed by Nevil Shute's scientifically based novel, *On the Beach,* which described how the massive and wind-spread radioactive fall-out from the use of atom, hydrogen and cobalt bombs in "the Third World War" had doomed to death the entire population of the earth.

We had also been inspired by Bertrand Russell's Open Letter in November 1957 to President Dwight D. Eisenhower and N. S. Khrushchev, Secretary of the Soviet Communist Party. Lord Russell pleaded with these two leaders to establish a cooperative co-existence between the United States and the Soviet Union, and to put an end to the hideous race in nuclear weapons. He asserted that "the supreme concern of men of all ways of thought at the present time must be to ensure the continued existence of the human race. This is already in jeopardy from the hostility between East and West and will, if many minor nations acquire nuclear weapons, be in very much greater jeopardy within a few years from the possibility of irresponsible action by thoughtless fanatics."

As we talked on, the idea emerged that we ought to take some sort of special action about a cessation of hydrogen-bomb tests and the ultimate abolition of nuclear weapons altogether. After discussing these questions for a week or so with our family and a few friends, we decided—as a first step—to make a direct appeal to President Eisenhower and Premier Bulganin* of the Soviet Union.

While we were in the process of drawing up our appeal, we were considerably encouraged by the petition filed on January 12, 1958, with the United Nations by Dr. Linus Pauling, Professor of Chemistry at the California Institute of Technology and a Nobel Prize winner. This petition, signed by more than 9,000 prominent scientists from forty-three countries, urged that prompt action be taken towards an international agreement "to stop the testing of all nuclear weapons." The statement declared:

"Each nuclear bomb test spreads an added burden of radioactive elements over every part of the world. Each added amount of radiation causes damage to the health of human beings all over the world and causes damage to the pool of human germ plasm such as to lead to an increase in the number of seriously defective children that will be born in future generations. So long as these weapons are in the hands of only three Powers, an agreement for their control is feasible. If testing continues, and the possession of these weapons spreads to additional governments, the danger of outbreak of a cataclysmic nuclear war through the reckless action of some irresponsible national leader will be greatly increased."

On January 18, 1958 we sent to President Eisenhower and Premier

---

*Succeeded as Premier by Nikita S. Khrushchev on March 27, 1958.

Bulganin almost identical Open Letters about suspending H-bomb tests. Although there had been excellent committees working towards this same goal and numerous petitions issued with this same end in view, we felt that for once a simple appeal from a husband and wife, a father and mother, might receive more attention than still another statement signed by a number of individuals. We released our Open Letters to the press in the United States, but the metropolitan newspapers ignored the story. Only two small dailies and two small weeklies gave it space. However, we thought the letters had some importance and that it was worthwhile to break through to the general public. Accordingly, on January 23 we published them in a half-page advertisement in the regular and international editions of *The New York Times*. The two Open Letters follow in full:

450 Riverside Drive
New York 27, N.Y.
January 18, 1958

To Dwight D. Eisenhower

Dear Mr. President:

In your recent State of the Union message you said: "The world must stop the present plunge toward more and more destructive weapons of war, and turn the corner that will start our steps firmly on the path toward lasting peace. . . ." Yet today the continued threat of a third world war that could annihilate mankind creates universal fear and darkens our hopes for the future. Despite many disarmament conferences over the past decade and now fresh attempts at substantial East-West negotiations, little real progress has been made toward disarmament in either nuclear or conventional weapons.

Repeated discussions on the part of the American, British and Soviet Governments have failed to achieve any agreement for a cessation of hydrogen-bomb tests. Yet the continuance of these tests, with their cumulative effect in increasing radioactive fall-out, constitutes a grave menace to the health and genetic soundness of the whole human race.

Since there appears to be slight prospect at present for an international pact to halt H-bomb tests, we urge, Mr. President, that your Administration take the initiative and stop further tests of this sort on a unilateral basis, for a temporary period of at least one year.

Such a move would catch the imagination of mankind and be a great dramatic action that might break the international stalemate and "start our steps," as you suggest, "firmly on the path toward lasting peace." It would give an immense stimulus to disarmament and the abolition of nuclear weapons altogether; and it would help make successful any serious East-West negotiations that took place after America's cessation of H-bomb tests. We can also hope that the Soviet Government would follow the example of the United States, thus paving the way for a formal agreement on the matter with the American Government.

It does not seem to us that the American Government and the American people have anything to lose by suspending H-bomb tests for a self-enforcing trial period. In fact, this proposal is clearly in the self-interest of both the U.S.A. and the U.S.S.R. Both countries, we understand, are already amply equipped with hydrogen bombs for military purposes. In any case, we do not think that either country intends to launch a military attack on the other.

We write to you as citizens who for twenty-five years have been active in work for international peace, and for American-Soviet understanding and cooperation. Today we note sadly that these aims are still far from being fulfilled. We make this earnest appeal to you, President Eisenhower, in the spirit of Albert Schweitzer's Declaration of Conscience, because we desire above all things to have our children and grandchildren, the American people and the Soviet people, and indeed all humanity, live in a peaceful world free from the burden of armaments and the dread of extermination.

Since it was the United States that first invented, manufactured and used atomic bombs, we believe that our nation has a special moral responsibility to take the lead in outlawing nuclear weapons. We are convinced that if your Administration halted H-bomb tests, it would mean a great advance toward peace. And all the peoples of the world would surely applaud the American Government.

We have sent a similar communication to Premier Bulganin concerning Soviet policy and are enclosing a copy for your information.

Corliss Lamont
Margaret I. Lamont

450 Riverside Drive
New York 27, N.Y.
January 18, 1958

To Nikolai A. Bulganin

Your Excellency:

In your New Year's message to President Eisenhower you spoke eloquently of "the great ardent dream of humanity—to create a firm peace on earth." Yet today the continued threat of a third world war that could annihilate mankind creates universal fear and darkens our hopes for the future. Despite many disarmament conferences over the past decade and now fresh attempts for substantial East-West negotiations, little real progress has been made toward disarmament in either nuclear or conventional weapons.

Repeated discussions on the part of the American, British and Soviet

Governments have failed to achieve any agreement for a cessation of hydrogen-bomb tests. Yet the continuance of these tests, with their cumulative effect in increasing radioactive fall-out, constitutes a grave menace to the health and genetic soundness of the whole human race.

Since there appears to be slight prospect at present for an international pact to halt H-bomb tests, we urge, Mr. Premier, that your nation take the initiative and stop further tests of this sort on a unilateral basis, for a temporary period of at least one year.

Such a step would catch the imagination of mankind and be a great dramatic action that might break the international stalemate; it would give an immense stimulus to disarmament and the abolition of nuclear weapons altogether, and it would help make successful any serious East-West negotiations that took place after the Soviet Union's cessation of H-bomb tests. We can also hope that the American and British Governments would follow the example of the U.S.S.R., thus paving the way for a formal agreement on the matter with the Soviet Government.

It does not seem to us that the Soviet Government and the Soviet people have anything to lose by suspending H-bomb tests for a self-enforcing trial period. In fact, this proposal is clearly in the self-interest of both the U.S.S.R. and the U.S.A. Both countries, we understand, are already amply equipped with hydrogen bombs for military purposes. In any case, we do not think that either country intends to launch a military attack on the other.

We write to you as individuals who for twenty-five years have been active in work for international peace, and American-Soviet understanding and cooperation. Today we note sadly that these aims are still far from being fulfilled. We make this earnest appeal to you, Premier Bulganin, in the spirit of Albert Schweitzer's Declaration of Conscience, because we desire above all things to have our children and grandchildren, the American people and the Soviet people, and indeed all humanity, live in a peaceful world free from the burden of armaments and the dread of extermination. We are convinced that if the Soviet Union took the lead and halted H-bomb tests, it would mean a great advance toward peace. And all the peoples of the world would surely applaud your Government.

We have sent a similar communication to President Eisenhower concerning United States policy and are enclosing a copy for your information.

Corliss Lamont
Margaret I. Lamont

We mailed our letter to President Eisenhower at the White House, and the letter to Premier Bulganin in care of Soviet Ambassador Georgi N. Zaroubin*

---

*Succeeded as Ambassador by Mikhail A. Menshikov on February 6, 1958.

at the Embassy of the U.S.S.R. in Washington, D.C. We sent copies of the two letters to Secretary of State John Foster Dulles, Ambassador Henry Cabot Lodge, U.S. Representative to the United Nations, and Andrei A. Gromyko, Foreign Minister of the Soviet Union.

Ambassador Lodge replied on January 23 with a short and polite acknowledgment. On January 31 Maurice S. Rice, Acting Chief of the Public Service Division, sent a brief note on behalf of Secretary Dulles, addressing the letter to "Miss Corliss Lamont." Meantime, on January 27 Ambassador Zaroubin had written as follows:

>
> Embassy of the U.S.S.R.
> Washington 6, D.C.
> January 27, 1958

LETTER FROM SOVIET AMBASSADOR

Dear Mr. Lamont:

I received your letter of January 18th together with a letter to Premier Bulganin on the subject of suspending H-bomb tests, and a copy of a letter which you and Mrs. Lamont have written to President Eisenhower. In compliance with your request I am sending these letters on to Moscow.

As far as the essence of the said problem is concerned, the position of the Soviet Union was stated in the Message of N. A. Bulganin to President Eisenhower and in the proposals by the Soviet Government on the relaxation of tension which I had the honor to convey recently to the President.

I am sending you herewith copies of those documents as well as some other material which presents the position of the Soviet Union on the problem concerned.

>
> *Sincerely yours,*
> Georgi N. Zaroubin
> *Ambassador*

The only editorial comment concerning our Open Letters came in the right-wing weekly, the *National Review* of February 8, 1958. It was naturally hostile.

National Review Editorial, February 8, 1958

History Moves On

There is not a Communist bone in Corliss Lamont's body, or in his wife's either. They are—it says so right here in a paid half-page ad in the Times—*merely citizens, American citizens that is, who "for twenty-five years have been active in work for international peace, and for American-*

Soviet *understanding and cooperation.*" Their ad, which consists of simultaneous and in large part identical letters to President Eisenhower and Premier Bulganin respectively, is written in the "*spirit of Albert Schweitzer's Declaration of Conscience*"; so that any apparent similarity between their position and that of the Communists is purely coincidental. They even put "American" before "Soviet" in "American-Soviet," and not only in the letter to Eisenhower but also in that to Bulganin.

But the similarity does leap to the eye: No international agreement to stop H-bomb tests has been achieved. The tests constitute a "*grave menace to the health and general soundness of the whole human race.*" Let Mr. Eisenhower, then, "*take the initiative and stop the tests on a unilateral basis.*" Let Gospodin Bulganin also take the initiative and stop the tests unilaterally. (*How they are both to take the initiative unilaterally the Lamonts don't say, but no matter.*) Such a move would "*catch the imagination of mankind.*" It would immensely stimulate disarmament, it would help "*make successful any serious East-West negotiations.*" The American government and the American people would lose nothing by it; neither would the Soviet government and Soviet people; it is "*clearly in the self-interest*" of all.

Only on one major point do the two letters differ: the Lamonts tell Mr. Eisenhower that the U.S., having invented and first used the atomic bomb, has "*a special moral responsibility*" to make the move, but say nothing of this special U.S. responsibility, nor of any special Soviet responsibility, to Bulganin. So history does not merely repeat itself: the Lamonts have begun *to keep secrets* vis-à-vis *the Soviet Union!*

Here is our reply to the editor, published March 8, 1958, with the *Review*'s brief comment:

To The Editor, *National Review*

Unilateral Defenselessness

In your comment [February 8] on our Open Letters to President Eisenhower and Premier Bulganin calling for unilateral suspension of H-bomb tests by the United States and Soviet Russia, your proofreader (and what proofreader is perfect?) permitted an error which garbled one of our main points.

We said that continuance of the tests "constitutes a grave menace to the health and genetic *[not* general *as in your quotation] soundness of the whole human race."* . . .

As for your implication that our letters were somehow Communist-inspired, we should like to call to your attention that neither the Soviet Government nor any Communist Party in the world has urged that the

USSR halt H-bomb tests on a unilateral basis.
New York City

Corliss Lamont
Margaret Lamont

The Communists are not that dumb.—Ed.

In spite of the *National Review*'s sarcasm and the opinion of several "experts" on Soviet affairs that it was "naive" to think that the U.S.S.R. would take such a step as we had suggested in our Open Letter, the Supreme Soviet of the U.S.S.R. voted on March 31, 1958 to suspend tests of all nuclear weapons on a unilateral basis. The Soviet Government, however, left the way open for a reconsideration of this decision if the American and British Governments continued their testing of atomic and hydrogen bombs. Foreign Minister Gromyko, in placing before the Supreme Soviet the suspension proposal of the Soviet Council of Ministers (the Soviet Cabinet), stated in part:

"It is a fact that scientists, military and political leaders realize perfectly well that the development of nuclear weapons has attained such a level that the explosion of one or two hydrogen bombs can destroy everything or nearly everything living on the territory of quite a sizable European state, and that these bombs can be delivered almost instantaneously to any point on the globe by means of rockets. . . .

"Determined to make the utmost contribution to achieving the great objective of ridding mankind of the nuclear war menace, the Council of Ministers of the U.S.S.R. submits the proposal to the Supreme Soviet that the Soviet Union unilaterally cease tests of all types of atomic and hydrogen weapons, as the first step in this direction. In putting forward this proposal the Council of Ministers of the U.S.S.R. acts on the assumption that this noble initiative of the Soviet Union, which is bound to meet the aspirations of millions upon millions of people in all lands, will be instrumental in improving the whole international situation and will be echoed accordingly by other nations possessing nuclear weapons and testing them."

It was after breakfast on the morning of Monday, March 31, that we first heard over the radio that Soviet Russia was discontinuing its nuclear weapons tests. We talked over this good news and then quickly decided that we would send a telegram to President Eisenhower. In another hour or so we wired the following message:

New York 27, N.Y.
March 31, 1958

TELEGRAM TO DWIGHT D. EISENHOWER

In view of the official Soviet announcement today suspending tests of nuclear weapons on a unilateral basis, we wish to remind you of our letters of January 18 to you and Marshal Bulganin suggesting that the

United States and the Soviet Union halt hydrogen-bomb tests for a trial period. Although we had no reply to our communication, we are taking the liberty of urging again at this juncture that the American Government stop nuclear weapons tests with their dangerous spread of radioactive fallout throughout the world.

In the name of reason and humanity, Mr. President, we appeal to you to cancel the nuclear weapons tests scheduled to begin this spring in the Pacific. This action would gain the gratitude of mankind and pave the way for a formal agreement among the Great Powers to ban nuclear tests and the production of nuclear weapons under adequate United Nations inspection. Such steps would immensely increase the security of our country, which can achieve its highest ideals and fulfil its great destiny only if there is permanent peace. We are convinced that Soviet Russia sincerely desires amity and cooperation with the United States.

And we believe that tens of millions of Americans stand with us in hoping that our Government will match the new Soviet move toward sanity in international relations. We urge that your Administration promptly put into effect policies calculated to regain for our nation its moral leadership in the cause of world peace. . . .

Corliss Lamont
Margaret I. Lamont

The *National Guardian*, a progressive newsweekly, was the only publication to comment on our original Open Letters to Eisenhower and Bulganin in relation to the Soviet cessation of nuclear weapons tests.

National Guardian Editorial, April 7, 1958

What moved Moscow?

Who can tell what tips the balance in the affairs of mankind? On Jan. 18 this year, Corliss and Margaret Lamont wrote to President Eisenhower and Premier Bulganin proposing that each, on his own initiative, halt bomb tests for a period of at least one year. They made the full text of the letters public on Jan. 23 through a large advertisement in the N.Y. Times. Such a move, they said to both heads of states, "would catch the imagination of mankind and be a dramatic action that might break the international stalemate."

On Feb. 28 the Guardian's *Editor-in-Exile, Cedric Belfrage, wrote to Nikita Khrushchev, expressing his awareness of the U.S.S.R.'s stated readiness to abandon bomb tests by agreement as a first and logical disarmament step which Belfrage called "the kind of principled position which genuine socialists expect of the leading socialist states." He reported a sentiment in Britain that the Soviets should abandon the tests unilaterally.*

He then wrote the following:

"Since I have no doubt that your country wants to give every possible lead that is consistent with its security, I suggest that there is a way to do so short of a definite and final announcement that it will abandon tests. That is, to announce that the U.S.S.R. will set off no more test explosions unless and until the U.S.A. and/or Britain set them off."

The Soviet decision to bar further tests, announced March 31 by Foreign Minister Gromyko as the first act of the new Khrushchev government, goes not as far as the Lamonts had suggested but a little farther than Belfrage had hoped was possible. The Soviets will "reconsider" their decisions—not resume tests forthwith—if other nations fail to follow suit.

Belfrage and the Lamonts are well-known here and abroad as longtime proponents of American-Soviet friendship. The Lamonts are probably the best known Americans working for this objective; Belfrage has visited the U.S.S.R. four times and, as his letter stated, "my paper, the National Guardian, has worked for this since it was born in 1948." Their views and their estimates of world approbation of such an action—as well as their deep personal conviction that the testing must stop, no matter who takes the lead to stop it—undoubtedly have been seriously weighed by those responsible for the U.S.S.R.'s epochal decision.

Yet the Soviets have not been without pressure at home for such a move—not for propaganda advantage, but because of the weight of scientific testimony to the ravages of radiation on world health and because the Soviet people, too, want the threat of nuclear war removed. The refusal of Soviet scientist Peter Kapitza to work on atomic weapons is well-known. Along with Kapitza, some 154 other Soviet scientists responded to the Pugwash Statement issued last summer by 20 atomic scientists from ten countries, professing "readiness for common effort . . . toward the prevention of atomic war, the creation of secure peace and tranquillity for all mankind."

From the White House we received no direct answer to our Eisenhower telegram; but early in April we received the following undated letter from the Chairman of the U.S. Atomic Energy Commission:

U.S. Atomic Energy Commission
Washington 25, D.C.

Letter From Lewis L. Strauss

Dear Mr. and Mrs. Lamont:

President Eisenhower has asked me to reply to your comment about nuclear weapons tests.

In view of the importance of this subject to our country and of the many factors involved, I want to give you a comprehensive answer. In addition, I am enclosing statements by Charles L. Dunham, M.D., Director of the Division of Biology and Medicine, Atomic Energy Commission, on fallout from nuclear weapons tests, and by Dr. W. F. Libby, one of my colleagues on the Commission, on the reasons why the United States must continue weapons testing in the absence of safeguarded disarmament.

President Eisenhower, in his December 15, 1957, cablegram to the Prime Minister of India stated: "I know that the subject of testing of nuclear weapons is of understandable concern to many. I have given this matter long and prayerful thought. I am convinced that a cessation of nuclear weapons tests, if it is to alleviate rather than merely to conceal the threat of nuclear war, should be undertaken as a part of a meaningful program to reduce that threat.

"We are prepared to stop nuclear tests immediately in this context. However, I do not believe that we can accept a proposal to stop nuclear experiments as an isolated step, unaccompanied by any assurances that other measures—which would go to the heart of the problem—would follow. We are at a stage when testing is required particularly for the development of important defensive uses of these weapons. To stop these tests at this time in the absence of knowledge that we can go on and achieve effective limitations on nuclear weapons production and on other elements of armed strength, as well as a measure of assurance against surprise attack is a sacrifice which we could not in prudence accept. To do so could increase rather than diminish the threat of aggressions and war." The full text of President Eisenhower's cablegram is attached.

I assure you that the members of the Atomic Energy Commission share your concern on this important matter and that the Government decisions regarding nuclear weapons testing have not been made lightly. The possible risks from continued weapons testing have been carefully evaluated by competent scientists, both within and outside the Atomic Energy Commission; by independent scientific organizations in the United States such as the National Academy of Sciences, and by numerous authoritative groups abroad such as the British Medical Research Council. In essence they conclude that the risks from the current rate of nuclear testing are small, exceedingly small, in fact, when compared to other risks that we routinely and willingly accept day in and day out during our lifetime.

The conclusion one must inevitably reach after balancing all factors is this—we have the choice of a very small risk from testing or a risk of the catastrophe which might result from a surrender of our leadership in nuclear armament, which has been, we believe, the deterrent to aggression since 1945. The cause for most serious concern is not the effect of radiation resulting from the tests to keep our weapons posture strong, but rather the effect of the infinite human devastation that would result from the massive use of nuclear weapons in warfare.

At the hearings of the Congressional Joint Committee on Atomic

Energy, held in May and June of 1957, Shields Warren, M.D., one of the country's most distinguished pathologists, Professor of Pathology at Harvard Medical School, Director of the Institute for Cancer Research at the New England Deaconess Hospital, Boston, and United States delegate to the United Nations Scientific Committee on the Effects of Atomic Radiation, closed his testimony with the following statement: "It would be inexcusable for us to jeopardize our own safety and that of the rest of the free world in order to eliminate a risk of as low an order of magnitude as is constituted by a reasonable program of weapons testing."

I have a wife, a son, and three happy young grandchildren. Yet I subscribe completely to Dr. Warren's views. I could not do so if I thought the welfare of my family threatened more by fall-out than by possible nuclear war. Many authorities in addition to Dr. Warren share his view and have families of their own to protect.

You will, I hope, agree that their decisions have not been lightly made. I understand your concern and hope that my reply has been helpful.

Sincerely yours,
Lewis L. Strauss
*Chairman**

Enclosures

We answered Admiral Strauss's letter on May 23:

New York 27, N.Y.
May 23, 1958

TO LEWIS L. STRAUSS
Dear Admiral Strauss:

We regret our delay in acknowledging your undated letter of approximately April 2 concerning nuclear weapons tests. Since we were away on a rather long trip, much of our correspondence had to be postponed.

We appreciate the careful presentation of your point of view and that of the scientists whom you quote. However, we are not persuaded of the merit or soundness of this position. As you know, highly respected scientists can be quoted on the other side of this vital question—that is, in favor of ending tests of nuclear weapons.

Our most basic objection is to your thesis that "our leadership in nuclear armament . . . has been . . . the deterrent to aggression since 1945." We cannot accept this statement or the general attitude which it represents. We

---

*Admiral Strauss retired as Chairman of the AEC at the expiration of his regular five-year term on June 30, 1958.

do not believe that our country, strong and dynamic as it is, should put its faith in a heavy armaments program or, specifically, in massive nuclear armaments. Nor do we believe that the Soviet Union or the other Communist nations intend to resort to military aggression. The best way for the United States to attain national security—and at the same time to exercise moral leadership for peace—is to enter into an international agreement for general disarmament covering both nuclear and conventional weapons.

You say that the risk of damage from radioactive fall-out is very small compared to other risks we undergo daily. Is that a reason for adding to the unavoidable and avoidable risks of daily life? And even if the risk from radiation is small at present (a thesis which we by no means accept), the effects of it will increase and be cumulative, and may damage future generations whose well-being is part of our present responsibility.

We were surprised that your letter made no mention whatsoever of the fact that the Soviet Union had suspended all nuclear weapons tests on a unilateral basis. It is tragic that the United States Government has done nothing to match this significant step on behalf of peace. On the contrary, our high government officials have actually harmed the cause of peace by not taking the Soviet move seriously, by calling it mere propaganda, "a gimmick," in President Eisenhower's words. We can only express the hope again that the United States itself will take concrete action by stopping further A-bomb and H-bomb tests.

Meanwhile, we regretfully note that in your CBS television interview of May 4 you impugned the motives of those who, like ourselves, have been urging the cessation of nuclear weapons tests, and stated that the campaign against nuclear testing is not "in the open." This seems a strange accusation, in view of the fact that the campaign in question has been carried on chiefly through public statements issued by scientists and others to the press, and through the entirely open activities of such organizations as the National Committee for a Sane Nuclear Policy and the American Friends Service Committee.

We intend to continue our own efforts against the testing of nuclear weapons and to press for complete nuclear disarmament on an international basis. We feel happy that our stand on these issues coincides with that of great world citizens such as Lord Russell and Albert Schweitzer, and with the more humane and enlightened opinion of mankind in general.

Sincerely yours,
Corliss and Margaret Lamont

Meanwhile, on April 16 the Soviet Embassy in Washington had forwarded to us a letter from Foreign Minister Gromyko, answering our Open Letter to Marshal Bulganin:

Moscow, U.S.S.R.
April 16, 1958

Letter From Andrei A. Gromyko
Dear Mr. and Mrs. Lamont:

Your letter of January 18 addressed to the Chairman of the Council of Ministers of the USSR in which you expressed your anxiety concerning the continuing tests of atomic and hydrogen weapons and called for consideration of the unilateral termination of these tests by the Soviet Union has been read in the USSR with great attention. In your letter you mentioned that you had made an analogous appeal to President Eisenhower.

We fully agree with the opinion expressed in your letter that the continuation of testing nuclear weapons represents a serious threat to man's life and health and that the cessation of these tests would represent a considerable step toward strengthening peace.

I should like to note that the Soviet Government has many times made concrete proposals on simultaneous termination by the Soviet Union, the United States and Great Britain of nuclear weapons tests. Unfortunately, the Governments of the United States and Great Britain have so far not agreed to it. I hope that it is already known to you that the Supreme Soviet of the USSR, prompted by the desire to set in motion the implementation of this very important measure and thus to make the first step toward ridding mankind of the danger of annihilating atomic war, adopted on March 31 of this year the Resolution on the Soviet Union's Unilateral Cessation of Atomic and Hydrogen Weapons Tests. Now it is for the other states possessing nuclear weapons, for their Governments and parliaments to say their word.

I would like to express the deep conviction shared by the Soviet people that all those who sincerely strive for the establishment of stable peace and friendship between the nations will persistently work for the termination of tests of the atomic and hydrogen weapons so that it will be achieved everywhere and forever.

Sincerely yours,
A. Gromyko

We replied to this letter as follows:

New York 27, N.Y.
April 28, 1958

To Andrei A. Gromyko
Dear Mr. Gromyko:

We appreciate your thoughtful letter of April 16. We were, of course, aware of the remarkable and significant action of the Soviet Union in deciding on March 31 to terminate nuclear weapons tests unilaterally. We rejoiced with hundreds of millions of other people throughout the world over this important step toward peace.

In order to follow up our original letter to President Eisenhower, we sent him the enclosed telegram. We are greatly disappointed that so far the United States Government has not seen fit to cease its tests of nuclear weapons.

Needless to say we shall continue to do all in our power, as individuals, and working with such groups as the Quakers and the Committee for a Sane Nuclear Policy, to influence our Government officials and legislators to end nuclear weapons tests at the earliest possible time.

With all good wishes.

Sincerely yours,
Corliss Lamont
Margaret I. Lamont

* * *

While it is true that the Soviet Union suspended its nuclear weapons tests shortly after its completion of an important series of such tests, that did not seem to us an adequate excuse for the U.S. Government to go ahead with its scheduled tests in the Pacific during the spring and summer of 1958. The Atomic Energy Commission (AEC) reported that as of March 31, the date of the Soviet suspension, the United States had set off a total of more than twice as many nuclear explosions as Soviet Russia. The score was ninety for the U.S. and thirty-nine for the U.S.S.R. As the *New York Times* stated on April 1, "Because of the longer and more sustained test program, AEC officials feel that the United States has a more advanced and versatile test arsenal than the Soviet Union." In our opinion this consideration made U.S. continuation of nuclear weapons tests all the more needless.

We are in favor of an international agreement for the ending of nuclear weapons tests that will put into effect an adequate United Nations system of inspection covering Britain, the Soviet Union and the United States. Contrary to the interpretation of the U.S. State Department, the Soviet Government has long been willing to accept such inspection, not only as applied to the testing of nuclear weapons, but also to the banning of their production and the destruction of stockpiles.

Highly placed and influential Americans, including officials of the AEC, have claimed that there can be *no* adequate inspection system because no instruments can be devised to register certain underground nuclear weapons tests. After the AEC had set off a small atom bomb in September 1957, 2,000 feet inside a Nevada mountain and 800 feet from its top, the

Commission announced that the blast was detectable only 250 miles away. But in March 1958 Democratic Senator Hubert H. Humphrey of Minnesota, Chairman of the Disarmament Subcommittee of the Senate Foreign Relations Committee, found out from the U.S. Coast and Geodetic Survey that the underground explosion had been recorded as far off as Fairbanks, Alaska, 2,300 miles from the blasted mountain. Later the AEC admitted its mistake, but called it an "honest error."

That the Commission, with boundless scientific facilities at its command, could have made such a boner seems almost incredible; and there have been many drastic criticisms of it. For example, Dr. Hugo Wolfe, acting Chairman of the Federation of American Scientists, declared that the AEC's "purpose was to mislead the American public and to influence public opinion against the idea of an agreement on inspected cessation of nuclear testing. In view of the gravity of the subject and its relation to the future welfare of mankind, I suggest that an official inquiry into the methods and viewpoints of the AEC is long overdue."

At about the same time, the National Committee for a Sane Nuclear Policy, a group of public-spirited citizens organized in the fall of 1957, issued a detailed report. It said that the AEC, which is required by law to safeguard the public from nuclear hazards, had failed to be candid about the dangers of radioactive fall-out from nuclear bomb testing. The report particularly emphasized that the AEC had neglected to point out the degree to which Strontium 90, the most dangerous element in fall-out, was being absorbed into milk and other foodstuffs. The National Committee also criticized the AEC for taking eleven and one-half months to make public the terrible effects of the H-bomb which the U.S. exploded at Bikini in 1954 and which exposed Japanese fishermen aboard the vessel *Lucky Dragon* to poisonous doses of radioactivity.

The AEC has also argued that the U.S. testing of nuclear weapons must be continued so that the so-called "clean bomb" may be perfected. AEC member Edward Teller, who is often called the "Father" of the H-bomb and who recently stated that "disarmament is a lost cause," has been especially vocal in supporting this theory of a clean bomb. In his press conference of April 30 President Eisenhower undermined to a considerable degree Dr. Teller's position by stating that less than half of the 1958 U. S. tests would be concerned with clean bombs. "I was told," said the President, "by the Chairman of the AEC that at least 40 percent of the tests have their principal purpose to get cleaner bombs."

Then a few days later Admiral Strauss, testifying as Chairman of the AEC before the Joint Congressional Committee on Atomic Energy, proceeded to undermine Mr. Eisenhower: "There will also be a number of detonations to observe the effect of explosions upon military structures and materials. *Excepting this latter category* which, strictly speaking, is not for weapons development, some 40 percent of the tests are related *directly or indirectly* to the development of weapons with greatly reduced fall-out—that is to say, to so-called clean weapons." [Italics ours—C.L. and M.I.L.] As I. F. Stone puts it in his *Weekly* (May 12, 1958): "It is impossible to tell *just what that 40 percent is 40 percent of*. It might easily prove to be only 20 percent of the total number of tests, perhaps more, perhaps less." What *does* seem clear, however, is that Admiral Strauss was indulging in double-talk and had misled both the President and the public.

Dr. Albert Schweitzer, whose "Declaration of Conscience" in April 1957 was a high point in the campaign against nuclear weapons, provides another sort of answer to the AEC in his new statement of April 1958, entitled "An Obligation to Tomorrow."

Dr. Schweitzer reminds the world that the much-publicized clean bomb is "only relatively clean. Its trigger is an uranium bomb made of the fissionable uranium-235—an atomic bomb as powerful as the one dropped over Hiroshima. This bomb, when detonated, also produces radioactivity, as do the neutrons released in great numbers at the explosion. . . . The 'clean' hydrogen bomb may be intended, I fear, more for display-case purposes than for use. The intention seems to be to convince people that new nuclear tests will be followed by less and less radiation and that there is no real argument for the discontinuance of the tests. . . . We are constantly being told about a 'maximum permissible amount' of radiation. What does 'permissible' mean? And who has the right to 'permit' people to be exposed to these dangers?"

If the Third World War takes place, what essential difference will it make, we may ask, if tens of millions of persons in the combatant nations are burned to a crisp by the terror weapon of the "clean" H-bomb or the horror weapon of the "dirty" H-bomb?

What the Eisenhower Administration does by continuing nuclear weapons tests is not only to expose the American people to more and more radioactive poisoning—and even the AEC now admits that the United States is "the hottest radioactive place in the world"—but also to imperil in similar fashion the populations of other countries both near and far. So long as the Soviet Union was testing nuclear weapons, it was equally responsible for the international diffusion of fall-out.

For a long time now the U. S. Government has imposed upon mankind yet another frightful hazard connected with nuclear weapons. On the pretext that the Soviet Union may at any moment spring a surprise military attack on the United States or its allies, our Strategic Air Command regularly keeps flying and armed with atom or hydrogen bombs numerous planes*—including many of those assigned to bomber bases all around the world.

In March 1958 a U.S. jet so armed accidentally dropped an A-bomb

---

*The British Government has to some extent done the same thing.

in South Carolina. The explosion left a crater thirty-five feet deep and seventy-five feet wide, damaging six houses and a church. Six persons were injured, but nobody was killed. The A-bomb did not go off, but the TNT for triggering it did. Although the AEC and Defense Department had repeatedly issued assurances that no such accident could release fall-out, they both rushed teams for radioactive decontamination to the area. Later the *New York Times* revealed: "An undisclosed number of accidents involving atomic bombs has occurred since the Air Force started carrying the perfected weapons in training and alert flights."

*   *   *

In the meantime the campaign for the termination of nuclear weapons tests, and for the total abolition of these weapons, goes on all over the world. For here is a cause that cuts across all national and class boundaries, across all economic, political and religious viewpoints, to enlist the emotions and intelligence of human beings everywhere who are concerned about the well-being of future generations and the survival of mankind.

The National Committee for a Sane Nuclear Policy continues to hold public meetings and to print forceful advertisements. It has established more than seventy local committees in cities throughout the United States. The co-chairmen of the National Committee are Norman Cousins, Editor of the *Saturday Review,* and Clarence E. Pickett, Executive Secretary Emeritus of the American Friends Service Committee; while members include Dean John C. Bennett of the Union Theological Seminary, Clark Eichelberger, Director of the American Association for the United Nations, and Norman Thomas, veteran Socialist leader. In spite of the anti-Communist position of the above individuals, the Committee has been widely attacked as Communist-inspired. This is part of a general press pattern in the United States to discredit those who are opposing nuclear weapons as Reds or tools of the Reds.

Another group doing splendid work against nuclear bombs has been the American Friends Service Committee (Quakers). This was one of the cooperating groups in a special committee which, on the Memorial Day weekend of 1958, staged a great Walk for Peace to Washington. The walkers finally reached the White House and paraded in front of it. One of their most effective posters read "Peace in the World or the World in Pieces."

Closely associated with the Quakers is a committee called Non-Violent Action against Nuclear Weapons, which in 1957 staged the Prayer and Conscience Vigil at the U.S. nuclear testing site in Nevada. It planned the 1958 voyage of Albert S. Bigelow, a captain in the U.S. Navy during World War II, and three other pacifists in the thirty-foot ketch *Golden Rule* to the Eniwetok Proving Grounds in the Marshall Islands to protest against the new U.S. tests in the Pacific. To thwart this demonstration, the AEC issued special regulations banning all unauthorized Americans from the test area of approximately 390,000 square miles of open sea. On May 1 the *Golden Rule* crew, through its attorney, the famed civil liberties lawyer, A. L. Wirin, argued in a Federal Court in Honolulu that the AEC was violating the long-established principle of freedom of the seas and the Marshall Islands trusteeship agreement.

Although the judge ruled in favor of the AEC and issued an injunction forbidding the boat to sail, the crew defied him by setting out twice. Each time a Coast Guard cutter intercepted the ketch and brought it back to Honolulu. After the second attempt, early in June, Skipper Bigelow was sent to jail for sixty days on a conspiracy charge, while the other crewmen received the same sentence for criminal contempt of court.

Mr. Wirin, with Francis Heisler as co-attorney, is also handling two other legal actions dealing with H-bomb tests: the suits of Bertrand Russell, Linus Pauling, Norman Thomas, Brock Chisholm, T. Kagawa, Martin Niemoller and some thirty-five others, including sixteen Marshall Islanders, to restrain the American, British and Soviet Governments from further testing of nuclear weapons. Although this court test has little chance of success, it possesses considerable educational value.

In England the movement against nuclear weapons has been a good deal more successful than in the United States, with Peace Walks and other mass demonstrations repeatedly taking place. In the first part of April thousands of Britishers took part in a huge march to Aldermaston, the site of the Government's nuclear bomb plant. Eight thousand persons were present at the final meeting in a field opposite the "death plant." A week later 12,000 people turned out for the giant rally called by the Labor Party in Trafalgar Square. Among the speakers on "Stop the Tests Now" were Hugh Gaitskell, head of the Party, and the militant Aneurin Bevan. The Campaign for Nuclear Disarmament, which includes in its ranks many M.P.'s, now has 183 local branches throughout the country. And a Nuclear Disarmament Mass Lobby Committee has been established to bring pressure on Parliament. In spite of all this, the British Government went ahead with the testing of a nuclear weapons device on April 28 at Christmas Island in the Pacific.

In India the whole population has long been united against the threat of nuclear weapons and their testing. Prime Minister Nehru and other Indian leaders have again and again spoken out against the nuclear menace. In April 1958 Mr. Nehru hailed the Soviet suspension of nuclear weapons tests, supported the Polish proposal for a zone in Europe from which nuclear weapons would be barred, and opposed Secretary Dulles's plan to supply such weapons to Western Germany.

In Japan there has naturally been a powerful movement against nuclear weapons ever since the summer of 1945 when the U.S. Air Force dropped the first two A-bombs on Hiroshima and Nagasaki (August 6 and 9 respectively), killing approximately 167,000 civilians and seriously injuring 60,000, with 324,000 otherwise afflicted. The Japan Council against A- and H-Bombs has rallied enormous support for its program and has set up a vast network of local chapters in cities, towns and villages. In 1955 it gathered 32,500,000 signatures for a petition presented to the Japanese Diet asking that body to demand that the United States, Soviet Russia and Great Britain stop all nuclear testing. The Diet adopted such a resolution in February 1956, being the first national parliament to take action of this kind. The Council publishes a first-rate monthly journal, *No More Hiroshimas!,* which ably summarizes in each issue the news of the anti-nuclear-weapons movement from every part of the globe. This Council called the Fourth World Conference against A- and H-Bombs at Tokyo in August 1958.

In many other nations, too, groups and individuals are active in the struggle against nuclear weapons; and we have been able to describe here only some of the highlights in this world-wide movement.

Coming back to our own country, we reiterate what we said in our Open Letter to President Eisenhower: "Since it was the United States that first invented, manufactured and used atomic bombs, we believe that our nation has a special moral responsibility to take the lead in outlawing nuclear weapons." This responsibility is all the more serious, in our opinion, because we think that there was no military need which justified the use of nuclear bombs against the defenseless Japanese civilian population of two large cities. At the beginning of August 1945 Japan was already on the point of surrendering, and the Soviet attack on the Japanese army in Manchuria was due to start, and did start, on August 8, two days after the bombing of Hiroshima. President Truman could easily and reasonably have waited another week or two before giving his fatal order, to see what would be the effects of the massive Soviet offensive; or he could have arranged a non-lethal public demonstration of the power of the A-bomb to convince the Japanese Government that its cause was lost.

In conclusion, we believe it is urgent that Americans by the million, regardless of political or other affiliations, redouble their pressures on Congress and the Eisenhower Administration to halt nuclear bomb tests, to work out a formal agreement with the Soviet Union to this end, and to negotiate a further treaty for stopping the production of nuclear weapons and for the destruction of existing stockpiles. Also we vigorously oppose any Congressional bill or government agreement to give other nations the technological information for manufacturing A-bombs and H-bombs.

We ask our fellow citizens to write President Eisenhower, to write their Senators and Congressmen, to write their newspapers; to initiate resolutions and action in church, labor, educational, scientific and peace organizations; to join local or national committees for the abolition of nuclear weapons testing and production.

Atoms for armaments and war, with all the tremendous expenditures involved, must give way completely to atoms-for-peace, the utilization of nuclear technology for the general economic and scientific advancement of mankind. At stake in this portentous issue is the very existence of the American people and the human race.

Postscript for Second Edition

Since this pamphlet was first published in July of 1958, important developments have taken place in the world-wide movement for the cessation of nuclear bomb tests. Two internationally sponsored reports issued by leading scientists in August were of special significance.

The first report was that of the United Nations Scientific Committee on the Effects of Atomic Radiation. The signers stressed the dangers to mankind of continued nuclear weapons tests and unanimously agreed that "radioactive contamination of the environment resulting from explosions of nuclear weapons constitutes a growing increment to world-wide radiation levels. This involves new and largely unknown hazards to present and future populations; these hazards, by their very nature, are beyond the control of the exposed persons. The Committee concludes that all steps designed to minimize irradiation of human populations will act to the benefit of human health. Such steps include the avoidance of unnecessary exposure resulting from medical, industrial and other procedures for peaceful uses on the one hand and the cessation of the contamination of the environment by explosions of nuclear weapons on the other."

The second report resulted from a seven weeks' conference in Geneva of East-West scientific experts, who came to the unanimous conclusion that if there were an international agreement for the suspension of nuclear weapons tests, violations could be detected and identified within certain specific limits. If the recommendations of this Committee are later put into effect, it seems probable that nearly 200 inspection-detection stations will be set up throughout the world, including at least twenty-five each in the United States and the Soviet Union.

Both the United States and Britain continued with their thermonuclear testing in the Pacific Ocean after the Soviet suspension of March 31. The U.S. Atomic Energy Commission not only carried through many huge nuclear explosions at the Eniwetok Proving Grounds, but also fired missiles with atomic warheads into the stratosphere over Johnston Island near Hawaii. According to Dr. Willard F. Libby of the AEC, fall-out from these missile tests will rain down on the entire world for the next ten years. The AEC also scheduled about ten tests in Nevada for September and October.

However, quickly following the Geneva report on detecting nuclear explosions, the U.S. and British Governments announced that they would be ready to begin talks with the Soviet Government on Friday, October 31, towards formally halting nuclear tests, and that they would at that time conditionally halt further tests for a one-year period. Premier Khrushchev, for the Soviet Union, accepted the suggested date. The conference will be held at Geneva.

The Eisenhower Administration stated that its projected suspension of nuclear weapons tests would be renewed from year to year only if "satisfactory progress is being made in reaching agreement on and implementing major and substantial arms control measures such as the United States has long sought." We consider this an unfortunate condition, because it ties up the abolition of nuclear testing once more with the question of general disarmament, upon which there may be disagreement among the Great Powers for a long time to come.

Furthermore, Secretary Dulles has indicated that in nuclear bomb discussions with the U.S.S.R. he would raise the question of inspection-detection posts being established in China, "to cover the possibility of testing being conducted by the Soviet Union within Communist China." But the diplomatic difficulties of bringing China into such an accord, some of them recently created by Mr. Dulles himself, are well-nigh insuperable at present.

The fact remains that despite some progress during the summer of 1958 towards an international cessation of nuclear bomb tests, the success of the coming conference on the subject is by no means assured. We stand by our telegram of March 31 to President Eisenhower that the United States should have followed the Soviet example and suspended nuclear testing. Since that did not happen, we urge the American people to bring every possible pressure to bear on the Republican Administration to enter promptly into an international treaty for the ending of both nuclear weapons testing and production.

September 22, 1958

C.L.
M.I.L.

About Margaret I. Lamont

Margaret I. Lamont (1904–1977) was Corliss Lamont's wife. She was a graduate of Barnard College and received an M.A. degree from Columbia University. She worked devotedly for such causes as civil liberties, the rights of racial minorities, international understanding and world peace.

After the United Nations was established Mrs. Lamont became an active volunteer for public education concerning the U.N. She traveled extensively with Mr. Lamont and visited the Soviet Union in 1932 and 1938.

13
A Peace Program for the U.S.A.
(1959)

Any realistic appraisal of international relations at present must reach the conclusion that in this realm mankind, far from making progress during the twentieth century, has actually retrogressed to a considerable extent. In many other spheres of human activity there have been great advances since 1900. But the First and Second World Wars, with their tens of millions of cruel casualties and their terrible economic destruction, have represented an appalling regression in international affairs.

Since the end of the Second World War, this deterioration has continued, with a far-reaching Cold War between East and West, a staggering armaments race and, above all, a piling up of horrible nuclear weapons whose testing and possible use menace the American people, the Soviet people and all humanity. Everyone knows that the massive radioactive fall-out from atom and hydrogen bombs in a Third World War would threaten the extermination of the human race and indeed of all forms of life upon this planet. Since 1945, when the U.S. Air Force dropped the first atom bomb on Hiroshima, international war has taken on a new dimension of frightfulness. If the United States and the Soviet Union, both of which are armed to the teeth with nuclear weapons, went to war today, neither country could win; it would be mutual suicide, with the allies of the main contestants and with neutral nations all sharing in the disaster.

Yet daily we live in the shadow of just such a catastrophe which might be sparked by a hot-headed or misinformed officer in the lower military echelons giving an order for an air attack on "the enemy." And so long as the danger of a nuclear conflict persists, we citizens of the twentieth century—with all our vast material and mechanical progress, with our atom splitting, our jet planes, and our earth satellites—we moderns will remain essentially uncivilized in our international behavior.

For humane and intelligent men in every country, then, the achievement of world peace must be an over-riding aim. And the fulfilment of this aim must take priority on the agenda of United States foreign policy. The best way, and the only sure way, for America to gain lasting national security is the establishment of peace and cooperation among all the nations of the earth.

Peace means the abolition not only of world war, but of medium-sized wars and little wars, such as that initiated by Britain, France and Israel against Egypt in the fall of 1956. Little wars, which may seem temporarily localized, are a noxious evil, not only because of the economic devastation and loss of life they entail, but also because in this day and age they may expand into big wars which sweep over the entire globe.

When I speak of international war, I do not mean to include genuine civil wars which may take place in this country or that. Much as I prefer a settlement of domestic issues in every land through peaceful and democratic methods, I do not think that we can deny the right of an oppressed people to resort to revolution. The United States, which itself came into being through revolution, should be the last country in the world to try to take away that right from other peoples. Since the end of World War II successful revolutions have taken place in the nations of Eastern Europe, in China, in Egypt and in Iraq; and a bloody anti-colonial revolution is going on at present in Algeria.

The refusal of the U.S. Government to recognize the right of indigenous revolutions in other lands has been one of the most disruptive factors in the post-war world. This is especially true in the Far East where for almost ten years the United States has artificially prolonged the bloody Chinese civil war through a military alliance with the ruthless dictatorship of Chiang Kai-shek and through bolstering his regime on the island of Formosa (Taiwan) with more than two billion dollars in aid. The Chinese situation erupted into crisis during the summer of 1958 when the Communist regime in control of the mainland began shelling the islands of Quemoy and Little Quemoy, which are situated only a few miles off the coast of China and are still occupied by Chiang's troops.

My first point for a United States peace program is that the Eisenhower Administration should at once withdraw all its military forces from the region of Quemoy and the other Chinese offshore islands, and from Formosa as well. The U.S. Government has no business at all interfering with Communist China's plain legal, moral and historical right to assert domain over the offshore islands.

Who with any feeling for reality can take stock in the Dulles-Eisenhower doctrine that American defense of Quemoy, which is less than seven miles from China and some seven thousand from San Francisco, is essential to the national security of the American people? It would make just as much sense for the Chinese People's Republic to claim that its security depends on its control of Santa Catalina Island off the coast of California. In his speech of September 11, 1958, President Eisenhower argued that the Chinese Communists, in attempting to recover islands which clearly belong to mainland China, were behaving like the Nazi and Fascist aggressors of the Thirties. There is not a shadow of historical justification in this comparison. Hitler and Mussolini repeatedly invaded other countries; but the Chinese Communists are using force only to take over part of their own country. And for Chiang these islands serve as a base for the constant harassment of Communist shipping and for his possible attempt to reconquer the mainland. The Chinese offshore islands belong with the mainland just as logically as Long Island and Staten Island belong with New York and the United States.

There is no doubt, either, that Formosa, forcibly annexed by Japan in 1895, likewise belongs to China. In December 1943 President Franklin D. Roosevelt, Prime Minister Winston Churchill and Generalissimo Chiang Kai-shek declared at the Cairo Conference: "All the territories Japan has stolen from the Chinese, such as Manchuria, Formosa and the Pescadores, shall be restored to the Republic of China." The Potsdam Declaration of 1945 reaffirmed this Allied commitment. And after Japan's surrender in 1945 Formosa was officially restored to Chinese sovereignty.

Formosa is less than 100 miles from the Chinese mainland. There is very little substance to Secretary of State Dulles's argument that the vital interests of the United States compel us to continue our support of the Chiang dictatorship on that island. I believe that the U.S. Government should withdraw its troops, its warships, its bombers, its nuclear weapons and its military advisers from Formosa and let the Chinese civil war take its course. The result would undoubtedly be the rapid collapse of the Chiang regime.

Beyond the question of the Chinese offshore islands and Formosa—and this is the second point in my peace program—we need a far-reaching change in America's general policy towards Communist China. Diplomatic recognition of the Chinese People's Republic by the United States is long overdue; and of course such recognition would by no means imply approval of the political and economic practices of the Communist government. This regime, which was recognized in 1950 by our closest ally, Great Britain, has shown indubitably that it is strong, stable and in complete control of mainland China. Under Communist leadership this vast country of some 650 million people, though subject to the rigors of dictatorship, has effected enormous economic progress, has abolished graft and other forms of corruption, has instituted equality for women, and has initiated far-reaching cultural advances.

The official line of the U.S. State Department is that the Peiping government is a puppet of the Kremlin. This is absurd. Communist China and Soviet Russia are equal partners in the socialist world; and there is increasing evidence that the Chinese are exercising more and more influence on their Soviet friends. The Communist revolution in China succeeded because that country, tired of the corruption, economic crisis and military defeat associated with Chiang's regime, was ripe for political change; because the Communists had the ability to exploit this internal situation; and because their military leaders were extremely capable. The fact that the Soviet Russians gave moral encouragement and general advice did not prevent the revolution from being essentially indigenous.

It is time, too, for the U.S. Government to give up its opposition to Communist China's admission to the United Nations. It is utterly irrational to deny effective representation in this organization to one-fourth of the world's population. And naturally the Communist government should have a seat on the Security Council in place of Chiang's. As the *Toronto Globe and Mail* has stated: "To pretend, in all solemnity, that a rump regime, decaying on a small island, is the true Government of China and has the sole right to speak for that mighty nation is folly. . . . In politics, as in everything else, nothing but disaster can come from evading reality."

Another folly connected with the U.S. attitude towards China is the long-standing Dulles ban which prevents American citizens, including most newspaper reporters,* from traveling to the Communist-ruled mainland and seeing for themselves what is going on there. Evidently Secretary Dulles does not trust Americans to make up their own minds about the Chinese situation; he is afraid of what their conclusions will be when they encounter the truth at first-hand. This is the same sort of head-in-the-sand blindness that characterized earlier Republican Administrations, in the 1920's, in their attitude towards Soviet Russia. The Republicans learn very little over the years.

My third point, following logically from what I have said about the Far East, is that the United States should cease its dangerous military intervention not only in Chinese affairs, but everywhere else as well. This would mean the withdrawal of U.S. forces totaling more than a million men from almost all of the approximately 950 American military bases

---

*In 1957 the U.S. State Department announced that 24 American newsmen would be permitted to visit China for seven months. In the same release the Department made clear it would not grant reciprocal treatment to Chinese journalists. Accordingly, the Chinese Government refused to admit the American reporters, a result that the State Department must surely have anticipated when it made its original—and hypocritical—announcement.

scattered in 73 countries throughout the world.

The old saying, "Mind your own business!" is a sound one for both individuals and governments. I want to see the U.S. Government mind its own business for a change. American military intervention in the Far East and the Middle East during 1958 exacerbated international tensions and in both cases led the United States to the brink of a general war.

Another important aspect of U.S. interventionist policy is that under the Eisenhower Administration the Executive Branch of our government has increasingly arrogated to itself the power to involve this nation in international conflict. Under the American Constitution, however, Congress alone has the right to declare war. But we have now reached the point where the President, through a *fait accompli* of military intervention utilizing nuclear weapons, can commit Congress and this country to a frightful hydrogen-bomb world war.

Thus we have a species of Executive *dictatorship* as regards the most significant question a people can face—the question of going to war. I believe that all Americans, regardless of their political persuasion, ought to feel deeply concerned over this unconstitutional procedure. What it means in concrete terms is that the Executive Department is violating the basic principle of the separation of powers among the three branches of government in our constitutional system.

When the Far Eastern crisis broke, Congress was not in session; but it *was* in session when in July 1958 President Eisenhower, completely bypassing the United Nations, sent the Marines to Lebanon on the absurd pretext that the revolt in Iraq showed that Soviet Russia and "indirect aggression" were threatening Lebanese independence. Yet before the President ordered military intervention, there was no opportunity for Congress to debate or vote on the merits of this momentous decision. And when one lone Democrat, Representative Reuss of Wisconsin, rose to criticize the President's action, he was immediately slapped down by Speaker Rayburn with the rebuke: "In times like these we had better allow matters to develop rather than make remarks about them."

Of course, the facts demonstrated that neither Premier Nasser of the United Arab Republic nor Premier Khrushchev of the Soviet Union engineered the Iraqi coup, but that it was carried through by a determined group of purely Iraqi military officers and Arab nationalists. A passionate and strong Arab nationalism is on the move throughout the Middle East. I believe that the U.S. Marines landed in Lebanon, as British paratroopers landed in Jordan, to intimidate the Lebanese people and the Arab populations throughout the Middle East.

The United Nations was functioning at its best when it arranged for the withdrawal of the American and British forces from the Middle East during the autumn of 1958. But this region is so important, with its immense oil resources and restive populations, that we need a peaceful and enduring settlement of Middle Eastern problems in general, preferably under U.N. auspices. Such a settlement must recognize the natural rights of the rising Arab nationalism in the area and the political and economic rights of Arab peoples who are still saddled with feudal dictators, usually supported by Western imperialism. The settlement must leave the Arab countries free to remain neutral in the Cold War. Finally, the U.N. must guarantee the present frontiers of the brave and progressive Republic of Israel, the only democratic state in the Middle East. An over-all settlement for the Middle East is my fourth point for world peace.

Fifth, Great Britain, the Soviet Union and the United States should immediately halt both the testing and production of nuclear weapons. It is common knowledge that the radioactive fall-out from atomic and hydrogen bombs is poisoning the air of this planet and penetrating the very food we eat and the milk and water we drink. In the summer of 1958 the U.N. Scientific Committee on the Effects of Atomic Radiation issued a unanimous report warning that explosions of nuclear weapons are contaminating the environment and creating serious health hazards to the human race, especially to children during their formative years. While it is highly probable that an agreement to stop nuclear weapons tests would be self-enforcing, a Geneva conference of East-West experts in August 1958 worked out a system of inspection and detection so that violations of an agreement would become known. If the three nuclear-weapons Powers do not succeed in agreeing on a formal treaty for the halting of the tests, I believe that each of the governments concerned should cease tests on a unilateral basis. Soviet Russia put into effect such a unilateral suspension for six months during 1958. The cessation of nuclear weapons tests, however, would be only a beginning; for the necessary goal is the complete abolition of these fiendish instruments of mass murder. Then the enormous potentials of atomic power could be harnessed entirely to the constructive purposes of peace and economic upbuilding.

Disarmament in nuclear weapons would pave the way, we may hope, for general and drastic disarmament in conventional weapons; in armies, navies, air forces, artillery and so on. This is my sixth point. There would also need to be a complete ban on bacteriological warfare and poison gas.

Not only do today's huge armaments serve as a constant temptation to reckless militarists to plunge the world into war, but they also represent the most colossal economic waste in the history of mankind. Out of the total $75 billion United States revised budget for 1958-59, approximately $48 billion, or 64 percent, was allocated to current military spending. If we add the interest payments, veterans' benefits and other expenses growing out of past wars, the total earmarked for purposes connected with war was approximately $60 billions, or 80 percent of the budget. Since the 1958 operating budget of the United Nations was about $55 million, we see that the U.S. Government spends more *billions* annually for military purposes than the U.N. spends *millions* annually for the cause of peace.

Or to put the matter perhaps even more graphically, the U.S.A. devotes approximately $164 millions per day to the purposes of war—about three times as much as the U.N. budget for an entire year. This $164 million is also to be compared with the total endowment, $135 million, of Columbia University, one of America's largest educational institutions. Think of the millions and billions that could be spent by the United States Government for peaceful projects for the permanent welfare of the American people if large-scale disarmament agreements were negotiated and the Federal military budget could be radically reduced!*

The official justification for the tremendous size of American armaments is that they act as a deterrent to the war-like designs of the Communist bloc and in particular of Soviet Russia. This claim that the Russians intend war does not stand up; it is a provocative political myth. Communists neither in the U.S.S.R. nor anywhere else aim to spread their doctrines and social-economic system through international conflict. The Marxists believe, in fact, that internal contradictions in capitalist countries will eventually lead to the establishment of socialism by the working class. In order to bolster its own self-defense, the Soviet Union has gotten tough along its frontiers, as it did in Finland and Hungary; but with this qualification the U.S.S.R. has an excellent record for peace.

In the Second World War the Soviets lost far more in casualties and economic destruction than any other belligerent. They do not want it to happen again. Soviet leaders as well as the masses of the people wish above all to devote their full energies to the further construction and expansion of socialism within the borders of the U.S.S.R. The Soviet Government can be depended upon to keep the peace and to uphold treaties for disarmament if only because of sheer self-interest. Of course, Soviet leaders carry on a great deal of propaganda about foreign affairs, but it is *propaganda for peace*. And indeed the American press is forever warning against the latest Soviet "peace offensive."

Furthermore, so far as armaments are concerned, Soviet socialism regards them as a tremendous drawback and a continuing obstacle to higher standards of living. Whereas in the capitalist economy of the United States the armaments boom is at present a primary factor in stimulating a high

---

*For example, I should like to see $25 billions eliminated from the U.S. arms budget and then allocated as follows: $5 billions to a vast Federal housing program; $5 billions to the extension of public education, scholarships and raising teachers' salaries; $5 billions to increased old-age pensions; $5 billions to national health insurance; and $5 billions to new hospitals and health centers.

degree of business activity, large-scale socio-economic planning in Soviet Russia is able to maintain a successfully functioning economy without the artificial stimulus of armaments production. The Russians, then, look upon far-reaching disarmament as both an essential international goal and also one very important for domestic well-being and development.

Disarmament would, of course, help small nations as well as large. One of the worst mistakes in U.S. foreign policy—and one that has played into the hands of the Communists—has been that our financial aid to other countries has been spent, under American pressure, primarily for military purposes instead of economic development. This has been particularly unfortunate for the underdeveloped nations of Asia and Africa, whose crying need is not more arms, but economic assistance and upbuilding. Furthermore, in several of the countries concerned—Burma, Pakistan, the Sudan and Thailand—democratic regimes have recently given way to dictatorships led by Army generals. And there is no guarantee how these military dictatorships will use the weapons supplied by the United States.

For instance, General Ayub Khan, after seizing power in Pakistan in the fall of 1958 and becoming head of the government, took a threatening attitude towards India. On December 11, 1958 the Indian Ambassador to the United States, Mahomed Ali Currim Chagia, expressed misgivings over the situation in a speech at the Waldorf Astoria Hotel in New York City. Mr. Chagia called attention to the fact that the United States is sending economic aid to India, and added: "At the same time, by giving arms to countries hostile to us, she is compelling us to spend more and more on our defense, and this diverts our resources from being used for the good of our people."

My proposals for nuclear and general disarmament naturally lead to point seven: Let us end the Cold War! Whichever side started this business, it has brought no real advantage to any of the countries involved. As stated in a recent advertisement signed by many eminent Americans, including Mrs. Eleanor Roosevelt, Clarence E. Pickett and James P. Warburg, the twelve years of Cold War have resulted in neither the containment of Communism nor the extension of democracy; and the United States stands in greater peril of annihilation than when the Cold War began.

The termination of the Cold War between the American-led bloc of nations and the Soviet-led bloc would bring a relaxation of tensions throughout the globe. It would mean normal trade once more between East and West, with the abolition of the economic embargoes which the United States and some of its allies have put into effect against the Communist world; it would mean the withdrawal of American troops and Soviet troops from all foreign countries; and it would mean a vast increase in cultural and scientific interchange between East and West.

The ending of the Cold War would go far in easing the most basic international antagonism of all: that between the U.S.A. and the U.S.S.R., the two rival giants on the world scene. The Soviet Union has obviously made many mistakes in foreign policy and has plenty of domestic shortcomings, especially in the field of democracy and civil liberties. Nonetheless the Soviets sincerely desire peaceful co-existence—and peaceful competition—with the capitalist countries. Soviet Russia and the other Communist-led nations never wanted the Cold War in the first place; and its termination is one of their chief objectives in international affairs.

No peace program today can neglect the problem of Germany, whose future affects so fundamentally the nations of Europe and indeed the entire world. And so my eighth point is that East Germany and West Germany should reunite, either under one federal government or as a closely knit confederation of the two main units. Whatever form German reunification takes, the German people must develop into a peaceful, democratic, *neutral* nation belonging neither to the American-led group of states represented by NATO nor the Soviet-led block of European countries allied for defense in the Warsaw Pact. Then, as Walter Lippmann has repeatedly suggested, Germany would serve as a buffer state between the Atlantic Powers, on the one hand, and the Eastern European People's Republics and Soviet Russia on the other hand.

The neutralization of Germany would fit in well with the sensible plan put forward by the Polish Foreign Minister, Adam Rapacki, that there should be established in Europe a denuclearized zone consisting of East Germany, West Germany, Poland and Czechoslovakia. Mr. Rapacki's plan also envisages a big reduction in conventional weapons within the proposed zone. The Rapacki plan would automatically prevent the United States and NATO from arming West Germany with nuclear weapons—a possibility that has alarmed workers for peace everywhere.

In the great, world-wide effort to establish permanent peace, all individuals and nations should strive, it seems to me, for a stronger, more effective United Nations, with expanding activities. This is my ninth point. In the Middle Eastern crisis of mid-summer 1958, the U.N. functioned well and worked out a compromise solution that maintained the peace. Too often in the past, one or another of the Great Powers has by-passed the United Nations in taking action on international problems when the U.N. could have been extremely helpful. One of the most important functions of the U.N. is of course to provide an international forum where world public opinion can express itself. Accordingly, the frequent hot debates at U.N. meetings serve a real purpose. It is far better for the representatives of opposing states to hurl bitter words at each other and to indulge in obvious propaganda than to have military planes start hurling nuclear bombs.

However, diplomatic negotiations outside the frame-work of the United Nations can still be very useful. So, finally, as point ten, I urge that a

Summit Conference of the heads of the Great Powers, similar to the one held in Geneva in 1955, take place as soon as possible to discuss the pressing problems of peace and to work out mutually acceptable solutions. I believe that if President Eisenhower and Premier Khrushchev met face to face and talked over frankly and sincerely the critical international difficulties facing mankind, they might make considerable progress. One advantage of such a meeting is that Mr. Eisenhower could carry on direct negotiations instead of proceeding, as usual, through the inflexible Secretary Dulles, with his dangerous brink-of-war strategy.

I have outlined here a ten-point peace program which, if followed through and put into effect, would surely be to the advantage of the United States, the Soviet Union and indeed all the countries of the world. Unless the U.S.A., in cooperation with the other Great Powers, adopts some such program, mankind will continue to face the harrowing danger of a Third World War which would set back civilization indefinitely and possibly destroy it altogether.

14
My Trip Around the World (1960)

Europe

During eight long years, from 1951 to 1958, the American State Department refused to renew my passport because of my publicly expressed dissenting views on domestic and foreign policy. Finally I sued Secretary of State John Foster Dulles in order to regain my natural right to travel, regardless of my political and economic opinions. I automatically won my suit and obtained my precious passport in June 1958, following the U.S. Supreme Court's liberal passport decision in the Rockwell Kent case.

Since I had not been able to travel across the seas for so long, I decided to make up for lost time and to circle the globe. Then, too, as a Humanist philosopher I have taught that the supreme ethical goal in life ought to be the happiness, freedom and progress of all mankind, regardless of nation, race or religion; but there was a lot of mankind I had never met face to face. And I viewed my six months' world tour as a chance to come into closer contact with distant countries and peoples, especially in the Far East, where I had not been before.

So, on the first day of spring, 1959—surely a day of happy omen— my wife and I set sail from New York on *La Liberté* across the Atlantic. For me the seven-day voyage was a rebirth into freedom. And when at last I glimpsed once more the familiar coasts of France and England, I felt that I was re-discovering much that had become, in many journeys of the past, an essential part of my being.

It was the greatest pleasure for me to return to England, a land of happy memories for me and one where I have many good friends. It was a delight just to stroll along the streets of London and through the splendid parks of that city. The English accent is always music to my ears, and I loved simply to listen to the English people talking together as I passed them by or they passed *me* by while I sat in the sun on a park bench, looking out upon places where not so long ago Hitler's bombers were creating havoc. Most of the war's debris has been cleared away, but even today a number of burnt-out squares remain as silent monuments to a determination that "it must not happen again."

Our little hotel on Half Moon Street was less than a block from lovely Green Park, which runs into Hyde Park, famous not only for its wide green lawns, but also as a free-speech center where radicals and dissenters and even crackpots can talk their heads off with no interference from the public authorities. There ought to be a Hyde Park of free speech in every city of the world, including our own United States. And as I listened to these orators in *London's* Hyde Park, I couldn't help reflecting how much better Great Britain had preserved *its* civil liberties since the end of the Second World War than had America. To be sure, during this period occasional violations of free speech have taken place in Britain, but the country has experienced nothing comparable to the far-reaching suppressions of our McCarthy era, the consequences of which are still etched deep in almost every sector of American life.

While I was in London, Parliament was in session, and I went over to the House of Commons two or three times to lunch with some of my friends in the British Labor Party. It was especially pleasant drinking coffee with them on the beautiful Commons Terrace overlooking the Thames and with a fine view up and down the river. We discussed at length the political situation.

I was particularly impressed by the program of the Victory for Socialism Council, led by Labor M.P.'s such as Harold Davies, Stephen Swingler, and Konni Zilliacus. This forward-looking group wants the Labor Party to become more militant in its socialist program; and to declare itself in favor of Britain's unilaterally halting both the further testing of nuclear weapons and also their manufacture. But the conservative leadership of the Party has rejected these proposals and has been soft-pedaling many important issues. That is one of the main reasons why the Conservative Party won such a sweeping victory in the general election of October 1959. As Mr. Zilliacus summed up the trouble, "Before we can beat the Tories in the country, we must beat the Tories in the Labor Party."

During our last weekend in England my wife and I made a pilgrimage to Oxford University where I studied at New College in 1924-25. That was one of the best years of my life. It was a joy to wander again around the University and to visit my old haunts. The New College garden, bounded on one side by the old city wall built many centuries ago, is as quiet and lovely a place as can be found anywhere. And in general the gardens of the 25 or so colleges that make up the University are unexcelled in their beauty, and give to one a rare sense of isolation from the outside world. As everyone knows, the creation and care of gardens in England have long since achieved the status of high art.

From Oxford we drove out ten miles into the rolling countryside to call on Mr. and Mrs. John Masefield, two of the oldest and best friends of my family. Mr. Masefield met us at the door of his house and was most cordial. He invited in the lady taxi driver to have some tea, but she declined. John Masefield, Poet Laureate of England and 81 years old, is in vigorous health and still turning out first-rate poetry. Only recently he began to make very successful vocal recordings of his poems. I don't know anyone who has a finer voice for reading aloud.

Although I am hardly a conservative in politics and economics, I do happen to be one as regards poetry, and still prefer poems that rhyme or scan. I was glad to find that here Mr. Masefield on the whole agreed with me. He said that our contemporary poetry in England and America lacks discipline and form. He likes very little of it and feels that current poets no longer dwell on themes of love and nobility. I consider John Masefield one of the truly great men I have known. The simplicity, honesty and ruggedness of his character, together with his continuing vitality, remind me of America's own dean of poets, Robert Frost.

I could go on indefinitely discussing England and the English, a wonderful country and a wonderful people. But in this pamphlet I have space only to describe some of the highlights of my long trip. And so I now turn to the Continent and especially Italy.

After spending a few days in Paris, ever a joy to the traveler, we relaxed at Nice on the French Riviera. Then on one long rugged day, with sensational views every few minutes, we drove the entire distance to Florence—along the Mediterranean Côte d'Azur, past the cliffs of Monaco, into northern Italy with its steep and mountainous roads, and finally down into the Florentine plain.

We stayed three weeks in Florence, which is of course one vast treasure-house of art. Our hotel room looked out over the River Arno to colorful hills where we could see the old city wall and towers that Michelangelo helped to construct back in the sixteenth century. Below us, along the river walk, strolled the people of Florence—buoyant and uninhibited. There were young couples with their arms around each other, old couples enjoying the sun and children skipping along. At our open window we had a splendid balcony seat to watch the world go by. And every so often a singer with a guitar would saunter past and serenade us.

With Florence as headquarters, we made expeditions in all directions to Italy's marvelous hill towns such as Siena, San Gemignano, Volterra, Perugia and Assisi. As you approach these magic cities from a distance, you see their graceful towers rising far away, then disappearing and reappearing according to the curve of the road and the structure of the Tuscan hills. We were living in a pervasive atmosphere of beauty where the loveliness of nature was continually merging with that of *human* creation. The hills and valleys were lush and green; and as twilight approached a golden glow suffused everything.

The history of this region is absorbing, but it often makes you sad. For the city states of Italy, at the height of their artistic flowering during the Renaissance, were continually assaulting one another. Not only were irreplaceable works of art ravaged during this period, but the flower of Italian manhood was killed off. Coming to a much later era, stiff fighting took place in and around Florence during the Second World War when the U.S. Army was driving out the Nazis. The retreating Germans shelled the bridges across the Arno and smashed all of them except the famed Ponte Vecchio. At this moment art lovers held their breath to see whether the Germans would bombard the rest of the city. It did not happen, but it was a close call. War is a terrible destroyer of the good and the beautiful.

The next highlight is Greece, *all* of it. This historic land was a very special experience for me, because I had never gone there before and because as a philosopher I was fascinated at seeing the places where Socrates, Plato and Aristotle walked, talked and lectured. We stayed in Greece several weeks and made Athens our headquarters. At least every other day we went up to the Acropolis, wandered through the half-ruined structures built in the Golden Age of Pericles, viewed from every angle the architectural miracle of the Parthenon, and looked out between its white marble columns, designed by Phidias, to the city lying below and to the shining sea in the distance. It was all the sheerest aesthetic ecstasy. And it continued even into the hours of darkness, for every so often the Parthenon was lighted up at night and we could see it from the streets of Athens.

We made many exciting explorations to cities such as Delphi, Corinth, Mycenae and Sunion, where on a headland an ancient and perfectly proportioned temple to Poseidon stands out dramatically. In *Don Juan* Lord Byron referred to Sunion's "marble steep"; and we saw there his signature carved into a marble pillar. Then came our five-day boat trip through the Greek Islands of the Aegean Sea, an adventure into the living past and the enthralling present, centering around legend-crusted isles like Crete and Rhodes and Delos.

As in Italy we were constantly drinking in vast panoramas of history along with the sublime art and the natural beauty. I took particular satisfaction in going out to the battlefield of Marathon and reconstructing from maps just how the Greeks drove back the Persians in 490 B.C. Here

I held up a whole busload of hurrying American tourists when I insisted on stopping to see the swamp that protected the Athenian right wing against a Persian cavalry charge. One plump angry lady in the bus demanded that a vote should be taken as to whether I be permitted to look at the swamp. For once I did not wait upon the democratic process, but quickly got out of the bus. There was a plaque at the edge of the ancient swamp, and I thought it would tell more about the battle. Instead, it stated that some years ago the area had been filled in as a mosquito-breeding hazard through the funds of John D. Rockefeller, Jr.!

In Greece even more than in Italy the ravages of innumerable wars are apparent. Athens, Sparta and the other Greek city states were at one another's throats most of the time. The Persians sacked much of the country; and later came barbarian invasions from the north. The most hideous war episode of all was in 1687 when the Turks placed a powder magazine inside the Parthenon, and the attacking Venetians scored a direct hit on the building with a mortar shell. This transformed the larger part of the Parthenon into a shambles. War is the most frightful enemy of art as of every other human value.

Yet despite the fact that almost all the architectural splendors of Greece, and much of its ancient sculpture, have been badly battered because of physical violence or plain neglect, what remains is so magnificent that we have in this small kingdom perhaps the greatest concentration of artistic glories in the world. And when I saw American bombers zooming over Athens from the U.S. military airfield nearby and heard talk about setting up a base for long-range ballistic missiles in Greece, I suddenly conceived the idea that the United Nations, with of course the agreement of the Greeks, should declare Greece an International Art Sanctuary and a permanently neutral state, something like Switzerland.

It would be under special U.N. protection, until the danger of war had passed away for all the nations of the earth. Let the United States, the Soviet Union and the rest keep hands off and place Greece outside the realm of power politics! Then this unique country that marked the birthplace of Western culture would carry on in lasting peace as a great Art Sanctuary, an enduring shrine of Beauty where art lovers, students and ordinary travelers could go forever for inspiration and aesthetic enjoyment.

From Athens I took a small but comfortable steamship to Istanbul, passing through the Dardanelles and sailing across the Sea of Marmora. At Istanbul I could look out from my hotel window across the Bosphorus to the green-clad hills of Asia Minor. But I must not stop here to describe what I saw and did during my two days' stay in Turkey's capital, nor to enter into my even more interesting weekend in Warsaw on my way to Soviet Russia.

The Soviet Union

In our long trip around the world we naturally spent considerable time in the Soviet Union where we had not been since 1938. Shortly after my return to America in that year I wrote: "It is my own feeling that the Soviet people are well-nigh invincible in an economic, moral and military sense. From without, Soviet Socialism can undoubtedly be set back, but hardly destroyed. . . . The very fact that, over a territory far larger than the United States and non-Russian Europe combined, Socialist economic planning has for many years been operating on a fairly efficient basis proves that *it can be done.*"

Twenty-one years later, in the summer of 1959, what I observed in the U.S.S.R. shows clearly that my earlier expression, "It can be done," has become a decided under-statement; now it is accurate to say that Soviet planning is carried out on so wide a scale and so successfully that the whole world, including the most conservative capitalists and economists, is taking note and reluctantly recognizing Soviet Russia's extraordinary achievements. After enormous setbacks resulting from the Nazi invasion, Soviet Socialism has come fully into its own and is operating with marked effectiveness in almost every sphere. And Soviet productivity not only proceeds with practically no unemployment, but is able to support certain social and cultural accomplishments that are quite remarkable.

I think especially of Soviet Russia's socialized medicine, which capitalist Britain is seeking to rival; of the U.S.S.R.'s impressive educational system, which has abolished illiteracy and forged dramatically ahead both in the field of general education and scientific training; and of recent technological wonders in the exploration of outer space and sending rockets to and around the moon. As to the educational system, it is difficult to work out exact figures for comparison; but I believe the soundest estimate available is that the Soviet Union allocates 10 or 15 percent of its national income to education, while the United States spends about 3 percent for the same purpose.

During June and July my wife and I saw at first-hand the great progress that has been made in the U.S.S.R. Moscow was in some ways hardly recognizable because of the tremendous building and municipal planning programs that have been carried through. A whole new city numbering some 250,000 has been erected on what used to be the outskirts. Everywhere as we drove around the Soviet capital there seemed to be beautiful broad boulevards—twice as wide as New York's Park Avenue—and fine new apartment houses. However, when we looked closely at the apartment houses, it was evident that some of them had been shoddily constructed and hurriedly finished to cope with Moscow's ever insistent housing needs.

We found that architectural styles had improved little since 1938 and were, with the notable exception of the unique subway stations, either drab or grandiose. From our hotel window we could see six of Moscow's new skyscrapers, including the University of Moscow, the Ministry of Foreign Affairs and two big hotels. The buildings looked splendid from a distance, but when you got close up the gingerbread decorations became obtrusive. The Soviet authorities themselves, including Premier Khrushchev, have become aware of these various defects; and there is now under way throughout the country a far-going movement for the improvement and modernization of architecture.

While we were in Moscow my wife and I of course talked with many different types of Soviet people, especially in the professions. Soviet individuals did not have the slightest hesitation to visit with us, or with other American travelers and foreign visitors in general from capitalist countries. It was a boom year for tourists in the U.S.S.R.; and of course among our fellow-travelers were ex-Governor Harriman, Vice-President Nixon, and seven governors of U.S. States whom we encountered on several occasions. A record number of Americans—more than 12,000 altogether—visited the Soviet Union during 1959.

One of the persons we saw most of was our old friend Vladimir Kazakevich, a Russian who for many years brilliantly taught and lectured in the United States on Soviet affairs. After the Cold War began, the U.S. Immigration authorities began to get rough with him; and he chose to go back to the Soviet Union rather than to endure insult and persecution from the McCarthy gang. Mr. Kazakevich has a good job in the American section of the Institute for World Economy and International Relations. He is one of the outstanding Soviet experts on America.

Another Soviet citizen who greatly impressed us was Professor of Psychology A. R. Luria, a most able teacher at the University of Moscow. I was particularly interested in his views on psychoanalysis. He stated that while most Freudian theories have zero for verification, Soviet psychologists do not discard psychoanalysis completely. They do, however, insist on proof for any psychoanalytic hypothesis. Professor Luria asserted that Freud gave too much emphasis to animalistic and biological factors in man, who also happens to be a *social* being.

During the Second World War the Soviet psychologists and physicians expected a great deal of neurosis in the Soviet Army and among the civilian population; but very little developed. Neurosis comes when there is trauma plus internal conflict, because you don't know what to do. During the war, Professor Luria went on, there was trauma without much internal conflict because everyone was part of a group and knew what to do. The pervading sense of WE throughout the Soviet Union has been and is a major factor in holding down to a minimum the incidence of neurosis and the disturbed personality.

Naturally I enjoyed talking with the alert editors of the Foreign Literature

Publishing House, which in 1958 issued a Russian translation of my book on American civil liberties, *Freedom Is as Freedom Does,* in an edition of 25,000 copies. Mr. P. A. Chuvikov, the head editor, told me that this edition sold out quite quickly; and it was only with some difficulty that he was able to find two copies for me. After Mr. Chuvikov had presented me with a handsome author's fee (in rubles), I discussed with him and his associates the whole question of the Soviet Union entering into some international copyright agreement that would cover the rights of foreign authors in the U.S.S.R. and Soviet authors abroad. This controversial matter remains in the domain of unfinished business. The lack of any Soviet copyright accord has aroused much resentment among foreign writers, many of whom are not even informed by their Soviet publisher when one of their works is issued in the U.S.S.R.

Still another delightful occasion in Moscow was the bountiful luncheon given us by Ludmilla Pavlechenko, famous woman sharpshooter who disposed of about 400 Germans in the Second World War. She visited the United States in 1942. The party at her comfortable apartment was warm and gay, with many toasts, both flippant and serious, drunk in vodka that flowed somewhat too freely for my limited capacity. Also present were Miss Pavlechenko's attractive husband and several friends.

One of my most interesting talks was with Soviet Foreign Minister Andrei Gromyko, whose office is far up in the new skyscraper where the Ministry of Foreign Affairs is now situated. I had known Mr. Gromyko when he was Ambassador to the United States and have always had a high regard for him. He had just come back from the Geneva Conference where he had labored long and arduously. In my opinion Mr. Gromyko is a most sincere and effective worker for international peace. It has often been stated that while the Soviet *people* really desire peace, their top leadership—"the scheming Communists in the Kremlin"—are secretly plotting war and aggression. Nothing could be further from the truth. As my conversation with Mr. Gromyko showed once more, both leadership and people in this nation are completely united in their will for world peace and better American-Soviet relations. I believe that Premier Khrushchev convinced a majority of Americans that this is so on his visit last fall to the United States.

Another current fable about the U.S.S.R. is that the Soviet people always look serious, troubled and sad. This is nonsense. We carefully observed the Soviet people in their offices and homes, in restaurants, parks and theaters, in the subway and on the streets. I have rarely seen more laughter and gaiety. People in any country are likely to look serious and preoccupied when hurrying to or from work; but when men and women in Soviet Russia relax, they show as much *joie de vivre* as individuals *any*where.

Yet another report sometimes appearing in the American press is that the Soviet Government has been depriving the people of food and other consumer goods in order to produce Sputniks, moon rockets and intercontinental missiles. The fact is that the planned economic system has been functioning so well that both technology and the standard of living have been developing rapidly in all directions. There is plenty of food throughout the U.S.S.R. today and the people look well fed. In fact the food was so tempting that I myself put on considerable weight. There are plenty of fine beverages, too. Soviet champagne compares favorably with some of the best French champagnes and costs about $3.00 a bottle. The Government recently reduced the price by 23 percent, partly to let it compete successfully with the more potent vodka. Unfortunately, drunkenness is still a problem in Soviet Russia.

Obviously, the Soviet Union has not made nearly as much progress in political democracy as in other fields. Yet there has been considerable relaxation since Stalin died and especially since Nikita Khrushchev became Premier. As Averell Harriman pointed out in a 1959 newspaper series on the U.S.S.R., the political prisoners in the concentration camps have been freed and have been rehabilitated into useful work. During my stay in Soviet Russia, I heard a good many criticisms of the Government. However, the Soviets have a long way to go to establish full civil liberties as we English-speaking peoples understand the term. The first step here should be the implementation of the 1936 Constitution, which specifically states: "The citizens of the U.S.S.R. are guaranteed by law freedom of speech, freedom of the press, freedom of assembly, including the holding of mass meetings, freedom of street processions and demonstrations."

My wife and I have always been a bit nervous about traveling by airplane; and so we felt some trepidation as we boarded the big Soviet TU 104 to go from Moscow to Tashkent on our first jet flight. We did not need to worry. For the Soviet jet operated smoothly and efficiently all the way.

We had long wanted to make a trip to the southernmost section of Soviet Central Asia, both to see the magnificent architectural beauties of the Moslem culture that so long dominated this area and also to study the functioning of the Soviet minorities policy in an enormous region where five major Turco-Tatar peoples intermingle with one another and with the Russians. We were able to fulfil our two main purposes during our fortnight's stay in Tashkent, capital of the Uzbek Republic, with side-trips in a 200-mile radius to such places as fabulous Samarkand, ancient capital of Tamerlane's earth-shaking empire, and the Fergana Valley, where a network of irrigation canals has transformed former desert lands into a most fertile agricultural district.

Wherever we went in Central Asia there seemed to be ample food, as in the Moscow area. In the towns and cities crowds of people were busy buying the abundant consumer goods that are available in the stores. The general standard of life, including the spheres of education and health, is fairly high in this vast region where before the 1917 Revolution a primarily nomadic and Moslem population maintained a precarious existence in poverty and squalor, ever facing the depredations of drought, famine and epidemic disease.

From everything we could observe, the different peoples in Uzbekistan all live together on a plane of equality, with the old racial prejudices and discriminations almost completely eliminated. Among the 444 deputies chosen for the Supreme Soviet of the Uzbek Republic in the last election held early in 1959, thirteen separate nationalities were represented. The most important minority is the Russian, with 62 representatives.

Another important fact to keep in mind is that out of the 444 deputies elected, 129 were women. This bears out our impression that in this huge territory the female sex, traditionally held in bondage there by the Moslem male, has made immense strides towards equality with men. Not only has polygamy been abolished by law, but also 99 percent of the women have discarded the heavy, long, black horse-hair veil which for centuries the Mohammedan religion demanded that all females should wear outside the home.

In Uzbekistan we enjoyed meeting and mingling with the dark-skinned and half-Oriental Uzbeks who make up the overwhelming majority in this land. They are a delightful and handsome people, with mobile, expressive faces, and the Uzbek children are a delight to watch. The girls wear their hair in two long braids hanging down their backs, and their dresses are brilliantly colored. The youngsters were frolicking everywhere like kids in any other country. Since it was extremely hot, with the temperature ranging from 85 to 95 degrees Fahrenheit, one of my favorite recreations was to go swimming in Lake Komsomol, in the city's biggest park, where I was able to relax with the Uzbek youth at play.

One of our most enjoyable afternoons in Uzbekistan was when we went to inspect the big Sverdlov Collective Farm (cotton) just outside Tashkent. We found it highly mechanized and operating most efficiently. After we had walked around for quite a while in the broiling sun, with the Chairman of the Collective as our guide, we retired to a shady veranda where they served us "tea" consisting of a small portion of green tea and very large portions of vodka, champagne and plov, a national Uzbek dish of meat and rice. The Chairman of the Collective raised his small vodka glass and proposed a toast to American-Soviet friendship. "Bottoms up," he said. Since my wife and I had chosen champagne, it was a bit difficult for us to drain our larger glasses. Nevertheless, we did it and then went gaily on to the next glass as I offered a toast to World Peace.

We drank a lot of other genial toasts, and a final one to the continued success of the Sverdlov Farm. Each time the Chairman repeated, "Bottoms up"; and we maintained the pace as best we could. At the end of the "tea" my wife and I and an American newspaper woman present had consumed two whole bottles of Soviet champagne! It is testimony to the high quality of that wine that none of us got either a headache or hangover.

Another afternoon we went to the most important mosque in Tashkent and witnessed an outdoor Moslem Prayer Service. At a Moslem religious service the men and women are segregated, and on this occasion all of the women were out of sight in the back somewhere. So we walked through the midst of some 1,000 silent, bearded Mohammedan males to the chairs reserved for our small party. Almost all these men were native Uzbeks, many of them very handsome and some, with shaved heads or bald heads, resembling Yul Brynner. It was a real thrill to hear the Muezzin call out repeatedly in a high-pitched voice, "Allah is great," and to see each worshipper, kneeling on his little prayer rug, bow down his head to the ground. I have never been so close to Allah before!

After the service the Mufti, head of the Moslem religion throughout Soviet Central Asia, gave us tea, fruit and lamb stew at a beautifully set table. We asked him many questions. He said the Moslems had complete freedom of worship in Soviet Russia, that they trained young men to be mullahs in special seminaries and freely distributed the Koran at the mosques. The Mufti was a dignified, charming man with seven children and five grandchildren. He was very sincerely concerned about world peace.

The Mufti explained that according to the Koran, the Moslem religion, wherever it is functioning, should cooperate with the established government. He and his associates, he told us, are cooperating with the Soviet Government and are on good terms with it. This is also the attitude of the Eastern Orthodox Church, by far the most powerful religious body in the U.S.S.R. The patriotic services of this Church during the Second World War led to greatly improved relations between religion and state in Soviet Russia. The Orthodox Church now actually supports the socialist economic system, which it does not find inconsistent with Christianity. The Soviet Government, on its part, has eliminated most of the crude anti-religious propaganda that was carried on until the Nazi invasion in 1941.

Towards all the people we saw in Uzbekistan I felt a deep warmth and should like to have remained among them indefinitely. But we had set out to circumnavigate the globe and had to move on. On our last afternoon we signed our names in the Tashkent guest book of Intourist, the official Soviet travel agency. By coincidence on the opposite page there was a statement signed by the seven American governors, who had left the day before, July 13. What they said is interesting:

On this day the undersigned have concluded a three-day stay in Tashkent, vital and inspiring capital of the Uzbek Republic. The warm friendship which has been extended to us by the people at every hand, the exemplary courtesy of all public officials, make us feel that our stay has been constructive. It will always remain in our memories as one of the most enjoyable experiences of our lifetime. We leave Uzbek and Tashkent with every wish for the protection of the ancient charm which has been so manifest and at the same time the continued business progress which has also been most conspicuous.

Signed:
> LeRoy Collins
>> *Governor of Florida*
>
> George D. Clyde
>> *Governor of Utah*
>
> John E. Davis
>> *Governor of North Dakota*
>
> Stephen McNichols
>> *Governor of Colorado*
>
> Robert E. Smylie
>> *Governor of Idaho*
>
> Robert B. Meyner
>> *Governor of New Jersey*
>
> Luther H. Hodges
>> *Governor of North Carolina*

Before breakfast on July 14 we drove out to the Tashkent airport and took another Soviet jet, this time bound for India. Reflecting on my trip through the U.S.S.R., I felt more convinced than ever that this socialist country run by Communists—with all its defects past and present—is a country with which the United States can and should cooperate in normal international trade, intercultural exchange, the banning of nuclear weapons, general disarmament and the establishment of enduring world peace. The U.S.A. and the U.S.S.R. will continue to disagree fundamentally on issues of economics and politics; but such disagreements need not stand in the way of peaceful, though competitive, coexistence between the capitalist and Communist blocs.

India

On a very hot morning in the middle of July my wife and I stepped into a Soviet jet at Tashkent and took off for Delhi. We flew over the towering Tien Shan, meaning "Celestial Mountains," over a part of Communist China's Sinkiang Province that juts out between the U.S.S.R. and India, then over the Himalayas themselves with their soaring, snowcapped peaks stretching out for hundreds of miles on either side, and finally down to our destination on India's wide northern plain. It was the most thrilling trip by air that we had ever made.

To reach Delhi took only about three hours. As we struggled through the Indian customs and out to a taxi, no less than six porters insisted on helping us to carry our seven bags—a sign of the immense poverty that burdens India—and I felt obliged to tip each one. The situation was in striking contrast to our experiences in Soviet Russia where tipping is now definitely frowned upon and where, having been rebuffed on several occasions, I finally gave up this pernicious custom altogether for the remainder of my stay in the U.S.S.R.

Delhi became the capital of India only in 1931; and the section that functions as the seat of government is known as New Delhi. It is a spacious and well-planned city, with fine government buildings, parks and apartment houses. The older section of the city, Old Delhi, where we spent much of our time, is more picturesque than the new part and also contains the chief slums in the metropolitan area. The appalling poverty of the Indian people was readily apparent to us when we walked or drove through the streets and alleys of Old Delhi. On every hand there were wretched beggars, both young and old, some of them quite disfigured. It is a horrible fact that beggar parents in this Eastern country will sometimes mutilate their children in order to make their begging more effective.

In Old Delhi, too, we saw at first-hand the meaning of cow worship in India. Often a cow would saunter across a main street along which we were driving in a taxi; the taxi would then have to make a detour, especially if the cow decided to lie down. When we were walking on the sidewalk, frequently a cow would be smack in our path. We watched cows calmly munching vegetables from vegetable stalls along the street; the owners could not interfere because the cow is a sacred animal and *must* be fed. Over all of India wander literally millions of cows, a large proportion of them diseased. They have the right of way over both human beings and vehicles.

There are also plenty of bulls on the loose. A professor who had taught at the University of Calcutta told me that one day a big bull wandered onto the campus. No one was pleased, but no one dared to prevent a sacred animal from munching the grass. A week or so later the bull charged and gored a student who was riding a bicycle through the campus. The young man almost died. Only then did somebody gently usher the bull off the university grounds, still free to roam and gore at will. There have been many instances of such bulls killing Indian men and women.

When we had tea with Malcolm MacDonald, British High Commissioner to India and son of England's first Labor Premier, Ramsay MacDonald, he told us that the cow situation had become worse since the establishment of Indian Independence in 1947. While the British were still in control, they did not interfere with cow worship; but neither did they encourage it. Shortly after Independence, however, the right wing of the Congress Party forced through a law prohibiting the killing of cattle throughout the whole of India. Monkeys, too, are sacred animals and constitute a destructive nuisance in many parts of the country.

Cow worship is of course closely tied up with the belief in reincarnation, which is a fundamental doctrine in the Hindu religion. The Hindus—and there are approximately 320 million of them out of India's 400 million population—are reluctant to take the life of any animal. They think that if you kill a cow, you may in effect be killing your grandmother or some other deceased relative.

Indian cow worship and the law against the slaughter of cattle prevent the utilization of what could be a very substantial source of fresh meat. This is a major reason why the vast majority of Indians are undernourished. Furthermore, the cows and monkeys eat tons and tons of food that ought to be going to human beings. I know of no other nation where the dominant religion has such a direct and deleterious effect on nutrition and health as in India.

When I visited Calcutta, I witnessed aspects of Hinduism that clearly belong in the category of primitive religion. One Saturday morning I went to the temple of the Goddess Kali, an important Hindu deity who has three eyes: one each for the past, the present and the future. In the stone courtyard of the temple, fire worship and animal sacrifice were going on. One Hindu family after another came in leading a little bleating goat and turned it over to the burly executioner. He pinioned the struggling animal in a sort of guillotine and quickly cut off its head with a big sharp knife. The head and the body fell to the pavement, and blood gushed out over the stones. Then a priest stepped forward, dipped his forefinger into the goat's blood and put a red blood mark on the middle of the forehead of each worshipper, including small children.

An old woman squatting nearby took over the head of each goat and cut away, for the priests of the temple, the parts suitable to eat. Dogs lapped up the pools of blood; and the sacrificer carried home the body of the goat to eat. For the Hindus the goat represents animal passion. When you sacrifice him, that symbolizes winning control over your own passions, killing them, as it were. After I had watched about five or six goats being sacrificed, I felt I couldn't stand any more.

So I walked out of the temple grounds and down the street outside. It was lined with beggars, some of them stark naked, seeking alms from the crowds who come to worship Kali. When four or five of these beggars spotted me as a foreigner and literally surrounded me, I broke into a run in order to escape.

Of course there is much that is splendid about India, including its magnificent art and historic buildings. The incomparable beauty of the Taj

Mahal can scarcely be exaggerated. Then there is this nation's firm stand for world peace and disarmament throughout the postwar period, the intellectual alertness of its educated class and the economic aspirations embodied in the Five-Year Plans that the Government has been carrying through in order to raise the standard of living and advance towards socialism. The Second Five-Year Plan started in April 1956, and runs through March 1961.

But the economic and social problems are so formidable that I do not see how Prime Minister Nehru, whom I admire as one of the leading statesmen of this country, and his Congress Party are going to solve them. The population of this subcontinent is increasing at the rate of at least seven million a year; and birth control is making only slight progress. One of Nehru's Cabinet ministers was recently quoted as saying that during the next decade probably some 15 million Indians would starve to death. That is one well-known way in which economic problems are "solved."

Although Prime Minister Nehru and the Congress Party are formally committed to the establishment of democratic socialism, the Indians I talked with told me that to a considerable degree only lip service is being paid to this aim. The Congress Party has not been *militant* in pushing through its economic and social programs, and many of its members are conspicuous for their apathy and lassitude. While my Indian friends did not look upon the Communist Party as the solution, they thought that the best hope for the ultimate success of Nehru and his associates was for them to acquire some of the militancy characteristic of the Communists.

As Walter Lippmann has put it, what is needed above all in India is "the organized pressures of a popular movement under government leadership so dynamic and so purposeful that it can inspire people to do voluntarily the kinds of things that in Communist China are done by compulsion." (*New York Herald Tribune,* December 11, 1959.)

A first priority for a truly militant policy on the part of the Congress Party would be the elimination of the graft that is widespread throughout governmental administration, both at the federal and the state level. Another priority would be the general institution of elementary efficiency. As Arthur Bonner, CBS correspondent who has lived in India for more than five years, states in his informative article, "India's Masses," "entering a government office is like stepping back fifty years or more. There are few filing cabinets and paper clips. Papers are attached by a string threaded through a hole in one corner and then wrapped in a folder tied together by another string. A code letter is pinned to the cover, and the name of the file is registered in a ledger. The file is then tossed on a shelf along with mounds of others. The registers are tossed somewhere else, and how any file is ever found again is a wonder." (*The Atlantic,* October 1959, p. 50.)

Looking back now on my globe-circling tour, I feel that my experiences in India were the most significant of the whole trip. For in no major country had I ever seen before such dreadful poverty, such a disease-ridden people, such backward religion and such abysmal and widespread ignorance. To me as an American the whole situation was a great shock, and a valuable shock. And it made me understand more fully the 1917 Communist Revolution in Russia and the 1949 Communist Revolution in China, since in those two countries living conditions for the masses of the people were similar to what exists in India today.

When the Chinese Communists won power in 1949, living standards were even worse in China than in India. A United Nations Statistical Bulletin, *National and per Capita Incomes, 70 Countries, 1949,* estimates the per capita income in India, in dollar equivalents, as $57, as compared with China's $27. These estimates do not of course tell the whole story about comparative standards of living, but there is no doubt that the Chinese level had been declining, owing to disastrous floods, wide-scale famine, civil war and international war.

The important point is that when a people numbering tens of millions or hundreds of millions, lives generation after generation in misery and semi-starvation, it is not difficult to comprehend why they may eventually explode into revolutionary violence in hopes that a new socio-economic system will provide for their basic needs and give them a better chance to enjoy the good things of this life. News of the dramatic economic upsurge in mainland China over the past decade is not only reaching the Indian intellectuals, but is also seeping through to the masses of the population. And unless India's Five-Year Plans bring about more rapid progress than at present, the example of Communist China will steadily grow more persuasive among the Indians and other peoples of the East.

Another point that India brought into focus for me was the whole relation between a country's economic system and the functioning of democracy. Political democracy in India today is weak and faltering, with Prime Minister Nehru frequently playing the role of an all-wise father. Max Lerner, commenting recently on the military dictatorships that have taken over in the Middle East and Southeastern Asia, stated: "The deeper truth is that most of the new Asian nations simply do not have the economic, political, administrative and social base on which a functioning democracy can yet be built. We are learning these days that a lasting democracy is the end-product of a long process of development, in which men learn in their daily lives to value and trust each other as equal persons, and leaders and administrators are trained to give them direction." *(New York Post,* October 23, 1959, p. 42.)

What I want to stress in this picture is the *economic* base as affecting the educational prerequisites for democracy. While I was in India I kept thinking of John Dewey's insistence that there cannot be properly functioning democratic institutions unless the people are sufficiently educated to possess the information and understanding for voting intelligently on public issues. Nobody can pretend that this is the case in India. And in this huge country there do not exist even the *material* necessities—in the way of schoolhouses, college buildings, pencils, paper, book publishing and the wherewithal for teachers' salaries—adequately to educate the electorate.

Thus 74 percent of the Indian population remains illiterate. Only some 50 percent of the children 6 to 11 years old attend primary school; about 10 percent of children 14 to 17 go to high school; and a mere 1 percent of men and women 17 to 23 are students at colleges or universities. Turning to other aspects of education important for political awareness, we find that the daily circulation of newspapers in India is 3.1 million for a population of over 400 million, while radio sets number a little more than 1.5 million. TV has been only recently introduced.

Again, reflecting on India's educational situation, I saw more clearly not only why right-wing dictators had been able to seize the governments in nearby countries with similar conditions, such as Pakistan, Burma and Thailand, but also why left-wing dictatorships had come into power in Soviet Russia and China. This statement leaves unqualified my immense preference for the use of democratic and peaceful procedures everywhere in the world for effecting economic and social change.

Hong Kong and Japan

From Calcutta I flew on to Bangkok, Singapore and Hong Kong. These are all fascinating cities, but I have space only to discuss briefly Hong Kong. Ringed with small mountains and on a bay studded with numerous enchanting islands, it is the most beautiful and dramatic harbor I have ever seen. It even surpasses San Francisco. Hong Kong boasts a long waterfront where you can watch Chinese junks and other boats being loaded and unloaded. Since there is a lively trade with Communist China, you can see plenty of Communist boats, flying their five-star flag, at the docks. On the myriad junks and sampans—"floating communities" as they are called—live thousands of families in cramped and squalid, though picturesque, quarters.

Since the Communist take-over on the Chinese mainland, more than a million refugees have fled over the border to Hong Kong, creating an enormous problem for the municipal authorities. Naturally these refugees are bitterly anti-Communist; but among the city's original Chinese population pro-Communist sentiment runs strong, even among some of the wealthier business men, who are proud to see China finally a free nation standing on its own feet and no longer subject to imperialist aggression and exploitation. Hong Kong in British hands serves as a valuable trade outlet and transshipment center for mainland China.

This British Crown Colony offers tourists a fine opportunity to buy a vast assortment of intriguing Oriental goods at low prices; and I myself started to purchase a few presents for my family and friends. Then I was stopped short by the discovery that the United States Government had put into effect a regulation that all articles, within at least 30 broad classifications, bought by Americans in Hong Kong would be confiscated by the U.S. Customs unless the buyer could obtain from the seller a Certificate of Origin certifying that the merchandise in question did not originate in Communist China or North Korea.

I was much incensed by this regulation whereby the American Government pushes its unrealistic and out-of-date Far Eastern policy to a ridiculous extreme, interfering with the right of Americans to buy what they want abroad. I also felt surprised that the British Government, which had reluctantly agreed to the U.S. procedures, would allow such an infringement of its sovereignty. The final result was that I bought very little in Hong Kong.

I remained only five days in Hong Kong, but it is a place where I would like to spend five weeks, five months, or indeed five years. From Kowloon, on the mainland side of the bay, I drove towards the small Sham Chun River which denotes the border line with the People's Republic of China, and was able to climb a little hill that gave me a view of two Communist towns a mile or so distant. That was the nearest I got to Communist China. I did not try to enter, because having only recently obtained a passport, I did not wish to have the U.S. State Department take it away from me and bar my traveling abroad for a long time to come.

Early in August I left Hong Kong for Tokyo on a Pan American Stratocruiser. The weather was clear as we flew over the Tokyo airport in the late afternoon, but instead of landing the plane started to circle. I quickly became aware that something was wrong; and when, through a fluke, I heard the captain talking with the airport about his left landing gear, I realized that we might be in for real trouble. Finally, the hostess told the passengers that we must prepare for a crash landing, because the left landing gear might not hold.

A number of passengers were ushered towards the rear, where I happened to be sitting. A Chinese mother and her two young children crouched between me and the back of the next seat. The children were frightened and crying, but I quieted them somewhat by singing a couple of American dance tunes. I remained outwardly calm, but felt terribly nervous. Then the plane came in. On the first bump the landing gear held firm; and I said aloud, "It held!" The flight officer opposite me said, "Wait for the second bump!" A moment later the second bump came, and everything was all right. We had made a perfect landing. As we descended from the Stratocruiser, I noticed six or seven fire engines drawn up on the airfield.

MY TRIP AROUND THE WORLD

In Japan I made Tokyo my headquarters, staying at the Hotel Imperial and frequenting especially the spacious and exotic old wing, which had been designed by architect Frank Lloyd Wright in the early twenties. I went on all-day trips through beautiful Nikko National Park and Hakone National Park; and then on a four-day tour to the lovely temple cities of Kyoto and Nara, and the atom bomb city of Hiroshima.

The Buddhist and Shinto shrines in Japan are impressive, but as works of art I did not think that they were as fine as the religious buildings in Thailand and India. The Buddhists, with their belief in reincarnation, are a strong and influential sect in Japan. I was struck by a story in the newspaper that there would probably be at least 1,000 suicides throughout the country when Crown Prince Akihito and his wife have their first baby. Each of the thousand individuals concerned is convinced that if he can arrange to die at the precise moment the baby is born, his soul will be reincarnated in it, and he will in effect become a member of the royal family and perhaps Emperor.

Surprisingly for me, Hiroshima turned out to be one of the most splendid harbors I ever visited—surrounded by jagged mountains and looking off to the colorful islands of Japan's big Inland Sea. Since I had taken an active part in the campaign against nuclear weapons, I was particularly interested in Hiroshima and explored it thoroughly in order to obtain as clear an idea as possible of what happened when a plane of the U.S. Air Force dropped the first atom bomb in history upon this city, August 6, 1945.

A party of four Japanese took me around. My official guide and interpreter had been a soldier in the Japanese Army and was stationed near Hiroshima when the bomb struck. The following day his unit was sent into the city to render aid. He gave me innumerable grisly, ghastly details. Most helpful also was Dr. Ichito Moritaki, Professor of Philosophy at Hiroshima University and Chairman of the Hiroshima Council against A and H Bombs. He had lost his right eye on A-bomb day. Two girl students who spoke English likewise accompanied us. One of them had been injured when the bomb fell.

I went through three Hiroshima hospitals. The first was the Atom Bomb Hospital, which administers only to patients suffering from the effects of the original explosion. Now, 14 years later, scores of people are still coming to this hospital for treatment every day. I saw many of them in the waiting room. The Director told me that in the first eight months of 1959, 27 Japanese A-bomb victims had died.

The second hospital, run by the Atomic Bomb Casualty Commission and partly supported by American funds, concentrates on research concerning the effects on human beings of the A-bomb explosion. It does not try to cure anyone, but its work is very important in a long-range sense.

The third hospital I visited is a small private institution run by Dr. Shima and built on the ruins of the old Shima Hospital, which happened to be the absolute center of the atom bomb strike. The 50 patients and ten staff members that day were simply obliterated in one minute or less. The hospital itself was completely destroyed. I talked at length with Dr. Shima himself, who fortunately was operating at a hospital in the country when the bomb fell. He told me he came back quickly to Hiroshima to help his patients, but all he could find was the charred body of the Head Nurse in the ruins of his hospital. The fact that the very center of the bomb's destructive power was a hospital ministering to the sick for the preservation of life seemed to me symbolic of the horror of nuclear weapons. It is a remarkable coincidence that at Nagasaki, too, the first direct center of the American A-bomb attack proved to be a medical institution, the Nagasaki Medical School.

What I saw and learned at Hiroshima was all rather grueling to me. And I came away completely persuaded that the United States made a terrible mistake in letting loose the A-bombs on Hiroshima and Nagasaki. In terms of dead, injured, suffering, and long-term effects on human health, these bombings were the most frightful military actions perpetrated against civilian populations in the history of human warfare.

During my three weeks in Japan I came to like its people very much. I have never known a people so polite, thoughtful and smiling—so pleasant in general. To everyone, including hotel personnel and taxi drivers, I returned the bows and smiles with equally deep bows and broad smiles of my own. I found this sort of give-and-take an amiable and heart-warming custom.

These Japanese traits I have been describing have often been ridiculed in the United States, but I believe they are sincere expressions of the Japanese character. Here we have an outstanding example of an essentially fine people being misled into nationalist aggression and eventual disaster by an autocratic and ruthless military clique. How could it happen? I have no pat answer to this paradox. Important factors, however, were undoubtedly the long tradition of strict feudalism in Japan, the fanatical Emperor worship and the tendency of the ruling class in recent times to imitate the most hardboiled features of German militarism and its Prussian code.

I hated to leave Japan just as I had hated to leave Hong Kong, India, Soviet Russia, England and Greece. Indeed, wherever I went on my six months' trip, I always wanted to remain much, much longer than I did. Every country, every city had something special to offer in the way of natural beauty or artistic achievement. But above all I liked the people, of every nationality, of every race and color. And the warm feeling I had always had for humanity throughout the earth was constantly reinforced by my day-to-day experiences and observations.

Human brotherhood extending over the globe is no mere dream; and the Humanist aim of working for the welfare and happiness of the whole family of man is the greatest and most worthwhile of all ideals.

15
The Crime Against Cuba
(1961)

Walter Lippmann, dean of American columnists, has referred to the Kennedy Administration's support of the anti-Castro military venture in Cuba as an appalling and colossal mistake. But the abortive 1961 invasion at the Bay of Pigs was worse than that. It was an outright crime against the Cuban people; and it was also a crime against the American people, against the United Nations and against world peace.

President Eisenhower must share the responsibility with President Kennedy for this enterprise in international immorality. As columnist William V. Shannon said in the *New York Post* of April 9, 1961: "Back in late 1959, the Eisenhower Administration decided to apply to Cuba 'the Guatemala treatment.' That is, the National Security Council gave C.I.A. Director Dulles the go-ahead to organize the Cuban exiles, train a military force and plan an invasion of Cuba."* On January 3, 1961, Eisenhower, partly in furtherance of this plan, severed diplomatic relations with Premier Fidel Castro's government.

In his 1960 election campaign, President Kennedy, on October 20, issued a special statement about Cuba, claiming that the Russians had established "a new satellite" there, and suggesting that the United States Government should help to strengthen the "democratic anti-Castro forces in exile, and in Cuba itself, who offer eventual hope of overthrowing Castro."

---

*In 1954 Eisenhower's team of the brothers Allen W. Dulles, Director of the C.I.A., and John Foster Dulles, Secretary of State, engineered the downfall of the progressive Guatemalan Government headed by President Arbenz. This was accomplished through covert U.S. military and other aid to the anti-government forces.

This statement by Kennedy aroused considerable misgivings among liberals and progressives, including myself, who had come out in support of his candidacy. But most of us felt that his tough attitude towards the Castro regime was political eyewash designed to catch right-wing votes. Subsequent events made it clear that we were guilty of wishful thinking.

In the early, pre-dawn hours of April 17, 1961, some 1,500 Cuban exiles and refugees—recruited, organized, subsidized and armed by the Central Intelligence Agency, a subdivision of the American Government—invaded Cuba. This army came in boats supplied by the C.I.A., with guns and tanks supplied by the C.I.A., and with fighting planes supplied by the C.I.A. The aim was to secure a beachhead in Cuba, to trigger a mass rebellion against Castro, and to set up a Provisional Government which would then get official American recognition and aid. The U.S. Joint Chiefs of Staff approved the military aspects of the blueprint for invasion, which was given the code name of Operation Pluto by the C.I.A.-Pentagon strategists.

The April 28th issue of *Time,* a magazine distinctly hostile to Castro, stated: "The invaders—all Cubans—were trained by the U.S., supplied by the U.S., and dispatched by the U.S. to carry out a plan written by U.S. military experts. President Kennedy knew D-day in advance and approved." To handle the anti-Castro forces, there were "six main training bases in Guatemala" and "two staging bases at Puerto Cabezas, Nicaragua, and tiny Swan Island off the Honduran coast.

"In recent weeks, the equivalent of fifty freight carloads of aerial bombs, rockets, ammunition and firearms was airlifted into Puerto Cabezas by unmarked U.S. C-54s and C-47s, in such quantities that on some days last month planes required momentary stacking. During Easter week, twenty-seven U.S. C-124 Globemasters roared in three or four at a time to off-load full cargoes of rations, blankets, ammunition and medical supplies at the U.S.-built airstrip at Retalhuleu, at Guatemala City and at Guatemala's San José airbase."

The U.S. Navy, at least, rendered direct aid to the expedition against Cuba. One of the Cuban invaders who later escaped to Miami writes in his diary, published in the *New York Herald Tribune* of May 5: "April 14—The flotilla is steaming toward our date with destiny. Two destroyers—I think they are North American—flank us." This information was confirmed from other rebel sources.

U.S. News and World Report (May 15) gave further details: "U.S. destroyers escorted the ships to within six miles of shore. A U.S. aircraft carrier was in escort, as well, but remained about thirty miles offshore. ... The B-26s of the anti-Castro forces flew from bases 600 miles away. They were escorted by U.S. Navy jets which peeled off about five miles from the beach, and left the B-26s on their own."

As history will permanently record, the Cuban Army and civilian militia smashed and smothered the invasion within three days, capturing more than 1,000 prisoners. Castro's tiny air force drove off or downed the enemy bombers, and sank most of the ships that had brought the invaders to the shores of Cuba. The entire Cuban people rallied to the support of the Government, and no sign of an uprising could be detected. Thus the long-heralded invasion to "liberate" Cuba ended in complete fiasco, with the Kennedy Administration that had backed this madcap venture discredited throughout the entire world.

The extent to which the U. S. Government was in charge of the invasion is further shown by the fact that just before it began, the C.I.A. hustled off José Miró Cardona, President of the Cuban Revolutionary Council, and the other leaders of this principal anti-Castro organization, to an isolated and abandoned airbase in Florida where they were held incommunicado. The C.I.A. then issued news releases in the Council's name, but without its knowledge.

According to *The New York Times* of April 26, these Cuban leaders "were kept from using the phone or from communicating with anyone on the outside. . . . Enraged, several of the Council members announced that they were leaving even if it meant being shot by the armed guards." Finally, Adolf A. Berle, Jr., President Kennedy's coordinator of Latin-American policies, and Arthur M. Schlesinger, Jr., another close adviser to the President, flew to Miami to calm down the Revolutionary Council. Apparently the C.I.A. thought that the Council leaders could not be trusted to be discreet.

Earlier the C.I.A. had also kidnapped seventeen anti-Castro volunteers, because it considered them too Left politically, and held them in a remote jungle camp in Guatemala for eleven weeks before and during the invasion (*New York Times,* May 7). This episode reinforces our general knowledge that the C.I.A., in lining up recruits for and organizing the Cuban expedition, was partial to right-wing elements, including former supporters of Batista. And the two "kidnapping" incidents together prove up to the hilt that the assault on Cuba was master-minded by the C.I.A., and that the Cubans involved, whether leaders or rank-and-file, were essentially captives of U. S. imperialism.

On the very day of the invasion, Dr. Raul Roa, Cuba's Foreign Minister, charged before the Political Committee of the United Nations that his country had been invaded "by a mercenary force which came from Guatemala and Florida and which was organized, financed and armed by the Government of the United States of America." Ambassador Adlai E. Stevenson categorically denied these accusations and declared: "The United States has committed no agression against Cuba. . . . I wish to make clear also that we would be opposed to the use of our territory for mounting an offensive against any foreign government."

Thus, as in the incident of the U-2 spy plane flight over the Soviet Union on May 1, 1960, the U. S. Government was caught red-handed in the Big Lie. Everyone who heard Mr. Stevenson speak in the U.N. knew that he was telling a diplomatic falsehood; and it was one that turned out to be most undiplomatic. For only a week later the White House gave out an official release on the Cuban affair, saying that "President Kennedy has stated from the beginning that as President he bears sole responsibility for the events of the past days."

The participation by the United States in a military assault on a country with which it was officially at peace was a dishonorable action totally opposed to the best in our traditions as a democracy. It constituted a cynical violation not only of America's ideals of international peace, but also of our laws, our Constitution and at least six international treaties, including our solemn agreements under the United Nations and the Organization of American States.

One of the neutrality laws violated went into effect on June 25, 1948, under Title 18, Section 960 of the U.S. Code, Annotated: "Whoever, within the United States, knowingly begins or sets on foot or furnishes the money for, or takes part in, any military or naval expedition or enterprise to be carried on from thence against the territory or dominion of any foreign prince or state, or of any colony, district or people with whom the United States is at peace, shall be fined not more than $3,000, or imprisoned not more than three years, or both." Sections 956 and 959 of Title 18 are also most relevant.

With President Kennedy's assent, the C.I.A. took such complete command of the Cuban invasion that it became in reality a U.S. act of war, if not *de jure,* at least *de facto.* However, under the Constitution (Article I, Section 8, Item 11) Congress alone has the right to declare war. Thus in the Cuban situation the Kennedy Administration—the Executive Branch of our Government—usurped the power of the Legislative Branch and went ahead on its own to involve the United States in military hostilities that conceivably could have led to a world-wide nuclear conflict.

The aggression against Cuba also was contrary to the United Nations Charter, Chapter I, Article 2, Sections 3 and 4. Section 3 states: "All Members shall settle their international disputes by peaceful means in such a manner that international peace and security, and justice, are not endangered." Section 4 requires: "All Members shall refrain in their international relations from the threat or use of force against the territorial integrity or political independence of any state, or in any other manner inconsistent with the Purposes of the United Nations."

Likewise the Cuban venture violated Article 15 of the Charter of the Organization of American States, signed at Bogotá in 1948 by both the United States and Cuba: "No state or group of states has the right to intervene, directly or indirectly, for any reason whatsoever, in the internal or external affairs of any other state. The foregoing principle prohibits not only armed force but also any other form of interference or attempted threat, against the personality of the state or against its political, economic and cultural elements."

The American Government's disregard of the U.N., O.A.S. and other international obligations of the United States is in itself a violation of our Constitution, under Article VI, Section 2: "This Constitution and the laws of the United States which shall be made in pursuance thereof and *all treaties made, or which shall be made, under the authority of the United States, shall be the supreme law of the land,* and the judges in every State shall be bound thereby, anything in the Constitution or laws of any state to the contrary notwithstanding." [Italics mine.—C.L.]

It was ironic that just two weeks after the landing in Cuba President Kennedy, signing a resolution that proclaimed May 1 as Law Day throughout the United States, said in part: "Law is the strongest link between man and freedom, and by strengthening the rule of law we strengthen freedom and justice in our own country and contribute by example to the goal of justice under law for all mankind."

The official reasons that the U.S. Government gave for its disregard of legal commitments, domestic and international, in the Cuban situation were that Premier Castro had created a Communist dictatorship in Cuba; that international communism had set up a base of operations in that country and was thereby violating the Monroe Doctrine; that Cuba—only ninety miles from American shores—had become a Soviet satellite; and that all this gravely threatened the national security of the United States.

An objective examination of the facts demonstrates that these charges against the Cuban Government are specious and mere pretexts for foreign intervention by means of force and violence. Nobody in his right mind can believe that the Castro regime, governing a little country with a total population of about 6,500,000—less than that of New York City—aims at military aggression against the United States. And Castro has repeatedly declared that he will work out the problem of the U.S. Naval Base at Guantanamo Bay through peaceful negotiations.

Since, therefore, Cuba does not represent any real menace to the security of the U.S.A., the American enemies of the Castro Administration are compelled to manufacture excuses for the most drastic action, including military invasion, against the Castro regime. These excuses must sound sufficiently plausible to delude the American people and world opinion. This explains the tremendous efforts—on the part of newspapers, magazines, radio, TV and the American Government itself—to whip up hysteria in the United States over the subject of Cuba. In this age, *nations as well as individuals can be victims of a frame-up.*

The revolutionary Government of Cuba came into power in January of 1959 as the result of an indigenous, non-Communist movement led by Fidel Castro to overthrow the reactionary and bloody dictatorship of Fulgencio Batista. The small Cuban Communist Party had long looked upon Castro as a well-meaning but blundering adventurer, and gave support to his 26th of July Movement only as it was nearing its final triumph. Throughout the Castro regime's brief existence of two-and-a-half years it has remained independent, while going steadily to the Left and experimenting with a socialist economy especially adapted to Cuban conditions and the Cuban people.

In this leftward trend Premier Castro's Administration was stimulated to a considerable degree by the hostile actions of the American Government and American business interests. Furthermore, when the Eisenhower Administration treated the Castro regime as a pariah and finally ruled out all American-Cuban trade, except in food and drugs, the Cuban leaders decided—with the very survival of their nation at stake—to fill in the void, especially in the absolutely essential trade in oil and sugar, by large-scale commercial agreements with Soviet Russia and Communist China. It was at this point that American Government officials, and most organs of public opinion in the United States, started to label the Castro government as "Communist" and to talk wildly of "the Communist bridgehead in Cuba" and "Soviet domination."

But it is important to remember that in our era former colonial or semi-colonial peoples throughout the world, from Indonesia in the Far East to Ghana and Guinea in Africa to Cuba in the Caribbean, have been winning national independence and at the same time setting up dynamically led republics that institute socialist programs in order to bring about rapid economic, social and cultural progress. It is essential to understand that when such regimes put into effect radical measures, as well as establishing close diplomatic and economic relations with the Communist bloc, this does not mean that they necessarily are Communist-controlled or are becoming Communist.

As Mr. Bella Doumboya, the representative of Guinea at the recently concluded session of the United Nations, said in a speech on Cuba before this body on April 17: "States engaged in the decolonization of their structure always discover, and are appalled by the fact that their economy is not adapted to the needs of their national life owing to foreign exploitation. Single crop economies are an essential characteristic of under-developed countries. A revolutionary government, in order to foster comprehensive economic development, is bound to alter the colonial shape of the productive system if it wishes to foster national output and the industrialization of the country.

"Contrary to accusations of Communist infiltration which circulate everywhere as soon as an under-developed country engages in bold reforms, it should be known that the acts which succeed the assumption of power are the ineluctable consequences of a life of dependence and frustration and derive mainly from the paramount claim of people hitherto subjected to a feudal regime. In countries where the national economy is under the control of foreign interests, misery and wretchedness is the lot of the indigenous population, all of whose labor power is occupied in the production of raw materials required for the continued expansion of the trusts.

"In the field of production, in order to facilitate new crops in line with the needs of the people, and to put an end to the exploitation of the peasantry, in order to call a halt to the inevitably catastrophic repercussions of this general situation on national output—in a word, in order to remedy the irrational utilization of land and bring to an end social injustice and misery, fledgling governments must always engage in historic acts which sometimes become the cause of ill repute for them."

Every word of Mr. Doumboya's address applies to what the Castro regime has been trying to do. If the American people and the American Government persist in misunderstanding the situation in Cuba and in other nations that have recently emerged into freedom, the effects on United States foreign policy and international peace will continue to be disastrous. For to ascribe home-grown movements toward national independence and socialism to some sort of Communist conspiracy directed from Moscow or Peiping not only vastly exaggerates the power of the Communist bloc, but also leads to provocative claims of Communist intervention or aggression when it does not exist.

On the other hand, the United States has its big Guantanamo base in Cuba; and maintains scores of other military bases fairly close to Soviet Russia and China, often in countries bordering upon them. As James Reston wrote in *The New York Times* of April 23: "Turkey, for example, has been getting from the United States far more power than Castro ever dreamed of getting from the Russians. The United States power, including even rockets with nuclear warheads, has been situated in Turkey for a long time, but the Russians, while annoyed by this fact, have not felt obliged to use their power to invade Turkey."

A flagrant attempt to inflame American public opinion against Castro is shown in the many reports published about the Cuban Air Force utilizing Soviet MIG jets against the invaders. *Time* even stated that some of them were flown by Czech pilots. That these stories were untrue is indicated by the United States Navy itself. A dispatch from the U.S. base at Guantanamo in *The New York Times* of April 20 states: "The sensitive radar on Navy ships here has picked up no trace of high-speed Cuban or Communist aircraft. Officials, therefore, are confident that there have been no MIG fighters in this area of Cuba at least. Nor has the Navy sighted any foreign submarines." This paragraph was omitted in a later edition of the *Times*.

During May, Senator Wayne Morse (D.) of Oregon, Chairman of a special Senate subcommittee on Latin American Affairs, reported that this body had heard "not a bit of evidence" that there was a single MIG plane in Cuba. According to Senator Morse, the Cuban planes that proved so effective in thwarting the rebel landing were of U.S. manufacture and had been sold to the old Batista government.

Castro's own comment on the make-up of his air force during the invasion crisis was, "Would that we had had a few MIGs in those days!" In any event the Castro regime has a right to purchase for its own self-defense MIG planes, or any other kind, from a foreign government.

Much of the American propaganda barrage against Castro has centered around Cuba's admitted lack of civil liberties and political democracy. This propaganda, in the first place, naturally fails to mention that the Cuban Revolutionary Government has rapidly developed full racial democracy, complete equality between the whites and the Negroes, who make up one-third of the population. Economic, social and political discrimination against colored people, a pervasive evil under the Batista and earlier tyrannies, has disappeared. As Joseph Newman reported in the *New York Herald Tribune* (March 23): "Castro and Guevara are literally adored by the large number of poor and humiliated Cubans, especially the Negroes. They see these two leaders as saintly and honorable men, dedicated to removing injustices and discrimination."

In two and one-half years the Castro regime has made far more progress towards unqualified civil rights than the United States, particularly in the South, during the entire 100 years since the Civil War began. Actually, many of the Americans who cry out against "the Castro dictatorship" hate and fear racial democracy, and are scared stiff that it might spread from Cuba to the continents of North and South America.

In the second place, our American propagandists do not point out that the Cuban Government has a democratic mandate in the sense that it is supported by the overwhelming majority of the people. This support stems from the fact that the Government has brought to the workers and peasants—the massive legion of the underprivileged—a higher standard of living, release from economic exploitation, vastly increased educational and cultural opportunities, the promise of continued progress, and a feeling of dignity and freedom at no longer being in bondage to U.S. imperialism. Had the C.I.A., the American State Department and President Kennedy known these things, they would not have made the miscalculation that the recent invasion would set off a popular uprising.

U.S. propaganda, in the third place, leaves out of the picture any reference to the relentless political and international pressures that have driven the Castro regime to certain dictatorial actions and policies. The outstanding foreign factor here has been the hostility of the United States, including its far-reaching economic embargo and culminating in April's military assault.

That aggression was hardly the sort of episode that could be expected to encourage democracy in Cuba, or in any other country confronted by similar circumstances. And the Cuban Government was certainly justified in putting into effect throughout the island far-reaching measures on behalf of public safety. It is well to recall that the National Emergency proclaimed by President Truman in 1950 during the Korean War is still in effect in the United States and has been utilized constantly for the curtailment of civil liberties.

There is, in truth, a large element of both inconsistency and hypocrisy in the American Government's call for "free elections" and political democracy in Cuba. It never made any such demands on Batista when he was in the saddle; nor on a number of other Latin American dictatorships that have been classified as part of "the free world"; nor on various other dictatorships allied to the U.S., such as those of Pakistan, Thailand, Saudi Arabia, Franco's Spain, Salazar's Portugal, and Chiang Kai-shek's Taiwan.

The real reason for the bitter opposition of the United States to the Castro regime is that it has put through radical social and economic reforms, nationalized the huge American property holdings in Cuba, freed the country from U.S. imperialist exploitation, established racial democracy and instituted a planned socialist economy that is functioning successfully. Above all, the Eisenhower and Kennedy Administrations have been afraid that revolutionary Cuba would serve as an example for other Latin American peoples to follow, and that it would inspire dangerous ideas even among the population of the United States.

In any case, so far as democracy is concerned, history has demonstrated that a basic law or principle of drastic economic and social change is that when a progressively oriented revolution takes place in *any* country, the new regime may feel obliged to put into effect draconian legislation and procedures in order to ensure its survival and the success of its program. This holds especially when the nation in question—like Cuba—has had little or no functioning democracy in the past, is throwing off a reactionary bureaucracy or tyranny, or is threatened by internal counter-revolution and military incursions from abroad.

The principle I have just enunciated clearly applies to the non-Communist Castro government and its efforts to build an indigenous form of socialism geared to the welfare of the Cuban people as a whole; it applies to the various revolutions towards socialism that have occurred elsewhere in the twentieth century; and it applies to our own American Revolution of 1776 against colonialism, when we were very hard on the Tories, some 100,000 of whom fled the country and suffered the confiscation of their property. In the chaotic and difficult conditions that faced the new American

Republic subsequent to victory in 1781, we were quite weak on democracy and civil liberties, even after the adoption of the Bill of Rights in 1791.

It would be well for Professor of History Schlesinger to remind President Kennedy that no presidential elections were held in the United States until 1789, more than seven years after the end of the Revolution; that even then George Washington was unopposed for President, as he was again in 1792; that the theory of our Founding Fathers, as written into the Constitution, made no place for political parties; and that two distinct parties did not come into existence until a good twelve years after the close of the Revolutionary War.

The eminent philosopher, William Ernest Hocking, Professor Emeritus of Philosophy at Harvard, in his book *Strength of Men and Nations,* stresses a consideration that is most pertinent to the Cuban situation: "In the worldwide effort to meet the needs of under-developed regions, it must be realized that a degree of dictatorship is inescapable for the first steps. . . . A people uneducated and uninformed, devoid of the habit of thinking out their own destiny, must proceed toward self-government under responsible guidance." And in such circumstances the people in general may well want "no gentle looseness of rein but a strict and determined command," just as midshipmen prefer a captain who "keeps a taut ship."

This discussion brings us back to the statement by Mr. Doumboya of Guinea that "fledgling governments must always engage in historic acts which sometimes become the cause of ill repute for them." As to such acts on the part of the Castro regime, as well as its obvious errors and excesses, the words of Lord Macaulay in his *Essay on Milton* (1825) are remarkably relevant:

"We deplore the outrages that accompany revolutions. But . . . the final and permanent fruits of liberty are wisdom, moderation and mercy. Its immediate effects are often atrocious crimes, conflicting errors, skepticism on points the most clear, dogmatism on points the most mysterious. It is just at this crisis that its enemies love to exhibit it. They pull down the scaffolding from the half-finished edifice: they point to the flying dust, the falling bricks, the comfortless rooms, the frightful irregularity of the whole appearance; and then ask in scorn where the promised splendor and comfort are to be found. If such miserable sophisms were to prevail, there would never be a good house or a good government in the world."

I said at the beginning of this essay that the U.S.-backed invasion of Cuba was a crime against the American people. This is true not only because it greatly increased international tensions and the danger of a horrible nuclear war, but also because it set at naught long recognized democratic principles and Constitutional safeguards in the United States.

In relation to Cuba, President Kennedy and his close associates acted as a tight little group of conspiratorial bureaucrats in violation of parliamentary procedures and the Constitutional separation of powers among the three branches of the U.S. Government. Prior to the invasion, Congress was not given the slightest opportunity to debate the Cuban issue; nor was it submitted to the Senate Committee on Foreign Relations, of which J. William Fulbright (D.) of Arkansas is Chairman, nor to that Committee's subcommittee on Latin American Affairs. However, Senator Fulbright, knowing about Operation Pluto in advance, almost alone among Administration leaders opposed it in a memorandum to the President. Of course the American people as a whole had no chance to express their opinion on the question of Kennedy's plunging them into the Cuban maelstrom. As Senator Morse put it in a speech on the Senate floor: "There is grave doubt as to the legality of the course of action our country followed last week in regard to Cuba. . . . Freedom is worth too much as a human system of government for us to surrender any of our freedom to *a police state system in the field of foreign policy,* dictated by denying to the people the knowledge of the facts of their own foreign policy." [Italics mine.—C.L.]

Kennedy's Cuban adventure constituted an Executive action running directly counter to the pronouncement in the Declaration of Independence about governments "deriving their just powers from *the consent of the governed."* [Italics mine—C.L.] As Mr. David Wise, White House correspondent of the *New York Herald Tribune,* wrote on May 2: "If a major foreign policy action—carrying with it the risk of war—must be prepared in secret, then should it be undertaken at all? And a corollary question being asked is how far down the road a democracy can go in emulating the tactics of its enemies before it wakes up one morning and finds it is no longer very different from its foes?"

After the invasion as well as before it, the Kennedy Administration pursued its policy of undemocracy, endeavoring to stifle a free and full debate on the crime against Cuba in Congress and in American organs of public opinion. The President arranged interviews with the highest ranking Republican leaders such as ex-President Eisenhower, former Vice President Nixon, ex-President Hoover, Governor Rockefeller and Senator Barry Goldwater. The aim was to secure Republican acquiescence in the Cuban assault and a bipartisan blackout on the whole business. In fact, during the first weeks after the invasion only Senator Morse spoke out in the halls of Congress against Kennedy's reversion to "the law of the jungle," as he called it. In the press there was plenty of criticism about how inefficiently the Cuban attack was handled, but precious little about its unethical and hypocritical character.

In a talk April 20 before the American Society of Newspaper Editors, President Kennedy compounded his mistakes of the past by indicating that there would be new ones in the future. "Let the record show," he declared, "that our restraint is not inexhaustible. Should it ever appear that the inter-

American doctrine of non-interference merely conceals or excuses a policy of non-action; if the nations of this hemisphere should fail to meet their commitments against outside Communist penetration, then I want it clearly understood that this Government will not hesitate in meeting its primary obligations, which are the security of our nation. Should that time ever come, we do not intend to be lectured on intervention by those whose character was stamped for all time on the bloody streets of Budapest."

These fighting words seemed to contradict the President's pledge of April 12 that "there will not under any conditions be an intervention in Cuba by United States armed forces"; and they were everywhere interpreted as not only a threat to the Latin American allies of the United States, but also as a warning that Kennedy might set in motion unilateral military intervention to encompass the destruction of the Castro government. It is no wonder that *The Nation* condemned this speech as "one of the most belligerent and reckless . . . ever made by an American President."

Developing further his undemocratic techniques, President Kennedy, in an address to the American Newspaper Publishers Association on April 27, urged the press to censor itself on behalf of national security. Angry at newspaper exposures of the C.I.A.'s cloak-and-dagger plot against Cuba, Kennedy asserted: "Every newspaper now asks itself, with respect to every story: 'Is it news?' All I suggest is that you add the question: 'Is it in the interest of national security?' And I hope that every group in America—unions and businessmen and public officials at every level—will ask the same question of their endeavors, and subject their actions to the same exacting test." To buttress his position, the President referred approvingly to the fact that in these "times of clear and present danger the courts have held that even the privileged rights of the First Amendment must yield to the public's need for national security."

In this manner President Kennedy expressed himself as favoring the current tendency in Supreme Court decisions to weaken civil liberties by making sweeping exceptions to freedom of speech as guaranteed in the Bill of Rights. I must add that the goal of every tyrant down the ages has been precisely to pressure and frighten the individual into *self-censorship,* so that he will not dare to speak up and protest publicly on controversial issues. When this happens a spirit of conformity and fear engulfs the nation, as in the United States at the height of McCarthyism. And if America's organs of public opinion now adopt the President's recommendations, this country will indeed be in a bad way.

In criticizing the President's speech, the *New York Post* (April 30) stated in an editorial: "Mr. Kennedy said 'no war ever posed a greater threat to our security' than the present crisis and that 'the danger has never been more clear and its presence has never been more imminent.' Such language usually foreshadows the suspension of civil liberties. That, of course, is not now the case; Mr. Kennedy explicitly asserted that he has no desire to establish the 'wartime discipline' under which the Communists continuously operate. Yet the surface impact and logic of his words is to encourage those who would create such a climate here." The *Post* was right.

President Kennedy's suggestion about newspapers censoring themselves aroused other strong comments in the press. Under the heading, "When the Government Lies, Must the Press Fib?" *I. F. Stone's Weekly* (May 8) stated: "The national interest in a free society is supposed to lie in the fullest dissemination of the facts so that popular judgment may be truly informed. It is the mark of a closed or closing society to assume that the rulers decide how much the vulgar herd shall be told."

In an editorial of similar purport entitled "The Right Not To Be Lied To," *The New York Times* (May 11) said: "A dictatorship can get along without an informed public opinion. A democracy cannot. Not only is it unethical to deceive one's own people as part of a system of deceiving an adversary government; it is also foolish." *The Christian Century*, a non-denominational and liberal religious weekly, assailed Mr. Kennedy's proposals to the press and claimed that they "carried an overtone of panic."

To summarize this part of my analysis, the Kennedy Administration has dealt a heavy blow to civil liberties through its intimate involvement in the invasion of Cuba, its brink-of-war policy towards the Castro regime and the President's two unfortunate speeches of April 20 and 27. At the same time our Government has given new heart and hope to every right-wing chauvinist in the U.S.A., and to every frenetic, anti-freedom group in the land, from the American Legion to the John Birch Society.

Plainly, the attack on Cuba was not only contrary to American ideals of fair play and the abolition of war, but also to our basic self-interest as a people and a nation. For the Cuban debacle seriously set back President Kennedy's genuine endeavors towards international peace; and lost the United States an enormous amount of prestige in every corner and continent of the earth, including Canada and Latin America, and among our allies as well as our acknowledged foes.

Joseph Barry well summed up the matter in the *New York Post* of April 23: "Whoever wins in Cuba, we have lost. The Cuban catastrophe has become an American tragedy. In its first 100 days the Kennedy Administration has virtually drained its initial favorable balance in the world's books. . . .

"Everywhere our principle of self-determination has been compromised by Kennedy's defense of intervention, however limited, in Cuba's destiny, and the promise—which to the world is a threat—to intervene heavily should its destiny not be the one we prefer. . . . The neutrals of the world, from Nehru to Tito, have been shocked. The new nations of Africa are fearful of what some already refer to as 'American neo-colonialism.' From Delhi is heard the dismaying doubt that 'the New Frontier may after all be just the old familiar brink.' "

In a letter to *The New York Times* printed on May 13, Cyrus Eaton, well-known Cleveland industrialist, pointed out the international implications of the American Government's failure to obtain dependable factual information concerning Cuba: "If our intelligence on Cuba, only ninety miles away, could be so erroneous and misleading, how much better is it likely to be on Czechoslovakia, East Germany, Hungary, Poland, Rumania, Bulgaria and the Soviet Union?

"From first-hand observation in Eastern Europe, I know that our diplomatic personnel deliberately maintain the most limited contact with government officials and practically none with the common man. . . . By seeking out the most extreme anti-Communist elements wherever it operates, the C.I.A. has largely cut itself off from reliable and useful intelligence."

Meanwhile, the Soviet Government had taken a firm and consistent stand on the Cuban situation. Premier Khrushchev in his note of April 22 presented to President Kennedy a series of reasoned arguments opposing the American attitude: "You simply claim," Mr. Khrushchev said, "some right of yours to employ military force when you find it necessary, and to suppress other peoples each time you decide that their expression of will constitutes 'communism.' But what right have you, what right has anyone in general, to deprive a people of the possibility of choosing their social and political system of their own free will?" Khrushchev concluded his message by urging once more that the Soviet Union and the United States work through to peaceful coexistence, with stable agreements on disarmament and other international problems.

In the United Nations on April 26, Valerian A. Zorin, head of the Soviet delegation, repeated his Government's pledge to come to the aid of Cuba in case it was subject to military intervention; and asserted that this promise "was given seriously, more seriously than the British pledge of help to Poland that helped to draw the Western allies into World War II." (*New York Times,* April 27.)

As for open U.S. military intervention in the future to get rid of Castro, Senator Morse was correct when he asserted on April 24: "I say to the Senators today that it is my judgment that if the United States seeks to settle its differences with Cuba through the use of military might, either direct or indirect, we shall be at least half a century recovering, if we ever recover, the prestige, the understanding and the confidence of one Latin American neighbor after another. . . . Cuba is not a dagger pointed at the heart of the United States, but is instead a thorn in our flesh."

However, Cuba need not even have become "a thorn in our flesh" had the Eisenhower Administration offered economic cooperation and assistance to the Castro regime when it took over early in 1959. America should have been glad at that time that there was a non-Communist revolution in the Western Hemisphere with far-reaching social goals and with intelligent idealists leading it. Here was a chance for the American Revolution to catch up with and participate in the great social revolution that has been sweeping the world during the twentieth century, a chance for the United States to befriend a struggling new regime and give guidance to a democratic reconstruction of the Cuban economy and political system.

Instead of grasping this unique opportunity, the American Government followed its usual policy of hostility towards a new order dedicated to radical social and economic reform, and did everything possible to weaken and undermine it. For the United States this was an extension of the attitude Walter Lippmann describes when he says: "We have used money and arms in a long losing attempt to stabilize native governments which, in the name of anti-Communism, are opposed to all important social change."

But it is not too late to retrieve the situation in regard to Cuba. Despite the American-supported invasion, only a week after it had been repulsed Premier Castro and President Dorticós said in a statement about Cuba and the United States: "We are willing to hold whatever discussions may be necessary to find a solution for the tension existing between the two countries and to arrive at a formula of peaceful coexistence, diplomatic relations and even friendly relations, if the Government of the United States so desires."

The U.S. State Department brusquely, foolishly and childishly dismissed this conciliatory gesture with the rejoinder, "Communism in this hemisphere is not negotiable."

However, there is no necessity for this being the final word if the Kennedy Administration will reconsider the whole matter in a spirit of reason and in the light of what is to the greatest advantage of the American people and lasting peace. In my opinion, President Kennedy should take the following steps:

1. Issue an unqualified pledge that the United States Government will not at any time in the future undertake military intervention against Cuba, either directly or indirectly.

2. Cease all further support to those Cuban exiles and refugees, on American soil or anywhere else, who are planning another invasion attempt to overthrow the Castro regime.

3. Announce that henceforth the United States Government will respect in full all international treaty obligations regarding Cuba.

4. Arrange the speedy resignation from the Central Intelligence Agency of those top officials who had primary responsibility for the C.I.A.'s ignominious role in the Cuban fiasco. Also replace Adolf A. Berle, Jr., the Administration's coordinator of Latin American policies, who has displayed an abysmal ignorance concerning Cuba.

5. Accept the Cuban Government's proposal for the re-establishment of diplomatic relations between the United States and Cuba.

6. Agree to negotiate the chief political and other problems that exist today between the two countries, including the questions of normal trade relations and proper financial compensation for the American property nationalized by the Castro regime. (Congressman Frank Kowalski [D.] of Connecticut made proposals along these lines in a speech in the House of Representatives on April 27.)

7. Agree to submit disputes on which agreement cannot at present be reached to the United Nations or the World Court.

8. Lift the ban against American citizens going to Cuba, re-establishing in this sector the precious right to travel.

9. Send to Cuba a special fact-finding commission of distinguished Americans to make a complete, impartial study of the situation there, so that the U.S. Government will have reliable information on the developments that have taken place under the Castro regime.

Suggested References

In this pamphlet I have not endeavored to describe in any detail the immense progress that Cuba has made under the Castro regime. For information about this aspect of the Cuban revolution I refer the reader to the following books:

Leo Huberman and Paul M. Sweezy, *Cuba, Anatomy of a Revolution,* Monthly Review Press, New York, 1960. Cloth, $3.50; paperback, $1.75.

C. Wright Mills, *Listen, Yankee: The Revolution in Cuba,* Ballantine Books, New York, 1960. 50¢.

Paul A. Baran, *Reflections on the Cuban Revolution,* Monthly Review Press, New York, 1961. 35¢.

16
My First Sixty Years
(1962)

On the evening of March 28, 1962, Mr. Casper Citron interviewed Dr. Corliss Lamont for a full hour on his radio program over Station WRFM, Hotel Pierre, New York. The interview follows.

CITRON: I'd like to welcome back to the Pierre a person who has been with us a number of times, a man who is well known in America: Dr. Corliss Lamont, a former Lecturer at Columbia, a philosopher, a writer, and a man who is today, actually right now, celebrating his 60th birthday. And we thought it might be a good idea to talk to him tonight and try to find out a little bit about what these past sixty years have been all about; how a man, particularly of his background, has come by some of the beliefs that he has; and of some of the things he has done in the last sixty years. So, Corliss, welcome back to the Pierre, and happy birthday.

LAMONT: Well, thank you, Casper. It's a great pleasure to be with you again, and especially to be celebrating my 60th birthday with you.
    You mentioned my background, and I suppose maybe I should start with that in tonight's discussion, because in my family circle there were a great many influences that have stood with me throughout my entire life.
    There was in my family a real freedom of discussion for all of the four children. My father and mother were very well-educated people; and we were always talking over the great important subjects of the day, whether they dealt with domestic affairs in the United States or international affairs, in which my parents were very much interested.

In addition to that, they had a very wide circle of most fascinating friends, both in America and abroad. Since my father and mother rather concentrated on England in their trips to Europe, they came to know a great many of the leading Englishmen of their day; and we had, for instance, visiting us fairly often in New York people like H. G. Wells, John Masefield and his wife, Lord Robert Cecil, and General Smuts of South Africa. And I can remember many times being at the dinner table with these persons and actually participating in conversations with them.

Of course this sort of informal discussion built up for me a very fine education, even before I went to college. I can remember some of the arguments, for example, that H. G. Wells participated in with my parents. Wells and I would take on my father and mother, both of us—Wells and myself, that is—being slightly to the left and in favor of some form of socialist economy. That was not only very stimulating but, of course, very informative.

And so it went for a large part of my earlier days. So that when I got to college, I had this very helpful background. And naturally my education at places like the Phillips Exeter Academy and Harvard University were also very important.

CITRON: Corliss, there's one question that, of course, I wouldn't expect you to come out with yourself, but I should ask. And that is: one thinks of the Lamont family as being a very wealthy family. And you didn't touch on this.

LAMONT: Well, certainly they were never in economic want, one may say. And it is a fact that in spite of my father's and mother's wealth, they were interested in liberal causes—in trade unions, and in the League of Nations, *especially* in international affairs. I could call them, on the whole, liberals in their public positions.

So that when it comes to the matter of economic status here, it's perfectly true that I myself have not been in want, either, at any time during my life. Part of my independence, I feel, and my willingness to take dissenting positions has stemmed to some extent from my feeling of economic security, due to the generosity with which my father and mother treated me.

CITRON: Well, one last question on that, Corliss. Was it your father or further back that this wealth came from, and where did it come from?

LAMONT: Well, here I think that it's rather interesting. My father, actually, was a rather poor boy to start with, the son of a Methodist minister in upstate New York. He worked his way through school and college. But then he went into banking, and became very successful. That is the story there.

And he, of course, was very generous with the funds that he acquired, and made very important gifts to all kinds of educational institutions.

CITRON: I hate to keep prying on this, but was it your father that was associated with Morgan?

LAMONT: My father was a partner in J. P. Morgan and Company from about 1910 on. He died, however, before Morgan went over into a union with the Guaranty Trust Company. So that that firm today is Morgan Guaranty Trust.

CITRON: Well, Corliss Lamont, let's leave that behind us, that pleasant topic of how one can have money and so forth. But it's much more important to find out what you did with it. And when you went to college, I imagine that you must have had some thoughts in your mind about philosophy, because you took a Ph.D. at Columbia in philosophy in 1932.

LAMONT: Well, it's true that I was interested in philosophy at a very early age. For one thing, my mother was a student of philosophy, and took an M.A. at Columbia herself, way back in 1898. And she talked over these philosophic subjects with me; so that was one of the discussions that went on continuously in the family circle; questions about God and immortality; and the meaning of the Bible, and all that sort of thing.

Actually, while I was an undergraduate in college, I wasn't quite sure what I was going to concentrate in. But a couple of years after my graduation, I came back to philosophy as the subject that I felt should be my field of concentration, and then went to both Columbia and Harvard graduate schools to study. I took my degree in 1932—that is, the Ph.D. degree—at Columbia, on a thesis entitled *Issues of Immortality,* which dealt with the whole question of personal survival after death. That has always been a fascinating topic to me, and remains so to this very day, especially now that I'm getting a little older and may have to go on to some other place before long.

CITRON: Well, now, you wrote a book, which I unfortunately haven't read—I don't know if it's still being published; but it's called *The Illusion of Immortality.* Could us tell us a little bit about that?

LAMONT: Well, that was—

CITRON: Is it still in print?

LAMONT: Oh, yes. That's still in print.

CITRON: Who is the publisher?

LAMONT: It's in a paperback edition now, sold by Philosophical Library. And it has gone into several editions, and still sells pretty well, because it's one of the few books that really tries to give a careful and thorough examination of the case against personal survival after death.

I had started out believing in immortality. But after my studies in philosophy, I came around to the position that we could not go on beyond the grave, except in the way of influence and through our children and descendants—that is, biological immortality. So I was forced to conclude that this was my one and only life. And I have operated on that basis for the last thirty years; and I think it makes a difference, because I feel that I am more concerned with what happens here, on this earth, than if I were looking forward to an after-existence, and I work a little harder and try a little harder to bring justice and happiness to people in this natural world.

CITRON: Well, Dr. Lamont, on this question of immortality, were there any reactions from such institutions as the Catholic Church or other church groups on this book?

LAMONT: It has been attacked fairly often by church people and church bodies. I don't think any particular church ever took it up in great detail. Actually, it has become, if I may say so, something of a reference book in many colleges and universities. And at Union Theological Seminary, for instance, the president of that institution, Henry Pitt Van Dusen, a good friend of mine, has used *The Illusion of Immortality*, my book, in some of his courses to show his students what he calls "the best argument" against the traditional Christian belief.

It isn't that Dr. Van Dusen agrees with me. But he is one of the teachers who wants to present to his students both sides of the question. This book has been used in that way in many places. And of course it is used that way in England, too, where there have been several English editions.

CITRON: Corliss Lamont, you mentioned how you feel that immortality must come through one's children. I neglected to ask you in the beginning: what have you done about children through the last sixty years?

LAMONT: Well, I followed the example of my father and mother, and like them, have been able to have four children, three daughters and a son. Two of my daughters are happily married. One of them has presented the family with two wonderful, beautiful grandchildren, whom I see a good deal of. And then I have another grandchild, who was born to my son and daughter-in-law up in Boston a year or so ago. I've been much blessed, I think, in the realm of children. And it's a great thrill to have grandchildren and to be a grandfather—even though it seems a bit queer sometimes to be called "Grandpa."

CITRON: What class were you actually in at college?

LAMONT: I graduated from Harvard in the Class of 1924. And in my class there were some very interesting, stimulating people: Senator Henry Cabot Lodge, Ambassador Lodge, was one of those I knew well in that class. Even in those early days, when we were both only about twenty years old, Lodge and I were on different sides of the fence; he always was conservative, and I always liberal or left. And another gentleman in the class who has meant a great deal to me is Charlie Poletti, who became—

CITRON: Lieutenant Governor.

LAMONT: —Lieutenant Governor, yes, of New York, and for a very brief period, Governor. We have had writers, too, like Oliver La Farge—who, incidentally, is the President of the Association on American Indian Affairs—a very fine man, a very gifted man, and whose early novel, *Laughing Boy*, I think it was, attracted me soon after I left college.

So that was a fine class. And at Harvard I continued what you may call the liberal education that I got in my own family circle. That is, at Harvard all kinds of ideas were presented to us students. And I got a chance—not just to hear the orthodox viewpoint, but liberal viewpoints and radical viewpoints as well. I think that Harvard still has that reputation and that sort of atmosphere, perhaps more than most other colleges. It is a place where there is plenty of room for dissenters. And as you will recall, we have had many eminent public men graduating from Harvard, who didn't exactly take the line of least resistance: for instance, Franklin D. Roosevelt, not to mention the present President of the United States.

CITRON: Dr. Corliss Lamont, after you took your Ph.D. at Columbia in 1932, you started to put into deeds your interest in civil liberties. And I believe it was in 1932 that you became a Director of the American Civil Liberties Union. Now, what was your earliest recollection of your interest in civil liberties?

LAMONT: Well, actually that went back to Harvard College, where I was always interested in trying to get unorthodox speakers to come and address the student body. And at one time I tried to get there people like Scott

Nearing and W. Z. Foster. I didn't succeed, actually, at that moment. But my civil liberties experience started then, when I was an undergraduate at Harvard. And then it blossomed after I graduated; and I really took it on as one of my main interests—as you say, becoming a Director of the American Civil Liberties Union, fighting through many crises with them, supporting really uncompromising freedom of speech for all individuals and groups in the United States.

And as I went on, I of course tangled with various government bodies myself. I not only tried to defend the civil liberties of other people, their free speech and their freedom of association, but I also tried to help establish civil liberties by speaking out frankly in all kinds of dissenting ways, so that I could become an active civil libertarian by expressing ideas freely myself.

CITRON: Well, now, Corliss, in the course of your interest in civil liberties you went before Senator McCarthy's famed committee, which led later to an indictment for contempt of Congress. Now, can you tell us exactly what happened there?

LAMONT: Well, that was, of course, a very remarkable experience for me: to be haled before McCarthy's committee by old Senator Joe himself, who came to New York especially for my hearing. My crime was that, like other authors, I had written a book which Senator McCarthy did not like because it was about Soviet Russia; it happened to be called *The Peoples of the Soviet Union*, and was about the racial groups in the Soviet Union. And McCarthy found that this book was on a U.S. Army bibliography. So that is why he summoned me before his committee, and started to ask me a lot of unconstitutional questions, about how I had prepared to write this book, whom I talked to about it, what my places of research were, and all that sort of thing.

I refused on First Amendment grounds to answer most of McCarthy's questions. And I told him plainly that my writings were outside the jurisdiction of his committee, which was supposed to look only into Government operations. And I was no employee of the Government. So I didn't consider that my books were a proper subject for his committee.

Also, freedom of the press was concerned, because here I had published a book, and that was no reason at all for McCarthy to start asking questions of me about it.

My case went to Congress. In the Senate, I was cited for contempt, although three Senators voted against the citation, including Senator Lehman of New York. And then—

CITRON: Who were the other two, Corliss?

LAMONT: Let's see, the other two were Senator Chavez of—

CITRON: New Mexico.

LAMONT: New Mexico, and Bill Langer of North Dakota.

CITRON: Right.

LAMONT: Langer was an erratic wonderful guy—

CITRON: And a Republican.

LAMONT: *And* a Republican. And he voted against the citation.

But anyway, the case went to the courts. I was defended by a brilliant civil liberties lawyer, Philip Wittenberg. We won first in a Federal District Court in New York City, where Judge Edward Weinfeld dismissed my indictment for the reason that McCarthy had no right to question me because his Committee had never been legally and constitutionally established. A Federal Appeals Court unanimously upheld this decision. This ruling set a precedent that meant the McCarthy Committee possessed no legal power or jurisdiction.

I was very happy, Casper, to really be involved in that battle. It was exciting; it was interesting; it was worth-while. And I think that I helped to nail—put a nail in McCarthy's coffin. Actually, if you look at his record in the courts, he won practically nothing at all. Of course, that was at a time when Congressional committees, especially his committee, were riding high. And they still remain a great menace to American civil liberties.

CITRON: Well, now, you're referring, no doubt, to the House Un-American Activities Committee.

LAMONT: Yes, that's right.

CITRON: I thought so.

LAMONT: And also, the Internal Security Committee of the Senate, because both of these committees are still operating today, calling witnesses before them for no good reason, ruining careers, smearing innocent people; and they really have constituted the spearhead of reaction and the witch-hunt in the United States.

CITRON: Well, now, since you brought up the House Un-American Committee, do you feel that there are any functions of this committee that are legitimate in your mind?

LAMONT: Well, actually no, because I think this committee is unconstitutional on its face, since the very resolution supporting it calls on the committee to expose un-American propaganda. And propaganda is the lifeblood of any democracy. Of course, we call propaganda what our opponents call education, and vice versa. But in a great political campaign, any time, whether it be for the Presidency or some other office, propaganda is really the heart of the matter—on both sides. So that when you start to make an investigation of propaganda, you are really investigating free speech and trying somehow to curtail free speech.

Therefore, the House Un-American Committee, I think, has no legitimate function, and is actually contrary to the Constitution in its functioning. Hence I stand with those who favor, very strongly, its total abolition.

CITRON: Well, now, Corliss Lamont, are you willing to admit that there is such—there possibly can be activity in the United States that is un-American?

LAMONT: Why—I hate the term "un-American."

CITRON: Instead of un-American, against the interests of the United States.

LAMONT: Of course there can be activities against the interests of the United States. There can be treason. There can be murder. Then there can be sabotage. There can be espionage. And actually, on the statute books, both Federal and State, we have plenty of laws to take care of all those crimes. And the government should go after any people—whether they're Communists or anybody else—who are guilty of those crimes.

But these committees of Congress actually are going after people who cannot be reached by any statute of the United States. And that is why it is mostly unconstitutional, because they pursue them in a sort of extra-legal way, and act as, really, courts of justice to condemn these people without the defendants having a chance to defend themselves according to proper legal procedures and regulations.

CITRON: Well, Corliss Lamont, you know you have admitted that there are possibly certain actions in this country that would be considered un-American, or non-American, or whatever terminology you would prefer. Also, we have a government that is divided into three branches: Executive, Legislative and Judicial. Now, you obviously believe in the right for cases to be tried in the courts; and you obviously believe in the Executive right for these cases to be looked into. But we have a Legislative branch of government; and if they can't look into such things in the Un-American Committee—where can they look into them?

LAMONT: Well, Casper, I—I happen to believe in this three-way separation in the Constitution. In fact, I continually stress it. And it is exactly that separation of powers which strengthens the case against the House Un-American Activities Committee, because it has again and again usurped the functions of the Judiciary and the Department of Justice. Now you ask who is going to look into these things if—

CITRON: From the Congressional view.

LAMONT: —from the Congressional viewpoint. The purpose of Congressional investigating committees—which I approve of—is to ascertain facts which are useful for legislation. But these witch-hunt committees don't do anything of the sort. They just keep trying to smear people. And they dig up information that everybody knows about already. So that I don't think they have any real function—from the legislative point of view.

But you see, it's not only the Legislative branch that oversteps its powers now and then. The Executive branch can overstep its powers too, as when the President of the United States has involved American military might in foreign countries in some war or other without the Congress having a chance to vote on it.

CITRON: One last question, Corliss, on this question of the House Un-American Activities Committee: would you allow the Committee to exist, in your own mind, if their fields were limited and their methods were changed?

LAMONT: Why, not under its present mandate from Congress, and not under the definition of "un-American," which, as I said before, is so really vague and sweeping that it can never be really limited to any one idea or group of ideas, or even group of activities.

Actually, if there ever were such a thing valid as an Un-American Committee, which I doubt, it would have to really investigate *actions*—illegal actions by groups and people which are not covered by other agencies of the Government. But you see, the Federal Bureau of Investigation takes care of all that.

CITRON: But that's the Executive end of the Government.

LAMONT: Yes, that's the Executive end. But the Legislative branch is not supposed to deal in uncovering criminal actions.

CITRON: But they are sort of a watchdog.

LAMONT: Well, they can be a watchdog, as I said, for legislative action and for digging up facts which are useful. Now, mind you, I'm in favor of the Congressional power of investigation in general. It's only three or four committees—like the McCarthy committee, the Un-American Activities Committee, the Senate Internal Security Committee—which have gone overboard in these investigations. You have a committee on banking, or you have a committee on commerce. And most of those committees stick to their knitting pretty well, and perform the limited function which is assigned to them by the House or the Senate.

But the witch-hunt committees are sort of roving committees which take the whole world—the whole world of the United States—as their jurisdiction, which I think is unfortunate, and actually illegal.

CITRON: Dr. Lamont, we could spend the whole last twenty-five minutes on this question of the House Un-American Committee; and I feel there's too much that I'd like to talk to you about that we haven't touched. But one point that you have sort of come to yourself, a moment ago, was about this question of foreign intervention on the part of the United States Government, from the Executive branch. Now, you're no doubt referring to such things as Cuba.

LAMONT: Well, Cuba first. You know, it was just a little under a year ago, Casper, April 17—I can never forget that date—when the United States, through the C.I.A., helped to stage that invasion of Cuba by Cuban exiles who were armed, organized, and financed by the United States Government. And I thought that that was really a terrible thing and that it went beyond the power of the Executive Department, because it was involving us in a little war, actually, without anybody discussing it in Congress—without Congress able to seize its prerogative, which is to declare war.

And I find a similar example again today in South Vietnam. There you have the United States Government, again, really embarking on a large-scale military intervention, sending all kinds of troops and machine guns and trucks and now helicopters to aid the tyrannical government of a fellow called Diem, who is an arch-reactionary and a very cruel dictator. And I don't like this, either.

There has been very little discussion of it among the people of the United States, practically no discussion in Congress. And again, I think the Executive—that is, President Kennedy here—is going beyond a so-called police action to embroil the United States in a real, though undeclared, war—which could flare up into a major conflict, and which could have the most serious consequences for the people of the United States.

CITRON: Well now, firstly, Corliss Lamont, on the Cuba situation I think that even the President feels that this was an ill-advised expedition in the form that it was accomplished, and that the C.I.A. had no business in fighting its own private wars. But let's not talk about the Cuban thing. There are three others that I would prefer to discuss.

First of all, I'm not going to talk about South Vietnam, on the basis that I feel that the action taken by the Executive branch—while it has not had the explicit approval of the Congress—has had a bipartisan White House breakfast approval from the very start of the conflict.

But there are three others that I would like to ask you about, and see what you think about our intervention: a) helping in the United Nations action in the Congo; b) our action in the Middle East of a few years ago; and c) the operation which was almost entirely American in Korea. What about those three?

LAMONT: Well, I think the Congo business under the aegis of the United Nations was a justified intervention, and that insofar as the United States supported that, in trying to bring peace and unity in the African Congo, that it was a good and justified action.

Now about Eisenhower's sending the Marines to Lebanon—four years ago, wasn't it?

CITRON: Yes.

LAMONT: In 1958. I thought that was a great mistake. And, again, it was the kind of Marine Diplomacy which we have come to frown upon in relation to Latin America, for instance. And it was not only a mistake because of sending armed forces, but the reasons were all wrong. It was all due to a revolution that took place down in Iraq, you will remember. And as soon as that revolution took place, throwing out a pretty dictatorial king, immediately there was a cry of Communism and that this was really all a Communist front, as it were.

Now, actually, it turned out to be nothing of the kind. These were just military men and nationalists trying to get in a better government in Iraq. But on the pretext that the Communists were threatening the whole Middle East, Eisenhower sent the Marines over there to prevent the Communist revolution from sweeping into Lebanon. Well, there wasn't any Communist revolution involved.

CITRON: But didn't the government request our intervention?

LAMONT: Oh, Lebanon?

CITRON: Yes.

LAMONT: It may well have done so. It may well have done so, but I don't think that that—

CITRON: It was on their invitation that we went in.

LAMONT: Yes. That does not, it seems to me, necessarily justify such an intervention. Actually, in South Vietnam today the government has requested help, sure; but that doesn't seem to me to make it right.

CITRON: What about the third case?

LAMONT: Now, as to Korea, there again I don't think it's quite as clear as in the Congo; but just the same I do think the invasion of South Korea by the North Koreans was a terrible act of international immorality, and that the U.N. cease-fire order should have been carried out by both South Korea and North Korea. Therefore, I think that there was justification for President Truman in sending in American troops, though I wish that he had not sort of jumped the United Nations on it. And I wish, also, that he had dismissed MacArthur earlier, so that MacArthur and the American Army would not have swept on to the Chinese border in North Korea, which brought the Chinese into the war, you see.

In other words, while part of the Korean operation was justified, part of it went, it seems to me, in a very wrong direction, which by bringing the Chinese in cost us thousands and thousands of American lives. And insofar as that happened, it was a mistake.

CITRON: Dr. Corliss Lamont, let's move into the field of international peace. Now, I have a quote from you which says: "I have been active in working for international peace and American-Soviet understanding." Can you amplify that?

LAMONT: Well, again I go back to my parents in those early days when they took me to Geneva, for instance, to take a look at the League of Nations when it was operating, back about 1924–1925. And I have maintained my very deep interest in international organizations for the prevention of war ever since that time. So that when the United Nations came along, after the Second World War, I became very much interested in that and have always been a firm supporter of U.N. principles and the U.N. Charter in general.

At the same time, looking over the situation from my own vantage point, it seemed to me that the most crucial place in the world which might make for war was in American-Soviet relations. And therefore, again quite early in the game, I became interested in trying to improve American-Soviet understanding.

I went to Russia two or three times, wrote a couple of books on that country, and tried to get across to the American public—and indeed the American Government—the fact that the Russians were very anxious to cooperate with the United States on peace. I think that was true *before* the Second World War; and I think it's been true *after* the Second World War.

But at any rate, I have maintained that interest right down to the present moment, and still believe that peace and understanding and coexistence between the Soviet Union and the United States are the key to world peace today.

CITRON: Well, Corliss Lamont, there are a number of things that have been going on that have served to amplify what you have said about peace between the East and West, which is in reality the two countries. And it might be of interest to our listeners to know what you might have done if you had been President Kennedy in the relationship with the Soviets in the last year.

LAMONT: Well, I need a lot of time to answer that question. I won't take all that time. But I will just outline a couple of things that come to mind. If I had been President Kennedy I would have sat down with Khrushchev and the Russians. I would have held a—

CITRON: Hasn't he done this?

LAMONT: Well, he hasn't held a Summit Conference. But that's only part of it, you see. I think—

CITRON: Well, he has met with Khrushchev.

LAMONT: Yes, he met with Khrushchev in Vienna a year or so ago. But it was very informal.

CITRON: Wasn't this sort of an awakening for Kennedy—that he had thought that he could sit down with Khrushchev? According to all the scuttlebutt, he came out a very worried man.

LAMONT: I'm not sure about that, Casper. I'm not sure whether that was the case or not. But I think that, instead of boosting American armaments by about eight or nine billion dollars, Kennedy should have accepted some of the Russian disarmament proposals. And that—

CITRON: Without safeguards?

LAMONT: *With* safeguards—that the Russians should disarm at the same time—and with other safeguards, too. And I believe that Kennedy went a little wild over the Berlin situation, and scared the Russians by his very tough attitude there and the threats on the part of the American Government that we would resort to nuclear war if necessary over the Berlin issue. I could never see that the Berlin issue really amounted to that much, or was that important.

But in general I think that the Kennedy Administration's whole attitude toward the Soviet Union is based on a wrong premise: namely, that the Soviet Union and the Communist states intend military aggression, if they can get away with it. I don't think that the Soviet Union has ever wished to spread socialism or communism through military aggression, or through wars, or anything of that sort. That is, they believe that the capitalist system is doomed anyway, and that the workers in each country will bring about their own change-over to a socialist system—in some cases, as Khrushchev said recently, through democratic processes.

In other words, the whole military build-up in the United States has been based all along on the idea that we must work up a mighty deterrent to that Soviet aggression that is always just around the corner. It was never around the corner. The Russians have never intended war. They suffered so in the First and Second World Wars that they are through with war so far as they can express a purpose of their own. And therefore, I think that this is a political myth which has been foisted on the American people to keep us nervous and even fanatical over the alleged Communist and Soviet menace.

CITRON: How do we know you're right, Corliss Lamont?

LAMONT: I think partly a study of the history of Marxist and Soviet documents, and their own efforts toward world peace, and their own principles, as demonstrated in, for instance, the League of Nations, even before the Second World War—where they were firmly in favor of collective security and tried hard to get the other Great Powers to come along on that basis against Hitler.

It's something, I suppose, that is very difficult to prove. And so far as disarmament is concerned, I don't ask that the United States should disarm unilaterally. But I do ask that we should try to enter into reasonable disarmament negotiations with the Russians—not only about conventional weapons but, of course, about nuclear weapons as well.

CITRON: Well, I'm glad you brought that up. Corliss Lamont, you were on this program not so long ago, after the Russians resumed nuclear testing.

And they, the way they did this, completely destroyed the moratorium that was understood, that we'd been dickering with them about for a number of years, constant meetings where we both had agreed not to test—and you yourself condemned the Russian attitude for restarting the nuclear testing. Now, is it out of sorts for Americans to say we cannot go into a new disarmament—or a treaty on banning atomic testing without adequate safeguards? Isn't this a perfectly normal reaction for us to take after what happened on the last thing?

LAMONT: Well, certainly it is. And I still condemn the Soviet Union for breaking the moratorium and going ahead with those tests. At the same time, I am sorry that the United States responded by going ahead with underground tests last fall, and that President Kennedy has now announced that we will go into atmospheric tests in all probability in April. I think this is a great mistake.

But you see, in addition, you talk about safeguards. All this talk about inspection of the Soviet Union, or the United States for that matter, to prevent nuclear testing, I think, has become quite irrelevant.

I think that, on the whole, both atmospheric testing and underground testing of nuclear weapons has become a matter that can be detected by foreign countries through the new mechanical devices. And I think that has been shown again and again in the last year or so. And as a matter of fact, the British at Geneva, in this last round of discussion, have been pushing toward that general conclusion.

In other words, an agreement to stop nuclear testing, both above and underground, is pretty much now self-enforcing, because as soon as there is a test, a violation, everybody else knows about it. So I don't think that it's necessary to harp on that particular approach so much. And I just say to myself, "Oh, ye gods! If they would only make just a start at stopping this nuclear testing and get the ball rolling, mankind would be much happier and we would be on the road to peace."

CITRON: Well, you mentioned that the Soviets as long ago as before World War II definitely wanted peace. Now, why will they not then allow us to have some kind of an inspection system set up whereby we would immediately now forego our testing of atomic devices in the atmosphere?

LAMONT: Well, they did accept the idea of inspection for a while. I imagine they really are, as they have hinted from time to time, afraid of spies and so on. I think that this is unfortunate; I think the Soviet Union should—if the United States insists—accept an inspection system for the stopping of nuclear tests.

CITRON: But they won't budge on this.

LAMONT: On the other hand, if the Soviet Union won't budge on it, I think the United States should make a treaty anyway. It's so terribly, terribly important to get that treaty to stop nuclear testing. And as I said earlier just now, a non-testing agreement seems to me to be self-enforcing.

CITRON: Well, Corliss Lamont, isn't this the situation that the two governments have been in for approximately three years? You talk about "if this" and "if that"—this is the position that they've been in: neither side will give in. We want safeguards; the Soviet Union doesn't want safeguards.

LAMONT: Well, you see, the question is what the safeguards should be—

CITRON: Well, inspection then.

LAMONT: —and how necessary they have become. I think that the whole idea of inspection has become far less necessary than it was earlier, because of these devices which even reveal our underground testing thousands and thousands of miles away.

CITRON: Well, Corliss, let's—this is something that has stymied the two governments for three years—let's move on to your attitude towards socialism. What do you feel that the future has in store for the United States democracy? Do you feel that there is some socialism in the offing? Or—

LAMONT: Well, let me, Casper, just go back for a minute to my basic philosophy, which I call Humanism, namely a philosophy which works for the welfare and progress and happiness of all mankind. What I have been moved by, motivated by, it seems to me, during the greater part of my life, is a kind of a compassionate concern for humanity. Some people would call it "love of humanity," in Auguste Comte's phrase. And also I rely primarily on the methods of reason and science in solving problems of a social and individual nature.

Now, it is this feeling for justice, I think, and the welfare of all humanity, which has led me to a belief in a democratic socialist economy as the best way out, not only for countries which are under-developed but for countries which are, you may say, even over-developed, like the United States.

And when I use my own intellect and thinking process to answer the question of how can we bring economic security and justice to the masses of mankind, I feel that some sort of collectivism—whether you call it socialism or not—is the answer.

Now, we have become increasingly collectivistic in the United States. We have little socialist experiments here and there, as in the Tennessee Valley Authority. And I think that as time goes on—

CITRON: Social Security?

LAMONT: Oh, Social Security, too. Yes. Yes, there are a lot of laws dealing with unemployment insurance and social security which were in the old socialist programs and which have been adopted by both Democrats and Republicans in the United States. So that we are moving steadily more in that direction. But we're not moving nearly as fast as other countries, where you have some kind of socialism established, as in the Soviet Union, Czechoslovakia and the eastern European states.

My own feeling is that it's too bad that socialism has come into power first in countries like Russia or China, which were terribly backward in a democratic sense, and which therefore found it pretty easy to go over from dictatorial feudalism to dictatorial socialism. What I want to see is one of the really democratic nations, like Great Britain or France or the United States itself, vote socialism into power so that we'd get a real democratic procedure bringing into effect this new sort of economy. In other words—

CITRON: Abolish the capitalistic system?

LAMONT: Well, it would nationalize the main instruments of production and distribution; and, yes, it would abolish capitalism in general, without, it seems to me, necessarily taking over all business in the country.

CITRON: What would you leave that the state would not take?

LAMONT: Well, a lot of the lesser businesses, perhaps part of the agricultural economy. When I say lesser businesses, I mean people who are employing only three or four workers, something like that. I would not be in favor, necessarily, under socialism, of group ownership of every little industry or every little service in the community.

CITRON: Well, in other words, would I be correct in assuming that you would advocate complete state ownership of industry in America except for the very smallest?

LAMONT: Well, not necessarily by the Federal state, but it might be by the city, as the subways in New York—

CITRON: It really wouldn't matter too much whether it was the city, State, or Federal, would it?

LAMONT: Well, it would matter only to this extent: that the key concept for me in the transition to socialism, and in the functioning of a socialist economy, is planning—economic and social planning. I don't dwell on the class struggle or that sort of thing at all. But using my own reason, I believe that life in our modern economies has become so complex that you must have some kind of over-all planning from central positions. One central position is obviously Washington, D.C.

CITRON: Don't they indulge in that?

LAMONT: They already have a good deal of planning. That's right.

CITRON: Council of Economic Advisors—

LAMONT: Surely.

CITRON: And so forth.

LAMONT: That's right. And I would extend it much further. But at the same time, I would allow for plenty of local autonomy in states and municipalities. I don't want everything controlled by the Federal Government under socialism. There's room for State planning in New York, for instance, or city planning in New York City, which can be very helpful.

And already, as you suggest, planning to some degree goes ahead. But under socialism, it would be expanded to an enormous extent. So that our general economic efficiency would increase, depressions and unemployment would be abolished, and the standard of living would go up much higher than it is even today.

CITRON: Aren't you forgetting what might happen to American initiative though?

LAMONT: Well, I'm not worried about that, because I don't think that initiative is brought into play solely by the profit system, the urge to make money under capitalism. All kinds of other things can stimulate individual initiative. After all, we have plenty of good, decent, efficient people working in the government service already, whose primary motive is not to make a profit on the stock market. I feel that the motivation of men can be bettered and transformed under socialism, so that they'll work just as hard—if not harder—than under the capitalist system or the old feudal system.

CITRON: Hasn't it been, though, the capitalistic system that has made or created the industrial might of America?

LAMONT: Well, certainly it has—because that is the system that we have operated with here ever since the American Revolution in 1776. We were never bothered with feudalism in the United States to any degree. We went right over to a form of capitalism from the start. And capitalism in many ways has done a splendid job; don't let's forget that.

But I think it has performed its task by developing the country in a technological sense, by bringing about the big industries and the new industries, and that it is time, finally, for socialism to take over.

CITRON: Well, Corliss Lamont, it's been a great privilege and very informative—certainly to me—to hear your views, which have taken sixty years to formulate, sixty years tonight. And I, needless to say, find some of your points of view I agree with; many of them I do not. But it's been interesting to take both sides of all these arguments. And I've certainly appreciated your taking time off in the last hour of your 60th birthday to come and talk to us here at the Pierre.

LAMONT: I've enjoyed it very much, Casper, and appreciate the chance, always, to talk with you.

Afterthoughts

In my autobiographical interview with Casper Citron, I was able to cover almost all of those fundamental interests and causes that have meant most to me during the first sixty years of my life.

We did not have time, however, to discuss the love and appreciation of Nature which have played a major role with me ever since I was a Boy Scout during the happy days of my youth in Englewood, New Jersey. My troop there took long hikes in the nearby woods, often on trails along the top of the Palisades of the Hudson. Thus it was that I early came to know intimately the rugged splendor of those cliffs and the magnificent views from the dramatic, rocky lookouts rising sheer above the river.

In the summer of 1914, when I was twelve, my father and mother took the whole family to a Montana ranch in the middle of the Rocky Mountains. From our cabins we could see snowcapped peaks in the distance. We rode horseback a great deal and sometimes went on camping trips into the exciting mountain country, our guide always carrying a rifle and constantly on the alert to the danger of a roaming bear. I learned, too, that summer the pleasures of trout-fishing while wading down the bed of a rushing stream and casting the fly into deep, eddying pools shaded from the sun.

Again, in July and August of 1915, our family traveled to the West, this time to White Pelican Lodge on the shore of Lake Klamath in Oregon. During these two extended trips to the Rockies, my parents introduced us to Crater Lake National Park, Glacier National Park, and Yellowstone National Park. I was thrilled by the beauty of these great outdoor recreation centers, and since that time have visited as many national parks as possible. I am convinced that America's broad network of state and national parks surpasses any comparable public park development in any country in the world. One of my pleasantest assignments at present is that of serving as a member of the Committee on the Appreciation and Conservation of Nature of the American Humanist Association.

Returning to the subject of the Palisades, about which John Masefield wrote his splendid poem, "The Western Hudson Shore," I should record that in 1929 my parents moved to a big house atop those cliffs near Sneden's Landing, New York, and lived there for close to twenty years. When my mother died in 1952, she willed to my younger brother Austin and me a score of lovely woodland acres fronting on the Palisades, and stipulated that this property should be maintained permanently in a wild and natural state. The Audubon Society of Nyack is the official custodian of this Lamont Sanctuary. I am its supervisor, and I take much pleasure in keeping the trails in good condition, sawing through and clearing away the trees that occasionally fall across them.

Exercise in the open air has always been my chief recreation; and I equally enjoy hiking, canoeing, skating, tennis, sailing, and surf bathing along a sandy beach. The queen of sports for me, however, has for many years been skiing. Since it is a bit dangerous, each December I say to myself that I am really getting too old for it. But when the snow starts to fall again on those beckoning slopes in New England and the Catskills, I am simply unable to resist the temptation. Ski weekends with friends or family have been among the greatest joys of my life.

The recognition of Nature's wonder and magnificence is not merely a personal enthusiasm for me, but is also a basic part of the philosophy of naturalistic Humanism. Humanists can find no Divine Father in or behind Nature, but Nature is truly our fatherland. We rejoice profoundly in the inexhaustible beauties and possibilities of this earth which is our home. We feel a deep kinship with the cosmos and with the myriad forms of life upon this planet. In our aesthetic and emotional response to a glorious sunset, to the infinite expanse of shining stars, to a foaming waterfall framed in evergreen, to the simple beauty of white dogwood or red roses, we Humanists attain a sort of naturalistic mysticism.

The appreciation of Nature, however, is by no means the only way in which the ordinary sensitive person can experience a state of what I like to call normal mysticism. With no supernatural explanation necessary, the spiritually alert individual frequently achieves natural ecstasies that bring an exalted and intensified sense of life. Listening to a Beethoven symphony, looking at Michelangelo's frescoes in the Sistine Chapel, viewing the skyline of New York City, reading one of Shakespeare's sonnets, knowing the thrill of artistic or literary creation, or being overwhelmingly in love—these consummatory experiences and many others constitute ultimate fruitions of the spirit and give to human life richest meaning.

Just as significant as such experiences is the feeling of joy in work, the deep satisfaction of liking your job and realizing how it contributes to the advancement of your fellow-man. As a Humanist, I reject the superficial view that all human actions are motivated by self-interest. To say that a brave soldier willing to give his life for the defense of his country, or a parent glad to make repeated sacrifices for the sake of his children, is moved primarily by personal self-interest is a shallow oversimplification and runs counter to the obvious facts of human nature. All normal people are capable of powerful emotions of altruism that come into play not only during periods of social crisis, but in the day-to-day problems of living in a family and in a society. The fact that you always act *as* a self does not necessarily mean that you must always act *for* self.

My common-sense ethical philosophy, then, is that men and women should intelligently *combine* self-interest and social altruism throughout their lives. Clearly, self-regard in the sense of keeping healthy, acquiring an education, and enjoying plenty of recreation is something to be encouraged for the welfare of both the individual and society. But in addition everyone ought to be concerned with the larger social objectives such as the good of his family, his city, his state, his country, and the world at large. The ideal of public service is one that the sincere Humanist always adheres to. And when there occurs a definite clash between personal self-interest and the social good, he puts the community first.

Long ago I discovered that the way to achieve happiness is not to seek pleasure directly, but to find work and other activities that are congenial, healthy, and socially significant, and then to let pleasure and happiness come as a by-product. If you can lose yourself, as it were, and indeed forget yourself, through absorption in an interesting craft or profession important for the community, then the chances are that the *joy in work* I mentioned earlier will overflow into your leisure hours and days, and that you will become a truly happy man. George Santayana phrases the central point with his customary acumen when he talks of interests that "so possessed the self that all thought of self was banished in pursuing them." (*The Realm of Spirit,* pp. 160–161.)

As a dissenter in the fields of philosophy, politics, economics, and international affairs, I have come into constant collision with orthodox opinion and orthodox persons, who tend to be dogmatic and intolerant. Bitter and unjust attacks have constantly been made on me; and I have been harassed by inquisitorial investigating committees of both the House and Senate, by the American Legion and by the F.B.I. Throughout these battles I have kept my eye on my main objectives of helping to establish complete democracy and civil liberties, international peace, the philosophy of Humanism and a better life for all mankind. Whatever the strains of social conflict, I have always on the whole enjoyed a good fight in a good cause. And I have been highly amused by some of the tactics used against me by the ultra-rightists.

For instance, when I recently went to lecture in San Diego, I found that the John Birchers and their supporters had set up there a Patriotic Information Bureau—with the telephone number, AT 1-1776! If you called this number, you automatically received the "Message of the Day." That Message, the day before my speech, was to warn the citizens of San Diego that I was coming to town to spread my dangerous doctrines! As it turned out, the meeting was quite well attended, and I am sure that the free publicity given out by the right-wingers was actually helpful in this regard.

Looking to the future, I cannot conceive that I shall ever voluntarily retire from working for the significant ideals and causes in which I believe. What happens to me almost daily is that after I have finished reading *The New York Times* at breakfast, I am full of indignation over the cruelties and injustices recorded in the news. This recurring indignation serves as a great spur to action.

Also I am continually inspired by such lion-hearted individuals as Professor Alexander Meiklejohn, ninety-year-old philosopher, former President of Amherst College and outstanding writer and crusader for civil liberties; Dr. Harry F. Ward, aged eighty-nine, former Professor of Christian Ethics at Union Theological Seminary and another great civil libertarian; William Ernest Hocking, also eighty-nine, Professor Emeritus of Philosophy at Harvard and still active in the cause of peace; and Bertrand Russell, just turned ninety, internationally famed British philosopher and the world's most eminent Humanist. All of these men, whom I am privileged to know personally, have effectively kept on with the good fight, despite their advanced years. And there are many others, women as well as men, who could be mentioned in this connection.

Since we stand willing to sacrifice our lives in line of duty—whether in times of war or times of peace—we should confront resolutely lesser evils such as slander, government prosecution, or imprisonment. Fighters for freedom throughout history have had to face similar, and often worse, ordeals. And we ought to remember that American liberals and radicals have suffered comparatively little during the past three decades as contrasted with comparable groups in Europe and Asia.

These are some of the thoughts that have come to me in contemplating my sixty years of full and diversified living. Finally, I would add that as we grow older, we dissenters should grow more militant instead of more timorous about the fundamental issues. For we who have lived half a century or more have already had a most interesting and varied existence, with probably a great deal of personal happiness and fulfillment. This is certainly true of myself. No dictator, no powerful demagogue, no tyrannical government, can take away our past. True, they may interfere with our future; but the important thing is that, no matter what the personal cost, we should continue to resist evil men and evil institutions as long as our hearts go on beating.

Our permanent rebellion is not a matter of force and violence; it is the daily rebellion of our spirits against the misdeeds perpetrated by the cruel, the stupid and the reactionary. In our struggle for a happier world and a more complete democracy, we find a constant challenge to our intelligence, our ability, and our perseverance in the face of formidable obstacles. And we march forward in the comradeship of sensitive and courageous friends who are the salt of the earth.

17
The Enduring Impact of George Santayana (1964)*

The Centenary of the birth of philosopher George Santayana (1863–1952) occurred on December 16, 1963. Several magazines and professional organizations gave due recognition to this important anniversary, with *The Humanist* and *The Journal of Philosophy* both publishing special Santayana issues.

The question naturally arises at this time as to whether Santayana is likely to attain a permanent place in the history of philosophy and culture. While there will undoubtedly be considerable disagreement on this matter, I believe that his name and influence will indeed be lasting, for three main reasons: first, because of the wide-ranging nature and general excellence of his work; second, because he gives a sound, telling and comprehensive presentation of one of the great living philosophies—Naturalism or Humanism; and third, because his superb literary style makes him a joy to read and will continue to attract people whose specialty is not necessarily philosophy.

As to my first point, George Santayana undeniably was a writer of enormous creativity, covering not only the whole vast field of philosophy, but also producing poetry, plays, essays such as those in *Soliloquies in England,* a first-rate novel, *The Last Puritan,* and a volume of fascinating

---

*All books by Santayana referred to in the text were published by Charles Scribner's Sons, except *Three Philosophical Poets* (Harvard University Press).

Sonnet XI, "The Poet's Testament" (Copyright 1953 Charles Scribner's Sons), "Epitaph" (Copyright 1952 Charles Scribner's Sons) and excerpts from various books by George Santayana are used by permission of Charles Scribner's Sons.

letters. In his youth at Harvard Santayana showed genuine artistic promise in his sketches. From his earliest books such as *The Sense of Beauty* and *The Life of Reason,* he maintained the highest standards of literary quality and displayed marked intellectual mastery of relevant subject matter. It is only the last volume published during his lifetime, *Dominations and Powers,* a collection of somewhat rambling and disjointed essays, that seems to me to fall below par.

The massive corpus of Santayana's work is broader in scope than that of John Dewey, for example, in that the latter published no poetry, drama, literary essays or fiction. But Santayana's reach was narrower than Dewey's in that while he accepted and relied upon the facts and methods of science, he did not in his writings go thoroughly into the specifics of scientific method, as did Dewey in *How We Think* and *Logic: The Theory of Inquiry.* Also unlike Dewey, Santayana wrote little on the theory and techniques of education.

Regarding my second point, George Santayana's exposition of Naturalism, which he sometimes prefers to call "Materialism" and which I prefer to call "naturalistic Humanism," is in my opinion outstanding among modern philosophers. This fundamental Naturalist viewpoint runs through all of his books on philosophy and through much of his other work. Furthermore, in his revised, one-volume edition of *The Life of Reason* Santayana presents an integrated and inclusive summary of the Naturalist philosophy that can be understood by the average educated person. The broad sweep of this classic work becomes clear from its main divisions: "Reason in Common Sense," "Reason in Society," "Reason in Religion," "Reason in Art" and "Reason in Science."

This sort of philosophic synopsis is something that John Dewey, for one, never achieved. Towards the end of his life Dewey was working on such a book, but lost the only copy of his manuscript when it was about two-thirds finished. In the English-speaking world at least, comparatively few of that minority group known as Naturalists, Materialists or Humanists have taken the trouble to write over-all outlines of their philosophies that could serve to educate the public. The fact that Santayana *has* done this, brilliantly and within the pages of a single book, constitutes another reason why his fame will not soon fade.

In his elucidation of Naturalism, Santayana is at his best in demonstrating that religious supernaturalism, taken literally, is simply bad physics and misleading science, but that taken poetically it becomes significant myth and symbol with moral overtones. "Reason in Religion" embroiders upon this theme in detail and stands out as one of the most able and convincing books ever written in showing that mature and educated individuals cannot accept as fact the existence of supernatural gods, spirits, powers or immortalities of any sort. Just because this volume treats traditional religion with understanding and restraint, it is especially persuasive. For as one of Santayana's characters in *Dialogues in Limbo* (p. 181) observes, "You will never enlighten mankind by offending them."

It is important to note that Santayana's father, Don Agustin, early gave encouragement to the familiar naturalistic analysis of religion that his son later developed. I have recently read over the revealing letters, in Columbia University's special Santayana Collection, that Agustin Santayana wrote from Spain to George, who was living near Boston, between 1873 and 1893. The elder Santayana repeatedly expressed his agnostic and anti-clerical views regarding religion. One passage, written when his son had just turned 21, struck me especially: "I am firmly convinced that the time is not far off when man will no longer be able to believe in anything supernatural, and that all religions are the inventions or creations of man—*like poems.* Then there will be no cults, nor priests. There will be only a feeling of wonder at what is beyond our comprehension." (My italics—C.L.)

Santayana died in 1952 at the age of 88; and while there are some inconsistencies in his philosophic system, particularly in relation to his doctrine of essences, he maintained his basic Naturalism to the end. Unhappily, however, there are a few critics who claim that he compromised in his old age, and who purport to prove their point by special reference to the book he brought out in 1946 when he was 83 years old—*The Idea of Christ in the Gospels or God in Man, A Critical Essay.*

A good example of this type of approach is to be found in a recent study *Santayana: Saint of the Imagination,* by Professor of English M. M. Kirkwood of the University of Toronto. (University of Toronto Press, 1961.) Mrs. Kirkwood starts out well in her book by combining in interesting fashion a running biography of Santayana with a survey of the main features of his philosophy. But towards the end of her volume she goes far astray in her interpretation.

Using as her text *The Idea of Christ in the Gospels,* she writes about Santayana: "He views the universe as significant largely because it operates mysteriously so as to glorify the Good." (P. 207.) Mrs. Kirkwood blithely makes this colossal *faux pas* in the teeth of numberless assertions elsewhere by Santayana to the contrary. Sufficient to refute her is a single dictum from *Reason in Common Sense:* "Only in its relative capacity can the universe find things good, and only in its relative capacity can it be good for anything." (P. 37.)

Mrs. Kirkwood buttresses her unfortunate misunderstanding of Santayana by the following passage from *The Idea of Christ in the Gospels* (p. 80): "But when God personifies *The Good,* the heart loves him already without having named him, and the new revelation comes only in the miracle that *The Good* should prove to be also the power that ultimately governs everything."

Taken by itself, this quotation might seem to support Mrs. Kirkwood's transformation of Santayana from a complete Naturalist into a Christo-Platonic saint. But the very next sentence in his book reads: "Such is the atavistic message, the glad tidings, brought by Christ." By entirely omitting this statement, Mrs. Kirkwood gives entirely the wrong impression.

Mrs. Kirkwood repeats this unscholarly procedure at the conclusion of her chapter "A Philosopher Completes His Task," where (p. 230) she quotes with a grand flourish from Santayana's *Dialogues in Limbo* (p. 67): "Religion in its humility restores man to his only dignity, the courage to live by grace. Admonished by religion, he gives thanks, acknowledging his utter dependence on the unseen, in the past and in the present; and he prays, acknowledging his utter dependence on the unseen for the future."

Again, Mrs. Kirkwood leads the reader to think that the quotation represents Santayana's own position, failing to point out that these words were uttered by the shade of "Democritus." For of course *Dialogues in Limbo* constitutes a philosophical discussion among seven different characters, each one of whom speaks for himself and none of whom necessarily expresses Santayana's ultimate opinions.

Curiously enough, so far as *The Idea of Christ in the Gospels* is concerned, the chief offender besides Mrs. Kirkwood is the Catholic Government of Spain. After he died in September, 1952, Santayana was buried in the special Spanish section—the Tomb of the Spaniards—of Rome's big Catholic cemetery, Campo Verano. In 1959 I visited this Pantheon, with cypress trees shading it on one side, and took detailed notes.

Santayana's grave stands out noticeably because it is the only one which has a raised marble slab; and his name and dates are incised on this in letters much larger than those in the other inscriptions. It is evident that the Spanish Ambassador to Italy, who is in charge of the Pantheon, wished to give Santayana preferred status in it. The Ambassador also had a passage from Santayana translated into Spanish and placed in bold block letters on a concrete wall next to his grave.

The legend reads: *"Cristo ha hecho posible para nostros la gloriosa libertad del alma en cielo."* ("Christ has made possible for us the glorious liberty of the soul in heaven.") After some research I discovered that the words in question are a free translation of the first two lines on page 167 in Santayana's chapter "The Resurrection" in *The Idea of Christ in the Gospels*. In this chapter the author explains what the story of the resurrection means to Christians. Again, a statement is disingenuously lifted out of context and utilized on behalf of a supernaturalistic ideology in which Santayana definitely disbelieved.

Shortly after his study of the Gospels was published, Santayana became aware that it was being widely misinterpreted. Thus in July 1946 he wrote David Page, an American editor: "Now nobody—not even good critics—seem to gather what my books say. . . . They report what they themselves dreamt while their eyes perused the pages. This is particularly true of *The Idea of Christ*. This book is a perfect illustration of the view of religion that I formulated in 1900 in the Preface to *Interpretations of Poetry and Religion.*" (George Santayana Collection, Columbia University Libraries.)

In 1951 Santayana wrote a letter to Warren Allen Smith, an American Humanist, explicitly repudiating any notion that in *The Idea of Christ* he was tending toward theism. He asserts: "My Naturalism is fundamental and includes man, his mind, and all his works, products of the generative order of Nature. Christ in the Gospels is a legendary figure." (*The Letters of George Santayana*, Daniel Cory, Ed., p. 408.)

Santayana was also well aware of certain age-long peculiarities of the Catholic Church. Amid the vicissitudes of World War II, he had retired at the age of 77 to a Catholic nursing home in Rome administered by English nuns. It was called the Convent of the Blue Sisters of the Little Company of Mary. About two years before his death, when his health had become increasingly delicate, Santayana expressed some misgivings about the Blue Sisters. In Daniel Cory's words (*Santayana: The Later Years*, p. 304):

"He said that in case I happened to be away when a final relapse overtook him, I was not to be misled by any reports that were circulated about his last hours. I must remember that he was living in a Catholic nursing home where it was more or less expected that a man should die like a Christian. So if I ever heard reports that there had been a sudden 'change of heart' at the end, I was not to believe, for instance, that he had requested 'extreme unction'; but perhaps it might be difficult to avoid receiving it, especially if he were in a semi-unconscious state."

Santayana repeated this warning to Cory several times. And sure enough something of the kind *was* attempted during the philosopher's last days, although the episode is not described in Cory's book. What happened was that a Catholic nurse suddenly refused to administer morphine, which the patient, very ill from cancer, required to ease his pains, unless he called in a priest to confess him. Santayana rebuked the nurse and murmured, "I shall die as I have lived." Fortunately, Cory was in constant attendance during the philosopher's terminal illness and was able to prevent any religious hoax from going through.

In spite of his basic naturalistic position concerning the chief problems in philosophy, Santayana always remained sympathetic to the Christian Church as an institution and particularly to the Catholic Church whose majestic and colorful rituals had an aesthetic appeal for him. As the late Professor William Pepperell Montague of Barnard College put it, there can be both "anti-clerical theists," like himself, and "clerical atheists." Obviously Santayana belonged in the latter class. And there is some pertinency in the quip of a fellow-philosopher, reputed to be Bertrand Russell, "Santayana thinks there is no God and that Mary is his mother."

* * *

In August of 1950, two years before Santayana's death, I had the privilege of visiting him in Rome. About 4 o'clock on a Friday afternoon I walked halfway up the ancient, narrow, cobblestoned Via Santo Stefano Romano, on Celian Hill near the Colosseum, and entered the outside gate of the Convent of the Blue Sisters. I went on past cypress trees and a well-groomed, typically English lawn to the front door, which was opened by one of the Sisters. She ushered me into a sitting room. Santayana in his dressing gown shuffled in and took me down to the end of the hall to show me the view of the old city wall. Then we went into his own simply furnished room for tea.

We talked for two hours without interruption, as I asked him question after question about his philosophy. Santayana was 87 at this time and not in the best of health, but he seemed to me exceptionally keen intellectually. Throughout our conversation I was impressed by how alert and sparkling were his eyes.

"I was brought up on English philosophy," he said, "but it never suited me. Then when I read the Greeks, I knew that was It. The way I think is the way Aristotle and the pre-Socratic philosophers thought, in a different idiom and in a different civilization. Socrates too much moralized philosophy and prepared it only too well for the topsy-turvy system of Christianity. When I was an undergraduate at Harvard, I used to carry around a pocket copy of Lucretius's *On the Nature of Things,* which a friend had given me. I would read it on the horse car. As for modern philosophy, I think that perhaps my greatest inspiration was Schopenhauer. I like his pessimism."

Santayana spoke of how much he loved to write. "That is why I have written so much," he said. "I have written for myself," he continued, "rather than for any public. I believe that some of my best writing was done when I was preoccupied, as during the First World War in England. I would go out walking alone all day, taking along a notebook, and would lunch on bread and cheese. That is how *Soliloquies in England* came into being."

When I got up to go, I did not expect to see Santayana again; but he suggested that I come back when convenient. So I returned Sunday afternoon for another rewarding talk. This time he was dressed in a brown cassock and looked a bit like a monk.

We soon got on to the subject of Santayana's essences. For him, he told me, they were really ideas and sensations respectively intuited and felt by human beings. When he describes the essences as eternal, he does not mean that they are everlasting, but that they are outside of and above time, like the defined concepts of the triangle and the oddity of 3.

As we chatted, Santayana made caustic comments about some of his opponents in philosophy and amusing personal observations on various people he had known. Two of his great-nephews had come to see him in Rome, one of them a brilliant boy who had been head of his class at Harvard. But, added Santayana scornfully, "this promising lad has gone into the manufacture of soap!" Our philosopher even censured the Pope, remarking that perhaps he had been foolish to declare the dogma of the bodily Assumption of the Virgin Mary to heaven. Was it any better, Santayana asked, than the big lies of the Russians, who now claimed that they made practically all the great scientific discoveries?

When I said my final Goodbye, Santayana told me he had been glad to see me and that it seemed to wake him up. His parting words were: "I shall be right here next year if I am still alive."

Though Santayana became distinctly a sort of hermit philosopher during the last half of his life, he always appeared happy to have serious-minded visitors from America and elsewhere come to call. After the U.S. invasion of Italy during the Second World War, he welcomed the numerous American soldiers and officers who interrupted his solitude. I was, then, only one of many persons who had long and fruitful talks with him. However, as Professor Horace M. Kallen, who was Santayana's Assistant at Harvard, once remarked, "Santayana is like the Pope; he does not return calls." The point is that despite his retirement from teaching and social life, he remained a friendly and understanding human being. And his bachelor isolation enabled him to find the time to produce a galaxy of thought-provoking books that will continue to interest and inspire intelligent individuals for a long time in the future.

*   *   *

Coming finally to my third point—Santayana's literary style—I believe that his prose, which I regard as the most beautiful in philosophy since Plato, will be an important factor in making his influence a lasting one. His command of English is all the more remarkable because he learned the language well only after he was 14, his native tongue being Spanish. I am aware of course that some critics, of whom Father Thomas N. Munson is typical, claim that Santayana's style is "florid." *(The Essential Wisdom of George Santayana,* p. 45.) I do not find it so. Santayana not only ranks with Bertrand Russell as one of the twentieth century's most readable philosophers, but also frequently delights us with brief nuggets of wisdom that in a single sentence brilliantly sum up a deep and complex thought. I have never known a philosopher who produced so many genuine aphorisms.

Some 35 years ago when I first began the intensive study of philosophy I started a notebook, continued up the present day, in which I recorded usable short quotations from the era of ancient Greece down to contemporary times. The entries from Santayana far exceed in number those from any other thinker. I here give some typical examples that afford considerable insight into Santayana's basic tenets:*

Typical Santayana Epigrams

Men became superstitious not because they had too much imagination, but because they were not aware that they had any. (Interpretations of Poetry and Religion, p. 108.)

That rare advance in wisdom which consists in abandoning our illusions the better to attain our ideals. (Ibid., p. 250.)

Fanaticism consists in redoubling your effort when you have forgotten your aim. (Reason in Common Sense, p. 13.)

In Aristotle the conception of human nature is perfectly sound; everything ideal has a natural basis and everything natural an ideal development. (Ibid., p. 21.)

Knowledge is not eating and we cannot expect to devour and possess what we mean. (Ibid., p. 77.)

Love is a brilliant illustration of a principle everywhere discoverable: namely, that human reason lives by turning the friction of material forces into ideal goods. (Reason in Society, p. 9.)

Love would never take so high a flight unless it sprung from something profound and elementary. (Ibid., p. 32.)

There is no tyranny so hateful as a vulgar and anonymous tyranny. It is all-permeating, all-thwarting; it blasts every budding novelty and sprig of genius with its omnipresent and fierce stupidity. (Ibid., p. 127.)

The fact of having been born is a bad agury for immortality. (Reason in Religion, p. 240.)

The virtue of the Greeks lay in the exquisite firmness with which they banked their fires without extinguishing them. (Egotism in German Philosophy, p. 141.)

---

*Hundreds of additional quotations showing the epigrammatic genius of our philosopher have been compiled by Ira D. Cardiff in a Santayana anthology, *Atoms of Thought* (Philosophical Library, 1964).

A string of excited, fugitive, miscellaneous pleasures is not happiness; happiness resides in imaginative reflection and judgment, when the picture of one's life, or of human life, as it truly has been or is, satisfies the will and is gladly accepted. (The Middle Span, p. 8.)

In each person I catch the fleeting suggestion of something beautiful and swear eternal friendship with that. (Ibid., p. 111.)

The truth is cruel, but it can be loved, and it makes free those who have loved it. (Introduction to Everyman's Edition of Spinoza's Ethics, p. xix.)

Existence, while it is the home of particular certitudes, is also a cage in which an inevitable and infinite ignorance sings and dies imprisoned. (Platonism and the Spirtual Life, p. 35.)

Like Polonius's cloud, she [Nature] will always suggest some new ideal, because she has none of her own. (Reason in Art, p. 201.)

Trifles, as Michael Angelo said, make perfection, and perfection is no trifle. (Soliloquies in England, p. 43.)

Compromise is odious to passionate natures because it seems a surrender, and to intellectual natures because it seems a confusion; but to the inner man, to the profound Psyche within us, whose life is warm, nebulous and plastic, compromise seems the path of profit and justice. (Ibid., p. 83.)

The dark background which death supplies brings out the tender colours of life in all their purity. (Ibid., p. 99.)

The length of things is vanity, only their height is joy. (Ibid., p. 116.)

The necessity of rejecting and destroying some things that are beautiful is the deepest curse of existence. (Character and Opinion in the United States, p. 233.)

Reason is not a force contrary to the passions, but a harmony possible among them. Except in their interests it could have no ardour, and, except in their world, it could have no point of application, nothing to beautify, nothing to dominate. (The Realm of Matter, p. 147.)

The life of theory is not less human or less emotional than the life of sense; it is more typically human and more keenly emotional. Philosophy is a more intense sort of experience than common life is, just as pure and subtle music, heard in retirement, is something keener and more intense than the howling of storms or the rumble of cities. (Three Philosophical Poets, p. 124.)

Through the tears of the historian there often comes a smile, and the evening of one civilization is the morning of another. (Dominations and Powers, p. ix.)

Those who cannot remember the past are condemned to repeat it. (As quoted in The American Treasury, Clifton Fadiman, Ed., p. 734.)

As Professor Irwin Edman of Columbia has said, Santayana's gift "for the sentence that distils a life, an argument, or an adoration becomes unmistakable. One does not need to have these jewels in their setting to note the brilliance with which each one of them shines. . . . One would like to examine the way in which adjectives that seem merely a surface felicity, serve really to carry on the argument, while the reader is pausing over their flagrant charm. . . . Lovers of literature are enchanted (and it is a good guess that they always will be) by a prose as supple and picturesque, as musical and as just as exists in our time." *(The Saturday Review of Literature,* December 16, 1933.)

In the same article Professor Edman states that Santayana "cannot avoid the perfect cadence and the image at once glamorous and distracting in its beauty." Here I must disagree with Edman. For while I am deeply stimulated aesthetically by the rhythmic march of Santayana's prose, I am no more distracted by it than by the melody of Lucretius's verse in *On the Nature of Things.* In other words, Santayana's style carries along with it his intended meanings in all their purity and implication, making him more rather than less easy to understand. The grace of that style extends even to Santayana's letters, as can be seen in the large volume edited by Daniel Cory that I have cited. I myself received some of those marvelous letters, the first one back in 1935 and the last in 1951.

I have been discussing here primarily Santayana's prose style, but would like to add a word about his poetry, which includes some of the finest poems in the English language. There are four volumes of verse, almost all of it written during the first part of Santayana's career, while he was still a teacher at Harvard University. They are: *Lucifer,* a drama in verse; *A Hermit of Carmel and Other Poems; Poems,* including most of the sonnets; and *The Poet's Testament,* published posthumously and containing a delightful play in verse about Plato and other Greek philosophers at the court of Dionysius the Younger in ancient Syracuse.

There follow three of my favorite Santayana poems, the first a sonnet that brings out the above-the-battle quality of his character:

SONNET XI

Deem not, because you see me in the press
Of this world's children run my fated race,
That I blaspheme against a proffered grace,
Or leave unlearned the love of holiness.
I honour not that sanctity the less
Whose aureole illumines not my face,
But dare not tread the secret, holy place
To which the priest and prophet have access.
For some are born to be beatified
By anguish, and by grievous penance done;
And some, to furnish forth the age's pride,
And to be praised of men beneath the sun;
And some are born to stand perplexed aside
From so much sorrow—of whom I am one.

EPITAPH

O Youth, O Beauty, ye who fed the flame
That here was quenched, breathe not your lover's name.
He lies not here. Where'er ye dwell anew
He loves again, he dies again, in you.
Pluck the wild rose, and weave the laurel crown
To deck your glory, not his false renown.

THE POET'S TESTAMENT

I give back to the earth what the earth gave,
All to the furrow, nothing to the grave.
The candle's out, the spirit's vigil spent;
Sight may not follow where the vision went.

I leave you but the sound of many a word
In mocking echoes haply overheard.
I sang to heaven. My exile made me free—
From world to world, from all worlds carried me.

Spared by the Furies, for the Fates were kind,
I paced the pillared cloisters of the mind;
All times my present, everywhere my place,
Nor fear, nor hope, nor envy saw my face.

> *Blow what winds would, the ancient truth was mine,*
> *And friendship mellowed in the flush of wine,*
> *And heavenly laughter, shaking from its wings*
> *Atoms of light and tears for mortal things.*
>
> *To trembling harmonies of field and cloud,*
> *Of flesh and spirit, was my worship vowed.*
> *Let form, let music, let the all-quickening air*
> *Fulfill in beauty my imperfect prayer.*

In this essay I have not had the space to analyze in depth the different aspects of George Santayana's work. I have given only a brief outline of why I believe that the renown of this thinker and writer will long survive the corrosive ordeal of time. He clearly stands out as one of the greatest Naturalist or Humanist philosophers who has so far emerged in the United States.

As Santayana's co-teacher and friend in the Harvard Philosophy Department, the late Professor Ralph Barton Perry, has written: "When all is said, there is no denying Santayana's genius and his place among the immortals. It is not difficult to disagree with his opinion, or to withhold the affection which he seemed not to ask, but it is impossible not to esteem him, and pay him homage as a great mind and a great spirit. To posterity his life and work will appear as one of the redeeming features of this troubled age."

18
The Tragedy of Vietnam
Where Do We Go from Here?
(1964)

by HELEN B. LAMB

President Lyndon B. Johnson in a speech to a Labor Conference in Washington, D.C. on March 23, 1964:

> The people of the world, I think, prefer reasoned agreement to ready attack. And that is why we must follow the Prophet Isaiah many times before we send the Marines, and say, "Come now and let us reason together."
>
> And this is our objective—the quest for peace and not the quarrels of war. . . .
>
> In every trouble spot in the world this hope for reasoned agreement instead of rash retaliation can bear fruit.

Why are Americans fighting and dying in far-away Vietnam? Are we anxious to protect American investments there? Does South Vietnam have strategic raw materials which our Government thinks we need? Is the country within the perimeter of U.S. defense and security? The answer to all these questions is NO. Then why have we poured first billions of dollars and now 23,000 American troops into South Vietnam?

The official United States position, as expressed repeatedly by President Johnson, Dean Rusk and others, has been that we are there because we want to "help" South Vietnam, we want to preserve "freedom" in South Vietnam, stop "aggression" against South Vietnam, and that our troops were "invited" to come to South Vietnam as "advisers" by the duly recognized

Government of South Vietnam.

These reassuring bromides emphasizing our noble intentions cannot conceal certain stubborn facts. We are taking sides in a strictly Vietnamese civil war. We are the only foreigners directly engaged in this war. The South Vietnamese Government which we are so eager to protect is virtually our own creation, as Senator Wayne Morse (D-Oregon) has recently pointed out. The Government of Ngo Dinh Diem which "invited" our military forces into South Vietnam was thoroughly exposed to the entire world as one which did not represent the will of the South Vietnamese people, but the power-grabbing proclivities of Diem's own family clan. Since the execution of Diem by his own officers, rival military factions have fought for power—that is, for American largesse, which keeps the generals in power and the war going.

American public opinion is beginning to question the huge outlays of funds and the sacrifice of American boys for the sake of propping up unpopular "strongmen" who cannot defend themselves from their own people and so cling desperately to us. Senator Ernest Gruening (D-Alaska) addressed the Senate on March 10 concerning United States military involvement in South Vietnam, and concluded: "This is a fight that is not our fight into which we should not have gotten in the first place. The time to get out is now before the further loss of American lives." Senators Allen J. Ellender (D-Louisiana) and Morse have expressed substantial agreement with him. Others, including Senator E. L. Bartlett (D-Alaska) and Majority Leader Mike Mansfield, have urged that we welcome President de Gaulle's effort to bring about a negotiated settlement.

How the War Started

How did this endless Vietnamese civil war start? The successive beleaguered governments of South Vietnam have been challenged by the revolutionary forces of Vietnamese nationalism. These forces are intent on the overthrow of any and all right-wing governments which are tied to America's apron strings. We call the guerrilla fighters Communists (Viet Cong). Actually the overwhelming majority of these revolutionary fighters are not Communists and the program they are fighting for is not a program to establish a Communist regime.

Originally, back in 1945, when the war started, it was not a civil war but a revolutionary war of liberation from French colonialism. The Vietnamese were led by the great revolutionary, Ho Chi Minh, Vietnam's leading Nationalist and Communist. He organized the Viet Minh, a coalition of different Vietnamese political parties and interests commanding widespread support among the Vietnamese, conservatives as well as radicals. Even the

Vietnamese Catholic hierarchy in North Vietnam supported Ho's revolution.

From 1947 on, the United States tried to convert this struggle for independence from French rule into an ideological war between rival right-wing and left-wing Vietnamese factions. To do this, the United States evolved a double strategy. We tried simultaneously both to help the French defeat the revolutionary Viet Minh and to force the French to grant formal independence to a conservative Vietnamese faction. This faction was built around the reinstated Vietnamese Emperor, Bao Dai, who had obligingly served as puppet head of Vietnam under the French colonial regime, as well as under the Japanese occupation during World War II, but had abdicated in favor of the revolutionary Viet Minh in 1945. Our double strategy was bound to fail because it was contradictory. The more we helped the French against the Viet Minh the less likely were the French to relinquish their hold on Vietnam.

Vietnam's George Washington

In the end, the French were forced out of Vietnam but not by our preachments. They were defeated by the Viet Minh at Dien Bien Phu because the Vietnamese people agreed with the Viet Minh that the war was a war of national liberation from French domination. And they did not believe the United States-French-Bao Dai claims that France would give Vietnam true independence or that Bao Dai was a genuine Vietnamese patriot to whom all Vietnamese should rally. Instead of turning against Uncle Ho, as Ho Chi Minh is affectionately called, very many Vietnamese loved and revered him as their great national hero, fought for him, worked for him, and carried on their backs the supplies for his army. He is the Vietnamese George Washington. To the end, Bao Dai was regarded as a French puppet and whatever concessions were grudgingly made to his Government by the French were attributed not to the magnanimity of the French but to the strength of the Viet Minh.

Following several years of struggle with no outside assistance Ho Chi Minh finally, after 1949, got some help from Communist China, but it was a tiny trickle compared to the avalanche of aid that the French and Bao Dai got from the United States. The United States poured over a billion dollars worth of military aid and defense support into the war at that time, thus making the French-Bao Dai army infinitely better equipped than Ho Chi Minh's peasant troops. This American aid merely prolonged the agony and greatly added to the casualty lists for both France and Vietnam. It did not alter the outcome.

As the war dragged on, the French became weary and reluctant to continue the fighting. They were alienated by what some Frenchmen suspected were America's efforts to displace them in Indochina. The French press questioned why French lives should be lost in America's anti-Communist crusade. To keep the war going, the United States offered a greatly expanded military aid program. But the French will for peace prevailed and a peace conference was finally scheduled in the spring of 1954 at Geneva, attended by all the Great Powers, even intermittently by the United States, though the Eisenhower Administration hoped it would fail.

Ho Makes Concessions

It did not fail. Ho Chi Minh, a past master at negotiation and compromise, made significant concessions in order to achieve a settlement. These concessions were the provisional partition of Vietnam at the 17th Parallel, an important face-saving device for the French as it allowed them to regroup their troops temporarily in South Vietnam rather than surrender to the Viet Minh. No Vietnamese wanted this partition. Even the Bao Dai delegation was against it. Two reasons impelled Ho Chi Minh to make this concession. First, the United States was threatening to expand the war and had offered France the use of the Atomic Bomb. And second, the partition itself was supposed to be temporary.

The Geneva Accords stipulated that within two years French troops had to withdraw from South Vietnam; and that the provisional governments of the two zones, the North under Ho and the South under Bao Dai and his Prime Minister, Diem, had to give way to a new all-Vietnamese government, freely chosen in a nation-wide election supervised by the International Control Commission set up to police the Agreements. The United States alone among the Great Powers refused to endorse the Geneva Accords, though we did at that time go on record as opposing the overthrow of these Agreements by force.

What Partition Means

After Geneva, it soon became apparent that the United States planned to subvert the Geneva Accords by subtle, indirect means such as the formation of SEATO (Southeast Asia Treaty Organization), and to continue the struggle under a different guise. We refused to accept the verdict of history. Our side, the French-Bao Dai team, had lost. But we did not let them settle down peacefully to carry out the Agreements.

How would we Americans have felt if at the end of our own Civil War between the States, a foreign power had said to the defeated Southern leaders, "We will support you; we will help you get ready to fight again;

you can ignore the peace terms and we will back you up. With our help you can get your secession after all; the South should be a separate country because its institutions and ideology are fundamentally opposed to those of the North." This is precisely what we have done in South Vietnam.

This American policy of insisting that Vietnam be permanently cut in two at the 17th Parallel with no intercourse, not even trade, between the anti-Communist South and the Communist North, outrages Vietnamese patriotism because it violates the integrity of Vietnam and threatens its very survival as an independent state. Instead of one strong country it creates two weak ones, neither of which is viable. North Vietnam needs the surplus rice from the South, and South Vietnam needs coal and industrial raw materials from the North. Thus the total divorce of North and South Vietnam has forced each half to turn elsewhere for trade and aid, North Vietnam to the Communist bloc and South Vietnam to the United States.

This precarious dependence on Great Powers, which belong to different power blocs and are locked in conflict with each other, fills thoughtful Vietnamese, whatever their politics, with great anxiety for the future of their nation. Vietnam is a small country at best and suffered in the past a thousand years of Chinese domination. The Vietnamese expelled the Chinese in 939 A.D. and maintained their independence except for short interludes until the French conquest beginning in 1858 and ending in 1954 with the country's partition. This division, so fraught with danger for the Vietnamese people, is like a time bomb.

What Price Confrontation?

The American policy of maintaining tension in this area through a hostile confrontation between North and South Vietnam has created in South Vietnam a country which cannot possibly stand on its own feet. South Vietnam has a smaller population than North Vietnam. The role the United States assigned to South Vietnam was that of virtually declaring war on North Vietnam. South Vietnam cut off all trade and normal relations between the two zones, making it necessary to build a military establishment way beyond the capacity of South Vietnam's own slender resources. South Vietnam has thus become chronically dependent on the United States. In consequence, the leaders of South Vietnam, from Ngo Dinh Diem on, have had to bear a double cross, the cross of being called American puppets and the cross of being held responsible for the continued partition of their country.

In addition to everything else that is wrong with a policy that insists on creating a sanitized anti-Communist bastion of the "Free World" out of South Vietnam, this policy of the U.S. made civil war in the South inevitable. Why? Because it involved a vigorous effort to root out all pro-

Ho Chi Minh sentiment in the South where he had and still has much support. In fact, before 1954 large areas of the South had been governed by the Viet Minh, which had already put through agrarian land reforms. Diem's Government tried to turn the clock back. With Diem's army, sent into the countryside to purge all those who had helped the Viet Minh or benefited from Viet Minh reforms, marched the landlords demanding back rents. There were protest demonstrations and brutal police repression until finally many in the rural areas, including members of the Cao Dai and Hoa Hao religious sects, fled to the jungles to organize an armed resistance.

A Grassroots War

This current revolution was made in South Vietnam. To quote from the famous French authority on Vietnam, Philippe Devillers:

> The point of view of most foreign governments, in the West especially, is that the fighting going on in South Vietnam is simply a subversive campaign directed from Hanoi. The DRV [Democratic Republic of Vietnam, i.e., North Vietnam], unable to get the better of Diem by means of diplomacy, and not daring to resort to direct action, has chosen to attempt to overthrow him from within, sapping tirelessly the foundations of the regime and spreading terror.
>
> The hypothesis is certainly a plausible one (and to formulate it serves the purposes of Communist propaganda); but it leaves out of account the fact that the insurrection existed before the Communists decided to take part, and that they were simply forced to join in. And even among the Communists, the initiative did not originate in Hanoi, but from the grass roots, where the people were literally driven by Diem to take up arms in self-defense.
>
> (From *The Chinese Quarterly*, Jan.-March, 1962)

The civil war has jettisoned all possibility of South Vietnam's becoming a showpiece for Western-style prosperity and freedom. It postponed indefinitely the emergence of those fragile exotic plants, civil liberties and Western parliamentary democracy. Because of the way the war has been conducted, the countryside has become increasingly aroused against the successive governments of South Vietnam and their American backers. Both sides use terror in this dirty war, but the government side has more terrible means for the mass extermination of people, livestock and crops. It has used poison chemicals, napalm bombs and long-range artillery supplied by the United States. Powered by American planes, death and destruction

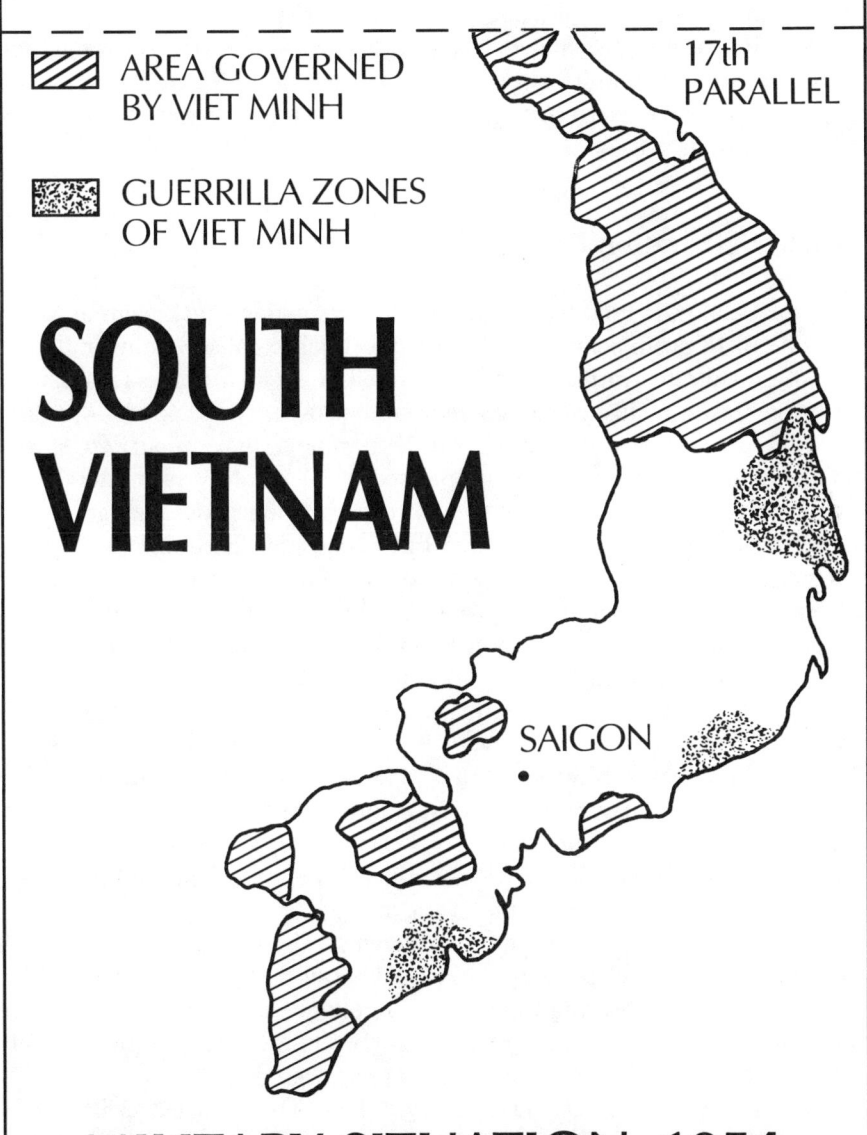

rain from the sky on a village's entire civilian population—on guerrilla fighters and passive bystanders, the rich as well as the poor peasants, the Catholics and the Buddhists, women, children and old men. These tactics suggest that the Government gave up long ago any hope of "winning" the people to its side.

What Is Liberation Front?

By the crucial year 1960 the Diem tyranny was under attack from all sides. A group of 18 prominent South Vietnamese intellectual and political figures issued a manifesto April 26th criticizing the Government for its total failure to bring freedom, justice, democracy and prosperity to South Vietnam. Even the military were disaffected. On November 11th a *coup d'etat,* staged by dissident army officers, was suppressed by General Nguyen Khanh, the present dictator. The failure of these efforts to bring about changes in the Government and the repression which followed led more and more Vietnamese to join the guerrillas, either from dislike of the Diem regime or fear for their personal safety. On December 20th, 1960, the guerrillas organized the National Liberation Front to coordinate the fighting against the Diem regime and to get some consensus on possible peace terms.

Like the former Viet Minh, the Front is a coalition of many groups—religious, ethnic and political—with several political parties, of which the Communist Party of South Vietnam plays an outstanding role. The main support for the Front comes from those South Vietnamese who have suffered most under the Diem rule—the poor peasants, certain Buddhist sects, the Cambodian minority and the ethnic tribes who live in the high plateaus. The Front's program reflects the needs and wishes of its present members as well as their desire to get more adherents. This means it is the typical program, not of a class war, but of a liberation movement against the tyranny of the overbearing South Vietnamese Government and its foreign sponsors. Therefore it has something for everyone and postpones really difficult controversial issues until freedom has been won.

At the head of the Front is Nguyen Huu Tho, a noted civil liberties lawyer, who during French rule had defended Vietnamese patriots arraigned before the courts of Saigon for their political activities on behalf of Vietnam's freedom. In 1950 he organized demonstrations against American arms shipments to Saigon, for which he was jailed by the French. After 1954, he became Vice President of the Peace Movement of Saigon-Cholon, working for the full implementation of the Geneva Accords. Considered subversive by the Diem Government, he was arrested in September, 1954, and held without trial until the guerrillas freed him in 1961. With no political affiliation himself, he heads the Front's committee of leaders from different political parties, religious sects and ethnic minority groups as well as representatives for different sectors of the population—students, women, peasants and so on.

Why the Front Has Grown

The Front has grown in a short time into a large organization, estimated to contain some 300,000 full and part-time fighters and from four to five million supporters, according to A.P. correspondent Malcolm Browne (*Providence Journal,* Feb. 9, 1964).

The Vietnamese people are attracted to the Front's program and propaganda. The Front makes peace proposals instead of war proposals. It advocates neutralism as a means of stopping the war and insuring Vietnam's independence. It demands that normal trade relations be resumed between North and South Vietnam and that ultimately negotiations take place between the two areas looking toward the reunification of Vietnam. It outlines a postwar program of economic development and social and political reform. It calls for a great extension of freedom by the removal of all restrictions which have been imposed by the South Vietnamese governments since 1954 on groups, local communities and individuals. Let us analyze the content of Front propaganda and compare it with the South Vietnamese Government's own propaganda line.

The most effective propaganda is of course the propaganda of deed and example. What is the tone of life in Saigon, controlled by the Government, and in the countryside that is controlled by the Front? In Saigon there are increasing extremes of wealth and poverty; new building is mostly luxury apartments. There are many signs of high life and Western influence— gambling and prostitution; and the twist, American jazz, American movies and American soldiers with a lot of money to spend. Everywhere there is evidence that the South Vietnamese Government depends heavily on the United States—3 billion dollars' worth of American aid since 1954, mostly in the form of imported consumer goods and weapons. Corruption and graft have become matters of common knowledge. According to the reports in the American press, the Saigonese appear to be either cynical or indifferent as to the succession of military *coups.*

Out in the rural areas where the Front is strong, equality is the keynote; all are poor. There is no corruption and no luxury. Life is difficult, austere and rigorous. People work hard and become fanatically dedicated to the cause of the Front. Instead of being dependent on handouts from abroad, they are very self-reliant and even improvise primitive weapons of their own. There are no foreigners in their midst. In consequence, their movement is an all-South Vietnamese movement and their cause that of patriotically ridding their country of all foreign—that is, American—interference.

What about North Vietnam?

American commentators assert repeatedly that North Vietnamese troops have committed aggression by invading the South. If this were so, it would not be a matter of foreign aggression, as North Vietnamese are still Vietnamese. But is it so? *New York Times* reporter David Halberstam reported on March 6, 1964, "No capture of North Vietnamese in the South has come to light."

To be sure, former Viet Minh soldiers are now fighting in South Vietnam, but they are South Vietnamese according to United States officials *(New York Times*, June 18, 1963). These are the Viet Minh regulars who had to regroup in North Vietnam under the Geneva Agreements of 1954. They thought they would be returning to their families in the South in 1956 after the promised elections. When Diem and the United States blocked these elections, many of these South Vietnamese filtered homeward over the famous Ho Chi Minh trail through the jungle of Laos. The Front does not need soldiers from North Vietnam. It is an insult to the South Vietnamese to imply that they do not make as dedicated, competent and militant fighters as their northern compatriots—when they are on the side of Vietnamese freedom. As to their supply of weapons, the United States made an official breakdown of a cross-section of weapons taken from the Viet Cong and only one in fifty came from the Communist bloc, as reported in the *Baltimore Sun*, Oct. 14, 1963, by its Far Eastern correspondent, Louis R. Rukeyser.

The whole rationale of guerrilla warfare presupposes that success depends on the support of the people, on raising local issues meaningful to the people, on local leaders and local self-reliance, with weapons either homemade or captured from the enemy. Peasants fight because they are defending their homes. So the Front stations its recruits in their own locale, whereas the government, fearing its soldiers may defect, stations them far away from their home base. The guerrillas destroy roads and bridges because these are the means of supplying the government troops, not the guerrillas' own forces.

The guerrillas fighting courageously in South Vietnam against such great odds know, however, that they have the unqualified moral support of all the socialist countries. Many student and peace organizations in non-socialist countries, even including the United States, have passed resolutions condemning the war and proposing an international conference to bring about peace through compromise and negotiation. The members of the Front have naturally the greatest sense of solidarity with their North Vietnamese compatriots who have a very special interest in the victory of the Front. This victory would mean not only the end of American interference in South Vietnam, but also the resumption of normal trade relations between North and South Vietnam looking toward ultimate reunification of Vietnam. These goals mean as much to a North Vietnamese as to a South Vietnamese. But the concrete aid that the North has provided for the struggle in the South seems to be slight, aside from educational and training facilities accorded South Vietnamese who manage to get to the North.

Coup Follows Coup

While the Front has grown stronger since 1960, the Government of South Vietnam has grown weaker, and its dependence on the United States has consequently increased. The attempted *coups d'état* in 1960 and 1962 failed, but were followed by others in 1963 and 1964 which were successful. These self-appointed military cliques kill or jail their predecessors, so that the only real thread of continuity in South Vietnam today is the American presence and American power, to effect American policies. Each clique clutches for our favor and announces that it wholeheartedly supports the American position. As long as the United States continues to pour men and money into South Vietnam, there will always be some Vietnamese who, with hands outstretched for more aid, will parrot the United States line on the war.

The relationship of all these governments to the United States has been basically that of a parasite to its host—with certain surface differences in the relationship being registered from one regime to the next. Diem and his brother Nhu wanted American money but not American advice. Diem was an obstinate, proud man absolutely sure he knew what was best for Vietnam, and so inevitably collided with American advisers who were equally sure that only they knew what was best for Vietnam. Diem and especially his smart brother Nhu became increasingly exasperated with American interference in how to win the war against the guerrillas, how to run the Government, and how to handle the Buddhist crisis. Their growing hostility to America tended to veil the Government's dependence on the United States and thus took some of the curse off the Front's charge that Diem was nothing but an American puppet. Friction mounted with the continued failure of the joint U.S.-Diem effort to destroy the guerrillas.

Finally, in the summer of 1963, the United States decided that the Diem regime had to go. We called for a "change in personnel"—just as if South Vietnam were the Ford Motor Co. and we its leading stockholders. Then by quietly discontinuing the commercial aid program, ultimate source of the military budget, we stirred the generals to act. We sloughed off Diem because he was not sufficiently puppet-like. With this "lesson" before them, the successors to Diem are not likely to get out of line.

The United States has leaped to recognize each new government in turn, and American officials solemnly announce on each occasion that *this* government represents the will of the South Vietnamese people. When our protégé, Diem, was overthrown, the population of Saigon went wild with joy and showered the military Junta with flowers and kisses. But this demonstration represented relief over the end of the Diem tyranny rather than support for the generals who succeeded it. Three months later when the Junta was itself overthrown, no one, Vietnamese or American, lifted a finger in its defense. For the new dictator, General Khanh, there were neither flowers nor kisses. The weary Saigonese merely asked, "General Khanh—who is he?" On the evening of his *coup* and the next day, General Khanh spent his time not in rallying the population to his leadership but, closeted with U.S. Ambassador Lodge, arranging for the continuation of American aid, which was quickly granted.

Khanh Acquires a Fortune

Shortly thereafter, General Khanh boasted that he had $10,000,000 and could therefore flee the country and lead a life of ease if he wanted to *(New York Herald Tribune,* Feb. 3, 1964). So far, he has chosen to remain and become the hero of *Life* magazine, which quotes an American "adviser's" description of Khanh as follows: "He is a hell of a fighter. He is the kind of leader who goes out into the field with his men and kicks them in the rear." (Feb. 14, 1964.)

American officials and General Khanh are still in the honeymoon stage. We praise him to the skies and he reciprocates. He asks our advice and he follows it, even to dispensing candies to the kiddies. According to newspaper reports he admits that the anti-Communist cause has no chance of survival without the most wholehearted United States support, and says, "Unfortunately, he [Ambassador Lodge] is the number one man in Saigon." *(New York Times,* March 13, 1964.)

Whenever General Khanh travels into the countryside, he is flanked by American army men or diplomats. It looks as if we were trying desperately to sell Khanh as our man to the doubting Vietnamese public. How can American officials be so naive? As the London *Times* pointed out last Sept. 3, ". . . anyone put into power by the Americans, or any other foreign power, would almost automatically forfeit any hope of gaining mass backing." The American embrace may well be the kiss of death for General Khanh in this sense.

Unquestionably the General is overdoing his puppetry. One wonders if he is not a veritable agent of the Front! For hasn't each new government clique accused its predecessor of working for neutralism and an accommodation with North Vietnam, i.e., of being a "traitor"? Perhaps the next dictator will so accuse General Khanh.

Civil Liberties for Whom?

Freedom is a great slogan used by both sides to rally people to their cause. Freedom from American intervention is the goal of the Front; freedom from Communism is the slogan of the Government. In the realm of specific civil liberties both sides claim to stand for the basic freedoms: freedom of speech, of religion, of assembly, of the press, and of political and trade union organization. The Front has the advantage of being the party not in power in Saigon. Government spokesmen cannot obscure their own very bad record on individual and group liberties. None of these basic freedoms has been respected.

General Khanh and the Junta before him inherited the whole Diem apparatus of tyranny and have not yet cleaned house. There are today some 28,000 political prisoners who are still in jail and who have never even been brought to trial. Under Diem the elections were rigged. Since Diem, there has been an out-and-out military dictatorship, with no elections in sight. General Khanh, the leader of the moment, brands all who disagree with him as either Communist or neutralist traitors. Even South Vietnam's top generals were held under house arrest, though no evidence had been presented against them.

General Khanh thus demonstrates a total disregard for due process of law in contrast to Nguyen Huu Tho, the head of the Front, whose efforts on behalf of civil liberties are well known. General Khanh's "freedoms" tend to be of the never-never-land variety, since they wait on final victory and unconditional surrender, conditions which appear daily to be more remote. In the meantime, General Khanh advocates not more freedom but more repression, reviving Diem's secret police and the hated strategic hamlet program renamed "new rural life program."

Government by Threat

The people of South Vietnam have been uprooted from their homes, impressed into forced labor, the peasants herded into "strategic hamlets" long distances from their fields. Here they live under police surveillance and under constant fear of reprisals because of their relatives in the Front. More and more hamlets have gone over to the Front, which besides the abolition of these practices advocates a return to village autonomy. The Front wants to accede to the villagers' desire to elect their own officials instead of having an army of government civil servants foisted on the village from above.

The freedom that is denied to individuals likewise is withheld from private enterprise. True, business firms cannot be driven into concentration camps, but can be and are subject to blackmail, as they were under the other anti-Communist governments of South Vietnam. Import licenses have been cancelled because the importer's politics were distasteful to one or another dictator. Now the Government has threatened to confiscate French investments in South Vietnam—banks, rubber plantations and a few industrial plants—unless these firms not only subscribe to the Saigon Government's present politics, but also put pressure on de Gaulle to make France do likewise! *(New York Times,* Jan. 23, Jan. 26, 1964.)

In contrast to the Government's threats to private investment and enterprise, the Front has offered protection to business interests, even foreign concerns, provided they play a productive role in the future economy of Vietnam. This is in line with its desire to obtain the broadest possible support, passive if not active, for its struggle against United States domination of South Vietnam. The rubber plantations have been forced to pay double taxes—to the Front in the countryside and to General Khanh's Government in Saigon. No wonder business wants a peace settlement!

The propaganda of the various South Vietnamese governments, one suspects, has been pitched to win not the Vietnamese, but American audiences —and assistance. Each ruling clique tries to make the issue Western Capitalist Democracy *vs.* Communism. Both these concepts are abstractions which have very little meaning to the average Vietnamese. The people, save for a few Western-educated intellectuals more at home in New York than in Vietnam's rural districts, have had no experience with Western political institutions. They have experienced, however, the South Vietnamese Government's curious amalgam of extolling freedom in theory but denying it in practice, and they are against it.

Freedom in Fact

Let us take, for example, the Montagnards, tribesmen who live in the mountains of South Vietnam, and whose culture, language and economy are entirely different from those of the lowland Vietnamese. They do not want rhetoric about the virtues of a two-party system. They want concrete safeguards for their distinctive way of life—and these the Front has promised. They want the right to dress as they please, wear long hair, live in the tribal long house instead of single family dwellings, use their own language in schools and courts, keep their old land-holding relationships and their inheritance of property laws. In all this they seek ethnic and cultural autonomy as it has already developed in North Vietnam where the Government, unlike that of the South, allows cultural diversity. The North has retained some of the old safeguards which the French provided against the ruthless Vietnamization of these primitive people.

The one great positive freedom which the Vietnamese do understand and have fought to achieve is not individual freedom—this is a Western import—but group freedom, especially the freedom from foreign domination. In the Vietnamese struggle against French colonialism, the Communist, Ho Chi Minh, was the great national hero and leader. Therefore, people associate national fulfilment and freedom with Communist leadership. No comparable leader to Ho Chi Minh has emerged in South Vietnam—Diem saw to that. Ho is admired and honored by millions of Vietnamese, both in the North and in the South, whether they are or are not Communist.

In areas where subject peoples have had to fight to win independence from their colonial masters, a term in jail becomes a badge of patriotism and an essential ingredient of the claim to leadership in the country's future. Nguyen Huu Tho meets this specification. None of the leading figures of any of the governments of South Vietnam since 1954 can qualify in this respect. They all either worked as administrators for the French or fought in the French colonial army against their own compatriots.

U.S. Objective: What Is It?

To the war-weary general public in Vietnam, peace is the paramount issue and the Front has captured it. The Front proposes an immediate cease-fire and a negotiated peace between contestants. The successive South Vietnamese governments, though unable to defeat the Front, have talked belligerently of fighting to the bitter end. Nothing less than total victory and unconditional surrender will do. The United States, which is the power behind General Khanh's shaky throne, has never proposed an over-all settlement. It is unclear for what goals we are urging the Vietnamese to fight so bitterly. As Stanley Karnow pointed out in the *Herald Tribune* (March 1, 1964), "What constitutes a satisfactory solution is something Washington will have to define just as it has yet to describe clearly its ultimate objective in Vietnam."

Why have we made no proposals for a settlement? Why is there no urgency to restore peace to this war-torn land, no suggestion of willingness to negotiate, no hint that we would be willing to make compromises if the other side did likewise? The United States is using South Vietnam as a guinea pig for trying out and testing under fire new weapons, equipment and tactics with which to fight guerrilla uprisings everywhere. If the war ended we would cease to have our "laboratory." Is this why there is no

American urgency for peace?

Why are the Vietnamese generals so reluctant to formulate peace proposals? Generals everywhere are trained to make war, not to negotiate settlements; the latter is the diplomat's job. Peace has certain very real hazards for the Vietnamese military. The generals would have to relinquish their power to civilian authorities. General Khanh says he would like to do this but would he? The end of the war would bring a drastic cut in the military budget because American aid would cease or be much reduced and because a truly civilian government would want to use most of South Vietnam's meager resources for economic development. Peace would thus mean that the power, prestige and pocketbook of the military clique would suffer. Is this why General Khanh offers mobilization for total war to the war-weary Vietnamese, and threatens to shoot or jail for life all those whom Khanh considers to be slackers? (*New York Times,* March 19, 1964).

Front Urges Negotiations

In contrast to the Government's reluctance to discuss peace, the Front has consistently advocated a negotiated settlement. Many Vietnamese welcome the Front's peace proposals, irrespective of their merits, simply because the people are so anxious to have peace. Actually the proposals do have the great merit that they are based on a true estimate of the facts. The main reality in South Vietnam is that the war is a *stalemate,* with the power of people and numbers on one side, and the power of superior material on the other. In the present contest there is a striking parallel with the former war between the Viet Minh and the French; today the Front controls most of the countryside at night, as the Viet Minh did formerly, while by day the Saigon Government controls the cities and the main roads, much as the French did. This stalemate is endless because if the United States tries to upset the balance by attacking North Vietnam, the war will be extended to a higher level of horror, since both sides can play the deadly game of escalation. The stalemate means that no one is going to win an unconditional surrender. If ever there is going to be peace, it can only come by a negotiated settlement in which both sides make compromises and adjustments.

The Front has proposed as a compromise the setting up of a new coalition government composed of representatives of the existing government, the Front and other Vietnamese organizations. General elections would follow, the franchise to be universal. The idea of compromise is spelled out further in the middle-of-the-road character of the program for economic development. The Front proposes that it be neither capitalist nor communist, but a mixed economy which permits private enterprise and promotes agrarian reform and economic planning.

It is vital to end this war by compromise, either the Front's or some other growing out of the peace negotiations which must come sooner or later. After a civil war, the soldiers do not retreat behind different national barriers; they have to settle down and live with one another in their own war-torn country. Compromise suggests self-respect and face-saving for all. It is the very antithesis of the "arrogance of victory and the venom of defeat," to use E. M. Forster's phrase, which could poison the atmosphere for generations to come. Therefore the quality of the peace, as well as the possibility of peace, depends on a negotiated settlement.

Neutralism Is Favored

Neutralism is tremendously popular in South Vietnam as the means for ending the war and safeguarding the peace. The Front has proposed it as part of its over-all compromise. As a neutral, South Vietnam would treat all countries alike—Communist as well as non-Communist. Neutralism means keeping all governments at arm's length, not allowing South Vietnam to be caught up in any nation's suffocating embrace. This would not preclude American aid or trade in moderation. It would preclude the stationing of troops by the United States, China or any other foreign country on South Vietnamese soil. Neutralism would commit South Vietnam to independence and self-reliance. If South Vietnam's neutralism were guaranteed by the Great Powers, those Powers would be committed to observe and honor this independence, and to check one another.

The desire for neutralism in South Vietnam is very strong and has existed for some time. It requires the withdrawal of American troops from the entire area. This is ardently desired even by some Vietnamese who are opposed to a formal commitment to neutralism by South Vietnam. They believe this American withdrawal would help to get the South Vietnamese Government—whichever general is in power at the moment—to the conference table. Ho Thong Minh, who runs the influential Paris journal, *Pour le Vietnam,* stresses this point particularly: that if only the Vietnamese are left alone, they can resolve their differences whether within South Vietnam or between North and South Vietnam. The American military presence stiffens the South Vietnamese government clique to the point where it is unwilling to entertain any thought of compromise and negotiation.

Neutralism is also valued in South Vietnam for its own sake. After all, neutralism is not an exclusively Vietnamese phenomenon, but rather represents a widespread longing of countries everywhere to steer clear of power politics and war. The alternative to neutralism is membership in a bloc. But for small, weak countries newly emerged from colonialism, this bloc membership means not partnership between equals but dependency, and evokes the specter of colonialism. Furthermore, a neutralist foreign policy represents the nation's best chance of survival, in the considered judgment of the leaders of many countries in Asia and Africa. Neutralism means offending neither side. Because little wars are safer than big ones, the Great Powers tend to work out their rivalry with each other via the small, weak countries which thus sink to being mere pawns. This is what neutralism tries to avoid.

The United States should understand this desire of new nations to avoid entangling alliances. When our country was young and weak we adopted this same foreign policy. But now our officials take the patronizing view that countries espousing neutralism are misguided and do not understand their true self-interest. By inference, only *we* know what is best for *them*. Despite U.S. pressures, most of the peoples of Southeast Asia have already adopted a neutral stance—Burma, Indonesia, Laos and Cambodia. Even Thailand (Siam) has a strong neutralist minority. Neutralism is in the Thai blood; Siam alone avoided becoming a colony in the 19th century, and achieved this feat by being a buffer between rival colonial Powers, the French and the British.

Government Fears Neutralism

As the Front has grown, so has the desire for neutralism, both within and outside the Front. The sentiment for neutralism has been very strong in the Vietnamese exile community in Paris, a community small in numbers and representing the well-educated business and professional people who were able to escape from the Diem tyranny. The leaders in this community have had political careers in Vietnam. Some of these have formed the influential Committee for Peace and the Reconstruction of South Vietnam under Tran Van Huu, former Prime Minister in Bao Dai's regime. This committee is working for the neutralization of South Vietnam. The repression of free speech and the press was so great under Diem that this Vietnamese exile community in Paris represented about the only opposition voice of the Vietnamese people other than that of the Front. While not all the Paris exiles are of one voice, a neutralist South Vietnam has become the dominant note.

After the *coup d'etat* in the fall of 1963 the repression in South Vietnam lifted temporarily and new viewpoints were allowed expression. Leading Buddhists, especially those from Central Vietnam where Buddhism is strongest, spoke out in favor of neutralism. So did some representatives of the Cao Dai religious sect. A new newspaper appeared, advocating neutralism, and was quickly suppressed. Alarmed at the widespread growth of neutralist sentiment, General Khanh cracked down and on Feb. 14, 1964, published a decree stating that anyone advocating neutralism would be subject to a military trial. The United States likewise grew jittery over the spreading enthusiasm for neutralism. We sent the armored missile cruiser, *Providence,* up the river to Saigon to quell the rising tide of neutralist feeling. As if this show of American force could undermine Saigon's longing for peace! Now, since the ruling dictator equates advocacy of neutralism with treason, neutralism again has no voice in Saigon. But it has many silent followers.

U.S. Opposes Reunification

Apparently the United States Government is opposed to the neutralization of South Vietnam for fear that it would soon lead to the peaceful unification of all Vietnam under Ho Chi Minh. Some form of Federation between North and South is likely to take place eventually, whatever our fears, and the issue will be decided by the Vietnamese people themselves, not by Americans. United States insistence on partition (we call it the sovereignty of South Vietnam) is viewed by many Vietnamese as a typical colonial tactic of divide and rule. Long before us the French had insisted on the partition of Vietnam into three zones. As a result, one of the slogans of the long struggle for independence from French imperialism was the reunification of Vietnam.

Both North and South Vietnam taken separately, as well as Vietnam taken as a whole, have suffered from the American policy of permanent partition, trade embargo between the two zones and their perpetual confrontation. The two zones have been weakened, but in different ways. North Vietnam has stressed self-reliance and self-sufficiency—using the limited Communist bloc aid largely for industrial development—so it has had to tighten its belt and convert an undue proportion of resources to food production. South Vietnam, on the other hand, has chosen the path of increasing an already overwhelming dependence on the United States— some 75 percent of its annual budget is derived from American handouts. Foreign trade figures show this same total dependence on the United States. Year after year South Vietnam imports goods, mostly consumer goods, valued at three or four times the value of South Vietnam's exports. This may be good for American business, but it is bad for Vietnamese independence and economic development and has reduced South Vietnam to a nation of mendicants.

But it is idle and frivolous to compare and contrast North and South Vietnam. Americans committed to the policy of permanent dismemberment of Vietnam like to play this game of pitting the North against the South from every vantage point, economic, social and political. But to Vietnamese nationalists, whether they are conservative or radical, Vietnam should be one country, not two. It is just a question of how this reunification is going to be achieved—by peaceful negotiation or by war.

Even Khanh Wants Reunification

The Front proposes the reunification of Vietnam by stages, beginning with the establishment of normal relations between the North and the South, that is, the resumption of trade and visiting back and forth. Later, after a coalition government has been set up representing all of South Vietnam, not just the military clique now controlling Saigon, negotiations can take place between the governments of the North and the South. The reunification could be worked out to the extent and at the pace that the South Vietnamese Government desires. Many Vietnamese not in the Front want to explore these proposals, since they represent what the great majority of the South Vietnamese people want, according to Le Quang, a leading spokesman for the large Cao Dai religious sect in South Vietnam (*La Tribune de Génève,* Dec. 27, 1962).

Even General Khanh is now proposing the reunification of Vietnam, not by peaceful negotiations but by force of American arms. His government-inspired demonstrations feature school children bearing aloft placards reading "We Want to March North." (*New York Times,* March 13, 1964.) Any effort by the United States to extend the war by bombing or blockading North Vietnam would not reunify Vietnam but destroy it, and could unleash World War III.

We Need New Vietnam Policy

As Senate Majority Leader Mike Mansfield has urged, the United States needs to reappraise its Vietnam policy. The world of 1964 has moved a long way from the world of 1954 when John Foster Dulles launched the futile and arrogant policy of treating South Vietnam as an outpost of the United States of America. Any new policy for Vietnam should help the Vietnamese to meet their own needs as they see them, instead of attempting to manipulate these long-suffering people for our purposes. Rather than opposing their deepest aspirations for a negotiated peace, let us work toward a conference between representatives of both sides to arrange a cease-fire.

Instead of opposing neutralism as a communist plot, let us accept it as representing the longing of the Vietnamese people to live at peace with each other and with the outside world. Let us call an international conference of all the Great Powers and the countries in Southeast Asia to explore the possibilities of Vietnamese neutralism and what contributions we and others can make, so that this neutralism can be as stable and viable as possible. To what acts of omission as well as commission could and should the Great Powers commit themselves to help Vietnam and other aspirants to neutralism attain their dream of non-alignment? Instead of trying to substitute ideological confrontation between Vietnamese factions for Vietnamese nationalism, let us accept the reality of Vietnamese nationalism and of its corollary, the reunification of Vietnam. Why not work with Vietnamese nationalism instead of against it?

Accepting Vietnamese nationalism means letting the Vietnamese decide on their own what kind of economic system they want and what type of relationship they want between North and South Vietnam. The famous domino theory, which regards the countries of Southeast Asia not as independent entities but as faceless dominoes doomed to fall in unison if any one of them alters its position, violates Vietnamese nationalism and the principle of self-determination. It says, in effect, the Vietnamese cannot decide what they want for themselves since whatever they do has repercussions elsewhere. (The assumption that Vietnam alone holds the dike for an anti-Communist Southeast Asian bloc is of course a myth, since most of the countries of Southeast Asia have already gone over to neutralism.) A policy of neutralism and the reunification of Vietnam should not be regarded by Americans as a defeat for America, but as a victory for the Vietnamese—since this is what they want.

President de Gaulle has done a great service in outlining the goals for a stable settlement—neutralization of Southeast Asia, reunification of Vietnam, agreement of Southeast Asian countries to respect one another's boundaries and consent of the Great Powers to respect the neutrality of the area. De Gaulle may also be able to help in working out the concrete means of achieving this goal. He can be a broker between the rival superpowers of China and the United States, as well as between hostile factions within Vietnam. France has great knowledge of the area and its people. France has an important stake in the area—substantial foreign investments, schools and religious and cultural missions. The Vietnamese middle class speak French, not English, and value French culture and education. In France itself there are many influential Vietnamese who are identified neither with the Front nor with the Government of South Vietnam.

Loose Federation Favored

Two peaceful ways of reuniting Vietnam have been proposed so far. The Geneva Accords provided for an internationally supervised election. In 1962 a new proposal was made by the National Liberation Front and seconded by the Government of North Vietnam. This program recommends a conference between the North and South Vietnamese governments. It gives South Vietnam equal weight with North Vietnam, even though South Vietnam's population is smaller. Reunification by a conference between the two governments could result in a different kind of relationship between the North and South, namely, a loose federation as opposed to a unitary state which would result from over-all elections. The conference plan appeals to many South Vietnamese middle class elements. A federation also appeals to many Vietnamese intellectuals, those in the Front as well as those outside it, who want South Vietnam to pave the way for parliamentary democracy in Vietnam.

Because this conference proposal presupposes that a new government will be set up in South Vietnam, a government which represents a united South Vietnam, instead of one torn apart by civil war, it implies two stages for the fulfilment of any stable settlement. For this reason it evokes the ghosts of past failure. The Geneva Agreements also were supposed to be fulfilled in two stages, but the second stage, that of the elections, never took place. Anxiety over fulfilment of the second stage can be dispelled if this time the United States signs the agreement, American troops are withdrawn, and the coalition government set up in the South is one of broad representation. This is a difficult course. Is there any reason, however, to believe that it will become any less difficult the longer negotiations are postponed?

Ho Needs a Settlement

As the civil war intensifies the peasants become more politically aroused—both by the Front's activities and by the war itself—the population of Saigon more war-weary, the government soldiers more rebellious and Ho Chi Minh more uneasy. The strains of war decrease his ability to remain neutral between the U.S.S.R. and China. By stepping up the war in South Vietnam and threatening to expand it to North Vietnam, the United States is doing its utmost to push North Vietnam into increasing reliance on the power of China. Then we turn around and accuse North Vietnam of veering toward China!

An end of the war and restoration of trade between North and South Vietnam would not only enable South Vietnam to live, but would give Ho some ability to maneuver in his delicate and skillful game of balancing Russian and Chinese aid and influence, thereby maintaining Vietnam's independence. When Ho's relations with the West are resumed, he will be even better placed to build and strengthen the true independence of Vietnam so that it may evolve toward political non-alignment. In this connection, it may be recalled that Vietnamese Communists are strong Nationalists. Like the Yugoslavs, they made their revolution on their own initiative and by their own efforts.

The War Must Stop!

Whatever the outcome of negotiations, the killing in Vietnam must stop. By interfering on the losing side, our country has doomed Vietnam to a continuing civil war which would have been over long ago save for our massive transfusions of money, material and men, to the faltering governments of South Vietnam. The terrible suffering of this dirty war is on our conscience. All the homeless, all the orphans, all the widows, all the tortures by the Government's soldiers to extract information and by the guerrillas to punish the informers, all the excruciating pain of burning human flesh from napalm bombs, all the thousands of Vietnamese dead, whichever side they were fighting for—all these horrors are being multiplied by the Johnson Administration's insistence that the war must go on.

And the American dead! As this is written, latest figures are 31 killed in the first 103 days of 1964. Americans killed, wounded and missing since Jan. 1, 1963 totaled 812. (Jacques Nevard in *The New York Times*, Apr. 14, 1964.)

Not a single additional American boy should die in this dirty, undeclared war that violates America's own highest ideals, the United Nations Charter and the basic rights of peoples everywhere to self-determination!

As Senator Gruening declares, "Let us get out of Vietnam on as good terms as possible—but let us get out." (March 10, 1964.)

Postscript, January 1965

Since the first printing of *The Tragedy of Vietnam*, the dirty war has been intensified and more Americans are fighting in it. There are more widows, more orphans, more peasants slaughtered or made homeless by air raids financed if not piloted by Americans. South Vietnam's military and political deterioration continues. Even in the little territory which the Government holds (perhaps 20 percent) the Government is contested by rival war lords, a great upsurge of Buddhist militancy, and the omnipresent Viet Cong. Coup follows coup in monotonous succession.

General Khanh has only survived by outright American intervention. Yet the honeymoon is over. In a desperate effort to secure Vietnamese support, Khanh has indulged in anti-American jibes, accusing us of meddling in South Vietnam affairs. He should know!

Peace sentiment and war weariness mount. We must cease to pressure the Vietnamese to subscribe to U.S. goals and instead allow the Vietnamese to make a peace settlement among themselves which all outside powers commit themselves to respect.

H. B. L.

About the Author

Helen B. Lamb is a long-time student of Asian political and economic problems. Having received her Ph.D. from Radcliffe College in 1943, she worked as a research analyst for the Foreign Economic Administration on the U.S. Government Guide Program for the American occupation of Japan. Subsequently she joined the Center for International Studies at M.I.T. where she did research on India. Her perceptive book *Economic Development of India* dealt with the impact of British rule on India's economy. For the last two years she has been making an intensive study of Vietnam in preparation for a book on the present crisis there. She went to Paris in 1963 to interview Vietnamese political exiles in that city and summarized her findings in an article in *The Nation*, "The Paris Exiles" (Aug. 10, 1963). Dr. Lamb has taught economics at Black Mountain, Bennington, and Sarah Lawrence colleges.

19
Vietnam:
Corliss Lamont *vs.* Ambassador Lodge
(1967)

Foreword

For some five years I have been active in opposing United States military intervention in Vietnam. In 1962 and again in 1963 I helped to organize Open Letters, signed by prominent Americans, to President John F. Kennedy, urging him to make peace in South Vietnam and to withdraw all American military forces. I have signed various protests to President Lyndon B. Johnson against his waging war on all Vietnam, have written letters to the press along the same line and have made numerous speeches on the subject.

President Kennedy's policy towards South Vietnam was bad enough; President Johnson's bombing of North Vietnam, starting in February of 1965, and his general escalation of the war, made the situation immeasurably worse. I have been critical of many aspects of U.S. foreign policy ever since we refused to join the League of Nations after World War I. But never before in my lifetime has the United States Government committed such far-reaching violations of morality, international law and ordinary human decency as in its conduct in Vietnam. And never before has a President of this country so continually and consistently deceived the American people about U.S. foreign policy or been so hypocritical in his pretense of seeking peace.

For example, no sooner had the Johnson Administration (December 19, 1966), through Ambassador Goldberg at the United Nations, requested Secretary General U Thant to make extensive new efforts towards a Vietnam peace, than news reports definitely revealed that a week earlier U.S. planes had dropped bombs within the city limits of Hanoi. These air raids destroyed sizable residential areas and killed or wounded more than 100 civilians. In dispatches to *The New York Times,* its crack reporter Harrison E. Salisbury described the vast bombing damage he had seen in both Hanoi and nearby suburbs.

In *The Times* of December 27 Mr. Salisbury states: "Whatever the explanation, one can see that United States planes are dropping an enormous weight of explosives on purely civilian targets. . . . President Johnson's announced policy that American targets in North Vietnam are steel and concrete rather than human lives seems to have little connection with the reality of attacks carried out by United States planes.

"A notable example is Phuly, a town about 25 miles south of Hanoi on Route 1. The town had a population of about 10,000. In attacks on October 1, 2, and 9, every house and building was destroyed. Only 40 were killed and wounded because many people had left town and because an excellent manhole-shelter system was available."

In another dispatch, appearing in *The Times* of January 2, 1967, Mr. Salisbury tells about U.S. bombings of Phatdiem, a complex of Roman Catholic villages near the Gulf of Tonkin: "In the district as a whole, officials said, there have been more than 150 attacks since 1965. . . . A half dozen Catholic churches in the village complex have been damaged, some severely. . . . The big central cathedrals are no longer used . . . because of danger to the congregations from air attacks . . . . Phatdiem has no visible military objectives."

The Salisbury reports clearly show, I think, that the Johnson Administration was concealing the facts when it kept repeating that U.S. bombers were strafing only military targets in North Vietnam. No "mistakes" and inaccurate bombing on the part of American pilots can account for their killing large numbers of civilians, destroying hospitals, schools and churches, and laying waste to residential areas on a wide scale. The conclusion must be that the United States Air Force in North Vietnam, as in South Vietnam, has been guilty of terror tactics against women, children, peasants and civilians in general.

I have known personally only one important official directly involved in the United States aggression in Vietnam. That is Henry Cabot Lodge, U.S. Ambassador to the South Vietnamese Government during both the Kennedy and Johnson Administrations, and my classmate in the Harvard Class of 1924. The crisis in Southeast Asia is so extremely serious for both the American people and the world at large that I have taken the unusual step of writing two Open Letters on the matter to Ambassador Lodge, one in November, 1965 and another in October, 1966.

My public debates with Henry Cabot Lodge started back in 1923 when we were both members of the Harvard Debating Union and often crossed swords there. In June, 1923, I wrote an article for the college monthly, *The Harvard Advocate,* entitled "Ideas for Irreconcilables," which argued in favor of the United States entering the League of Nations. Mr. Lodge opposed this proposition. My article was partly an answer to his "Political Sentimentalists" in an earlier issue of *The Advocate.* I claimed that he had grown "morbidly sentimental about sentimentalism."

It is worth noting that in my undergraduate days I also disagreed drastically with Mr. Lodge's grandfather, the first Senator Henry Cabot Lodge, regarding his hostile attitude towards the League of Nations. My parents, too, Thomas W. and Florence C. Lamont, thought that the senior Lodge did a great disservice to America and world peace by leading the fight against the League in the U.S. Senate. Thus the Lamont-Lodge dispute stretches over three generations.

My two Open Letters to Ambassador Lodge overlap to some extent, but for the record it seems worth while to print both of them in full.

C.L. 1967

Lamont to Lodge, 1965

315 West 106th Street
New York, N.Y. 10025
Nov. 1, 1965

Ambassador Henry Cabot Lodge
U.S. Embassy
Saigon
South Vietnam

Dear Cabot:

You will recall that as classmates in the great Harvard Class of 1924 we both helped to found the Harvard Debating Union during our college days and that you and I had brisk exchanges of opinion at its meetings. Ever since that time, more than forty years ago, we have carried on a running debate concerning basic issues that have confronted our country and the world. You consistently maintained a conservative position, and before long became a prominent member of the Republican Party. I must say that in my judgment you were always one of the better Republicans.

Now our disagreement has become more far-reaching and fundamental than ever because of your active support, as American Ambassador to South Vietnam, of the Johnson Administration's cruel, illegal and immoral war of aggression in Vietnam. Furthermore, you were willing to become Ambassador a second time precisely when Marshal Ky, the new Premier of the South Vietnamese government, had proclaimed that his great hero was Adolf Hitler.

Like Secretary Rusk and the U.S. State Department, you have pretended that South Vietnam was established as a permanent independent state in the Geneva Accords of 1954, whereas you well know that the division of Vietnam into South Vietnam and North Vietnam was designed as a temporary measure and that the Accords provided for all-Vietnam elections in 1956 to unify the country. You must be aware, too, that it was the United States and its puppet, President Diem of South Vietnam, that refused to permit these elections and thus clearly violated the Geneva treaty.

As Walter Lippmann has pointed out: "While our government endorsed the Geneva agreements, and especially the provision for free elections, it opposed free elections when it realized that Ho Chi Minh (President of North Vietnam) would win them. Gen. Eisenhower states this frankly in his memoirs. Since that time we have insisted that South Vietnam is an independent nation." *(New York Herald Tribune,* April 20, 1965.) What all of this adds up to is that in this matter the United States has been guilty of double-dealing and a failure to honor its pledged word.

The inscription on the seal of Harvard is *Veritas,* a motto that has deep meaning for Harvard men. Do you really think, Cabot, that you are serving Truth when you join in distorting the meaning and history of the Geneva Accords that are so basic to understanding the situation in Vietnam?

Again, every objective observer knows that the National Liberation Front in South Vietnam, with its military arm—the so-called Vietcong—is leading a nationalist uprising supported by the vast majority of the population. The fact that Communists strongly back this revolution and share in its leadership does not nullify its indigenous character. What we have here is the resolute and unyielding effort of a former colonial people to assert its freedom. Opposing this is a white Western nation, the U.S.A., determined to re-impose shackles such as France maintained for almost a century. As the noted British historian, Arnold Toynbee, tells us, the Vietcong struggle is part of a world-wide "revolt of the 'native' majority of mankind against the domination of the Western minority."

The Vietcong guerillas possess effective modern weapons in considerable quantity, but only a trickle of arms reached them from North Vietnam (at least up to February, 1965). It is the United States that has been the main source of supply. For the guerillas have obtained their guns chiefly from deserters bringing in American-made arms or by capturing such arms from the apathetic troops of the South Vietnamese Government.

In spite of these well-recognized facts, the U.S. Government last

February, when it realized the Vietcong was winning the civil war, suddenly started intensive bombing of Communist North Vietnam on the specious ground that that country all along had been invading South Vietnam and bore the major responsibility for the troubles there. Johnson and his military advisors invented this line in order to justify their own savage aggression against North Vietnam.

This crass propaganda issuing from the White House you, Cabot Lodge, have supported all the way in public statements. In your heart of hearts, can you possibly think that this is *Veritas?* U Thant of the United Nations was right when he said in reference to Vietnam: "In times of war and of hostilities, the first casualty is truth."

You have also misled your fellow-Americans by claiming that the U.S. Government's purpose in Vietnam is to save freedom and establish democracy. In fact, starting with the brutal dictator Diem, the United States has bolstered up one puppet dictatorship after another in Saigon—nine different governments in the past two years—as successive military coups have taken place. These South Vietnamese governments rule through police-state methods of crude violence, terror and torture. None of them would have lasted a week without the military support of the United States.

Actually, the main purposes of the President and the Pentagon in Vietnam seem to be experimentation with new military weapons and strategy; the arresting of the epic struggle of the colored races to throw off the burden of the white man; and the setting up of a huge military and air base in Southeast Asia. Such a base, of course, would be a constant threat to Communist China. Incidentally, it is absurd to claim, as some Administration spokesmen have done, that China is responsible for the revolutionary upsurge in South Vietnam and for the continuance of the war.

In all frankness, Cabot, how can you sleep nights when you sanction the horrible and wholesale slaughter by U.S. bombers of women, children and peasants—of non-combatant civilians in general—throughout Vietnam? In the past few months American planes have repeatedly dropped napalm and heavy-duty bombs indiscriminately on South Vietnam villages where a few Vietcong were "reported" to be. Here is what a U.S. Air Force officer recently told the Associated Press: "When we are in a bind, we unload on the whole area in order to save the situation. We usually kill more women and children than we do Vietcong." In North Vietnam, our bombers have destroyed hospitals and patients, schools and school children, residential houses and civilians. Owing to the terrific bombings in South Vietnam, more than 600,000 destitute refugees have fled to the coastal cities.

You are among those responsible not only for the killing of scores of thousands of Vietnamese, but also for the death of more than 1,000 American soldiers who have resolutely given up their lives in this futile, useless war 10,000 miles from our Pacific Coast—a madcap adventure in which the United States has already wasted billions of dollars collected from American taxpayers. The probabilities are all against our winning this conflict, even if our trigger-happy President sends 1,000,000 troops to Vietnam. We cannot win because of the jungle terrain, because the overwhelming majority of the Vietnamese people is opposed to the U.S. intervention and because no stable, effective government can be established in Saigon.

Yet the United States build-up increases at a rapid rate. Some 150,000 U.S. ground troops are in South Vietnam, while thousands more Americans participate in the war from warships, carriers and planes located outside of the country. On June 30, 1964, a well-known U.S. diplomat was asked what he thought would be the consequences of massive American involvement in Vietnam. His answer was:

"Well, that means we become a colonial power and I think it's been pretty well established that colonialism is over. I believe that if you start doing that you will get all kinds of unfortunate results: you'll stir up antiforeign feeling; there'll be a tendency to lay back and let the Americans do it and all that. I can't think that it's a good thing to do."

My dear classmate, do you know who said that? Why, it was none other than the Honorable Henry Cabot Lodge, then serving his first term as Ambassador to South Vietnam. So now that long-suffering country is, as implied by your own words, fast becoming a U.S. colony. Are you hoping soon to become Governor of the fifty-first American state—South Vietnam?

Please consider carefully that if the President keeps on escalating this Vietnam conflict and grabbing more and more Asian real estate, the Soviet Union and Communist China will surely react with far more effective countermeasures than they have used hitherto. Herein lies a terrible danger. For continuing escalation could finally erupt into the Great Nuclear War that would bring untold devastation to the U.S.A. and many other countries. Johnson and you, Cabot, are gambling with the survival of our nation and of the human race itself.

Addressing you now as a former Senator, there is a special point I want to make: As a member of the U.S. Senate for many years, you ought to be much concerned with the prerogatives and powers of that august body as set forth in the American Constitution. Today, President Johnson is usurping the functions of both the Senate and the House of Representatives by taking this country into a *de facto* war in Vietnam and thus by-passing the Constitution's pronouncement in Article I, Section 8, that Congress alone has the power to declare and make war.

You, as an ex-Senator, should be one of the first to protest against the President's dictatorial flouting of the Constitution—an obvious illegality that is contributing towards the breakdown of democratic government in the United States. Another example of Johnson's dangerous misuse of the Executive function was his dispatch of 20,000 Marines to the Dominican Republic last spring to prevent a liberal regime from coming to power. (See Senator Fulbright's notable speech of September 15, 1965.)

I should think that you, Cabot, as a former U.S. Ambassador to the United Nations pledged to uphold its Charter and international law in general, could not but suffer many qualms of conscience in upholding the President's current foreign policy. For the Administration's brutal course of action in Vietnam flagrantly violates the Charter of the United Nations, the Geneva Accords of 1954, the principles laid down at the Nuremberg Trials of Nazi war criminals, and the 1949 Geneva Conventions of the International Red Cross dealing with the "rules of war."

As a member of the United States diplomatic corps, you cannot be unaware that President Johnson's Vietnam venture has seriously set back American influence and prestige virtually everywhere in the world. Johnson has been able, through judicious arm-twisting, to obtain token support here and there, but even America's own allies are really appalled at our Vietnamese policy. On the shelf for the duration are the pressing tasks of working out disarmament agreements regarding both nuclear and conventional weapons. And in general, to cite Walter Lippmann again, "The war in Vietnam is blocking the progress of the nations, including that of Red China itself, towards the peaceable coexistence and accommodation which is the predominant need of all the peoples." *(New York Herald Tribune, Oct. 12, 1965.)*

The way out of the Vietnam mess is clear. There must be a cessation of U.S. bombing in all of Vietnam and a general cease-fire; a peace conference that includes the National Liberation Front as an independent authority in its own right, and the various nations directly involved; and a settlement that returns to the original Geneva Accords. This would mean the complete withdrawal of the United States Army and all other foreign troops from South Vietnam; a guarantee against any foreign military bases in that country; and elections to enable the Vietnamese people freely to choose their own government in accordance with the long-established principles of self-determination.

It is often said that America would lose face if it gets out of Vietnam without winning a clear-cut victory. But the United States has already lost so much face because of its barbaric conduct in Vietnam that this argument has little merit. In all truth, our country would gain great prestige by retiring from Vietnam, just as did France and President de Gaulle when they finally agreed to Algeria's independence.

Of course, a negotiated settlement in Vietnam would be helpful to the Communist countries as well as the capitalist. The self-interest of every nation is served by peace. Thus the position I have presented is essentially pro-

American and pro-humanity. It is a position shared in general by millions of American teachers, students, writers, clergymen and workers, as well as such eminent individuals as President de Gaulle, Senator Gruening, Senator Morse, Professor Linus C. Pauling, Bertrand Russell and Arnold Toynbee.

In conclusion, then, I urge you, Cabot Lodge, to stop abetting President Johnson's evil actions and designs in Vietnam. It would be an enormous pity at this advanced stage of your career for you to fatally tarnish your reputation by qualifying as a leading War Hawk. Resign your ambassadorship and rebuild your public image before it is too late! The highest patriotism is not militaristic; it is to strive for justice and peace and that international amity which is the best assurance for America's national security. Come home and help transform the Republican Party into the great American Peace Party, opposed to U.S. military intervention in Asia, Latin American or anywhere else. On that platform you and the Republicans might well win another election.

Sincerely yours,
CORLISS LAMONT

P.S. Because of the pressing importance of the Vietnam issue, I am treating this communication as an Open Letter and am sending it to our fellow Harvard classmates.

Postscript

Lodge did not answer my letter while he was still in Vietnam. But more than 19 years later, on Aug. 2, 1984, he sent me the following note from his residence in Beverly, Mass.:

> Dear Corliss,
>
> Regarding your open letter of November 1, 1965 concerning me: You were right. We were wrong and we failed. I should have resigned sooner.
>
> Thank you for your most interesting book [*Yes to Life*] which I am reading with avidity.
>
> Best wishes always.
>
> Cabot

Lodge resigned as U.S. Ambassador to South Vietnam in the spring of 1967. He died Feb. 27, 1985.

Lodge on Vietnam

On September 13, 1966 the World Journal Tribune *of New York printed a letter from Ambassador Lodge on Vietnam. I sent a reply refuting his statements to the* World Journal Tribune; *but this newspaper, which in general supports the Lodge-Johnson position on Vietnam, refused to publish my communication. This is what prompted me to write my Second Open Letter. Lodge's letter to the* World Journal Tribune *is as follows:*

In sending best wishes to the new World Journal Tribune, I am sure I speak for many Americans who realize what this newspaper can mean to the nation as well as to New York. The fact that I am an old Herald Tribune man gives me a special interest.

This may be an appropriate time, too, to summarize why the suppression of aggression in Viet Nam is important—especially so important as to justify the present active involvement of the United States.

To give a brief answer to a big question. I submit, first that to suppress aggression is morally right since the suppression of aggression has a high priority on the list of the purposes of the United Nations which are embodied in its charter. And the United Nations Charter is the most widely adhered to code of behavior for nations.

Then, to the United Nations Charter should be added the Southeast Asia Treaty and the numerous acts by Congress on the subject which give our involvement in Viet Nam not only a moral but a legal base.

Finally, our involvement is a matter of prudence and wisdom, sagacity and self-defense.

If the Communist aggression against Viet Nam were to be successful and we were to be expelled and they were to seize the country, a situation of danger would be created which could scarcely be exaggerated and which would make our present situation seem as safe as a church.

No one recognizes this more than the leaders of the other Asian countries. They know if Viet Nam goes under, the repercussions would come soon in Thailand, the Philippines, Malaysia and Taiwan. History shows that aggression feeds on itself and that one aggression encourages another.

Do we want to wait until the aggression is lapping at the shores of Japan and Australia, bringing on the world-wide holocaust which a threat to these countries would involve?

Clearly such a defeat would shake confidence in us not only in Asia, but also in the Atlantic community. It would thus endanger peace everywhere.

Clearly, the United States is not trying to be policeman for the whole world. We are not making our stand on the peaks of the Himalayan Mountains. But neither should we wait to defend our country until the enemy is either on the sands of Waikiki Beach or on the sands of Cape Cod.

For this great Vietnamese sweep of coast, with one of the greatest food producing areas of the world at its southern end, to fall to the aggressor would be a direct threat to our security in this shrunken world.

If you look at the map, you can see this country is in the middle of Southeast Asia—a sort of strategic keystone. What happens to it affects all of Southeast Asia. But it also has a direct and vital effect on us.

The American fighting man who is here today is quite simply and plainly fighting for his country.

HENRY CABOT LODGE
U.S. Ambassador to South Viet Nam.
Saigon.

Lamont to Lodge, 1966

315 West 106th Street
New York, N.Y. 10025
October 6, 1966

Ambassador Henry Cabot Lodge
U.S. Embassy
Saigon
South Vietnam

My dear Cabot:

For over forty years, ever since we graduated together in the great Harvard Class of 1924, we have been corresponding on public issues. Our letters have been frank and hard-hitting. We have almost always disagreed, but sometimes have learned new facts or viewpoints from each other.

Today, continuing with our lifelong debate, I write you in great distress of mind because I am so concerned over President Johnson's illegal and immoral war in Vietnam, and your own active role in it as Ambassador to the South Vietnamese Government. Recently, in a letter printed in the *World Journal Tribune* of September 13, 1966, you make an unqualified defense of American policy in Southeast Asia on the grounds that our nation must halt "Communist aggression" in Vietnam. But as Senators Gruening and Morse point out, the real aggressor there is the U.S.A.

Your letter, dear classmate, achieves virtually a world's record for inaccuracy. You talk loosely, for instance, of the United Nations Charter justifying the U.S. venture in North and South Vietnam. As a former American Ambassador to the U.N. you know perfectly well that this claim is not true. You also know that U Thant, the Secretary General of the

United Nations, is firmly opposed to American military intervention in Vietnam, that he has called the war "one of the most barbarous in history," and that he is on record as asserting that if the American people "only knew the true facts and the background to the developments in South Vietnam," they would agree that "further bloodshed is unnecessary."

You give no indication that you have read U Thant's important statement of September 2, 1966, about Vietnam: "The cruelty of this war and the suffering it has caused the people of Vietnam are a constant reproach to the conscience of humanity. Today, it seems to me, as it has seemed for many months, that the pressure of events is remorselessly leading toward a major war, while efforts to reverse the trend are lagging disastrously behind. In my view the tragic error is being repeated of relying on force and military means in a deceptive pursuit of peace. I am convinced that peace in Southeast Asia can be obtained only through respect for the principles agreed upon at Geneva in 1954, and indeed for those contained in the Charter of the United Nations."

Your letter to the *World Journal Tribune* attempts to bamboozle the readers of that newspaper by omitting any mention of the Geneva Accords of 1954 to which U Thant refers. It is impossible to understand the situation in Vietnam without knowledge of these agreements that divided the country into South Vietnam and North Vietnam only on a temporary basis, provided for all-Vietnam elections in 1956 to unite the nation, and stipulated that there should be no foreign military bases or foreign armed forces in either South or North Vietnam. The United States Government promised to respect this treaty and to make no effort to subvert it by violence.

When the American Government and its puppet, the dictator Diem, refused to let the 1956 elections take place, a thoroughly indigenous revolution led by the Vietcong started against the South Vietnamese Government. It soon became a popular movement of wide proportions. Massive American military intervention to suppress this revolution and bolster faltering dictatorships has not only clearly violated the Geneva Accords, but also has transformed the United States into an outright aggressor. If Ho Chi Minh's Government finally retaliated by sending substantial forces into South Vietnam, it was only after Johnson in 1965 had begun the ruthless bombing of North Vietnam and had landed tens of thousands of U.S. combat troops in South Vietnam.

You, Cabot Lodge, like President Johnson, Secretary Rusk and Secretary McNamara, would like to erase from the memory of man the Geneva Accords and the other facts I have cited. The aim is to attempt the frame-up of a whole country, to mislead the American people and the world into believing that North Vietnam is the aggressor instead of the power-mad big bully—the United States of America. Do you really think that such disingenuous tactics on your part conform to *Veritas,* the motto on the seal of Harvard that you and I in our college days swore to uphold?

The reason why all Johnson's peace proposals are dishonest and phony is precisely that instead of being directed to the main contestant in the South Vietnamese civil war—the National Liberation Front and its military arm, the Vietcong—they are directed to the Government of North Vietnam and throughout make the false assumption that it is an aggressor state. Unfortunately, you have strongly supported the President's position here. It is obvious that Hanoi will never approve or attend a Peace Conference that at the outset assigns Ho Chi Minh's regime a criminal status.

In modern times many ambassadors have been mere messenger boys for their governments. But as Ambassador to South Vietnam you have been much more than that; you have played a major role since your first appointment by President Kennedy in 1963 in both formulating and effectuating policy. Utilizing your own special study of counter-insurgency as taught by the U.S. Army, you have helped plan military strategy. You have advised American generals on how to combat the Vietcong and Vietnamese generals on how to stage coups to install new U.S. stooges. Indeed you have functioned a good deal of the time as a Major General, which is your rank in the U.S. Army Reserve Corps. And you have consistently taken "the hard line."

So I say to you, Mr. Major General, that you bear prime responsibility for what Walter Lippmann has called "the escalation of frightfulness" in Vietnam; for the indiscriminate napalm and saturation bombing of innocent women, children and peasants in South Vietnamese villages; for the defoliation of the countryside by noxious chemicals dropped from the air, and for the cruel and extensive bombing of North Vietnam. The reckless and inhuman nature of U.S. air strikes becomes tragically clear in the repeated "mistakes" of American planes in killing scores of Vietnamese in "friendly" villages and even annihilating our own troops.

You share responsibility, too, for the flourishing of U.S. sponsored prostitution wherever American troops are quartered in South Vietnam. The American military has transformed the beautiful city of Saigon into one of the biggest brothels in history. Commenting on the prostitution the Americans have created, a Catholic Sister in Saigon has stated: "I think the Vietnamese resent this more than anything else about the expanding of the war, more even than the bombing." (*New York Times,* August 4, 1966.) There is no sign, sir, that you as U.S. Ambassador have said anything or done anything to halt this crime against morality and the women of Vietnam.

Meanwhile the total American military commitment in Vietnam goes up and up, with well over 315,000 troops there now, not to mention 60,000 sailors in the Seventh Fleet off the coast. U.S. casualties likewise become higher and higher, with the official figure now at more than 5,400 men killed in combat and more than 30,000 wounded. The cost to the American taxpayer mounts correspondingly, with the Vietnamese war taking now at least $15 billion a year to finance. The April 1966 issue of *Fortune* magazine, for which you were once a consultant, estimates that as the conflict escalates, the total expense annually will rise to $21 billion. At the same time our domestic inflation also escalates, and our enormous expenditures in Vietnam further increase the growing deficit in the U.S. international balance of payments. There can be no doubt, either, that the colossal costs of our madcap venture in Southeast Asia are seriously handicapping the Great Society program.

No matter how many soldiers Johnson pours into Vietnam and how much of our treasure he spends for the killing of Vietnamese, the United States can never win this war. The Pentagon estimates that in a guerilla operation of this kind the United States must have for victory a ratio of 10 to 1 against the enemy. Even if Johnson sends over 1,000,000 men, it is not too difficult for the Vietcong and North Vietnamese to provide 200,000 additional fighters to match them in the jungle terrain. And if the U.S. raises the ante to 2,000,000, then China will come in and easily marshal 400,000 men. This is why General MacArthur and all our military experts have in the past warned against the United States becoming involved in a major land war in Asia. What we are doing in Vietnam is to sink deeper and deeper into the worst military trap in our history.

You, General Lodge, are caught in this same trap and are throwing your reputation, earned in peaceful and useful public service, down the drain in a futile effort to put across Johnson's evil designs in Vietnam and Southeast Asia. And as the brutal American attack on Vietnam continues, the danger steadily increases, as U Thant warns us, of a major conflict involving China, the Soviet Union and nuclear weapons. Such a nuclear war would be the greatest catastrophe that has ever come to America and the human race.

It is no wonder that peace-loving people and peoples all over the world are aghast at what the militarists of Washington are doing. It is no wonder that Pope Paul is greatly worried and exclaims, "We cry to them in God's name to stop." Even America's official allies are horrified. I should think that the plan of the Bertrand Russell Peace Foundation to try as "war criminals" you and other members of the Johnson Administration would give you pause. It is well to remember what our Declaration of Independence says about having "a decent respect to the opinions of mankind."

Pro-consul Lodge (as they call you in Europe), you are directing a U.S. colonial administration in South Vietnam and yet you pretend all the while that you are trying to save democracy in that country and guarantee its right of self-determination. No government in Saigon since the days of Diem could have lasted one week without the military protection of the United States. That is true of the South Vietnamese Government today, led by Premier Ky, the dictator who proudly proclaimed that his great hero was Adolf Hitler.

And what about the other members of the ruling junta? Here is what Senator George S. McGovern of South Dakota revealed about them on June 30, 1966: "I call attention . . . to the blunt fact that all but one of the South Vietnamese generals who represent the military junta fought with the French against their own people in the war for independence which followed World War II. Would not this be roughly comparable to having eight or nine Benedict Arnolds attempting to run the U.S. in the years that followed our own war of independence 175 years ago?"

Of course Senator McGovern's suggestion is entirely sound. And how can you, Ambassador Lodge, a veteran of World War II and a 100 percent American all the way through—how can you, sir, endure being the boon companion and faithful partner of the Benedict Arnolds of Vietnam? Is this the way to carry on the spirit of our great American Revolution of 1776?

Way back in our student days you had a special appreciation of French civilization and French culture, and I admired your command of the language. Today you are a member of the French Legion of Honor. Why, then, do you fail to appreciate the wisdom of President de Gaulle and his associates, who have repeatedly stated that the only road to lasting peace in Vietnam is for the United States to carry out a phased and total withdrawal of its forces, so that the long-suffering Vietnamese can settle their own destiny without outside interference? A U.S. agreement for such a withdrawal, for a general cease-fire with both the Government of North Vietnam and the National Liberation Front, and for a return to the 1954 Geneva Accords is the intelligent, sane way out for America, for President Johnson and for you, Cabot Lodge. It is the only sure way of your getting rid of the Albatross that you so heedlessly hung around your neck three years ago.

When in 1962 de Gaulle, defying the imperialists and reactionaries, withdrew the French Army from Algeria and gave that country its independence, practically the entire world applauded. And France gained mightily in prestige. The United States could win equal prestige throughout the earth if it brought home its army, navy and air force from Vietnam.

If you yourself could see the light sufficiently to support this move and try to persuade Lyndon Johnson of its merits, you would go far in rebuilding your public image that has been so tarnished by your role as a leading War Hawk. Since the American people are daily growing more and more fed-up with the Vietnam war, they would feel grateful to any U.S. official who made a real and honest attempt to terminate the conflict. It is time for our beloved country permanently to halt its military intervention in foreign lands and steadfastly to uphold again the traditional American ideals of international peace and cooperation. World peace is the best guarantee for the national security of the United States and the welfare of the American people.

Because of the transcending importance of the Vietnam issue, I am treating this communication as an Open Letter and am sending it out to various interested persons. Over the years I have been your chief antagonist in the Harvard Class of 1924; and am today its only member, indeed the only Harvard alumnus in general, who feels it necessary to condemn openly your part in America's aggression against Vietnam. I believe that I am fulfilling a patriotic duty in doing so, both as regards the Harvard community and the public at large. It is possible that eventually our correspondence may prove to have some historic importance. And I am confident that in judging between us, history and the conscience of America will find you to have been terribly wrong about Vietnam.

Sincerely yours,
CORLISS LAMONT

Afterword

My two Open Letters to Ambassador Lodge received considerable publicity in the press, both in the United States and abroad. I presented and commented on the 1966 letter at the Sunday forum of the Boston Community Church on December 11. The Minister of the Church, the Reverend Donald G. Lothrop, had invited Ambassador Lodge to debate me in person, but Mr. Lodge declined. Mr. Lothrop then asked Ambassador Lodge's son, George Cabot Lodge, to represent his father, but he also declined. Accordingly, in order to have the Ambassador's viewpoint fairly presented, Mr. Lothrop drafted Edmund C. Berkeley, a Harvard graduate and well-known businessman, to read to the audience Mr. Lodge's letter in the *World Journal Tribune*. Mr. Berkeley made it clear, however, that he did not agree with Ambassador Lodge.

To update some of the statistics in the 1966 letter, I find that as of this writing over 465,000 members of the U.S. Armed Forces are taking part in the Vietnam conflict—405,000 on land and 60,000 at sea. This is exclusive of men in the Air Force involved in bombing flights from Guam and Thailand. The American casualties haven risen to more than 7,000 killed in action and more than 40,000 wounded. And the latest reliable figure for the cost of the war to the United States is $25 billion a year. As Walter Lippmann says, President Johnson, because of these tremendous expenses, "has all but brought the so-called Great Society to a stop."

February, 1967   C.L.

20
The Meaning of Vietnam and Cambodia (1975)

Essays, Open Letters and public messages by two concerned Americans who fought against United States aggression in Southeast Asia for thirteen years, 1962–1975.

Foreword

We have rejected and still reject, the attempts of President Ford, Secretary of State Kissinger and the U.S. Establishment in general to sweep under the rug the cruel, immoral and unconstitutional war of aggression waged, directly or indirectly, by the United States for thirteen years, 1962–1975, in Southeast Asia. When Mr. Kissinger said in April, 1975, "The Vietnam debate has now run its course," he was trying to cover up the hideous role that the United States Government had played in South and North Vietnam, and his own responsibility for some of the worst aspects of the American terror.

If the United States in the future is to have a rational and humane foreign policy truly committed to international peace, the American people must fully understand and evaluate the Big Bully imperialist character of the U.S. military intervention in Vietnam, Cambodia and Laos. We hope that this pamphlet will make some contribution to the understanding that is needed to the development of a genuinely peace-loving United States and to the establishment of permanent international peace.

All the public messages in this pamphlet were written jointly by Corliss and Helen Lamont, except for the Open Letter to President Kennedy of

---

Co-authored by Helen Lamb Lamont, who was the wife of Corliss Lamont. She died July 21, 1975, shortly before this pamphlet was published.

April 11, 1962, composed by Mr. Lamont. We are grateful to Mr. Taylor Adams of New York City for many helpful suggestions in the readying of our public pronouncements. We believe that it is worthwhile for the historical record to assemble these various documents in one publication.

CORLISS LAMONT
HELEN LAMONT

THE NEW YORK TIMES

Wednesday, April 11, 1962

AN OPEN LETTER TO PRESIDENT JOHN F. KENNEDY

Against U.S. Military Intervention in South Vietnam

Signed by 16 American Citizens

Dear President Kennedy:

As individuals who believe that the only security for America lies in world peace, we wish to ask you why at present the United States is sending its Army, Navy and Air Force to bring death and bloodshed to South Vietnam, a small Asian country approximately 10,000 miles from our Pacific Coast.

In other words, since you have the ultimate responsibility in this matter, we want to raise with you the question of the American Government's massive military intervention in South Vietnam to bolster up the corrupt and reactionary dictatorship of Ngo Dinh Diem. According to reliable newspaper reports, the United States has sent nearly 5,000 troops to South Vietnam, together with enormous quantities of small arms, machine guns, artillery, and helicopters to transport the soldiers of the Diem Government. In addition, Mr. President, you have set up a special U.S. Military Assistance Command for Vietnam.

All of these measures are calculated to thwart the will of the South Vietnamese people who have been fighting year after year in a broad, country-wide movement, made up primarily of peasants, to get rid of the tyrannical Diem Government. While a proportion of Communists are active in this movement, and there may be some support from North Vietnam, there is substantial participation in it by non-Communists. And considerable opposition to dictator Diem is anti-Communist, as witness three attempts by the military to overthrow his Government, and two exiled political groups, the Democratic Party and the Free Democratic Party, both with headquarters in Paris.

The United States intervention in Vietnam is in specific violation of the 1954 Geneva Agreements which marked the final defeat of France in

Indochina and which established Cambodia, Laos and Vietnam as independent countries. These treaties prohibited foreign troops and foreign military bases in Vietnam, limited military advisers to 685, banned fresh military supplies except for replacements, and provided for national elections in 1956 to establish a single, unified government for both North and South Vietnam. The American Government through its intervention has clearly violated all the military prohibitions of the Geneva pacts; and it supported President Diem in his illegal refusal to go through with the promised plebiscite.

United States troops have been definitely taking part in military operations in South Vietnam; and U.S. casualties are piling up, including the 93 Army men who lost their lives when a Super Constellation crashed on March 16 while flying them from San Francisco to Saigon. It is evident that the United States is involved in a real, though undeclared, war. Yet neither Congress, which under our Constitution alone has the power to declare war, nor the American people have had an adequate opportunity publicly to air and debate the present policy of your Administration in South Vietnam. And you yourself, Mr. President, have given out only the scantiest information about this dangerous situation. We must agree with the Republican National Committee, in its official publication *Battle Line,* that you have a "clear responsibility to make a full report to the people" as to the extent of American intervention in South Vietnam.

The most persuasive statement we have found about the need of more information in such a perilous situation as this nation confronts in South Vietnam was made by you, Mr. President, in a speech on the floor of the United States Senate, April 6, 1954, about the Vietnam crisis of that time. We are taking the liberty of quoting a few passages from your address as printed in the *Congressional Record* of that date:

> The time has come for the American people to be told the blunt truth about Indochina. . . . But the speeches of President Eisenhower, Secretary Dulles, and others have left too much unsaid, in my opinion—and what has been left unsaid is the heart of the problem that should concern every citizen. For if the American people are, for the fourth time in this century, to travel the long and tortuous road of war—particularly a war which we now realize would threaten the survival of civilization—then I believe we have a right—a right which we should have hitherto exercised—to inquire in detail into the nature of the struggle in which we may become engaged, and the alternative to that struggle. Without such clarification, the general support and success of our policy is endangered. . . .
>
> To pour money, materiel, and men into the jungles of Indochina without at least a remote prospect of victory would be dangerously futile and self-destructive. . . . I am frankly of the belief that no amount of American military assistance in Indochina can conquer an enemy which is everywhere and at the same time nowhere, "an enemy of the people"

which has the sympathy and covert support of the people. . . .

For the United States to intervene unilaterally and to send troops into the most difficult terrain in the world, with the Chinese able to pour in unlimited manpower, would mean that we would face a situation which would be far more difficult than even that we encountered in Korea. . . .

The facts and alternatives before us are unpleasant. . . . But in a nation such as ours, it is only through the fullest and frankest appreciation of such facts and alternatives that any foreign policy can be effectively maintained. In an era of supersonic attack and atomic retaliation, extended public debate and education are of no avail, once such a policy must be implemented. The time to study, to doubt, to review and revise is now, for upon our decisions now may well rest the peace and security of the world and, indeed, the very continued existence of mankind. And if we cannot entrust this decision to the people, then, as Thomas Jefferson once said: "If we think them not enlightened enough to exercise their control with a wholesome discretion, the remedy is not to take it from them but to inform their discretion by education."

It seems to us, Mr. President, that all of your comments as Senator in 1954 apply to what your Administration is doing in 1962 in regard to South Vietnam. In 1954 you expressed the belief that "no amount of American military assistance" could bring victory for the United States in Vietnam where there exists "the most difficult terrain in the world." We must have the same doubts about American victory today; and some high Washington officials have themselves conceded that it might take years—perhaps as much as a decade—to defeat the guerrillas of South Vietnam.

Most important of all, as you said in 1954, "The time has come for the American people to be told the blunt truth. . . . We have a right . . . to inquire in detail into the nature of the struggle in which we may become engaged, and the alternative to that struggle." Both Communist China and the Soviet Union have warned the United States Government that its "undeclared war" in South Vietnam constitutes a peril to world peace. Are we running the risk of becoming embroiled in another large-scale conflict such as the Korean War, Mr. President, or even in a nuclear-bomb war?

Frankly, we believe that the United States intervention in South Vietnam constitutes a violation of international law, of United Nations principles, and of America's own highest ideals. We urge, Mr. President, that you bring this intervention to an immediate end and that you initiate a special international conference to work out a peaceful solution to the crisis in Vietnam, as you have endeavored to do in Laos.

The people of South Vietnam have suffered enough. Having fought eight long years to win independence from France, they have been compelled to fight seven more years, 1955-1962, to achieve independence from dictator Diem and the United States, which has maintained him in power. It is time to end the ordeal of the South Vietnamese people and to permit them to enjoy the fruits of liberty and the pursuit of happiness.

THE NEW YORK TIMES
Wednesday, April 3, 1963
AN OPEN LETTER TO PRESIDENT JOHN F. KENNEDY
For Ending the War and Making Peace in South Vietnam

Signed by 62 American citizens

Dear President Kennedy:

We strongly urge you to heed the mounting opposition of American public opinion to U.S. intervention in South Vietnam, and to make far-reaching changes in our policy in that troubled area before the situation deteriorates further.

The truth is that the United States Army, with more than 12,000 soldiers and officers in South Vietnam some 10,000 miles from home, is fighting to bolster up an open and brutal dictatorship—that of President Diem—in an undeclared war that has never received the Constitutional sanction of the United States Congress. It is, moreover, as *The Nation* (Jan. 19, 1963) stated, "a dirty, cruel war—as dirty and as cruel as the war waged by French forces in Algeria which so shocked the American conscience."

Today our Army is no nearer victory than a year or more ago when the big American build-up started. The anti-Diem guerillas, led by the Vietcong, have captured more and more American weapons from the apathetic Diem troops and are increasingly using American-made rifles, machine guns and mortars to shoot down American helicopters operated by U.S. fliers. The number of Americans killed and wounded steadily grows. South Vietnam could become America's Algeria.

Kennedy's 1954 Speech Cited

You yourself, Mr. President, in a speech in the Senate on April 6, 1954, about the Vietnam crisis of that time, were 100 percent right when you said, in criticism of President Eisenhower's policy: "To pour money, materiel, and men into the jungles of Indochina without at least a remote prospect of victory would be dangerously futile and self-destructive. . . . I am frankly of the belief that no amount of American military assistance in Indochina can conquer an enemy which is everywhere and at the same time nowhere, 'an enemy of the people' which has the sympathy and covert support of the people."

That 1954 statement still holds true and points up the fact that the anti-Diem rebels, while receiving some help from Communist North Vietnam, represent a broad, indigenous, nation-wide movement; and that the United States has become increasingly involved in a conflict that it cannot win despite its tremendous military power. *For the American Government is caught up in an impossible dilemma.* The more aggressively it pursues the war—the more money, planes, tanks, guns and military personnel it pours into South Vietnam—the more Diem looks like an American puppet. Every time American planes, manned by American "advisers" and Diem soldiers paid from U.S. handouts, bomb a peasant village, burn a peasant's rice hoard, kill a peasant's water buffalo or drive a peasant from his ancestral lands, the Viet Cong gets more sympathy and more recruits from the local population.

More and more, as death and destruction increase, the issue becomes, in the eyes of the Vietnamese people, that of American interference and control versus Vietnamese independence and self-determination. But the days of the white man's domination of Asia are over, whether that domination be in the form of an outright colony, protectorate or alliance, or by guile, blandishments and "advice."

Diem Flouts Democracy

Ever since 1954 the United States has been working for an "American" solution for Vietnam—that is, to keep the country divided, so that at least one segment of it remains under Western control and becomes a bastion of anti-Communist strength. To achieve these ends, America has supported the tyrannical Diem regime against the National Liberation Front, a coalition of different political parties, ethnic groups and religious communities in which the Communist Party plays a leading role. These elements, as well as other groups outside the Front, have resorted to guerilla fighting or military coups to unseat Diem, because he has refused to allow normal democratic procedures for political opposition and an orderly change of government.

To keep him in power as "our man," the American Government is spending in South Vietnam at least $500 million a year. But as Senate Majority Leader Mike Mansfield (D-Mont) pointed out in his little known Commencement address at Michigan State University (June 10, 1962): "There is no longer any escaping the fact that after years of enormous expenditures of aid in South Vietnam, that country is more, rather than less, dependent on aid from the United States. Vietnam's independent survival is less rather than more secure than it was five or six years ago."

U.S. Defies Geneva Accords

The solution launched by the late Secretary of State, John Foster Dulles, and later adopted by your Administration, Mr. President, has been in violation of the Geneva Accords of 1954 which were devised to bring peace to war-torn Vietnam. The Great Powers that participated in that settlement solemnly declared that Vietnam was one sovereign country, not two, and that the provisional zones of North and South were to be united in 1956 by all-Vietnamese elections under international supervision. The Geneva Accords also aimed to keep Vietnam out of the Cold War by their provisions against military bases and military alliances, and for limiting both military equipment and the number of military advisers in the interim period before the elections.

Is it not finally time, Mr. President, for your Administration to end its abortive and unilateral effort to bring about a military solution in South Vietnam through American might, and instead, utilize diplomacy and international negotiation, as was done successfully in Laos? Such negotiations could either restore the original Geneva Agreements or put into effect some other plan that would lead to peace and to the disengagement of all Vietnam from the Cold War.

Returning to Senator Mansfield's speech, we agree with him that the whole American policy in Southeast Asia and South Vietnam requires painstaking re-examination. And we further agree with him that America's recent approaches of "deep involvement and enormous cost . . . are doubtful because they bring upon us a vague responsibility for the internal evolution of the nations of Southeast Asia, a responsibility which no nation can discharge for another in this day and age, a responsibility which is the right and duty of the people and leaders of these nations themselves to assume, a responsibility which, after many costly decades, we relinquished in the Philippines with no intention of assuming elsewhere."

"Most Disturbing," Say Senators

A searching report on Southeast Asia issued February 25 by a bipartisan Senate group headed by Senator Mansfield supports these same general propositions. And in reference to South Vietnam it significantly adds: "It is most disturbing to find that after seven years of the Republic, South Vietnam appears less, not more, stable than it was at the outset, that it appears more removed from, rather than closer to, the achievement of popularly responsible and responsive government."

We respectfully petition you Mr. President, as the Chief Executive of this nation and the Commander-in-Chief of its Armed Forces: (1) to consider seriously the advice of Senator Mansfield and that of the special

Senate group he heads; (2) to discard what Walter Lippmann has called "the Dulles system of Asian protectorates"; (3) to halt U.S. military intervention in South Vietnam; and (4) to call a special international conference, perhaps under the auspices of the United Nations, to work out a peaceful solution.

THE NEW YORK TIMES

Thursday, October 2, 1969

MR. NIXON:

Let's have done with wiggle and wobble

These token troop withdrawals and phony draft reductions—they are *not ending* the Vietnam war. They're soothing syrup to keep us quiet back home, while the slaughter goes on.

More than 9,000 American boys have died in Vietnam since YOU took over, President Nixon. After your promised withdrawals, 484,000 troops will still be left—to kill and be killed.

Jan. 1, 1961, through Sept. 20, 1969, witnessed:

TOTAL AMERICAN DEAD 45,352
TOTAL AMERICAN WOUNDED 252,059

Stop the gimmicks and sweet talk, Mr. President, and MAKE PEACE NOW! Insist on a coalition peace government in Saigon; and carry out a total withdrawal of U.S. forces in Vietnam.

On Oct. 15, as part of the Vietnam Moratorium, students and teachers throughout America will leave their classes to talk with their fellow-Americans about the madness of the war. Listen to them, President Nixon, when they ring your doorbell!

THE NEW YORK TIMES

Sunday, October 26, 1969

MR. NIXON:

The best way to stop inflation is to stop the war!

Why not tell us the *whole* truth, Mr. President? The greatest single cause of the high cost of living today is the Vietnam war.

You didn't mention this in your speech about inflation. You didn't tell us that the Vietnam conflict is costing U.S. taxpayers at least *30 billion dollars a year!*

The cost of living *has gone up 20%* since Johnson began to escalate the war in 1965.

This runaway rise in prices parallels the steady rise in U.S. War Casualties. From Jan. 1, 1961 through Oct. 18, 1969 the figures are:

TOTAL DEAD (including non-combat) 45,871
TOTAL CASUALTIES 302,721

More and more businessmen think the war is crippling our economy. The Stock Market has the jitters, and the cost of food, clothing and services *keeps on mounting!*

HEED the great Moratorium of Oct. 15th!
INSIST on a coalition peace government in Saigon!
ACT to stablize our economy by a total, speedy withdrawal of all U.S. armed forces from Vietnam!
Stop inflation—by stopping the war!

THE NEW YORK TIMES

Sunday, May 7, 1972

BOMBARD THE WHITE HOUSE AND CONGRESS WITH MESSAGES TO STOP THE U.S. BOMBARDMENT OF VIETNAM

To our fellow American parents and grandparents:

President Richard Nixon, who repeatedly has promised to take the United States out of the Vietnam War, has intervened full blast once more by his bombings in North and South Vietnam. Our double-talk President, as his speech of April 26th shows, will continue the cruel and immoral U.S. aggression indefinitely unless the American people stop him.

The war policies of Nixon and the Pentagon mean that our sons and our grandsons, our nephews and our great-nephews, still stand in danger of being sent to die or be mutilated in a senseless, hopeless war. And there is always the possibility that the Vietnam conflict will erupt into the Third World War.

Write, telegraph, telephone President Nixon, your Senator, your Congressman for the immediate withdrawal of all U.S. Armed Forces from Southeast Asia.

Demonstrate, meet, march, speak out, vote for peace and against the Vietnam War!

THE NEW YORK TIMES

Sunday, May 27, 1972

STOP NIXON FROM MAKING ANOTHER VIETNAM IN CAMBODIA

President Nixon is continuing the war in Indochina with his savage B-52 bombings in Cambodia, destroying villages, ruining farms and crops, killing and maiming numerous civilians.

Nixon, using American taxpayers' money, bombs and kills to support the reactionary government of Lon Nol, brought into power by a U.S.-sponsored coup that sent into exile Prince Norodom Sihanouk. It is the National United Front of Cambodia that is fighting Lon Nol in a genuine civil war to restore Sihanouk as head of a government of National Union. Nixon, however, dishonestly pretends that it is only the Communists who are opposing Lon Nol.

Nixon's military intervention in the Cambodian civil war, without Congressional authorization, is unconstitutional and a reckless extension of illegal Executive power. It could lead the United States into another Vietnam.

Support the Congress in passing bills that bar Nixon and the Pentagon from expending funds—directly, by transfer or by any other means—for waging war in Cambodia or anywhere else in Indochina! Support the Congress in any constitutional showdown with the President over these issues! The American people want the U.S. military completely and permanently out of Southeast Asia.

Write, telegraph, telephone your Representative and Senators for the immediate cessation of U.S. bombing in Cambodia!

Make the White House make peace!

THE NEW YORK TIMES

Sunday, May 11, 1975

DON'T LET HENRY KISSINGER BAMBOOZLE YOU WHEN HE SAYS "THE VIETNAM DEBATE HAS NOW RUN ITS COURSE"

The Debate on Vietnam Is NOT Over

The hideous war is finished, the American debacle completed, and the most evil enterprise in the history of United States foreign policy ended. But the American people must understand fully what happened, and why, in Vietnam, if we are now to have a foreign policy that is rational, humane and truly committed to international peace.

Let us not forget or forgive those unscrupulous U.S. Government leaders and other important figures in this country who were responsible for the cruel and criminal American war of aggression in Vietnam—a conflict that brought death to more than 56,000 in our Armed Forces, and that killed, maimed or made homeless millions of Vietnamese in both South and North Vietnam.

We believe that the best answer to Mr. Kissinger and a superb summary of the shameful Vietnam venture was made in a sermon on Sunday, April 27, by the Reverend Stephen H. Fritchman at the First Unitarian Church in Los Angeles, of which he is Minister Emeritus. We reprint below the most relevant parts.

Corliss and Helen Lamont

The Reverend Stephen H. Fritchman

Two days ago Secretary of State Kissinger told the American Society of Newspaper Editors, meeting in Washington, several astonishing things, but I limit myself to one paragraph from his speech. He declared: "In Indochina our government undertook a major enterprise for almost fifteen years. We invested enormous prestige; tens of thousands died, and many more were wounded and imprisoned; we spent over $150 billion, and our domestic fabric was severely strained. Whether or not this enterprise was well conceived does not now change the nature of our problem. *The Vietnam debate has now run its course.* The time has come now for restraint and compassion . . . Let us all now abide by the verdict of the Congress—without recrimination or vindictiveness. Let us look to the future."

I have come into this pulpit fairly often for 27 of the past 30 years since Japan surrendered in World War II and Ho Chi Minh declared (September 2, 1945) the existence of the Democratic Republic of Vietnam, a single nation—no Mason and Dixon line of North and South. That Declaration of Independence from the French colonials and the retreating Japanese occupiers, spoken in Hanoi, used deliberately words written by Thomas Jefferson: "All men are created equal. They are endowed by their Creator with certain inalienable rights: among these are life, liberty and the pursuit of happiness."

Recalling the promises made by the victorious powers of World War II, the Vietnamese leader also declared: "We are convinced that the allied nations, which at Teheran and San Francisco have acknowledged the principle of self-determination and equality of nations, will not refuse to acknowledge the independence of Vietnam." We now know, since Daniel Ellsberg released the Pentagon Papers to the American people, that President Ho Chi Minh tried to enlist American support for independence by sending letters to President Harry Truman. There is no evidence that Harry Truman ever responded. Henry Kissinger cannot compel me to forget those outrageous betrayals of 1945 by the allied powers.

No, Mr. Kissinger, I shall not silence my tongue, nor encourage amnesia, nor accept the blinders of the American media or of our government during the past thirty years of involvement by our diplomats from John Foster Dulles to yourself. Nor can I be silent on our industrial corporations that made billions on the arming of the French, the South Vietnamese and our own military forces. Do not ask this congregation to forget their own agonized labors for peace, their lost sons, both in the military and in the refuges made possible in Canada and other countries.

There is now a possibility that a united Vietnamese nation may again be attained, in spite of the millions dead in a modern genocide that beggars description, in a country defoliated, bombed, burned; a people of great historic dignity and culture, divided, invaded, starved and tortured.

The American bloodbath of napalm, gunfire, flame-throwers, fragmentation bombs, and all the other weaponry used, has I hope ended. The United States as a foreign invader has at long last been forced to leave, as were the French at Dienbienphu a decade ago—and the Japanese, before us.

This editorial statement this morning is simply my own public rejection of all those persons, led by Henry Kissinger, who want me to forget the Phoenix operation of the CIA which killed 20,000 anti-war civilians; who want me to forget the massacres and the carpet bombing of city after city—by Presidents Johnson and Nixon, and the earlier extension of the war from the days of Eisenhower and Kennedy, until this very year, by Gerald Ford. I will not forget the kidnapping of Indochinese children in recent days by those who would thus seek to have me forget the deaths of thousands of children in villages and ricefields for over two decades.

And we shall continue the telling of the fearful story of Vietnam to our friends, our children, our teachers, our ministers, our media pundits, our historians, our fellow workers, and our politicians, so that the crimes shall never be repeated nor the lies be retold. No, Henry Kissinger—don't count on me! As long as I am alive I shall remember Vietnam, as I remember the crimes of the Warsaw Ghetto, and Lidice, and Belsen, and Hiroshima, and Nagasaki.

THE NEW YORK TIMES

Sunday, June 1, 1975

TO OUR FELLOW AMERICANS!
DON'T LET PRESIDENT FORD AND HENRY KISSINGER DELUDE YOU ABOUT CAMBODIA!

Once again in the fracas over the Mayaguez the United States Government is trying to deceive and mislead the American people. President Ford and

Secretary Kissinger pose as brave, noble patriots saving the honor of America. But in reality, despite all their flag-waving, they have dishonored our country by a murderous, bomb-happy, senseless response to a small incident that, given a little more patience, could have been peacefully settled through diplomacy.

President Ford sent to their death not only many Cambodians, but over 40 Americans, a larger number than the 39-man crew of the Mayaguez, all of whom are safe. He grossly violated Thailand's sovereignty and stated policy by landing some 1,100 U.S. Marines in that country. And he clearly violated the 1973 Congressional law that forbids "combat activities by U.S. military forces in or over or from off the shores of North Vietnam, South Vietnam, Laos or Cambodia."

The President also flagrantly violated the United Nations Charter. Gullible Congressional leaders unthinkingly and emotionally supported Mr. Ford's action.

Wilfred Burchett, veteran journalist of many years in southeast Asia, was repeatedly proven correct in his reports during the Vietnam War. We believe that he is also correct in his article in the *Guardian* of May 28 where he analyzes the Mayaguez affair. We reprint below the most relevant portions of his dispatch entitled "U.S. Attack: Aggression Pure and Simple."

Corliss and Helen Lamont

Wilfred Burchett

The Mayaguez incident and the accompanying savage U.S. bombing of the Cambodian mainland demonstrates that President Ford and Secretary of State Henry Kissinger haven't learned a thing from the recent imperialist debacle in Indochina.

It is becoming clearer every day that this latest episode in the U.S. tradition of gunboat diplomacy was a deliberately provoked pretext for showing the tattered U.S. flag in Southeast Asia.

It is also becoming increasingly apparent that Ford and Kissinger have again miscalculated and that Pentagon press briefings to the contrary, the U.S. has suffered another significant political and military defeat by the Cambodian people.

The evidence pointing to the sham character of the whole affair is overwhelming.

Why else would the U.S. bomb the Ream airport on the Cambodian mainland two hours and 42 minutes after Washington was informed that the Mayaguez was being released?

Why else would the U.S. bomb oil refineries and other installations in Sihanoukville, causing—according to Cambodian officials—"very great losses in human lives," when 57 minutes earlier it was known that the crewmen had been released and 36 minutes earlier President Ford was informed that the crewmen had been safely recovered?

As the full extent of U.S. casualties is grudgingly revealed, it will become increasingly obvious that "protection of American lives and property"— the excuse offered for the renewed U.S. aggression against Cambodia— was of little concern to the White House and the Pentagon.

As the admitted casualty toll has risen—the Pentagon now says 15 U.S. personnel died and 3 others are still "missing"—an immense shadow has fallen across the picture of imperialist "invincibility" Kissinger has tried to project.

The Defense Department did not announce until May 21—nearly a week later—that an additional 25 Marines were lost even before the operation started. These men crashed to their deaths while being moved from their home base in Thailand to the Utabao base to take off for the wholly unnecessary attack at Koh Tong island.

So the U.S. death toll, now more than 40, has already exceeded the number of crewmen on the Mayaguez—to say nothing of the fact that the lives of these 39 were never in danger in the first place.

Behind the wildly extravagant press accounts of the U.S. military operations against Koh Tong island is an even more startling reality. The invasion of the island—far from being the spectacular victory the Pentagon has claimed—was another crushing military defeat for the U.S.

Despite a numerically superior force of Marines supported by naval and air bombardment—including seven-and-one-half-ton bombs, the biggest in the U.S. arsenal, the invading force was unable to secure and consolidate a beachhead.

The Pentagon was reportedly "surprised" at the fierce defense the invading force encountered. They shouldn't have been. The Cambodian troops defending Koh Tong are veterans of five years of the people's war to liberate their homeland. Although outnumbered by the Marines and without the benefit of air force or navy, they repulsed the attackers decisively, inflicting heavy casualties.

The incredible incompetence of U.S. intelligence was further exposed when it became apparent that the military never knew exactly where the crewmen of the Mayaguez were until they appeared alongside the U.S. destroyer Wilson—unharmed except for wounds inflicted by the U.S. "rescue" planes.

What was it all for, really? To boost the egos of Ford and Kissinger? To show the world that the U.S. is not a "pitiful, helpless giant"? Kissinger's declaration that the U.S. was not a "paper tiger" went over with most of the world with about the same impact as Nixon's insistence that he was "not a crook."

The fact is that Washington has covered itself with shame and ridicule in this affair. Its prestige, or what is left of it, has taken another plummet, especially in Asia. It proved that it has learned nothing from its defeats and is still intent on doing a maximum of damage in Indochina.

In a statement of principled dignity, the Cambodian government made its own position clear: "The Cambodian nation and people appeal to the people of the world, to the American people, to American youth and to peace-and-justice-loving personalities. If in the future there are more incidents of this nature, we ask you not to give any credence to them, but to vigorously denounce and condemn them. The Cambodian people and nation have no intention of seeking trouble with anybody and, incidentally, they have neither the possibilities nor the means to do so. We make use only of our rights to protect our sovereignty and territorial integrity."

Addendum on the Mayaguez Affair

Our message of June 1, 1975 in *The New York Times* does not make clear that President Gerald Ford's hasty orders violated the War Powers Resolution which requires the President to "consult" with Congress "in every possible instance" before sending American Armed Forces into action. But in this instance the President merely *informed* a few Congressional leaders *after* the event. In no sense could this be considered consultation. The Lawyers Committee on American Policy Towards Vietnam sums up the situation:

> Mr. Ford was informed of the seizure of the Mayaguez at 7:40 A.M., Monday, May 12. Orders for the beginning of the military operation off Cambodia were issued at 4:45 P.M. Wednesday, May 14. There were 57 hours within which the President had the time to consult the Congress. It is clear that President Ford like his predecessors, does not take seriously the laws enacted by the Congress, even though the Congress spends weeks and months in the enactment of legislation.

Our message in the *Times* did not register, either, the supine way in which both Senators and Congressmen, instead of calling Ford to account for violating the law, rushed pell mell to step aboard the President's War Bandwagon. And we cannot consider it an accident that a week or so later, with fake patriotic fervor at a high pitch, the Congress voted overwhelmingly to adopt the Administration's huge defense budget of more than $100 billion.

C.L.
H.L.

21
Trip to Communist China:
An Informal Report
(1976)

When in 1949 the Chinese Communists succeeded in overthrowing the government of Chiang Kai-shek, the world witnessed one of the greatest revolutions of modern times, as significant for mankind and as far-reaching in its effects as the Russian Revolution of 1917. The Chinese Revolution brought about the establishment of a planned socialist economy in a country larger then continental United States and with a population in 1976 of more than 800 million, constituting about one-fifth of the people of the earth. During the 27 years since 1949 Chinese socialism has had its ups and downs, but on the whole has made enormous progress.

I had never been to China and was especially desirous of seeing the people, the land and the functioning of the new economic system. Hence in the spring of 1976 I joined a group tour organized by the radical American newsweekly, *Guardian*. The trip took place from May 8 to June 1, lasting the regular three weeks of the standard group tour to Communist China. There were 23 other Americans from different parts of the United States on this tour. Selected as "political activists," they made a congenial and interesting company. The cost was $2,300 per person. At present the best way to get to China is to join a tour organized by some newspaper or an organization such as Promoting Enduring Peace, the US-China Peoples Friendship Association and the Smithsonian Institution.

We traveled more than 2,000 miles in China and visited six major cities—Peking, Anyang, Chengchow, Wuhan, Changsha, Shanghai—and two minor cities, Linshien and Shaoshan, the birthplace of Chairman Mao

Tse-tung. The China Travel Service was in charge of our tour and did an excellent, efficient job throughout. Three crack interpreters were assigned to the group. They not only interpreted, but also answered the numberless questions we asked about the new China. The hotel accommodations were all first-rate—twin-bed rooms each with a private bathroom. Every room had a laundry bag marked with the number of the room. You threw your clothes into it in the morning and got them back in the evening. No need to fill out a laundry slip. The Chinese are very honest and most of the hotels didn't give us keys for our rooms. They were left unlocked. No member of the group had anything stolen. The official currency is the yuan, at present valued at 56 cents in U.S. money.

The food was quite good on the whole. We always had an American breakfast consisting of eggs, toast and coffee or tea. Lunch and dinner were Chinese, which meant a lot of fish, some meat, a bowl of rice and excellent soup. Soup comes *last* instead of first in the Chinese meal. Good Chinese beer, 3 percent alcoholic content, was served with lunch and dinner, as was a sparkling orange drink. You could order canned orange juice extra at breakfast for a very cheap price.

Happily, our first stop was Peking, the capital and a very beautiful city. The first thing we learned was that no tips are permitted or received throughout China. This was good news for me, since I have always despised the custom of tipping. During our first morning in Peking we saw some of the traditional sights such as Tien An Men Square, the greatest public gathering place in all China, where the People's Republic was proclaimed in 1949, and site of the Great Hall of the People, where the National People's Congress meets and where most of the important diplomatic conferences are held.

We walked through the monumental Tien An Men Gate to the Forbidden City, a huge compound where the emperors lived and to which the ordinary Chinese was forbidden entrance. Now the City is open to everyone. It is a stunning place, with beautiful buildings and pagodas on every hand and interior decorations of highest artistic quality. In her little book, *Far Eastern Diary, 1920,* my mother, Mrs. Thomas W. Lamont, wrote about The Forbidden City: "We passed to the big court, a magnificent court with five white marble bridges and five doors in the huge gate. . . . I think there is no court in the world so beautifully and so nobly proportioned." I had the same reaction 56 years later. The Forbidden City as a whole is an architectural paradise; and visiting it was for me a profound aesthetic experience equal to that of viewing India's Taj Mahal.

The next day we drove by bus to the Great Wall of China, about two hours north of Peking. We made all our excursions by bus. That famous Great Wall extends over valley and mountain for more than 3,000 miles and was built to keep the "barbarians" out of China. It is 18 feet wide. Hence we were able to walk and climb along it for a half-mile or so. American astronauts circling the earth said that the Great Wall was the only human construction they could see.

At my hotel in Peking, I enjoyed getting up before breakfast and watching the thousands of workers ride by on their bicycles. Travel by bike extends all over China. And since there are comparatively few automobiles, buses or trucks, there is virtually no air pollution stemming from machine exhausts in any Chinese city. Of course going to and from work on a bicycle is good healthy exercise. Peking alone has 2,000,000 bicycles.

The few cars one sees are government owned, on government business, or belong to foreign embassies. "Will China ever turn to private car ownership? Probably not. The Chinese are well aware of the undesirable effects of dependence on private cars in many Western countries: high rates of traffic deaths and injuries, congestion, air and noise pollution, depletion of oil resources, and the high cost of individual upkeep. Producing cars on a large scale would also mean diverting vast resources from projects which have far higher priority for the Chinese such as mechanizing agriculture and developing a modern industrial state." ("Private Cars? Who Needs Them?" by Chieu Chang, *New China,* Sept. 1976, pp. 11-13.)

Another fascinating place near Peking is the Summer Palace situated on lovely Kun Ming Ho Lake and a recreation retreat for the Chinese Emperors and royal families as far back as 1,000 A.D. We walked the length of the Long Corridor with its gorgeous Painted Gallery and thence to the fabulous Marble Boat. After the British, in savage imperialist style, had burnt down most of the Palace in 1860, the Empress Dowager Tzu Hsi rebuilt it in 1888 with funds that had been officially assigned to the Chinese Navy. Would that we in America could appropriate funds from the Navy to build a splendid palace of art! After a fine luncheon in one of the Palace restaurants, we concluded our visit by going for a jaunt on the lake in a barge towed by a motor launch.

Now I turn to the socialist economic system in China. Early in the game, Chairman Mao Tse-tung and the Communist leadership decided that agriculture must be given priority, to feed an enormous population that often in the past suffered from hunger and famine. Now practically everyone is well fed and healthy. We drove out to the Nanyan People's Commune about 30 miles outside Peking. A Commune consists of a number of villages and collective farms. In this Commune there were 10,000 families, 40,000 people and about 5,200 acres of land. A Commune is supposed to grow enough food to feed itself and to send some surplus to the national government for distribution in the cities. The government aims to hold to a minimum the need for transportation and wants each Commune to be as self-sufficient as possible. The typical Commune not only produces rice, corn and other foods, but also has construction facilities, factories for light industry, retail stores, medical units and a Home for Respect of the Aged where very old people are taken care of. Work in the Nanyan Commune is carried on by 16 production brigades divided into 116 production teams. The Commune possesses a few tractors and trucks, but mechanization is not crucial when so much manpower is available. Each peasant family may have, if it so wishes, a private plot where it can grow its own vegetables.

The Chinese Commune is actually a large agro-industrial combine and represents the principle of *decentralization* that is a fundamental feature of the Chinese economy. The Commune exercises a great deal of local initiative and local responsibility, but of course operates within the general framework of the governmental and nation-wide Five-Year Plans. A new Five-Year Plan started in 1975. The Soviet Union has been experimenting with a somewhat similar agro-industrial unit called an "obyedinenie" (combination), administered by a Council of Collective Farmers.

Decentralization is also the order of the day in Chinese cities where large living units called Neighborhoods function efficiently. In Peking we visited the Temple of the Moon Neighborhood with a population of 150,000, 4 main streets, 5 hospitals, 10 restaurants, 23 groceries, 3 theaters, 2 clubs, 2 parks and a number of medical clinics. Again, self-sufficiency is the aim.

While the Communist regime is able to provide the necessities of life for China's vast population, the leadership realizes that the country does have a population problem. For this reason the authorities recommend that women do not marry until they are 25 and men not until they are 28. Married couples are urged to have only two children. Birth control techniques are encouraged. Full equality for women is guaranteed as a constitutional right. The Chinese frown upon pre-marital and extra-marital sex. Such pursuits, the government believes, steal time, energy and purposefulness from the building of socialism. In regard to sex relations, Communist China is for the time being distinctly puritanical.

From Peking we took a train to Anwang and a small city by the name of Linshien. It was a four-hour ride. I managed to get a window seat and expected to catch up on my reading. However, as soon as the train moved out of the city, I noticed a line of rather small, recently planted trees about 15 feet beyond the tracks. Hence the light kept flickering through these trees and made reading impossible. This experience brings out the fact that the Chinese have put across a tremendous tree-planting program since the Revolution of 1949 as part of the agricultural upsurge. Trees preserve the soil and hold the moisture in. The trees that prevented my reading were probably designed in addition to screen the passing trains.

Linshien before the Liberation, as the Chinese call the successful Communist Revolution, had been in the center of a vast valley continuously afflicted by drought. There was a fine river, the Changho, on the other side of the mountains, not large but dependable for plenty of water. The Communists decided to bring that water to the drought-stricken valley by constructing a big tunnel right through one of the mountains. The youth in the area were especially important in hewing this Red Flag Canal out of solid rock for half a mile and with rather elementary tools. We stood at the exit of the Canal from the mountain and watched the water sweep forward to three other main canals connecting with it and thence to a thousand sub-canals that irrigated the whole valley. Inside of two years it became one of the most productive agricultural regions in China. To manage the tons of available water many reservoirs were built, as well as 300 pumping stations and 50 hydro-electric plants.

The Linshien achievement underlines the fact that similar irrigation projects have been completed throughout China. Also the big rivers have been tamed and harnessed for agricultural production. In the old days the two largest rivers, the Yangtze and the Yellow, would burst forth in enormous floods every couple of years—floods that ruined huge portions of farming land and killed off millions of peasants. All that is now a thing of the past. And the lands that were formerly flooded are to a large extent now being cultivated by the peasants. The result has been a vast increase in the growing of rice, wheat, corn and other crops, with total agricultural production at least doubled since 1949. I think that the flood control and irrigation throughout China are the must impressive accomplishments of the Communist regime. And I am moved by the sheer drama of it all.

At Linshien we also visited a middle school. There the children, about 10 to 17, staged a marvelous ballet with singing. It was not just hopping around, but intricate and almost professional dancing. And the kids were in themselves beautiful. Here is the program by title:

1. Welcome Americans
2. Barefoot Doctors are Like Sunflowers
3. Picking Cotton on the Other Side of the Red Flag Canal
4. War Situation Prevails at Red Flag Canal
5. Deliver Grain to the State
6. Singing of a Hundred Birds
7. People of All Nationalities Love our Great Leader, Chairman Mao

I must comment on two of the ballet numbers, and first on the reference to "Barefoot Doctors." Not long after Liberation the Communist leadership decided that the peasant population was receiving inadequate medical care. Accordingly, Chairman Mao issued a call for medically trained people to volunteer for work in the countryside. Thousands of youth responded, especially in the south of China where it tends to be warm. So the young paramedics, who had had three to six months' training in a hospital, frequently went barefoot and soon became known as "Barefoot Doctors." When the movement spread north, the doctors on the farms and Communes wore shoes, but the term "Barefoot Doctors" stuck.

Another ballet at Linshien had "All Nationalities" in its title. This refers to the fact that there are 54 national minorities in China, comprising about 5 percent of the population. Each nationality has a considerable measure of autonomy, with the right to speak its own language, have it taught in the schools and used for newspapers and books. But it is obligatory also to learn Chinese. In Peking we spent an entire afternoon at the Institute of Nationalities located in a large complex of buildings.

From Linshien we went by train to Chengchow and Wuhan, cities far in the interior of China and five or six hundred miles from the ocean. At Chengchow we stood on the banks of the Yellow River and saw the great dyke system the Communists had built. At Wuhan we drove back and forth over the big Yangtze Bridge constructed by the Communists and connecting north China with south China. For thousands of years a ferry was the only way to cross the river, and trains needed two or three hours for transit. This was the place, too, where Chairman Mao took his famous swim across the Yangtze in 1966. He later wrote a little poem about it:

> *Now I am swimming across the great Yangtse,*
> *Looking afar to the open sky of Chu.*
> *Let the wind blow and the waves beat,*
> *Better far than idly strolling in a courtyard.*

Chairman Mao also stated: "Swimming is an exercise in struggling with the forces of nature, and you should toughen yourselves in big rivers and seas." In general, the Chinese have not only taken up swimming in a big way, but many other sports as well. For instance, tens of millions play pingpong. And the Chinese stress physical exercise programs and setting-up exercises that can be done to the beat of radio music at fixed times during the day.

We made a special visit to the University of Wuhan overlooking a beautiful lake. A Professor of Microbiology, Dr. Gow, gave us a briefing about the University. He spoke perfect English and was most congenial. He took a Ph.D. at Yale University in 1935 and also studied at the Rockefeller Institute. On all of our excursions to schools, factories, Neighborhoods, Communes and so on, the first thing was a briefing by the head person, with tea for each individual in the room. The person in charge always spoke in Chinese, which was translated by one of our interpreters. Then we asked questions. A member of the group acted as chairman. After the questions were finished we would go on a tour of the place.

Because I am a teacher, I was selected as chairman at the Wuhan University briefing. At the start I said to Professor Gow: "I bring you greetings from Columbia University where I taught and Harvard University where I graduated." The most significant point that Professor Gow stressed was that every student in the three-year course for graduation, must spend three months of each year working on a farm or in a factory. Many members of the faculty and administrative staff follow the same course. This educational policy helps to break down the separation between intellectual and manual work, and especially gives the student an intimate understanding of peasant and proletarian life. The same procedure applies to all the approximately 500,000 college students in China. At Antioch College in Ohio a somewhat similar type of training has gone on for many decades.

Progress in education has been spectacular under the Communist regime. Illiteracy, which ran to around 80 percent in the old China, has been almost eliminated. In numbers the university, middle and primary school students make up more than one-fifth of the total population. Education through the college and graduate school levels is free for all qualified individuals.

At Wuhan also we went through a mammoth factory, an iron-steel combine with six coal mines, four blast furnaces and 70,000 workers, of whom more than 10,000 are women. It is a very impressive plant. The lowest wage is 40 yuan per month and the highest 320 yuan for engineers. From interviews at Communes, Neighborhoods, factories and educational institutions, we learned that the average wage in China is about 65 yuan a month. With the yuan worth 56 cents, that makes $37.00. Some skilled workers receive more than 100 yuan a month. In the present stage of Chinese socialism, wages are paid according to the individual's ability and skill, with seniority also a factor. Men and women are paid equally for the same work. Prices are cheap. The average person pays 2 yuan monthly for full medical care, though it is provided free to trade union members. Rent of a city apartment with four rooms, including kitchen, toilet and running water, costs 5 yuan per month.

From Wuhan to Changsha we went by train, arriving at Changsha in time for a late supper. We were entering the dining room at the hotel when one of the interpreters appeared waving a one-yuan note. The interpreter said someone had left the yuan on the train in compartment 18 and would the occupant of No. 18 please claim the note. So that person spoke up and recovered his yuan. This incident is a good example of the strict Chinese honesty.

I must add a further word about medicine. In the 27 years since the Revolution, the new regime has succeeded in practically eliminating the main epidemic diseases of China, such as malaria, smallpox, T.B. and V.D. It is a healthy country and sanitation has made enormous strides. One morning in Changsha I woke up with a little cold. It didn't amount to much, but I called in a doctor just to see what it would be like. So a pretty young lady of about 25 came to my room with an interpreter about 9:30 A.M. I told her the cold was not serious, but that perhaps she could give me some pills to knock it out. Presto! She presented me with Vitamin C and Tetracycline, the very pills my New York doctor recommended to stop a cold!

The weather on our trip was mild and sunny, much like New York City in the spring. However, there was one day of rain at Changsha. That afternoon we were supposed to take an airplane for Shanghai. I began to get nervous about flying in a rainstorm. And I was happy when the Chinese cancelled the flight. We stayed an extra day at Changsha and flew to Shanghai the next morning. The Chinese are careful about air travel and do not like to fly in bad weather.

So we finally reached Shanghai, the largest city in China, with a population of more than 10,000,000. Our hotel was close to the harbor and it was easy to walk out to the edge and see the multifarious ships go by. It was fascinating, too, to wander out before breakfast to the park strip along the waterfront and watch the Chinese doing their vigorous and complex setting-up exercises.

We visited another school at Shanghai and a so-called Children's Palace, a recreational center for children. When I stepped off our bus at the Palace, a lovely little Chinese girl about 10 came forward and took me by the hand. I wasn't sure at first what this meant, but it quickly became apparent that she was to be my guide. She led me to the central room, sat beside me during the briefing, then led me to the various other rooms where activities were going on. Finally, she led me back to the bus and I said goodbye. Her name was Happy Ting. I found her guidance very touching. Chinese schoolchildren seem alert, intelligent and hard-working. The ballets and other shows they put on for us indicated that they are being trained in the arts and in aesthetic appreciation.

In China, even though it remains a dictatorship, they don't shoot their dissenters; they "re-educate" them. And that procedure applies also to the highest officials. Teng Hsiao-ping, recently dismissed just as everyone thought he would succeed the deceased Chou En-lai as Premier, is not in jail, but thinking things over and going through the process of re-education. I think Mr. Teng may well make a come-back some day. The same spirit of re-education and rehabilitation governs the treatment of crimes and disputes among the Chinese people. A local Council of Conciliation carries out the main investigation and hearing, attempting to solve through medication and conciliation the problem or controversy in question. The sentence for a designated offender is usually re-education rather than jail or some other kind of punishment.

The re-education process also applied to the tens of thousands of prostitutes of the old regime. After a period of re-training they became functioning workers in the socialist system. Not only has prostitution been eliminated, but also opium, harmful drugs, graft and corruption. The regime of Chiang Kai-shek, President of China before Liberation, was noted for the graft among government officials at all levels.

There is neither unemployment nor monetary inflation in China at present. Gradual economic progress will in all probability continue, including a more highly developed industry. But the Communists are determined that they will not permit the bad by-products of modern technology that have brought pollution and other evils to the United States and other capitalist nations. Experts are already working on this problem. Complete socialism remains the goal. And the spirit of the Chinese workers and peasants is well summed up on the widely distributed pins reading "Serve the People." In the Shanghai Airport that motto was extended by a quotation from Chairman Mao on a big streamer saying, "Serve the People of China and the World."

I have 39 pages of double-spaced typewritten notes on my Chinese trip, but have hit only the highlights in this pamphlet. At this stage of socialist development, with the emphasis still on agriculture, I am convinced that the Chinese are doing well. Since Liberation, the general standard of living has gone up dramatically in terms of food production, health, housing, clothing, education, employment opportunity, wages and cultural amenities. The people everywhere we went seemed dynamic, dedicated and fairly happy. At the local level, in Commune or factory, there is a good deal of "participatory" democracy. People speak up, criticize and put up big character posters with a message. However, I do not want to imply that there are no defects or unsolved problems in the socialist program or that China has become a Utopia.

The disastrous earthquake of July 28, 1976, which killed tens of thousands of Chinese and engulfed Peking and large sections of northeast China, proved a great test for the Communist regime. From all available accounts, that regime handled the crisis with remarkable efficiency and energy, proudly refusing the aid offered by several foreign countries. The Peking Hotel, where our group stayed while in Peking, was damaged. And most of the citizens of that city took to the streets with beds and other equipment, putting up temporary tent-like shelters where they stayed for some three weeks.

Another *Guardian* tour of 24 American teachers was actually in the Peking Hotel when the earthquake struck at 3:40 A.M., with a later tremor at 5:30 A.M. The entire building was rocking back and forth. After another severe tremor in the evening, the Americans were calmly evacuated from the hotel and spent the night in a bus parked outside. The next day the Travel Service flew them to Shanghai to spend the five days during which they had been scheduled to remain in Peking.

Guardian correspondent Jay Steele, the leader of the tour, wrote a first-hand report about the earthquake in which he stated: "The most impressive thing that we saw was the amazing organization and calmness of the people of the whole city lining the streets, most of whom were building shelters. . . . This meant that millions of people were in the streets. There was incredible discipline and collective spirit. . . . Not once did we see any disorder or signs of panic." (*Guardian*, Aug. 11, 1976.)

* * *

I shall conclude with a word about Communist China's foreign policy. I am critical of that policy, particularly in its attitude toward the Soviet Union. Both countries must share some blame for the bad relations between them. But today Chinese hostility toward the U.S.S.R. exceeds, in my opinion, the bounds of reason and constitutes a sort of compulsive, automatic anti-Sovietism. This was most recently demonstrated in Angola where the Chinese opposed the Soviet-backed Popular Movement for the Liberation of Angola (MPLA), which happily in the end won state power, defeating FNLA and UNITA supported by China and the United States.

The Chinese Communists now make the fanciful claim that what they call "Soviet social imperialism" is a greater menace to the peoples of the world than aggressive, militaristic American imperialism. At the same time the Chinese decry détente between the United States and the Soviet Union and urge Americans to put an end to it. This would mean a revival of the Cold War. I, who have worked for American-Soviet cooperation and détente for more than forty years, find the Chinese position here dangerous to peace and quite unreasonable. I cannot possibly accept the Chinese leadership's premise that war between the U.S.A. and the U.S.S.R. is virtually inevitable.

The sound attitude for Americans, especially liberals and radicals, is to maintain critical sympathy toward both China and the U.S.S.R. and to counsel cooperation in place of hostility between those two great countries. Perhaps we need an American Association for Chinese-Soviet Friendship!

We should press, too, for the U.S. Government to establish full diplomatic relations with the People's Republic of China, including official recognition, and to withdraw all military forces from Taiwan (Formosa). All this is in line with the Nixon-Chou En-lai Shanghai Communiqué of February, 1972, signed by both parties. In that Communiqué the United States agreed that Taiwan was a part of China and an "internal matter" for the People's Republic. The American Government has so far failed to withdraw from Taiwan and unfortunately has been sending it arms since 1974 at the rate of about $200 million a year. When this island is again integrated into China proper, the Communist government will in all likelihood establish it as an autonomous republic of China.

TRIP TO COMMUNIST CHINA: AN INFORMAL REPORT

On September 9, 1976, Chairman of the Communist Party, Mao Tse-tung, died after a long period of illness. He was one of the great revolutionary leaders in all history and one of the great statesmen of the modern era. With able associates like Chou En-lai and Chu Teh, he led the Communist Party against fearful odds to victory in the Revolution of 1949; and, despite some serious mistakes, guided the Chinese people successfully towards the new life of socialism. With Mao gone, it is quite possible that a committee rather than a single person will carry out his governing functions.

I believe that the "pragmatists," who are the moderates, will in due course probably win out over the "radicals" in the Communist Party. This would mean a greater emphasis on industrialization and a gradual relaxation of the unremitting enmity towards the Soviet Union, an attitude especially bound up with Mao. A policy of cooperation with the U.S.S.R. would bring important practical benefits to China and immensely help the cause of world socialism. But nobody in the West knows for sure what is going to happen in Communist China and perhaps the Chinese themselves don't know.

22
Adventures in Civil Liberties
(1977)

Restriction of free thought and free speech is the most dangerous of all subversions. It is the one un-American act that could most easily defeat us.
—Justice William O. Douglas

In writing an essay on civil liberties, there are at least four approaches that I might take. First, I could render an historical account of civil liberties since the year 1900, no doubt going into many details during this period. Second, I could give a review of the present situation, let's say over the past four or five years and extending up to the present day. Third, I could tell about the work of the main civil liberties organizations: the American Civil Liberties Union, where I was on the Board of Directors from 1932 to 1954; the National Emergency Civil Liberties Committee of which I have been Chairperson since 1963; and the Bill of Rights Fund, a less well-known organization of which I was President from 1954 to 1965. However, I shall take a fourth approach, namely, recounting my personal involvement in civil liberties battles, court cases and crises.

My first real involvement in a civil liberties issue was over fifty years ago at Harvard College from which I graduated in 1924. In the beginning of that year I was the undergraduate head of the Harvard Union, an organization which offered a social life to the students, provided a speakers program and also facilities for pingpong, pool and other indoor sports.

This essay is based on an address given by Dr. Lamont at the New York Society for Ethical Culture.

We had lecturers like the one who talked on Arctic explorations of the twentieth century, and another on wildlife in darkest Africa and a third on the flora and fauna of the Amazon River. All rather unexciting for most of us. I grew a bit restive myself and thought that the Union ought to have some speakers who discussed topics that were really interesting to the students of Harvard University.

So one day at a meeting of the Union Executive Committee I proposed a slate of different speakers: namely, William Z. Foster, who had led the great steel strike of 1920 and later became Chairman of the U.S. Communist Party; Eugene V. Debs who at that time was still in jail for speaking out against World War I; and Scott Nearing, who had recently been dismissed from the University of Pennsylvania for his radical views on economics. Mr. Nearing is very much alive today and, at over ninety years of age, is still firing away, writing and lecturing. My platform of speakers was not well received. The committee voted it down decisively and it caused great furor in Harvard circles. But we did succeed in slightly liberalizing the speaking program of the Harvard Union. That spring they put on some really controversial topics. That was, you may say, a matter of academic freedom, the right of students to hear speakers whom they wanted and were interested in.

Ten years later came the great battles for Trade Union organization, starting with the Roosevelt regime. After Franklin D. Roosevelt had been elected in 1932, we had a situation in Jersey City where there was a mayor named Frank Hague; and Hague took the position "I am the law," and his law was that there should be no workers organized into trade unions in Jersey City, so that the employers could do pretty much as they pleased. Well, one fine day in 1934 the Civil Liberties Union, of which I was already a Director, sent me over to picket on behalf of the Furniture Workers Industrial Union. I walked up and down for about twenty minutes with a sign and at the end of that time a couple of policemen came by with a police van and arrested me. They led me into the van and hauled me off to jail. The thing I best remember about that Jersey City jail is that they made me remove my necktie, shoelaces and belt, so that I wouldn't commit suicide.

I was in jail only a few hours, because the Civil Liberties Union very promptly got me bail, and I came out and went home to New York City for a pleasant supper. Yet, because I was in jail even for a short time I was immediately given the title of Jail Bird for Civil Liberties, a title I accepted with pleasure. We won the battle in Jersey City. Of course, we appealed my arrest right away, but there were other cases in the courts ahead of mine; and before my case even came to trial, we had won the right to organize workers in Jersey City because the higher courts of New Jersey cracked down hard on Mayor Hague. My case was then automatically dropped.

During the next ten years I was involved in little struggles here and there, and with my work in the American Civil Liberties Union. My next big case was in 1946 when I was subpoenaed by the Un-American Activities Committee of the House of Representatives. This Committee had been set up some years before, and after World War II became the greatest possible menace to civil liberties in the United States. They subpoenaed me as Chairman of the National Committee of American-Soviet Friendship and demanded that I bring with me to their hearing in Washington all our correspondence and financial records since the organization was founded. We considered this a violation of the First Amendment. We didn't think that the Un-American Committee had a right to investigate us at all and that its mandate for "the investigation of Un-American propaganda" was unconstitutional on its face. So I refused to bring those papers. I had a very heated session with J. Parnell Thomas, the Chairman, who later went to jail for graft, and with John E. Rankin from Mississippi, who shouted at me at the top of his lungs, and wanted to know why I hadn't told the American people about the crimes of Soviet soldiers everywhere throughout Eastern Europe.

Anyway, the House cited me for contempt of Congress because I didn't bring the papers. But actually I did not have custody of those papers. The Director of the organization had the responsibility for them. The U.S. Attorney General soon dropped my case because he knew it couldn't stand up in the Courts. The Un-American Activities Committee much later was transformed into the House Internal Security Committee. In January of 1975 that House Committee was abolished and we were finally rid of that evil institution, the Un-American Activities Committee.

Proceeding for another decade and a half, I come to an even more important encounter with the governmental authorities of the United States, when in 1953 I was subpoenaed by Senator Joseph McCarthy to appear before his Senate Sub-Committee on Government Operations at the U.S. Courthouse in New York City. And it was an odd reason for which he had subpoenaed me. Joe McCarthy blew his top because he found that a U.S. Army bibliography had listed a book by me called *The Peoples of the Soviet Union*. That was a book entirely on the racial and national policies of the Soviet Union; it wasn't a defense of their economic system or their political system. It was an attempt to show what the 177 nationalities of the Soviet Union were doing and how they were treated and what rights they had under the Soviet Constitution.

I hadn't known that my book was on the Army bibliography and was rather pleased at first, until I learned that it was there so that when American troops invaded the Soviet Union they would know how to treat those various minority peoples. I went down to the Courthouse, of course, and one of the first things I noticed was a gentleman sitting way off in the left-hand corner of the room, and I recognized him as Louis Budenz, that famous ex-Communist turncoat who was always swearing that this or that person was a member of the Communist Party. He was there frankly to intimidate me.

I told Mr. McCarthy at the start that I wasn't a member of the Communist Party, because I knew he was going to ask me that question and I wanted to spike his strategy. Then I refused to answer about twenty-five other questions that he did ask me. Those questions dealt with who helped me write that book on the Soviet Union, what members of the Communist Party were advising me, and whether there was an agent of the Soviet Government cooperating with me. I refused to answer all these questions on the ground that they violated freedom of the press and my freedom of scholarship; and that anyhow to investigate me was outside the scope of Senator McCarthy's Committee, since I was in no sense an employee of the United States Government. Nonetheless, the U.S. Senate cited me for contempt of Congress, with a possible sentence of a year in jail and a fine of $5,000. Three Senators voted against the contempt citation: Herbert Lehman, Democrat of New York; Dennis Chavez, Democrat of Arizona; and "Wild Bill" Langer, Republican of North Dakota. A personal friend, Senator Leverett Saltonstall of Massachusetts, made a speech declaring that I was "an honest man," but then voted for the contempt citation.

Philip Wittenberg, a noted New York City lawyer, handled my case and it never came to trial because we moved to dismiss the indictment; and Judge Edward Weinfeld in New York City did dismiss it in July of 1955 for the reason that, as my attorney had shown, the McCarthy Committee had no right to conduct an investigation of me. A Federal Court of Appeals unanimously upheld the Weinfeld decision in 1956; and because of that unanimity, the Government did not proceed with another appeal.

It is worth noting that in that period McCarthy forced into the courts about eight cases of persons whom he had gotten cited for contempt of Congress. He lost all eight cases. That is a good example of how during the McCarthy era the U.S. Courts, including the Warren Supreme Court, upheld civil liberties quite well, although never 100 percent. However, some of those who won against McCarthy in the courts lost their jobs because of all the smear publicity.

As to McCarthy himself, you just looked at his face and you knew he was a scoundrel. I was happy that by beating him in the courts, I put a nail into his political coffin. And it was no sorrow to me that a few years later he was deposited in a real coffin, after dying from hepatitis and too much liquor.

Now I mentioned *The Peoples of the Soviet Union* as the book on account of which McCarthy came after me; and it is significant to know that the FBI in their heroic attempt to protect America went to my publisher, Harcourt Brace, and asked, "Was this book financed by Moscow?" An absurd question for one of the most prosperous publishers in the United States. The FBI agent knew perfectly well the answer would be negative, but he wanted to indicate to the publisher that the FBI did not approve of the book and did not approve of me. Now what publisher after a visit from the FBI is going to be enthusiastic about publishing the next book by that author? Isn't he going to say, "I don't want to get in trouble with the FBI again"? The FBI did exactly the same thing with another publisher, Philosophical Library, which issued a book of mine called *Soviet Civilization.*

Even Canada succumbed to the McCarthy virus. In May, 1956, I was on a continental speaking tour and was scheduled to give two lectures at the First Unitarian Church of Toronto under the auspices of the Toronto Humanist Association, a philosophical organization that was completely non-sectarian and non-political. My topics were "Humanism and Civil Liberties" and "Humanism versus the Traditional Religions." When my train from Detroit to Toronto stopped at Windsor, Ontario, Canadian immigration officials came on board, arrested me and had me deported back to Detroit as an "undesirable visitor." Within hours the news of this incident had spread widely, and angry protests exploded in the Canadian press and Parliament. "Cut out this nonsense," said the *Toronto Globe and Mail* in an editorial castigating my deportation.

In fact, the protests became so serious and widespread that the next day the Canadian Minister of Immigration, John W. Pickersgill, reversed my deportation. At the same time he excused the earlier action on the grounds that the National Council of American-Soviet Friendship, which he called "a Communist front," had arranged my lectures. This was an absolute lie, since that organization had nothing whatever to do with my tour. The consequence of my deportation was that I missed my first meeting and a TV broadcast. However, I managed to arrive at the Toronto church just in time for my second address, by racing 250 miles through the rain in a drive-your-own car. I am reasonably certain that the FBI or CIA, or both together, incited the Canadian authorities to the nonsense of my deportation.

In that mad and maddening era of McCarthyism we had trouble with passports. I had engaged a passage on the "Queen Mary" with my wife and family to go abroad in the summer of 1951 and I thought I would easily get my passport renewed. But then suddenly the State Department put on the passport three questions about membership in the Communist Party. And though I had publicly declared my non-membership in the Communist Party about a thousand times, I refused to sign those forms, and for that reason was denied a passport for seven whole years. My stand was a matter of principle. There were no legitimate grounds for the State

Department to make political qualifications for an American citizen to obtain a passport. I got a letter from Mrs. Knight in the Passport Department saying, "Mr. Lamont, we are very sorry, but we think it is contrary to the best interests of the United States to have you travel abroad at present." And what was I going to do traveling abroad? I was going to go to museums, see the sights, visit friends and do a little research, but they always thought I was going to conspire somehow against the United States. Anyway, I sued the U.S. State Department to obtain my passport.

This passport nonsense went on for quite a while and instead of going to Europe that summer of 1951 we went to Mexico and had the time of our lives. You know, we might never have gone to marvelous Mexico except for the State Department refusing my passport. You don't need a passport to go to Mexico, and there I met Diego Rivera and David Alfaro Siqueiros, both noted Communists. Rivera insisted on painting my portrait and I really enjoyed Mexico immensely. Leonard Boudin, perhaps the most brilliant constitutional lawyer in the United States, was handling my passport case in the courts and also that of artist and writer Rockwell Kent. In the spring of 1958 the Kent case went to the U.S. Supreme Court. It was way ahead of my case and the Supreme Court ruled that the State Department's new forms were unconstitutional, stating that it could not make political qualifications for someone to get a passport. That was a great victory for civil liberties and the right to travel. After the Kent decision, my case was dropped because I didn't need to get a court ruling any more. And I soon obtained my passport.

Now we'll leap to 1963 and talk about the law that Congress passed requiring the Postmaster General to screen all incoming mail from foreign countries, except first-class sealed mail, for Communist political propaganda. If the Postmaster found something containing even one sentence of alleged Communist political propaganda, then he was to send a postcard to the addressee saying in effect, "Do you really want to receive this subversive literature?" And if he wrote back No, the Post Office destroyed the literature and if he wrote back Yes, the Post Office mailed the literature to him. My lawyer, Leonard Boudin, found out a little later that, when the Post Office sent the literature to the addressee, it also sent his name to the Un-American Activities Committee. And then the Un-American Committee would subpoena that poor guy who was getting some piece of mail from China or the Soviet Union or Poland, and he would be in trouble.

Well, anyway, I got a postcard informing me that a copy of the *Peking Review* was addressed to me and was being held by the Post Office in San Francisco. I hadn't subscribed to the *Peking Review* but somebody was sending me this magazine. I was rather annoyed at getting the postcard, and instead of returning it and saying, "Yes, I do want it," I sued the Postmaster General. I sued him on the grounds that he was violating my

First Amendment rights, that he was delaying the delivery of something I wanted to read and that this was all in violation of the Constitution. We lost the case in the District Court and also in the Federal Appeals Court, and then we went to the U.S. Supreme Court.

I remember going down to Washington in May 1965 with Mr. Boudin and sitting in the Supreme Court courtroom and hearing all the arguments. Boudin, of course, was brilliant and the Solicitor General of the United States rather weak and wobbly, like many other government officials. A delegation of students from the Harvard Law School was there to listen to the arguments before the Supreme Court. Only a month later the decision was announced in the case of *Lamont* v. *Postmaster General*. We were as surprised as could be that the Court decided 8 to 0, unanimously, that the statute was unconstitutional on First Amendment grounds. Justice Douglas wrote the main opinion saying that this law was unconstitutional because it interfered with the "unfettered exercise" of First Amendment rights. This was the first time in the history of the Supreme Court that it ever declared a Congressional statute unconstitutional on the grounds it violated the First Amendment. So we were all very pleased about that.

Now we jump another decade to the years 1975 and 1976 and the operations of the Freedom of Information Act which gives American citizens who think that the FBI or the CIA has a file on them the right to see the file in question. In 1975 Mr. Boudin and I made a guess, a reasoned guess, that there was a file on me at both the CIA and the FBI. That guess turned out to be true in both cases. After correspondence for about eight months in a delaying action the FBI confessed that it had a file on me of 1,800 pages, later admitted to be about 2,000 pages. I was somewhat surprised at the size of the file, but then my friends started to congratulate me. Anyway, early in 1976 we finally obtained 274 of those pages, and the FBI held back the other 1,726 "in the interest of national security and foreign policy." That was a lot of material I was not permitted to see. We appealed the matter in an administrative way to the Deputy Attorney General of the U.S., and also sued in the courts to get those 1,700-odd pages in my FBI file. In November, 1976, the Government surrendered to the extent of releasing to me all but 300 pages, with a number of names deleted. We are continuing our appeal for the release of the final 300 pages.

I forced myself to read most of my FBI file, and it was really very boring because they had monitored my radio speeches, and copied my articles and pamphlets. They could have gotten all this from me free. But they had to assign an agent to do all this work and I had to read it many years later. Nonetheless, I found some very important and amusing material. For instance, in 1961 John Kenneth Galbraith was appointed Ambassador to India by President Kennedy and he had to have a security check by the FBI. They came after Galbraith in a big way and one of the questions they asked was: "Professor Galbraith, why were you living fourteen years ago in the same apartment house in New York City as Corliss Lamont?" Well, Galbraith took an attitude of what you might call affronted dignity and brushed the matter off humorously by calling it a case of "dangerous cohabitation." So you see we have a new crime—not only guilt by association but guilt by cohabitation. Incidentally, Senator Javits of New York and his wife lived for a while in the same apartment house and I suppose they have kept it secret all this time. The building was 450 Riverside Drive, owned by Columbia University.

There was another incident there which was quite significant. One day the elevator man, Johnny, stopped me and said, "You know, there was an FBI man here asking me about you." I said, "Why Johnny, what did he say?" This was some twenty years ago and I'll try to reconstruct the conversation. The FBI agent said, "What does Mr. Lamont say on the way up in the elevator?" Johnny answered, "He don't say much." FBI agent: "Does he ever mention Soviet Russia?" Johnny: "No, I can't remember that." Then the FBI man became very firm and said, "Well, I suppose he *did* talk to you about Communism?" Johnny: "No, he never mentioned that." Johnny was getting nervous at this point because he felt he was failing a test and that somehow he must supply some valid information to a Government agent. So he said to the FBI man, "Well, I tell you, Mr. Lamont sometimes carries a tennis racquet." We will stop there, except that I must add that about a year later a U.S. Government employee was quizzed by the FBI as to why he had played tennis doubles with me.

About this same time the FBI came around to a friend of mine and asked him a number of questions about me. One was, "Does Lamont have a grand piano?" Another was, "Is he influenced by women?" I enthusiastically plead guilty here in the affirmative. Has there been a single man in the history of the human race who was not influenced by the female sex? The FBI question about women was so absurd it must have been invented by J. Edgar Hoover himself!

The FBI perpetrated its greatest outrage against me and my family when it engaged a member of my parents' staff to spy on me at the Lamont summer place on the island of North Haven, off the coast of Maine. The man in question was supposed to report with whom I played tennis and went sailing during my summer vacation, and to tail me in general. Again, absurdity to such a degree that we are justified in saying FBI stands for *Federal Bureau of Idiots.*

I could go on for a long time about my FBI file, and I do want to add this one thing that I learned from other sources. For many years the FBI came into my bank at the end of every month and looked at all my cancelled checks and then demanded that they receive copies of them in Washington. Well, this was against the law and has made me more nervous than anything else because I am always afraid of filing a tax return that isn't quite accurate. With the FBI maybe reporting all these checks to the Internal Revenue Service, I might get into real trouble, but nothing like that ever happened. For all I know, the FBI is still looking at my cancelled checks.

I will just mention in passing my CIA file, of which I have more than 300 pages. The CIA snoopers opened every letter I ever sent to the Soviet Union for twenty-five years and every letter I received from the Soviet Union. They photostated those 300 pages of letters and then sent me the photostats of the photostats; like the FBI, they are holding back a large number of pages of what they call very sensitive material. Even a postcard that I sent to the Soviet Union or received from there was photostated. What I was doing mostly was to correspond with an old friend, a former brilliant economics instructor at Columbia University by the name of Vladimir Kazakevich. He was a Russian emigré who returned to his homeland in 1949. We had quite a correspondence on economics and politics and I just hope the CIA read that stuff and got educated. I am now suing the CIA for the remainder of my file and for $150,000 damages for violation of my right to privacy.*

The CIA's opening of my letters was entirely illegal; and when they secretly investigated the Washington Ethical Society, a domestic organization, and its able Leader Edward L. Ericson, that also was completely out of bounds. For the Central Intelligence Agency has no right to spy on domestic organizations or to intrude into domestic dissent. Its Congressional charter definitely forbids it to engage in domestic activity. When Mr. Ericson obtained part of his CIA file, it consisted primarily of copies of his public addresses and of his monthly messages to the Society. Thus it was much like my FBI file. Incidentally, during the Vietnam War the CIA was illegally spying on fifteen other Washington-area organizations besides the Ethical Society.

The last episode I shall mention pertains to a non-governmental organization, the American Civil Liberties Union. Early in 1940 the ACLU passed an anti-Communist purge resolution, which became a model for trade unions and other non-governmental organizations in their own participation in the great anti-Communist witch-hunt. The Civil Liberties Union soon activated its new anti-civil liberties resolution in May of 1940 when it expelled Elizabeth Gurley Flynn, a devoted upholder of civil liberties, from the Board of Directors merely because she was a member of the Communist Party. This put into effect guilt by association, a concept which the ACLU had always opposed. I and nine other members of the Board

---

*In 1975 Federal District Judge Jack B. Weinstein rendered a hard-hitting decision against the CIA for its unconstitutional conduct toward me. See p. 378.—C.L.

voted against Miss Flynn's expulsion.

Many years later, in 1968 (Miss Flynn had died in 1964) I edited and published the full stenographic text of the Flynn hearing under the title of *The Trial of Elizabeth Gurley Flynn by the American Civil Liberties Union*. At the same time I petitioned the ACLU Board of Directors to rescind posthumously Miss Flynn's expulsion. My petition was not even presented to the Board. It was only some seven or eight years later that members of the Board read my book, which had been sent to them by Mr. George Slaff, a Los Angeles attorney and Vice-Chairman of the ACLU, who had become much concerned over the Flynn case. The final result was that in April of 1976, thirty-six years after the event, the ACLU Board of Directors passed by a large majority a resolution rescinding Miss Flynn's expulsion and apologizing to her. This was an important victory for civil liberties and a principled, courageous act on the part of the American Civil Liberties Union. I am happy that I played some part in bringing it about.

* * *

So what does all this add up to? It clearly means that the struggle for complete free speech and civil liberties must be unceasing, even in a country like the United States that does have strong democratic institutions. I have fought for civil liberties for more than fifty years. Yet I know that the battle will never be permanently won. However, I think that at present we are making progress in the defense of the Bill of Rights. The exposures of the CIA and the FBI have alerted the American people to the danger of unscrupulous government bureaucracies running wild and heedlessly violating both the Constitution and U.S. criminal law. With the cooperation of the Carter Administration, Congress will surely enact legislation restricting the activities of the CIA and FBI and providing for proper Congressional supervision.

At the same time the détente with the Soviet Union and the Communist world is matched by a domestic détente in which the old anti-Communist witch-hunt of the McCarthy days has largely subsided. In the realm of motion pictures, for instance, many formerly blacklisted persons have made a comeback. And Hollywood is now producing pictures, such as "The Front" with Woody Allen, that publicly expose its anti-civil liberties purges during the years of anti-Communist hysteria.

With a liberal Democratic Administration in power in Washington, I believe that the time is ripe for a great renascence of civil liberties in this country.

23
The Myth of Immortality
(1979)

In October, 1978, the civilized world was amazed and shocked over the mass suicide of some 900 members of the People's Temple, a recently organized American religious cult, at Jonestown in the tiny country of Guyana in South America. The leader of this esoteric cult was the Rev. Jim Jones, a charismatic figure who had extraordinary powers of eloquence and persuasion over his followers. He promised them a beautiful and happy immortality after death and told them that the time to die had come, by drinking a mixture of cyanide and purple Kool Aid. That hundreds of adult Americans, healthy of body but sick of mind, should literally carry out his directive shows to what dangerous extremes fanatical religion can go and the deep-felt lure of belief in blissful survival beyond the grave.

In this essay I shall attempt to analyze the age-long concept of personal immortality according to the methods of reason, modern science and common sense.

At the outset, however, we must recognize that there are at least five types of immortality that are worth discussing:

First, there is biological immortality through one's children and descendants. Of course, this does not apply to childless couples; and any family line may eventually die out.

Second, we have social immortality, that is, the impact and influence on future generations, both by famous individuals whose names may endure as writers, statesmen, scientists, assassins or what-not, and the average person.

The Garvin Lecture in Lancaster, Pennsylvania, 1974.

Third, based on the scientific law of the indestructibility of matter, there is material immortality, the indestructibility of the physical elements of the human body. This holds true even if the body is cremated.

Almost every thinking person would agree that these first three forms of immortality exist.

Fourth, we must consider reincarnation in human or animal form, wherein the soul of a dead individual enters or infiltrates the embryo or just born body of another human being or animal. Reincarnation is a particularly fundamental doctrine in the Buddhist religion and in India.

Fifth, we come to personal immortality, the enduring, unending survival of the conscious human personality after death. That is and always has been the most basic issue; and in this essay I shall discuss primarily this form of immortality. Down the ages the question of personal survival has been a constant and important subject of controversy in religion and philosophy. We must sympathize with those millions upon millions of human beings who, having lost their loved ones through death and finding this life full of suffering and unhappiness, have nourished the religious promise that beyond the grave a happier existence will be their lot.

I think that in general the problem of personal immortality has been more significant than the existence of God. The American philosopher, William James, stated: "The popular touchstone for all philosophies is the question 'What is their bearing on a future life?'" And he went on to say that for most men God has been primarily the guarantor of survival beyond the grave.

More than half a century ago, when I was twenty years old, I became seriously interested in the subject of immortality. At that time I was an active member of the Presbyterian Church and a convinced believer in a future life. My interest was strengthened by an aunt and uncle who were Spiritualists. My aunt was an amateur medium and brought me messages every now and then from her dead son Joe, who was my deceased cousin. On my twenty-first birthday she presented me with a poem entitled "A Man Thou Art Today," supposedly dictated to her by Joe. This implied traffic with the dead was quite stimulating to me, though I only half-believed it was authentic. My interest in the idea of immortality continued so great that I took up studies on the subject at Columbia University. I still believed in a hereafter. My research resulted in a Ph.D. thesis in philosophy under the title of *Issues of Immortality*. It was published as a book in 1932.

The main point in my thesis was to show that almost all immortality ideas rely upon some form of the unity of personality and body. (I am using the words "personality" and "soul" interchangeably in this essay, but prefer the term "personality," because it is less tied up with traditional concepts.) This living unity of personality and physical organism is an example of the metaphysical principle of the unity of form and matter.

Every manifestation of matter has a certain definite form or structure definable as a stone, a tree, a man or something else. In man the personality is the form, matter the body.

Religious acceptance of this doctrine is most clearly seen in the Bible. The Old Testament Hebrews could not conceive of a robust, happy afterlife without the body. They either looked upon death as the end or thought the enfeebled spirits of the dead went to a sad and somber place called Sheol. The ancient Greeks had a similar view of life after death in what they called Hades. According to Homer, the shade of Achilles told Ulysses: "Better to be the hireling of a slave and serve a man of mean estate than to be ruler over all these dead and gone." Plato wanted such passages to be deleted from the poets, because he thought that they would make warriors less willing to give up their lives in war.

Returning now to the Bible, we find that the New Testament Christians had a very different attitude towards post-mortem existence. Their brilliant solution was the resurrection of the natural body become glorified and incorruptible. The orthodox Christian conception of the resurrection and immortality brings out clearly that body and soul must be inseparable in the after-life just as in this life. The foundation stone of Christianity is faith in the bodily resurrection of Jesus into the realm of immortality as recounted in the New Testament. The resurrection extends to everyone, and it is to be the identical body of this world, without a hair or fingernail missing, that rises from the tomb. The Roman Catholic Church still forbids cremation for its members because it psychologically weakens belief in the resurrection of the corpse. Primitive religions also associated immortality with the body. The ancient Egyptians, for example, believed that a desirable future life was bound up with the mummification and preservation of the dead, natural body.

But in modern times more and more people in the Western world have become unable to believe in the literal resurrection of the body. Yet, in the immortality ideas of certain modern religious sects it is clear that some sort of body is necessary in the hereafter. The Spiritualists give the soul an *etheric* body. The Swedenborgians have invented the *crystalline* body. The Theosophists talk of *astral* bodies. And the Modernists in Protestant churches, like that brilliant preacher, Harry Emerson Fosdick, assume the existence of *spiritual* bodies in the future life as essential vehicles for the personality or soul. Reincarnation supplies the departed soul with a body, even if it be that of a monkey or cobra, as we know from a study of the Buddhists and Hindus in India. There is a strong Buddhist following in Japan. When I was traveling in that country in 1959, I read in the newspapers that since Crown Prince Akihito and his wife were expecting a baby very shortly, it was estimated that at least 1,000 suicides would probably take place so that the dead person's soul could enter the body of the baby at the precise moment of its birth. The individual thus reincarnated then might one day become Emperor. That's how seriously the idea of reincarnation can be taken.

More than 2,000 years ago Lucretius summed up the situation in his great poem, *On the Nature of Things:*

> *Again, feeling doth prove that mind is born*
> *Along with body, and with it step by step*
> *Doth grow, and equally must waste with age.*
> *For e'en as children totter with a weak*
> *And tender frame, so doth a slender wit*
> *Attend thereon; but as with riper years*
> *Their strength doth wax, wisdom will grow apace*
> *And force of mind gain increase. And at last,*
> *When time's stern strength hath sapped the frame, and loosed*
> *Are all the limbs, their powers benumbed, anon*
> *The wits are lamed, tongue raveth, mind is shaken,*
> *All things give way and in one breath are fled.*
> *'Tis meet, then, that the nature of the mind*
> *Should all be scattered likewise, e'en as smoke*
> *Into the high-flung breezes of the air;*
> *Since side by side with body do we see*
> *It brought to birth, and side by side they grow,*
> *And worn with age together droop and fade.*

Psychology, especially, demonstrates the unity of body and personality. The mind and thinking processes are vital to the sense of personality, to the development of the personality and to most of the activities of the personality. Those thinking processes are centered in the cerebral cortex which has more than ten billion neurons or nerve cells. In the brain's cortex the different interneuronic connections, actual and possible, approach infinity. Our memory patterns are laid down in this extraordinary cortex; and memory is of crucial importance for personal immortality because it is necessary for connecting the mortal and the immortal self, just as it is essential for connecting the self that goes to sleep at night with the self that awakes in the morning. In the body as a whole there are 265 trillion cells. And one must ask, "Really, can all those numberless intricacies of body and brain be resurrected as functioning entities on the great Day of Judgment after the corpse has decayed in the grave for untold eons or been reduced to ashes in the crematory?"

We also need to remember that mind in man comes into being only through social intercourse, through the give-and-take of language and speech in the family and the larger community. We are born with brains; we *acquire* minds by association with other minds. Thus, there is an inseparable connection between the body-mind-personality and the human community. This fact further undermines the dualist psychology.

In this discussion the scientific Law of Parsimony is of particular significance. This law holds that any scientific explanation be based on the fewest possible assumptions that succeed in accounting for all the facts. Sir Arthur Conan Doyle, the creator of Sherlock Holmes, came to think that the spirits of the dead could be contacted and even believed that invisible fairies tended the flowers at night. We discard this charming idea about fairies because the science of botany adequately explains in naturalistic terms why flowers grow or do not grow. They don't *need* the help of fairies. The Law of Parsimony rules them out as an unnecessary assumption.

The dualist assumption of man having a separable, supernatural soul violates this same law because such an assumption is superfluous for explaining the emotional profundities and intellectual powers of human beings. The infinite intricacy of the brain and its cerebral cortex are fully competent to sustain the manifold activities and impressive achievements of human personalities. To add a special soul to a man's native equipment is like conjuring up little devils or demons as the cause of insanity or hysteria. Physicians still believed in the devil theory well into the nineteenth century; and I gather from the newspapers that many of our fellow citizens are coming back to it today. The Catholic Church has never given up belief in *The* Devil and a multitude of little devils.

To summarize, the sciences of biology, medicine and psychology have accumulated an enormous amount of evidence pointing to the oneness and inseparability of personality and physical organism. The Law of Parsimony leads to the same conclusion. It is inconceivable that the characteristic mental activities of thought, memory and imagination could go on without the cooperating potencies of the brain and cerebral cortex. Moreover, the monistic view of the nature of man is supported or implied by Christianity and other religions which insist that soul and some kind of body are necessary for the after-life. Since I am unable to believe in any of the supernatural bodies offered, the research and reflection I carried on after the publication of my first book on immortality led me to conclude that it is very, very probable that death marks the end of the conscious personality. This is the theme of my later book, *The Illusion of Immortality* (1935).

What my Ph.D. thesis showed was that Christianity in its main divisions, primitive religion, modern cults in the West and reincarnation in the East, all stressed the necessity for some sort of body in the after-life and thus lent support to the monistic psychology of the unity of body and personality. Looking at the various alternatives, I concluded that the best way to achieve immortality is through the resurrection of the natural body, or through its continuing to stay alive on this earth.

As to the prolongation of individual human lives, the science of medicine has made such advances during the twentieth century that the average length of life has been greatly extended in many countries. Life expectancy in the United States is now a little over 73. The science of medicine is still grappling with old age diseases such as heart attacks and hardening of the arteries. Even if those diseases are finally overcome, it is doubtful if medicine can prolong human lives indefinitely. This is because the billions of cells in the human body will probably wear out and cease to function properly. It is barely conceivable, however, that far in the future a man might live to the age of 969, which the Bible tells us Methuselah reached.

Scientific experiments have recently been made with rats that were injected with a drug that prolonged the life of their body cells. Other experiments claim to show that if a man's body temperature were reduced from the normal 98.6 Fahrenheit to 88 degrees, for instance, he would then be able to live, other things being equal, to the age of 200.

Then there is the Life Extension Society, which claims that if you freeze a man at the moment of dying and then resurrect him and thaw him out fifty or a hundred years later, the doctors will be able, because of advances in medicine, to cure him of the disease from which he originally died. Then he might keep on living indefinitely. The advertising slogan of the Life Extension Society is "Freeze, Wait, Reanimate!" It is true that some unicellular animals and bacteria frozen for centuries into Arctic tundra or Antarctic ice have come alive when thawed out. But we must doubt whether the same result would take place in the case of a very complex organism such as man, with the circulation of the blood always a vital factor.

In California in 1967, retired Professor of Psychology James H. Bedford died at seventy-three. As soon as he was pronounced dead, various chemicals were injected into his body, which was then quickly frozen in dry ice. A few days later the dead body was immersed in liquid nitrogen for storage at 196 degrees below zero centigrade. This experiment is being conducted by the Cryonics Society of California, an organization for the study of life at extremely low temperatures. The cost for Professor Bedford and his family was $10,000.

We have to admit that these experiments are on the right track, because they do proceed on the basis of body and personality being inseparable. And such experiments remind us of the solid truth that the only way to become immortal is to stay alive forever in this natural world. Then we actualize the original meaning of *immortality* as "not-death."

When we turn from religion and philosophy to science, we find conclusive evidence of the intimate and inseparable association of body or physical organism, on the one hand, and personality, including the mind, on the other hand. This inseparability is the central feature of what we call the *monistic* or Aristotelian psychology as contrasted with the *dualistic* or Platonic psychology. Psychological dualism assumes that man is fundamentally a two-ness, with a separable, supernatural soul entering the body at the moment of conception.

Modern biology, psychology and medicine all give strong support to the monistic viewpoint.

Biology shows that the species man is the culmination of a long evolutionary process that began at least three billion years ago when the first living forms appeared on this earth. Personality and mind appear only when the physical organism has reached a very complex stage, as in the human animal. Mind came towards the end, not the beginning, of evolution as it has developed up till now. It is the complexity of the brain in man, and especially of the cerebral cortex, that gives him the power of thought.

Just as in the evolution of species, mind and personality appear when bodily organization has reached a certain stage, so it is in the history of every normal human being. Neither the embryo nor the newborn infant possesses the distinguishing features of mind. The laws of heredity and of sex, all based on genes, are fundamental in determining what sort of personality develops.

As I said earlier, the resurrection of the dead body is in some ways the most sensible way to save the day for immortality. But that is a miracle that in this modern age I and probably a majority of the human race cannot possibly believe in.

And this solution in any case has a fatal flaw. The world refuses to come to an end and no resurrection has taken place, despite the repeated predictions of the Seventh Day Adventists. Meanwhile, the souls of the dead are supposedly biding their time in places like purgatory; but they do not have their original bodies with them. And their survival as naked souls, as it were, runs into all the difficulties I have pointed out in relation to personal survival in general.

I deeply regret that personal immortality seems impossible. Having just turned seventy-seven, I do not relish at all the prospect of complete extinction within the next ten years or so. As the sole survivor of my original family, I would like nothing better than to awake after death in the Utopia that is heaven and to be once more with my beloved parents, brothers and sister; and to mingle with my many dear friends who have passed on.

However, the main motive for my desiring an after-life, as for most other people, is the simple wish to keep on living. We are enjoying life on this earth, or a lot of us are, and we want to keep it up. And so, since we have to die, we would like to go on living somewhere else. It is an extension of the instinct for self-preservation. The idea of personal immortality, if we exclude the concepts of hell and purgatory, is a beautiful myth or dream. But we should not treat the dream as reality.

The sonnet "Transient" by Don Marquis deals with this theme:

> *Give up the dream that Love may trick the fates*
> *To live again beyond the gleam*
> *Of dying stars, or shatter the strong gates*
> *Some god has builded high: give up the dream.*
> *Flame were not flame unless it met the dark—*
> *The beauty of our doomed, bewildered loves*
> *Dwells in the transience of the moving spark*
> *Which pricks oblivion's blackness as it moves;*
> *A few more heartbeats and our hearts shall lie*
> *Dusty and done with raptures and with rhyme:*
> *Let us not babble of eternity*
> *Who stand upon this little edge of time!*
> *Even old godheads sink in space and drown*
> *Their arks like foundered galleons sucked down.*

It is worth-while to note that although I reached a negative conclusion about immortality, I started out with a strong bent in favor of the belief. And now I still hold to the *dis*belief, though I have a strong desire to enjoy a long and lively post-mortem existence. I have tried to follow the facts wherever they have led and to use my reason in interpreting the facts. And I have continually kept in mind George Santayana's epigram: "That rare advance in wisdom which consists in abandoning our illusions the better to attain our ideals."

In my own case the knowledge that when I am dead, I stay dead, has stimulated me to greater activity and to work harder on behalf of such goals as social justice, civil liberties and international peace. I believe that giving up the illusion of immortality helps men and women in general better to achieve their this-earthly ideals. Frequently in the history of the West the belief in immortality, with its heaven and hell, has cut the nerve of effective action in this world. That belief has sometimes even functioned as an apology for war. Here is a report referring to the Korean War by *The New York Times* of September 11, 1950: "Sorrowing parents whose sons have been drafted or recalled for combat duty were told yesterday in St. Patrick's Cathedral that death in battle was part of God's plan for populating the kingdom of heaven." That was Monsignor William T. Greene of the Roman Catholic Church.

But do not let us think that the Catholics can outdo the Church of England. Dr. Geoffrey Francis Fisher, former Archbishop of Canterbury, has this to say: "The hydrogen bomb is not the greatest danger of our time. After all, the most it could do would be to transfer vast numbers of human beings simultaneously from this world to another and more vital one into which they would someday go anyhow."

But my prize statement in connection with war came from a Captain in the United States Army who in a letter to me criticized my book *The Illusion of Immortality* on the grounds it might undermine the morale of the Army. I do not think it ever did undermine that morale, because I doubt if any soldier ever read the book except that one Captain. There were no orders reported from the Defense Department of the United States. In his letter the Captain went on to say that we in the Army "regard death as no more important than a nose bleed." Just like a nose bleed! Wouldn't that be wonderful, if true? Well, if death is really that unimportant, then why worry about sending millions of young men to their doom in international wars?

Of course, these quotations I have been giving do not tell the whole story. There have been plenty of devout believers in immortality who have been militant fighters for social justice.

We often hear the classic statement that the denial of immortality leads to a philosophy of "Let us eat, drink and be merry, for tomorrow we die." Certainly the Humanist philosophy that I support is in favor of good food, good drinks and a merry time for all. But if this life is the sole opportunity for self-enjoyment and merriment, it is also the only opportunity for human achievement, working for the social good, expressing love towards one's family and friends, and contributing to the welfare and progress of humanity as a whole. And the greatest heroism of all is to die for a cause when you don't believe in a hereafter and have no hope of a reward in heaven.

In the Communist countries of the Soviet Union and China, the denial of personal immortality is official doctrine. Whatever we think about the situation in those nations, and whatever valid criticisms of them we have, the Chinese and Soviet peoples work hard and energetically despite their general belief that this life is all.

But we do not have to go so far afield to find out that disbelief in immortality does not usually turn people into playboys, drunkards and drifters. Here in the United States there is a strong Humanist movement whose adherents reject belief in personal immortality or any form of the supernatural. Humanists are usually very active people and militant on behalf of all sorts of good causes such as civil liberties, international peace and the conservation of Nature. In general, the best way to avoid preoccupation with the prospect of death is preoccupation with useful and happy activities here and now. But death almost always causes a great deal of strain, sorrow and unhappiness. One important antidote for these natural reactions is to understand fully the meaning of death in Nature.

In most religions death has been regarded as a great enemy of mankind, if not the greatest. Christianity has looked upon death as a punishment for the sins of Adam and Eve. Such attitudes have been a significant factor in the development of immortality ideas. If there is a life beyond death, then death—the great evil—is defeated. And Christianity has always been a death-conquering religion, as witness the dead Jesus allegedly rising from his tomb into eternal life.

In the cultures of the West, the somber, negative aspects of death have been constantly stressed. People think of death primarily when some close relative or friend dies, when hundreds of men and women lose their lives in an airplane accident, or when millions of human beings meet death in a world war. And every normal person tries to avoid death as long as he can. But if we study the phenomenon of death objectively, we find that it has positive aspects and on the whole is perhaps more a friend than foe of man.

When living animals first came into existence on this planet, they were one-celled organisms, like the amoeba and protozoon. They reproduced by dividing into two parts. *Binary fission* is the scientific name. Such organisms simply kept on dividing and were, barring accidents, biologically immortal. They could be killed in an accident, but they never died of natural necessity, as do we and all the higher animals. Then, after untold millions of years, sex came into being. That was one of the greatest occasions in the history of this earth, in the history of evolution, in the history of life. It has never been sufficiently noted or celebrated. For Nature's invention of sex made the species man possible.

When did it happen? The biologists do not really know. Perhaps it was about two billion B.C., perhaps a billion years ago; or somewhere between one and two billion years ago. Sex speeded up the evolutionary process because sexual reproduction resulted in enormous variety and large numbers of organisms. This gave an added chance for mutations. When animals became male or female, death by natural necessity became a most important factor in evolution. Death prevented the earth from becoming overpopulated with the numerous forms of life that evolved. Death made room for the mutations that finally resulted in man. Death rid the planet of unprogressive species and gave serious meaning to Natural Selection and the Survival of the Fittest. Without sex—and death that served to control it—man would never have appeared. Death was apparently the biological price for sexual differentiation.

So death all along was to a large degree the friend of man. And death is still a friend by holding down the surging population of the human race and all other living forms. Death is especially the *friend of future generations,* for whom there would be no room unless death cleared the way. If our aim is to bring about the greatest happiness of the greatest number, death is a most valuable ally. For year after year, decade after decade, it opens the way for the largest possible number of individuals, including our own descendants, to experience the joys of living.

Life, then, affirms itself *through* death, which was brought into existence by life and derives its entire significance from life. In the dynamic and creative flux of Nature the same living organisms do not go on indefinitely, but retire at a certain stage and so give way to newborn and lustier vitality. Man is not exempt from this biological law, and he should accept it with courage and understanding. The American novelist, Anne Parrish, has beautifully expressed these truths: Each one of us "must die for the sake of life, for the flow of the stream too great to be dammed in any pool, for the growth of the seed too strong to stay in one shape. . . . Because these bodies must perish, we are greater than we know. The most selfish must be generous, letting his life pour out to others. The most cowardly must be brave enough to go."

Another fact about death, a very significant by-product, is that it enables the human race to sustain itself on this earth. Almost all of man's food is the result of death: meat, fish, fowl, vegetables, eggs, fruit, cereals. Coal, oil and peat originate in decomposed organic substances. All objects made of wood, such as tables and chairs, houses and boats, come from dead trees. And paper, too. Wool for clothing and leather for shoes originate in death. Dead and dying leaves give us the varied and magnificent colors of autumn trees and foliage. Yes, death is built into everyday activities of the human species and we rely upon it in many different ways.

What is bad about death is when it comes prematurely or painfully, in terrible accidents or in more terrible wars. Death is a blow of such magnitude and finality that I think it is always a tragedy for the person who dies or his relatives, or both. Premature death—in childhood, youth or middle age—is the greatest tragedy. When death is a release from painful and incurable illness, it is still tragic that death should be the only cure. Even the death of old people, men and women in their eighties and nineties, seems to me a tragedy, and often a real loss to the community. For many of them are wise and useful citizens with broad experience.

It is always too soon to die, even if you are three-score years and ten or four-score years and ten—indeed, no matter how young or old you may be. Hotspur's cry in *Henry IV* echoes down the ages, "O gentlemen! the time of life is short; to spend that shortness basely were too long." We all have the familiar experience of looking back on life and finding that it has all gone by with appalling swiftness. And most of us over fifty have a haunting sense of transiency. So it is that I sympathize with everyone who ever longed for immortality.

In this discussion of death, we can see that there is a clash between value and non-value. Death, as I pointed out earlier, makes room on this earth for the newborn generations of humanity. That is an undeniable value. At the same time death eliminates human personalities with their almost limitless possibilities for growth, achievement and happiness; death kills off individuals who have reached the peak of social functioning, and causes deep shock and enduring sorrow that results from the loss of loved ones.

All this adds up to a great non-value. Thus both value and non-value are inherent in the institution of death.

Finally, on the meaning of death I wish to quote a passage from *Science of Life* (1929) by H. G. Wells, G. P. Wells and Julian Huxley:

> The individual has, so to speak made a bargain. For the individual comes out of the germ-plasm and does and lives and at length dies for the sake of life. It is a bit of the germ-plasm which has arisen and broken away, in order to see and feel life instead of just blindly and mechanically multiplying. Like Faust, it has sold its immortality in order to live more abundantly.

I think it is worth-while to try to offset, as much as possible, the sting of death. Helpful in this connection is emphasis on the ideas of biological immortality and social immortality, both of which reason can accept as valid. The classic expression of social immortality is George Eliot's poem, "The Choir Invisible." I quote the first and last stanzas:

> *Oh may I join the choir invisible*
> *Of those immortal dead who live again*
> *In minds made better by their presence: live*
> *In pulses stirred to generosity,*
> *In deeds of daring rectitude, in scorn*
> *For miserable aims that end with self,*
> *In thoughts sublime that pierce the night like stars,*
> *And with their mild persistence urge man's search*
> *To vaster issues....*

> *This is life to come,*
> *Which martyred men have made more glorious*
> *For us who strive to follow. May I reach*
> *That purest heaven, be to other souls*
> *The cup of strength in some great agony,*
> *Enkindle generous ardor, feed pure love,*
> *Beget the smiles that have no cruelty,*
> *Be the sweet presence of a good diffused,*
> *And in diffusion ever more intense.*
> *So shall I join the choir invisible*
> *Whose music is the gladness of the world.*

It is time now to say a word about the Spiritualists, Extra-Sensory Perception, "E.S.P." as it is called, and Abnormal Psychology in general.

The Spiritualists, of course, are positive that there is an after-life and claim to be in constant touch with the souls of the dear departed. I have been to numerous seances and, as I said earlier, was in close contact with one medium, my aunt. She brought messages from "the other side" to my father, who was her brother, as well as to me. I recall that on one occasion she had a very important message for my father from a banking associate, J. Pierpont Morgan, the Elder, who had died in 1911. The world-shaking communication turned out to be, "Tom, you are doing a fine job." My parents were not impressed. Spiritualist mediums on the whole tend to transmit messages that are so general that they can apply to any person, dead or alive. If just one message from the beyond would give the name of a murderer and lead to his conviction, it would be more convincing.

Some of the mediums who receive alleged messages from the other world call their procedure by the fancy name of *Clairaudient Dictation.*

In the Preface to my book *The Illusion of Immortality,* I stated: "I would welcome heartily any concrete evidence or valid reasoning tending to establish man's immortality," and I still stand by that. Mrs. Shirley C. Jenney responded to this invitation by sending me her book, *Fortunes of Eternity,* a volume of poems she had received in Clairaudient Dictation from the spirit of Percy Bysshe Shelley. I read these poems carefully, but have to report regretfully that they are not up to the standard of Shelley's poems when he was a mere earthling. Anyway, Mrs. Jenney did not convince me that I was wrong about immortality.

Mediums claim to be in touch with many famous personalities of the past, including William Shakespeare and Jesus Christ. Some years ago a medium in New York City wrote a book entitled *The Autobiography of Jesus.* She said that the spirit of Jesus himself had dictated the manuscript to her. She has not yet found a publisher for this volume, but personally I think it might be a best-seller.

A medium will occasionally come through with a bit of extraordinary information which she says is from a person who has died. I am very doubtful of this. There is a new hypothesis being considered now that would help explain such messages. As we know, the brain not only has electric currents active within it, but also gives off waves of radiation, which may form definite patterns. A so-called medium might be sensitive to radiation waves that had come originally from a deceased person before he died, and were floating around in space. From these waves she might be able to decipher some information. In this case it would be the radiation that had survived, not the soul of the dead individual.

If telepathy, which I think is a plausible possibility, exists, that could account for some of the more mysterious communications of mediums. But telepathy in itself does not prove human survival after death, since presumably it means communication between two living individuals. And Extra-Sensory Perception, even if shown to exist, cannot prove the actuality of immortality. These various phenomena all belong in the field of Parapsychology; and it is certainly worth-while to study and analyze them in an objective scientific way.

During recent years a new proof has been offered of survival after death based on the work of Drs. Elisabeth Kübler-Ross and Raymond Moody, author of *Life After Life* (1973). Both of these researchers assert that many persons pronounced clinically dead have later revived and claimed that while they were "dead" they were aware of being out of their bodies and often in another world where they were warmly greeted by deceased relatives and friends. In his book Dr. Moody gives many carefully formulated examples. But the fact is that if a human being supposedly dead does revive and live on, he never died in the first place. What he may report about the period when he was totally unconscious or "dead" are obviously dreams and not to be taken as objective descriptions of another world.

I have discussed various kinds of immortality. But there is still one variety I have not mentioned. I suggest that in place of any kind of individual immortality, we concentrate on the *immortality of the human race.* In order to achieve that goal, there are certain obstacles we must overcome in the near future, as soon as possible.

First, there is the danger of a world-wide nuclear war, in which death-dealing fallout could bring about the extinction of all mankind and most life upon this planet. The continued production of nuclear weapons by the Great Powers is simply mad. The armaments race in both conventional and nuclear weapons still continues. The United States maintains a huge number of military bases and troops abroad at the cost of tens of billions of dollars. These enormous armaments are a menace to both America and the world at large.

Second, there is the danger of the peoples of the world so polluting the waters, the air and the environment in general that the earth will become uninhabitable for human beings. I think that we are getting control of this situation in the United States and other countries.

Man's ultimate fate is of course bound up with the sun, which some day will not give off enough heat to maintain life on this planet. The late Harlow Shapley, Professor of Astronomy at Harvard, estimated it will be ten billion years before the sun cools off that much. Other astronomers say it will be five billion or less. These various figures are all quite speculative. Such vast stretches of time seem to be practically immortality in itself. In any case, we must not accept inevitable doom. Modern science is only some 400 years old. Imagine what advances science will have made in 400 million years or four billion years.

The development of atomic energy opens up vast possibilities for the future. Scientists are already talking of sending up artificial suns to encircle the globe. Other scientists talk of utilizing nuclear power to speed up the revolution of the earth around the sun, so that our planet would get nearer to the sun as its heat diminished. And it has long been dreamt that humans will eventually be able to emigrate to other planets in space-ships when and if this earth becomes uninhabitable.

Whether or not these speculations have validity, it is exciting and consoling to think that in other parts of this infinite universe, including our own galaxy, forms of life different from or similar to humankind may have been evolving. Citing Professor Shapley again, he states "we can no longer doubt but that wherever the physics, chemistry and climates are right on a planet's surface, life will emerge and persist." And if extra-terrestrial life *has* emerged here and there, it is possible that beings more highly developed than man have evolved.

It is a fact that in the observable universe billions upon billions of stars exist—10 to the 21st power. There are 150 billion stars just in our own galaxy. It is reliably estimated that if only one out of a million stars in the universe has at least one planet, there are in the cosmos planets numbering 10 to the 15th power, which means 100 trillion. And if only one planet in a million is of a sort that can support life, there are at least one billion such planets in the universe. The distinct probability that life exists scattered throughout the universe may mean that life, if not man, is immortal in this stupendous cosmos.

But for human individuals in this remarkable twentieth century, I suggest again that it is none too soon for us to be thinking about and striving for the immortality of the human race. I am convinced that the advance of science and of international cooperation may result in such further conquests of Nature that human life and civilization can be indefinitely prolonged. As a Humanist, I refuse to load the dice by reading the actualization of human hopes and ideals into the stars, the drift of history or a Divine Providence that underwrites the future on our behalf. Man stands alone and cannot romantically expect that his story is necessarily going to have a happy ending. Man's future is up to man. I believe that he has the ability, courage and intelligence to win out, with all the nations and peoples of the earth marching forward together to attain life eternal for humanity.

24
Militant Activist at 84
(1986)

Looking back on my life at the age of 84, I have mixed feelings. I have already published an autobiography, *Yes to Life* (1981), and I could write another entire book frankly giving an account of the serious mistakes I have made. In spite of that, I believe that on the whole my life has been worth-while, both because of my contributions to the public welfare and because I have enjoyed what I was doing, especially the battles in which I have been involved and frequently won. I have stood firm for my dissident views and have consistently sustained about twelve main activities. As a vigorous octogenarian I continue to work hard—writing, speaking and combatting most of the policies of the Reagan Administration.

My foremost concentration has been in philosophy, especially the philosophy of Naturalistic Humanism (sometimes called a religion). This way of life, relying primarily on the methods of reason, science and democracy, rejects belief in all forms of the supernatural; and considers our supreme commitment as the welfare, progress and happiness of all humanity in this one and only existence. The Humanist watchword is *compassionate concern* towards our fellow human beings. This philosophy asserts that there is no Divine Providence or God guiding and helping mankind, but that men and women, possessing true freedom of choice, bear the full responsibility for solving their problems, whether personal or social. My book, *The Philosophy of Humanism,* is the acknowledged reference work in America for the Humanist viewpoint.

I first became interested in Humanism when, working for a Ph.D. in philosophy at Columbia University, I chose the question of personal immortality for my dissertation. I received my degree in 1932 with a thesis entitled *Issues of Immortality*. Although I was a firm believer in survival after death when I began my study, I became an equally firm disbeliever at its conclusion. And three years later in 1935 I published *The Illusion of Immortality,* a Humanist extension of my Columbia thesis, showing that personal survival beyond the grave (or crematory) is very, very improbable. This volume has been cited as the best refutation in the English language of the idea of immortality.

I still support its conclusions, although in my old age I strongly desire a hereafter. I have found my this-earthly existence far too short for all the things I wanted to do. Like most persons, I wish that I could relive my life. The vagabond years have passed so swiftly and I constantly feel the sting of transiency. Andrew Marvell's lines ever haunt me:

> *But, at my back, I always hear*
> *Time's wingèd chariot hurrying near.*

And, like John Keats,

> *. . . I have fears that I may cease to be*
> *Before my pen has glean'd my teeming brain.*

My most poignant thought is that this life has been my one and only chance to experience happiness and to serve mankind; and that when death inevitably strikes, I must sink into total unconsciousness and oblivion, while earth and life persist for billions of years and the vast universe of Nature whirls on and on forever.

After the publication of the First Humanist Manifesto in 1933, I soon was calling myself a Humanist and became active in the American Humanist movement. Later I joined the American Humanist Association (A.H.A.), the chief organization trying to educate the people of the United States on the Humanist viewpoint. I also wrote occasional articles for *The Humanist,* a bi-monthly magazine issued by the A.H.A. I served for a while on the Board of Directors of the A.H.A. and finally became its Honorary President. In 1973 I signed Humanist Manifesto II together with thousands of other dedicated Humanists.

I must say a word about those persons who consider Humanism a religion and therefore prefer to call themselves "religious Humanists." I think that Humanism is a philosophy, but have cooperated closely with the religious Humanists for many years. In fact, Naturalistic Humanists are in accord with key ethical and social principles of Christianity and other religions. It is well to keep in mind that several Unitarian ministers were initiators and signers of the First Humanist Manifesto. One of them, the Rev. Edwin

H. Wilson, was Executive Director of the American Humanist Association for a dozen years. He became a close friend. Other warm friends were the Rev. Stephen H. Fritchman, for many years the crusading pastor of the First Unitarian Church of Los Angeles; and the Rev. Everett M. Baker, Dean of Students at the Massachusetts Institute of Technology and inspiring advocate of international peace and understanding.

In 1981 I was suddenly drawn into the socio-religious maelstrom stirred up by a new organization, the so-called Moral Majority and its right-wing religious fanatics. The Moral Majority was founded in 1979 by the Reverend Jerry Falwell, Tim LaHaye and associated Baptists of fundamentalist faith. They all denounced secular Humanism and Humanists in general as "the root of all evil" in America and the world at large.

In this assault on Humanism I became intimately involved after Mr. LaHaye published *The Battle for the Mind* (1980), the "bible" of the Moral Majority. He reprinted in his book some thirty-six passages from my *The Philosophy of Humanism* to demonstrate the horrors of that viewpoint. This was perhaps the greatest tribute I had ever received as an author. Yet I was not pleased.

For LaHaye was using me as a whipping boy to support his wild exaggerations about Humanism. He states: "Most people do not realize what Humanism really is and how it is destroying our culture, families, country, and one day, the entire world. Most of the evils in the world today can be traced to Humanism, which has taken over our government, the United Nations, education and most of the other influential things of life." I should like to laugh off LaHaye's absurd statements, except that the Moral Majority reaches millions on its radio and TV outlets and its President, Jerry Falwell, is a close advisor of Ronald Reagan. The truth is that the malicious anti-Humanist campaign of Falwell and his evangelical allies is somewhat similar to Senator Joseph McCarthy's witchhunt in the 1950s against Communists and alleged Communists.

Perhaps the most effective comment on the Moral Majority's nonsense is a stanza from the satiric poem, "A Humanist Manifesto" by Curt Sytsma of Des Moines:

> *In every age, the bigot's rage*
> *Requires another focus,*
> *Another devil forced on stage*
> *By hatred's hocus-pocus:*
> *The Devil used to be the Jew*
> *And then it was the witches;*
> *And then it was the Negroes who*
> *Were digging in the ditches.*
> *The devil once was colored pink*

And labeled communistic;
Now, all at once, in just a blink,
The devil's humanistic.

The American Humanist Association is only one segment of the Humanist movement in the United States. There is also the Fellowship of Religious Humanists, the North American Committee for Humanism and the Humanist Institute, the function of which is to train individuals for Humanist leadership. In addition, the Ethical Union and most of its member Ethical Societies are essentially Humanist in their philosophy. Their close cooperation with Humanists is seen in the International Humanist and Ethical Union (I.H.E.U.) with headquarters at Utrecht, Holland.

Yet despite these various Humanist organizations and their unceasing educational endeavors, the Humanist movement in general has made little progress in America since the issuance of Humanist Manifesto I more than half a century ago. The Humanist Association has never had more than about 6,000 members and is down to about 3,700 today. The upsurge of rightist religious groups during the recent past is undoubtedly holding back the Humanist cause. Now in my final years I feel unhappy about this situation. The only answer for Humanists is to keep the torch burning and to go on working for the Humanist philosophy, buoyed up by the belief that there are millions of Americans who are actually Humanists, but who do not wish to acknowledge it publicly or who do not even know the word.

Almost as important as philosophy, there has been my vigorous support of civil liberties in which I have served on the Board of Directors of the American Civil Liberties Union, as President of the Bill of Rights Fund and as Chairman of the National Emergency Civil Liberties Committee. My first serious encounter with government repression came in 1934 when, representing the A.C.L.U., I went over to Jersey City one day to picket peacefully on behalf of the Furniture Workers Union, which was on strike. The city police soon arrested me and hauled me off to jail in their van. They took my fingerprints and made me remove my necktie, shoelaces and belt to prevent me from committing suicide.

Within a few hours I obtained bail and went home to New York City for a pleasant supper. After a few weeks the higher courts of New Jersey cracked down on Mayor Hague of Jersey City and held in a case ahead of mine that the picketing was legal. My case was then automatically dropped. Just the same I was dubbed as a Jailbird for Civil Liberties. And I came to consider even this slight experience of arrest and jail as a valuable initiation into the great struggle for civil liberties.

After World War II, I tangled continually with U.S. Government authorities. Especially upsetting to me was the refusal of the State Department to renew my passport after I had engaged passage for myself and family for a trip to Europe in the summer of 1951. The only excuse the State Department gave for this violation of my right to travel and civil liberties was: "It is contrary to the best interests of the United States to have you travel at present."

The real reason was that the Government wished to punish me for criticisms of its domestic and foreign policies and to warn other dissenters. For seven long years I was unable to obtain a passport, until in 1958 the U.S. Supreme Court decided in the case of painter Rockwell Kent that it was unconstitutional for the State Department to make political qualifications for granting a passport to an American citizen. That was a memorable victory for the right to travel, and my lawyer, Leonard B. Boudin, saw to it that I was at once granted a passport.

My most important civil liberties case came in 1953 when Senator Joe McCarthy summoned me to appear before the Senate Permanent Subcommittee on Government Investigations, of which he was Chairman. The reason he had subpoenaed me was that a U.S. Army bibliography had listed a work of mine entitled *The Peoples of the Soviet Union,* a study of the history and rights of the 177 nationalities that make up the U.S.S.R. McCarthy asked me some twenty-five questions about who helped me write the book, what members of the Communist Party advised me and whether some agent of the Soviet Government had cooperated with me. I refused to answer all of his questions on the ground that they violated freedom of the press and freedom of scholarship, and that anyway an investigation of me was beyond the scope of McCarthy's Committee. Nevertheless, McCarthy persuaded a pliant U.S. Senate to cite me for contempt of Congress, with a possible sentence of one year in jail and a fine of $1,000. An official indictment followed.

Philip Wittenberg, a New York City lawyer, handled my case, but it never came to trial because we moved to dismiss the indictment for the reason that the McCarthy Committee had no legal or constitutional authority to investigate me or anyone else. The truth was that McCarthy's Committee had never been officially established, with its powers designated, by its parent Committee on Government Operations. In 1956 a U.S. Appeals Court unanimously upheld the decision of a Federal District Court judge, Edward Weinfeld, who had dismissed my indictment as unconstitutional. I was the first McCarthy defendant to demonstrate the total illegality of his Committee and thus set a precedent that could be used successfully in the legal defense of any persons subpoenaed by him.

Despite its illegality, the McCarthy Committee roamed the country for several years calling before it liberals, radicals, Humanists, pacifists, trade unionists and intellectuals in most professions. It put them through a galling inquisition, often ruining their reputations and bringing about the loss of their jobs, even when the courts of justice sustained their cases.

As to McCarthy himself, he was not only an unscrupulous political demagogue, but personally an unpleasant and repulsive character. If you just looked at his face, you intuitively knew that he was a scoundrel of the worst type. He raised hatred of Communism and the Soviet Union to new heights. Although McCarthy was finally discredited, particularly through a U.S. Senate resolution condemning his conduct, he left permanent scars on the body politic.

I mentioned *The Peoples of the Soviet Union* as the volume on account of which McCarthy sought to discredit me. And it is significant to realize that the Federal Bureau of Investigation, in its heroic attempt to protect "national security," went to my publisher, Harcourt Brace, and asked a McCarthy-like question, "Was this book financed by Moscow?" This was a ludicrous query for one of the most prosperous publishers in the United States. The F.B.I. agents knew perfectly well that the answer would be negative, but they wanted to indicate to the publisher that the F.B.I. did not approve of either my book or me.

Another of my civil liberties cases that merits special attention erupted in 1963 and concerned a Congressional statute, typical of the prevailing anti-Communist climate, that required the U.S. Postmaster General to screen for Communist propaganda second and third class mail from foreign countries. If he or a subordinate found such propaganda in a book or magazine, he was to send a postcard to the addressee saying in effect, "Do you really want to receive this subversive literature?" If the addressee answered "Yes" the Post Office mailed the literature to him and also sent his name to the House Un-American Activities Committee.

One day in 1963 I received a postcard telling me that the San Francisco Post Office was holding a copy of *Peking Review* addressed to me. But instead of replying, I straightaway sued the Postmaster General for violating my First Amendment rights and acting as a censor in the delivery of something I wished to see. It was a clear-cut issue of an American citizen's right to read and right to know. I appealed my suit, again under the guidance of attorney Leonard Boudin, to the U.S. Supreme Court. In 1965 that Court ruled unanimously that the statute was unconstitutional because it interfered with the "unfettered exercise" of First Amendment rights. This was the first instance in its history that the Supreme Court had held a Congressional law unconstitutional due to its violation of the First Amendment. Since that time the case of *Lamont* v. *Postmaster General* has repeatedly been cited in support of litigation upholding civil liberties.

My bad experiences with the Federal Bureau of Investigation and the Central Intelligence Agency belong in the category of civil liberties, because of their repeated disregard of my right to privacy. The F.B.I. was on my trail for several decades, ever attempting to obtain proof that I was a member of the Communist Party, a charge that I had denied at least a hundred times. Through the Freedom of Information Act I discovered that this agency had a file on me of almost 2,800 pages, of which I obtained over 2,000. Looking through that treasure-trove I discovered that the F.B.I. repeatedly indulged in absurdities. For instance, when Professor John Kenneth Galbraith needed security clearance in 1961 for his appointment as Ambassador to India, the F.B.I. asked him why he had lived in the same apartment house as I at 450 Riverside Drive in New York City. Galbraith was affronted by this ridiculous question and spoke of the new crime of "dangerous co-habitation."

Another idiotic ploy by the F.B.I. was its infiltration of my parents' staff at their summer residence on the island of North Haven, Maine, by hiring the caretaker to tail me whenever I visited the island. He reported on whom I played tennis with, sailed with or had to lunch. I had always been on friendly terms with this man, who finally became conscience-stricken and made a full confession to me long after my father and mother were dead.

My relations with the C.I.A. were less complex and extended than those with the F.B.I. The C.I.A., during a period of twenty years, simply opened and copied all letters, about 155, that I had sent to the United States from the Soviet Union or received there. Under the Freedom of Information Act I obtained photostats of the C.I.A. photostats and proceeded to sue this vicious agency for $150,000 damages for violation of my right of privacy and the Fourth Amendment of the Bill of Rights. At the trial the C.I.A. admitted openly that its actions had been illegal and unconstitutional, but necessary for the sake of "national security," the stock excuse the U.S. Government uses whenever it subverts the Constitution.

Judge Jack B. Weinstein of the Federal District Court in Brooklyn handed down a most sympathetic decision in my favor, but awarded me only $2,000. He also directed the C.I.A. to write me a letter of apology, which it did in due course. The Judge was particularly incensed over two "love letters" that I had written to my wife, Helen. He declared: "Illegal prying into the shared intimacies of husband and wife is despicable."

More important than the C.I.A.'s unlawful opening of letters is the fact that, instead of remaining as an intelligence agency, it has become a secret paramilitary arm of the U.S. Government, managing the overthrow of leftist and Socialist governments, as in Chile; and engaging in covert terroristic actions such as the mining of Nicaraguan harbors. In addition, the C.I.A. is now the conductor of psychological warfare and disinformation campaigns against the Soviet Union and other Communist countries. Every decent American should be appalled and ashamed that his government sanctions the outrageous and unethical practices of the C.I.A.

Another major enterprise has been my work in education. I started as an Instructor in Philosophy at Columbia College in 1928, teaching not only philosophy but also the Introduction to Contemporary Civilization. This course began with the Middle Ages and came down to the 20th century, interweaving a history and analysis of politics, economics, philosophy and science. The assigned reading relied especially on Professor John H. Randall's distinguished book, *The Making of the Modern Mind.* In giving the course I found that I was growing increasingly liberal in my opinions and finally became a radical espousing a planned and democratic Socialism.

Later I shifted to the Columbia School of General Studies where for twelve years I gave a course on the philosophy of Naturalistic Humanism. From this course I drew extensive materials for writing *Humanism as a Philosophy,* later retitled *The Philosophy of Humanism.* I lectured on the same subject for several years at The New School for Social Research. I also taught courses on American-Soviet affairs at the Summer Schools of Cornell and Harvard. In 1971 I became a Columbia University Seminar Associate participating in a program of special seminars on important subjects meeting about once a month during the academic year. My own Seminar analyzes the many-sided topic of death.

I graduated from Harvard in the Class of 1924 and have been a loyal alumnus of that University. In 1984 I celebrated the sixtieth reunion of my Class at Cambridge. However, my major academic connection has been with Columbia, where I took a Ph.D. in philosophy in 1932. I taught there, as I have said, for many years and have maintained a continuous relationship by serving on the Advisory Council of The Friends of the Columbia Libraries and working closely with the Rare Book and Manuscript Library. In cooperation with its discerning Librarian, Kenneth A. Lohf, I helped to establish special collections for artist Rockwell Kent, poet John Masefield and philosopher George Santayana. In 1974 the University awarded me The Columbia Libraries citation for Distinguished Service and in 1984 named a Reading Room after me at the splendid new headquarters of the Rare Book and Manuscript Library.

Next, there are my unceasing efforts on behalf of international peace and disarmament, stressing at present the reduction and abolition of nuclear weapons. When I was still an undergraduate at Harvard I became an ardent supporter of the League of Nations and founded a College League of Nations Society. I was strongly in favor of the United States joining the League and argued on and off with my conservative Republican classmate, Henry Cabot Lodge, who opposed that move. After World War II, I naturally backed the United Nations and have been critical of the American Government's hostility towards it.

I came out from the start against the brutal and fruitless United States aggression in Vietnam that cost the lives of more than 58,000 American troops and several million Vietnamese. My wife, Helen Lamb Lamont, and I published a number of advertisements in the press denouncing Presidents Johnson and Nixon for the savage U.S. war against Vietnam. I also wrote an Open Letter, Nov. 1, 1965, to Henry Cabot Lodge when he was U.S. Ambassador to South Vietnam in which I severely criticized the American government's policy and his part in putting it into effect.

Nineteen years later in 1984 Mr. Lodge sent me a note answering my Open Letter and stating: "You were right—We were wrong and we failed. I should have resigned sooner. Thank you for your most interesting book which I am reading with avidity. Best wishes always." Lodge's admission was an important victory for me, but also showed he had the integrity to admit a serious mistake.

In 1983 I militantly opposed the Reagan Administration's invasion of Grenada and its covert military and terroristic operations in the secret war against Nicaragua. Important in revealing U.S. aggressive foreign policy are the stupendous amounts—about $300 billion for 1986—allocated to defense in the national budget. The billions wasted on the Pentagon and nuclear weapons are the largest item by far in causing the enormous federal budget deficit year after year and in increasing the total federal debt to more than $2 trillion.

I always coupled my enthusiasm for the League of Nations and the United Nations, which celebrated its 40th year in 1985, with firm support of the International Court of Justice, usually known as the World Court. I was shocked by President Reagan's decision in January 1985, to take no part in the World Court proceedings dealing with Nicaragua's suit against the United States for violating international law by supporting paramilitary attacks by rebels in Nicaragua and by mining its harbors. To quote *The New York Times,* "This is the first time that the United States has walked out of a case in the World Court, in defiance of the Court's rules, since joining the tribunal in 1946. . . . At the State Department a spokesman said Nicaragua's case at the World Court was 'a misuse of the Court for political and propaganda purposes.'"

In my judgment the U.S. action was disgraceful, dishonorable and hypocritical. It betrayed America's traditional ideals of international peace and transformed our country into a lawless, bullying nation that relies on violence and military measures in place of peaceful and diplomatic procedures. As Anthony Lewis states (*New York Times,* Op-Ed, Jan. 21, 1985): "The Reagan Administration feared that the court proceeding would bring out the facts of its aid to terroristic activities and focus attention on its violation of treaties." Thus the U.S. withdrawal from World Court jurisdiction meant that President Reagan was trying to avoid accountability by concealing the truth and was negating the American people's right to know, a basic civil liberty.

The Reagan Administration made the situation even worse when in October 1985 it announced that the United States would refuse to litigate any "political" case whatever before the World Court. I thought this was international sabotage.

Important in my peace work have been my steady efforts for better American-Soviet understanding and even limited cooperation. While I am most critical of the Soviet Union's lack of civil liberties and treatment of dissenters, the Communist dictatorship has made notable achievements in other fields such as science, medicine, public health, care of women and children, education and national planning. On the whole the record of the U.S.S.R. in attempting to control nuclear weapons has been better than that of the United States, which initiated the nuclear arms race by the horrible and immoral atom bomb destruction of Hiroshima and Nagasaki in Japan, with more than 200,000 civilians killed.

It weighs heavily with me that during most of my adult life hate of the Soviet Union and fear of Communism in general have played such an important role in American politics and foreign policy. The deplorable McCarthy era was based primarily on anti-Communist hysteria; and now the same sort of uncontrolled madness is rife throughout the United States, with the Reagan Administration frequently leading the way. However, we can hope that the Geneva Summit meeting in November 1985 between President Reagan and Soviet General Secretary Gorbachev will reduce American-Soviet tensions and bring about genuine progress towards the limitation of nuclear armaments.

Then there has been my career as an author. I have written altogether some twelve books and edited six. The most important of my studies concern philosophy: *The Philosophy of Humanism, The Illusion of Immortality and Freedom of Choice Affirmed,* a denial of universal determinism and an insistence that at the moment of making a choice between two or more alternatives every normal human being possesses an element of spontaneous freedom, no matter how conditioned and limited by past or present circumstances. For the sixth edition (1981) of my book on Humanism I added a new Introduction entitled "Exposing the Moral Majority," in which I answered the vicious attacks on the Humanist philosophy by Jerry Falwell and his frenetic band of religious zealots.

Other volumes of mine cover civil liberties, Socialism, the Soviet Union, poetry and the history of the Lamont family. My authorship culminated in 1981 with an autobiography, *Yes to Life*. In addition I have produced innumerable magazine articles and more than twenty booklets in my series of Basic Pamphlets.

My latest literary effort has been as Editor of *Collected Poems of John Reed*. Soon after I entered Harvard College in the Class of 1924, I heard about a famous member of the Class of 1910, John Reed (1887–1920). I then read his great book, *Ten Days That Shook the World,* admittedly the best eyewitness account of the 1917 Communist Revolution in Russia. After my graduation I became increasingly interested in Reed's adventurous career and was favorably impressed by the American movie, *Reds,* which portrayed much of Reed's life.

Understandably I was quite excited when, working one day with materials of Columbia University's Rare Book and Manuscript Library, I opened a battered loose-leaf notebook, the titled contents of which read: "The Collected Verse of John Reed, submitted in partial fulfillment of the degree of Master of Arts, Faculty of Philosophy, Columbia University, June, 1947." I had been vaguely aware that Reed had written some poetry from time to time, but to my knowledge it had never been collected in one volume. I felt that I had made a real literary discovery and in due course decided that this unknown Master's Essay, hidden away in Columbia's archives, should be published to round out the dramatic story of John Reed. Accordingly, I arranged publication of the manuscript by Lawrence Hill & Co. of Westport, Connecticut, so that Reed's *Collected Poems* was issued in paperback during the spring of 1985.

Not to be overlooked has been my rejection of the capitalist system and my belief that a planned and democratic Socialism is best suited to fulfill the needs of the American people and all other peoples. I oppose Capitalism because of its continuous cycles of prosperity and depression, because of its inability to eliminate unemployment and poverty, because of its plundering of our planet for the sake of financial profit and because of its initiation of wars and immense armaments. In the 20th century, Capitalism brought about two terrible world wars, with death for tens of millions of soldiers and civilians throughout much of the earth. And later capitalist United States waged an unprovoked war of aggression against Vietnam, threatened Central America with military intervention and piled up huge arsenals of nuclear weapons that had the potential of destroying all humanity.

In my view the fundamental advantages of Socialism lie in its functioning for use instead of profit and its instituting over-all socio-economic planning through public ownership of the main means of production, distribution and finance. I would leave any business employing fewer than six persons in private hands. While much national planning is necessary under Socialism, in America decentralization at the state, county and municipal level would be encouraged. Socialist planning for abundance, democratically administered, permanently overcomes the contradictions of Capitalism. I summarized my socialist views in a book, *You Might Like Socialism: A Way of Life for Modern Man* (1939).

The concept of planning is not difficult to understand. Every mature man or woman plans for daily living, work and recreation. If you buy tickets for a play on a certain date, that is planning ahead for pleasure. Every successful capitalist business must plan carefully and within its budgetary limits. The same holds true of national governments and their different departments. Socialism simply lifts planning to a higher and more complete level. It no more does away with individual freedom and initiative than does city planning in regulating automobile traffic for the common good.

Socialism will not be established in the United States for a long time. It took five hundred years for Capitalism to win control over most of the world. And the transition from Capitalism to full-fledged Socialism may also require several centuries. This point must be kept in mind when we make judgments about the existing Communist dictatorships. The Soviet Union, China, and smaller countries have all been attempting to establish Socialist economies, but have found the task most difficult and have not yet developed beyond the primary stages of Socialism. Progress in human affairs usually takes place slowly and graphically illustrates "the inevitability of gradualness," though sometimes there are quick spurts in some nations, especially in case of far-reaching revolution.

A happy variant in the story of my life has been my profound interest in and appreciation of poetry. I have given support to both The Poetry Society of America, of which I was Vice-President for several years, and the Academy of American Poets, of which the late Mrs. Marie Bullock was the energetic President. The Academy received from my mother, Mrs. Florence C. Lamont, a large bequest for the establishment of a Lamont Poetry Prize to underwrite every year the publication of the winner's book of poetry.

The lasting friendship of my parents and me with British Poet Laureate John Masefield has given an added glow to my feeling for poetry. When I was a student at New College, Oxford, during the academic year 1924–25 I met Mr. and Mrs. Masefield, who lived about four miles out of town on Old Boar's Hill. The Masefields were very kind to me. I would often bicycle to the Masefield house, Hill Crest, for tea or supper and then revel in coasting down the long incline back to Oxford. After supper, Masefield would occasionally read aloud some of his favorite poems. His voice was mellow and haunting. After I got back to my lodgings at Oxford at the home of the Julian Huxleys, I would jot down what I could remember of Masefield's comments in the margins of my volume of his *Collected Poems*. That invaluable book is still in my library. Sir Julian became a close friend and one of England's leading Humanists.

I have long admired John Masefield's poetry, whether his long narrative poems such as "Dauber," "Reynard the Fox," and "Right Royal," or his shorter poems and sonnets. Some of his sonnets deal with distinctly philosophic themes. What delights me especially in Masefield's verse is its rhythmic flow combined with skillful scanning. One can almost sing his poems. So much of modern verse seems to be merely prose in successive lines, giving the *appearance* of poetry but not the real thing.

I have published several books in the realm of poetry: *Remembering John Masefield,* which consists mainly of the Poet Laureate's letters to me; *Lover's Credo,* a slender sheaf of poems; and as Editor, *Man Answers Death, An Anthology of Poetry.* In addition I was co-Editor, with my nephew Lansing Lamont, of *Letters of John Masefield to Florence Lamont.*

From an early age I was an energetic outdoor person. For many years I belonged to the Boy Scouts and liked their motto, "Do a Good Turn Daily." I have relished every aspect of Nature's beauty and magnificence, from the starry heavens and foaming waterfalls to flowers dancing in the breeze. Naturally I have always been keen for the conservation of forests and animal life. We must conserve and extend environmental values wherever possible. I am enthusiastic about America's superb National Parks, many of which I have visited. I recall with rapture Glacier National Park in Montana, the Grand Canyon of the Colorado, Yosemite in California and Grand Teton in Wyoming, where I spent two summers riding and hiking.

I have enormously enjoyed sports and done well at them. I played on soccer and baseball teams at St. Bernard's School, and on hockey teams at Phillips Exeter and Harvard. I remember with joy skating for miles up the winding Exeter River. Also I rode horseback, climbed mountains, cut trails, canoed on lakes and rivers, fished for trout in sparkling streams and went on camping trips in Montana and Oregon. Later I concentrated on tennis and skiing, while in my old age I have turned to long walks and the fascinating game of doubles croquet. During many summers in Maine I did a lot of sailing, including racing and exploration of the lovely pink-white granite islands in Penobscot Bay.

Undoubtedly my vigorous and life-long pattern of exercise was a major factor in my general good health. I had my appendix removed in my early thirties, but after that encountered no serious trouble until I became eighty. Then I underwent a risky heart operation in which my failing aortic valve was successfully replaced with the healthy valve of a pig. All gratitude to the pigs!

I register with deep feeling how much I have appreciated family life, starting with my beloved father and mother, and going down the line to sister and brothers, wives, children, grandchildren, step-grandchildren, grand-nephews and numerous other affectionate relatives. To render a lasting tribute to these relationships, I edited a stout volume, *The Thomas Lamonts in America* (1962), Thomas W. Lamont being my father. This book traces the Lamonts back to Scotland and the Clan Lamont, which came into being in the 13th century. Centuries later many Lamonts, beset by religious wars and the murderous Campbells, migrated to Northern Ireland (Ulster). Then about 1750 my branch of the family sailed across the ocean to America. I am proud of the resolute, centuries-old Lamont tradition.

As far back as I can remember, the center of family life was the dinner table. My parents invited for dinner poets such as John Masefield and Walter de la Mare, novelists such as H. G. Wells and Francis Brett Young and statesmen such as Lord Robert Cecil and Jan Christiaan Smuts of South Africa. I was often at meals when they were guests and drank in the fascinating conversation. The Lamont table was an open forum where significant subjects were discussed and debated with everyone speaking openly and frankly.

When I had established my own home, with a wife and four children, we followed the same pattern. And at Thanksgiving, Christmas and New Year's I often read aloud an appropriate poem or a prose piece that I had myself composed, such as a Thanksgiving Invocation.

No survey of my life can be complete without noting my chief amusements and recreations. Much of my recreation has been, as I have indicated, in the realm of outdoor sports. For indoors my favorite games were bridge and chess. Since I have lived in New York City for about sixty years, I have found it easy to obtain entertainment in the evening at the movies, the theater or the ballet. For many years Katharine Hepburn has been my special enthusiasm in motion pictures. I believe she is America's greatest actress. I was able to become a good friend, to go on walks with her in Central Park or atop the Palisades and even to exchange an occasional letter.

I had a profound love for music of almost every variety, although I preferred concerts to the opera. Music led me to greatly enjoy dancing, at various hotels and particularly at the Rainbow Room at Rockefeller Center. I became quite partial to musical comedies and before long was learning and singing the theme songs from such plays as *Oklahoma* and *Finian's Rainbow*. All this resulted in Folkways Records in 1977 producing and selling, in celebration of my 75th birthday, a long-playing record of thirty-six selections sung by me. It was well received.

Some mention must be made of my philanthropies. My parents bequeathed to me funds far greater than I could ever personally need. This situation created for me an ongoing social responsibility as to how to dispense my extra funds generously and wisely. This responsibility has sometimes proved a heavy burden because of the numberless financial appeals pouring in by mail, phone and telegram. At the same time, my inherited wealth has enabled me to help many deserving organizations, committees, journals and institutions, and to come to the rescue of many individuals. In the year 1984 I made over a hundred substantial tax-deductible donations, and many more without tax deductions.

In general I have concentrated on grants in the fields of civil liberties, the Humanist movement, international peace, poetry and the conservation of nature. For example, I have made large gifts for the furtherance of peace projects to Amherst College, Harvard University and the University of Wisconsin. I also established a Civil Liberties Professorship at the Columbia Law School. And I have founded the Half-Moon Foundation, with a considerable endowment, to carry on after my death by making grants to institutions in my special fields of interest.

People have frequently asked me how it could happen that I, born and brought up in an affluent family, supported liberal and leftist causes most of my life. My answer is threefold: first, I have profound compassion and sympathy for my fellow human beings; second, I possess genuine freedom of choice when deciding between different alternatives; and third, I depend on the use of reason in analyzing the basic problems that have faced America and the world. Actually, many Americans with backgrounds similar to mine have reached similar conclusions. Of course, with an independent income I was able to confront government hostility with no fear of losing economic security for myself and my family.

Finally, it seems appropriate to conclude this essay with a listing of the various special Awards presented to me from time to time. They are as follows:

1955   *New York City Teachers' Union Annual Award*
"For valiant and unswerving defense of intellectual freedom."

1972   *First John Dewey Humanist Award* from the American Humanist Association
"For distinguished contributions to the philosophy of humanism."

1974   *The Columbia Libraries Citation for Distinguished Service*
"The Trustees of Columbia University in the City of New York make known to all men by these presents that Corliss Lamont has been awarded the Columbia Libraries Citation for Distinguished Service. . . ."

1977   *Humanist of the Year Award* of the American Humanist Association
"For life-time dedication to Humanist philosophy and action."

1981   *Peace and Justice Award* from the Westchester Peoples' Action Coalition
"To Corliss Lamont, whose keen intellect, profound humanism and unceasing dedication to civil liberties, enhanced with the soul of a poet, has moved this world a little closer to his vision . . . the liberation of the human spirit in a world of beauty, and a world at peace."

1981   *Gandhi Peace Award* from Promoting Enduring Peace
"To Corliss Lamont, in appreciation of your boldness, courage and enduring commitment to the causes of civil liberties, human rights and world peace. Through your concern and dedication for upholding human dignity in all aspects of life, through your extensive writings, court actions and leadership in the fields of philosophy, humanism and civil rights, you have demonstrated the highest traditions of mankind in your efforts to help all people to achieve a full and meaningful life."

1983   *Stephen H. Fritchman 'Heretic' Award* from the First Unitarian Church of Los Angeles
"For outstanding achievement in the cause of social progress."

1984   North American Committee for Humanism, The Humanist Institute:
"Because Corliss Lamont has become the spokesman of Humanism through his many writings
Because he has courageously defended free speech and human rights against the intimidation of bigots and political opportunists
Because he has championed the ideal of a single humanity with equal dignity for all
Because he has generously supported the work of humanism throughout North America
Because he has done more to publicize the ideas and values of Humanism than any other living person
We offer tribute to him and declare that Corliss Lamont is an honorary Member of the North American Committee for Humanism, 29th March, 1984."

1984   *Ethics in Action Award* from Westchester Ethical Humanist Society
"In recognition of a lifetime exemplifying ethics in action."

1985   Humanist Counselor Hall of Fame.
"For lifetime service to Humanism and Humanity."

1987   *The John Phillips Exeter Award.*
Presented by the Trustees of Phillips Exeter Academy to an Exeter graduate who exemplifies in high degree the lofty ideals and nobility of character of the School's founder, John Phillips.

25
The American People's Right to Know
(1987)

For more than sixteen years the National Emergency Civil Liberties Committee has been waging an unceasing campaign on behalf of the American people's Right to Know against the successive Administrations of Presidents Richard Nixon, Gerald Ford, Jimmy Carter and Ronald Reagan. Our procedure has usually been to print an advertisement in the Sunday *New York Times*. The Right to Know is also the right to truth and is the most fundamental civil liberty of all, encompassing freedom of speech, freedom of assembly, freedom of the press, freedom of religion, freedom to read, freedom to listen and freedom to travel.

Our first public message on this subject was published in the *Times* in May 1970 in protest against President Nixon's secret invasion of Cambodia as part of America's illegal, immoral and brutal military aggression against Vietnam. In this disaster more than 58,000 United States troops and some two million Vietnamese lost their lives.

The latest and in some ways most outrageous example of violating the Right to Know exploded in November 1986 when it was revealed that President Reagan, with no notice to Congress, but assisted by the C.I.A., had secretly carried on a series of complex dealings with hostile Iran, including the illegal U.S. delivery of arms to that country. And a large amount of the financial profits were diverted to the Nicaraguan Contras and the rebels of Afghanistan and Angola.

Altogether, the National Emergency Civil Liberties Committee has published a total of eleven messages centering around the Right to Know. These reports have been signed by Corliss Lamont, Chairman of the organization, Edith Tiger, Director, and Leonard B. Boudin, General Counsel. The messages have been well received by the public. The last one printed in this pamphlet, "The American People's Right to Truth From Their Government," appeared in the *Times,* October 26, 1986. The Contents gives a listing of the eleven advertisements.

Corliss Lamont, Editor
December, 1986

Contents

1970—An Urgent Constitutional Message *(About President Nixon's invasion of Cambodia)*
1975—C.I.A. and F.B.I. Spying Violates American Rights *(Wire-tapping and other secret surveillance greatly endanger Bill of Rights)*
1978—An Important Victory for Civil Liberties *(About the C.I.A. unconstitutionally opening mail)*
1983—Constituional Crisis *(About the unconstitutional invasion of Grenada)*
1984—Who is Running the Country? *(About the C.I.A.'s secret war against Nicaragua and the abuse of executive power)*
1985—The World Court and the Right to Know *(President Reagan's withdrawal from the World Court regarding Nicaragua)*
1985—Nuclear Secrecy and the Right to Know *(About deploying U.S. nuclear weapons around the world)*
1985—President Reagan's Assault Upon the World Court and the People's Right to Know *(About the U.S. boycott of the World Court, mining Nicaraguan harbors and supporting the Contras)*
1986—The People's Right to Know *(Is Nicaragua becoming another Vietnam?)*
1986—The World Court and the Rule of Law *(About the Reagan Administration's defiance of the World Court)*
1986—The American People's Right to Truth From Their Government *(About the Reagan Administration's Campaign of Disinformation)*

THE NEW YORK TIMES

Sunday, May 10, 1970

AN URGENT CONSTITUTIONAL MESSAGE

The Country is in a State of Justified Alarm.

President Nixon's invasion of Cambodia, and his resumption of aerial bombing of North Vietnam, has created a grave constitutional crisis for our country. It raises equally serious problems of international law and of public morality.

In the guise of exercising his powers as Commander-in-Chief of the Armed Forces, the President has committed the lives of Americans and Asians to a further extension of an undeclared and illegal war. This is a violation of Article I, Section 8, of the United States Constitution—which explicitly gives Congress alone the power to declare war. In taking this action President Nixon could not even rely on the specious authority of a Tonkin Gulf resolution. He has acted against the will of the Congress and the people, who have indicated at every opportunity available to them their desire to withdraw American troops from Indo-China as expeditiously as possible.

The President has extended the scope of an aggressive war in disregard of the principles urged upon the world by the United States at Nuremberg.

The President has violated his campaign promises and his post-election commitment to withdraw American troops from Vietnam. He has made a cruel joke of his declared intentions to reduce their numbers, to create a volunteer army, and to reduce the voting age requirements. How many young men will volunteer for such an army in such a war, and how many will survive to cast their votes?

What can the American people and their elected representatives do to protect themselves against a Chief Executive who is subordinating them and all branches of government to his own will? We suggest that the Congress, the judiciary, members of the armed forces, and all other citizens must consider what steps can legally be taken—and must be taken—to protect our constitutional liberties.

> 1. *We believe that the Congress has the duty—by joint resolution or statute—to rescind all military appropriations, to direct that no monies be henceforth expended for military action in Indo-China, to require the immediate cessation of such action, and to mandate the return of American men and women now in Indo-China to the United States.*
> 2. *We believe that if the President does not abide by the Constitution he should be impeached and removed from office.*
> 3. *We believe that the judiciary must meet its responsibility of passing judgment on the conduct of the President and the illegality of the war. How can the rule of constitutional law in this nation survive if the Courts continue in their policy of abstention from their basic responsibility?*
> 4. *We believe that in the present situation no American citizen is under a legal obligation to enter or remain in the armed forces until these issues have been resolved. We believe that servicemen, as well as*

those about to be inducted, should institute appropriate legal proceedings to save them from complicity in an illegal war.
5. *We believe that the labor movement must finally cast aside the corrupting influence of the military-industrial conspiracy and awaken to its moral responsibility in this crisis. Our country now faces the unusual situation in which a general strike can serve to restore constitutional government, check our violations of international law, and rescue us from the moral abyss into which the President has plunged us.*
6. *We believe the administration of the United States is now in the hands of a man who has made political capital of a debased and cynical conception of "law and order." It is time for all men and women of good will to join to restore constitutional law and moral order before they are utterly destroyed.*

THE NEW YORK TIMES
Sunday, April 13, 1975
C.I.A. AND F.B.I. SPYING VIOLATES AMERICAN RIGHTS

The C.I.A. The F.B.I. They're watching you. If you've ever attended an anti-war demonstration, written a letter of protest to the White House, known any civil rights or anti-war activists, if you've ever received mail from a Socialist country, then you're a dissenting American. Someone to be watched. Listened to. Spied on.

You may not remember precisely. But through secret wire-tapping and the collection of secret files, the C.I.A. will remember, the F.B.I. will remember.

It doesn't matter that the Bill of Rights gives every American the right to dissent, guarantees to every citizen the right to speak without fear, to assemble peaceably, to print freely any opinion, and to petition the government for a redress of grievances. It doesn't matter that the Bill of Rights protects us against unreasonable search and seizure, of our homes, our papers and effects.

Our rights, our irreplaceable rights, no longer matter. The freedom of the individual absolutely guaranteed by the Bill of Rights is eroding, weakened before the persistent and anti-democratic onslaughts of the C.I.A. and F.B.I., who by their own admission have consistently violated our civil liberties. Our rights are being lost because these agencies are out of control, and because Americans do not care.

Well, we care. We are the National Emergency Civil Liberties Committee. And for twenty-four years we have been passionately fighting to save the rights of the American people, in test cases involving freedom of speech, press, religion. The right to assemble and travel freely. To remain silent in the face of inquisition. To refuse to fight in an immoral and illegal war. To enjoy the right to dissent.

We have fought hard and we have won some victories. But now, with the Bicentennial approaching, there is hope for a real rebirth of the American spirit and the American freedoms. Therefore, the NECLC urgently demands the following of Congress:

1. The establishment of a Congressional watchdog committee to scrutinize the activities of all intelligence gathering agencies.
2. The establishment of controls requiring the C.I.A., and any other intelligence gathering agency not now under Congressional jurisdiction, to make full disclosure of its funding methods and expenditures.
3. The immediate release of all files on American citizens illegally obtained by the C.I.A., F.B.I., or any other intelligence gathering agency, and the return of such files to said citizens.

It is not too late. To change. To be free. To speak your mind. We urge you to write to your Senator and Representative and demand the protection of your Constitutional rights. (If you're not sure who your Congresspersons are, call us.) Too often, Congress ignores the people's voice. That voice must be a roar. Write. Ask your family to write. Ask your friends to write. Know what is happening to you and do something about it.

And we ask for your support, to continue the fight we have waged for twenty-four years. The fight to know, to inform Americans of their rights, and to protect those rights where it is most important, in the Congress, and in the Courts.

Help us.

Don't take your Constitutional rights for granted. You might wake up one day, and find them gone.

THE NEW YORK TIMES

Sunday, March 12, 1978

AN IMPORTANT VICTORY FOR CIVIL LIBERTIES

Corliss Lamont wins financial damages from Central Intelligence Agency for its unconstitutional opening and copying of 155 letters to and from him in suit sponsored by National Emergency Civil Liberties Committee

In a decision handed down February 17, Federal Court Judge Jack B. Weinstein of the Eastern District of New York awarded $2,000 to Corliss Lamont for the C.I.A.'s gross violation of his privacy, and directed the United States Government to send him "a suitable letter of regret" for the C.I.A.'s illegal actions. NECLC attorneys Leonard B. Boudin and Michael Krinsky represented Dr. Lamont.

Judge Weinstein's Opinion

Corliss Lamont had over 100 pieces of correspondence to and from various people in Russia opened by the C.I.A. The letters were copies. The F.B.I. was furnished with the copies to add to the extensive files it was in the process of accumulating in the course of its own work.

Mr. Lamont has written and lectured extensively on a variety of subjects, including philosophy and civil liberties. Eighty-eight letters dealt primarily with aspects of humanism and were directed to Vladimir Kazakevich, a friend the plaintiff had met while both were lecturing at Columbia University; these letters included various pamphlets and articles published by Mr. Lamont which, because they were attached to the letters, were duly copied and filed in the archives of the F.B.I. and the C.I.A. In addition, a series of letters to plaintiff's counsel, Leonard Boudin, dealt with various aspects of civil liberties, some apparently arising from Mr. Lamont's position as a leader in the American civil liberties movement and related activities. Still other letters were directed to friends and members of the Lamont family.

Mr. Lamont's reaction to his discovery of these illegal mail openings was one of "surprise," "indignation," "depression," and a "sense of failure" upon realizing that his life-long work on behalf of civil liberties had not prevented this major breach of his own rights is understandable. It is apparent, however, that this doughty and sophisticated fighter for civil liberties quickly recovered from his depression. It is unlikely that he, or any other sensible person actively engaged in the everlasting struggle for freedom in our beloved country or elsewhere expects perfection in his lifetime. The damages were similar to those suffered by plaintiff Wilson.

There are, however, two Lamont letters which require separate consideration. They were characterized by plaintiff as "love letters" to his wife. In describing the opening of these letters on the witness stand Mr. Lamont was obviously deeply upset. While he was some 70 years old when he wrote them and his years have now exceeded the biblical span, his emotional reaction is understandable. It should have been foreseen by the C.I.A. Illegal governmental prying into the shared intimacies of husband and wife is despicable. (The Court has not read the letters—it had more than enough of the demeaning process of reading other men's letters to their loved ones as a young naval officer assigned from time-to-time to censorship duties on his ship.) The letters of plaintiff to his wife will be sealed by the Clerk of the Court.

Plaintiff Lamont is awarded $2,000.00 provided the government furnishes a suitable letter of regret. Twenty-five percent shall be paid as a legal fee.

The sums being awarded are in large measure symbolic. They probably substantially underestimate the deep sense of personal affront and the psychic loss suffered by a distinguished man of the world writing to friends, associates and his wife. Certainly the wound to his sense of freedom and pride in our Constitution is enormous.

Were there fewer possible plantiffs, the Court might have considered larger symbolic awards for those plaintiffs who had a number of letters opened over a span of time. Plaintiffs have made a powerful argument that repeated intrusions warrant more compensation, if only as an indication that the courts are sensitive to both the quantity and the quality of a constitutional violation. But the Court must be practical; the number of possible plaintiffs runs into the thousands and the possible damages, even at the modest level fixed by the Court, into the millions. These damages will not be paid by the bunglers responsible for the wrongs, but by the taxpayers, who were unaware of the program.

Jack B. Weinstein
United States District Judge

THE NEW YORK TIMES

Wednesday November 9, 1983

CONSTITUTIONAL?

We are in the midst of a constitutional crisis. The President wages an illegal war in Nicaragua and orders an unprovoked invasion of Grenada. These acts violate the war-making powers of Congress.

The greatest military power in the world sends its marines, navy and air force to bomb Grenadian buildings, kill innocent civilians, and take over the government. Our President makes transparently false excuses and bans the press to conceal the facts from the American people.

The invasion of Grenada is an act of war and illegal under:

    .... The Constitution of the United States
    .... The Charter of the United Nations
    .... The Charter of the Organization of American States
    .... The Neutrality Act of 1948
    .... The War Powers Act
    .... The Nuremberg Charter and Judgment.

The censorship and containment of the press was an attempt to mask these violations of law and in itself violated the First Amendment of the Constitution.

Congress has been delinquent by its failure to condemn the President's aggression.

We citizens must not default in our responsibility. We must exercise our First Amendment rights of speech, assembly and petition:

1. *Demand the withdrawal of all American forces from Grenada and its adjacent waters;*
2. *End the war against Nicaragua;*
3. *Call for a congressional inquiry to determine whether impeachment is appropriate.*

CONGRESS MUST ACT. SO MUST YOU.

Exercise *your* First Amendment rights and honor *your* Constitutional obligations. Come to Washington on Saturday, November 12th. Join more than 100 peace, civic and religious groups, and unions and others in a massive march to the White House to protest intervention in Central America and the Caribbean. Write or wire your Congressional representatives.

THE NEW YORK TIMES
Sunday, May 13, 1984
WHO IS RUNNING THE COUNTRY?

The President has asked us to back his foreign policy. Bill, how can we back his foreign policy when we don't know what the hell he is doing? . . . This is an act violating international law. It is an act of war.
—Senator Barry Goldwater
to C.I.A. Director William Casey,
April 9, 1984

There is a lot of talk about not trying to overthrow the government, but the facts speak for themselves. Unless you're trying to do this, why else would you mine their harbor?

—Senator Patrick Leahy

In early April, the press revealed that the Central Intelligence Agency was directly involved in mining Nicaraguan harbors. Senators Goldwater and Moynihan accused the Administration of concealing from their Senate committee the information about covert activities required by law. While members of Congress expressed outrage, the rest of us were left wondering "who is running the country: The President? The C.I.A.? The Pentagon?" Whatever became of government by and for The People? What happened to the open government we were promised after the Watergate break-ins and cover-ups?

From the invasion of Grenada to the not-so-secret war in Nicaragua, we see abuses of executive power and the exercise of an invisible government. This violates the American people's RIGHT TO KNOW.

We believe that there can be little doubt that this executive misconduct constitutes "high crimes and misdemeanors." Nor is Congress blameless in this matter. The press seems to know more about what is happening than does Congress. In its disinterest in the existence of both covert and overt war Congress has abdicated its constitutional responsibility to the American people.

The National Emergency Civil Liberties Committee demands an end to President Reagan's dictatorial abuses of executive power, to covert activities and secrecy in government. And we say that it is time the people know who is running the country. If you agree, join with us to bring an end to the invisible government.

THE NEW YORK TIMES

Sunday, February 3, 1985

THE WORLD COURT AND THE RIGHT TO KNOW

An Open Letter to the American People

In his Inaugural Address January 20 President Reagan spoke eloquently of the great American ideals that he and his fellow-citizens must strive to uphold. Yet only two days previously the President had directed that the U.S. Government take no further part in the World Court proceedings dealing with Nicaragua's suit against the United States for violating international law by supporting paramilitary attacks by rebels in Nicaragua and by mining its harbors. This dishonorable boycott of the World Court betrays America's historic ideals for international peace and for the rule of law throughout the world. President Reagan is clearly a man of many contradictions.

As Anthony Lewis states in his excellent article on Presidential powers without accountability (*New York Times,* Op-Ed Jan. 21), "The Reagan Administration feared that the court proceeding would bring out the facts of its aid to terrorist activities and focus attention on its violation of treaties." Thus the U.S. withdrawal from World Court jurisdiction means that President Reagan is again trying to avoid accountability by concealing the truth and is violating the American people's basic civil liberty, *the right to know*.

THE NEW YORK TIMES

Sunday, February 24, 1985

NUCLEAR SECRECY AND THE RIGHT TO KNOW

Secrecy Is Incompatible With Democracy

In a special dispatch from Washington, D.C. the *New York Times* on Feb. 13 disclosed that the Reagan Administration has had "contingency plans to deploy nuclear weapons in Canada, Iceland, Bermuda and Puerto Rico." On Feb. 14 the *Times* revealed that these plans also included the Azores Islands of Portugal in the Atlantic, the Philippines, Spain and the British island of Diego Garcia in the Indian Ocean. The very listing of the eight locations concerned makes the whole business seem both dangerous and absurd.

More important, none of the governments involved even knew about the existence of these plans, which could prove a grave threat to their peoples. With regard to Puerto Rico, the contingency plans jeopardize the 1967 commitment of the U.S., when she signed the Treaty for the Prohibition of Nuclear Weapons in Latin America.

Since the American people know nothing about this scandalous, secret and hide-and-seek nuclear game perpetrated by the Pentagon and President Reagan, the public's right to know, a basic civil liberty, has once again been violated.

THE NEW YORK TIMES

Sunday, October 27, 1985

PRESIDENT REAGAN'S ASSAULT UPON THE WORLD COURT AND THE PEOPLE'S RIGHT TO KNOW

On January 18, President Reagan directed that our government take no further part in the World Court proceedings dealing with Nicaragua's suit against the United States for violating international law by supporting rebel paramilitary attacks and mining Nicaragua's harbors. This dishonorable boycott of the World Court was a betrayal of America's historic ideals of international peace and of the rule of law.

In October the Reagan Administration took another step backward, announcing that it will refuse to litigate any "political" cases before the World Court, a term our government will define as it pleases, from case to case. All disputes between nations are by their very nature political cases. Ours is the first nation therefore to radically undercut the Court's jurisdiction in international disputes.

The Administration's unilateral withdrawal from World Court jurisdiction in the Nicaragua case and the recent statement generally abrogating its jurisdiction flout the rule of law, and are attempts to avoid accountability to world opinion and to deny the American people's right to know.

—What are the real reasons underlying these extreme measures effected by our President?

—Are they but the prelude for further aggression?

THE NEW YORK TIMES
Wednesday April 9, 1986
THE PEOPLE'S RIGHT TO KNOW
THE MOST BASIC CIVIL LIBERTY

Is Nicaragua Becoming Another Vietnam?

VIETNAM

1964: President Johnson claims a North Vietnamese attack upon the U.S.S. Maddox which was sent into Vietnamese waters as a provocation.

Result: Congress passes the Gulf of Tonkin resolution prepared prior to the incident and then used by Johnson as "functionally equivalent" to a declaration of war and authority to send U.S. fighting forces to Vietnam for the first time.

(The North Vietnamese attack was never proven according to leading scholars.)

NICARAGUA

In March 1986 President Reagan dramatically charged that the Nicaraguan lawful "hot pursuit" of Contra forces to their Honduran bases was an "invasion." He failed to reveal that this was one of hundreds of similar unchallenged incidents over the last three years; he pressured Honduras to complain and brought American military forces into the area of conflict in violation of the War Powers Act.

Result: Senate votes for military aid to Contras and House leaders begin to falter.

For four years the Reagan Administration has directed the Contras in their killing of thousands of Nicaraguan adults and children, and destruction of schools, hospitals, crops and farms in the name of the American people.

The United States Government has walked out of a proceeding in the International Court of Justice in order to avoid a judicial determination of the facts of U.S. aggression.

DO YOU KNOW ENOUGH ABOUT WHAT THE PRESIDENT IS DOING AGAINST NICARAGUA TO BE SURE THAT IT JUSTIFIES THE DEATHS OF NICARAGUAN CIVILIANS AND POTENTIALLY THOSE OF AMERICAN CITIZENS?

THE REMEDY

WRITE YOUR REPRESENTATIVES IN CONGRESS:
1. To defeat Contra aid;
2. To initiate an immediate and full investigation by the Senate Foreign Relations Committee and the House Committee on Foreign Affairs;
3. To return to the World Court for its adjudication of the Reagan Administration's attack upon Nicaragua.

THE NEW YORK TIMES
Sunday, July 20, 1986

THE WORLD COURT AND THE RULE OF LAW

On June 27, 1986, the International Court of Justice issued its judgment that our government's military and economic attacks on Nicaragua violated international law and the Treaty of Friendship Commerce and Navigation between the two countries.

The opinions and judgment of the Court are the first independent and impartial adjudication of the facts and of the controlling law. Yet, the Reagan Administration has announced that it will defy the Court's adjudication and judgment.

We, the American people, cannot accept our government's repudiation of the rule of law. It would violate our international obligations and lead to international anarchy.

On June 26, the House of Representatives regrettably voted to give military aid to the Contras, and the matter is now before the Senate.

Such military aid would violate the Court's order that the Reagan Administration cease and refrain immediately from such unlawful action. Now that the American people and the Congress know the facts, it is a matter of national honor, as well as legal obligation, that the Administration should comply with the World Court's decision and act upon its reminder of the need of both parties to cooperate with the Contadora process. This will constitute a significant message to the world that America is returning to its traditional ideals of international peace and justice for all humanity.

THE NEW YORK TIMES
Sunday, October 26, 1986
THE AMERICAN PEOPLE'S RIGHT TO TRUTH FROM THEIR GOVERNMENT

Two extraordinary revelations of governmental misconduct on a national level call for every citizen's immediate action: (1) the Administration's "disinformation program," particularly with respect to Libya; and, (2) the Administration's involvement in the war in Nicaragua.

I

Bob Woodward of the *Washington Post* recently revealed that Admiral Poindexter of the National Security Agency had proposed a disinformation program to make false statements to the press for the alleged purpose of "destabilizing" colonel Qaddafi of Libya. This program was actually adopted, possibly with some modification, and the government gave false statements to the press and through it to Congress and the American people.

The United States Supreme Court has held that the concealment or obstruction of relevant information is unconstitutional. This was the holding in *Lamont* v. *Postmaster General* and *Kent* v. *Dulles,* two important test cases of the National Emergency Civil Liberties Committee. But "disinformation" is far worse. It is deliberately misleading the American people.

It also reopens the question of whether the Administration lied to its selected Congressmen whom it "consulted" before its bombing of Libya.

Further, the Administration's disinformation notice that we were prepared to bomb Libya was a dangerous provocation. The Administration recognized that there was a risk that its threats might provoke "terrorism" but it stated internally that it was prepared to take that risk.

II

The Nicaraguan government's capture on its territory of an American, Eugene Hasenfus, carrying arms for the Contras, is another revelation of the Reagan Administration's direct involvement in the war against Nicaragua which the International Court of Justice has said violated international law. The captured American was an employee of the C.I.A.'s conduit airline used in Vietnam. The Administration's evasions were properly met by *The New York Times* editorial characterizing them as lies.

THE REMEDY

All Americans concerned with truth in government, and the people's right to know, should request their representatives in Congress to conduct open hearings:

(1) in which all the documents relating to the disinformation program are disclosed;

(2) the Administration is required to reveal what it told and showed the few Congressmen on the April bombing of Libya and what it actually knows about the sources of the terroristic atttacks upon American citizens;

(3) the Administration is required to reveal its actual involvement and, in particular, that of Vice President Bush in the Hasenfus affair and in our other military activities in Nicaragua.

26
Jesus as a Free Speech Victim (1987)

by CLIFFORD J. DURR

Introduction

Both Christians and non-Christians regard Jesus Christ primarily as a religious martyr and the founding father of the religion of Christianity. Very few worshippers, writers or people in general have thought deeply of the free speech and civil liberties implications in the persecution and execution of Jesus. Yet he stands out unmistakably as the most illustrious civil liberties victim in the history of religion.

Mr. Durr, with faithful reliance on the four gospels of the New Testament, tells the story in a simple and persuasive way, showing that the priests, the Pharisees and the business interests all wanted to get rid of Jesus because of his outspoken attacks upon them and his general opposition to the Establishment of his day. Thus the Bible itself reveals that the vigilante treatment of Jesus constituted a typical civil liberties case with the issues of freedom of speech, opinion, worship and of "due process of law" directly involved.

Durr's booklet, a publication of the National Emergency Civil Liberties Committee in 1981, is even more relevant today than when he wrote it some 40 years ago. For we are now confronted in the United States with a group of religious fanatics, led by the so-called Moral Majority and Liberty Federation, that is viciously attacking the American Bill of Rights, organizing boycotts of television programs, promoting the censorship of books that present the Darwinian theory of evolution or having a liberal slant, demanding their withdrawal from public school libraries and even pressuring librarians to reveal the names of borrowers of materials of which they disapprove. All of these actions blatantly violate the American people's Right to Know, our most basic civil liberty.

These fundamentalist religious zealots and televangelists, with vast millions of dollars at their disposal and a huge network of radio and TV outlets, believe that they are in direct touch with God and that his word as expounded in the Bible and interpreted by them is the absolute truth. Their intolerance of liberals, Humanists and civil libertarians knows no bounds. The number of misstatements in their literature and propaganda is simply enormous. Yet they profess to follow Jesus, who said "The truth shall set you free."

The right-wing religious fanatics have also been instituting suits in support of their censorship programs. For instance, in Alabama 600 Christian fundamentalists brought suit against the State Board of Education for the removal from public schools of a large number of textbooks which they claimed were promoting "the religion of secular Humanism." On March 4, 1987 a Federal district Judge, Brevard Hand, ruled in favor of the plaintiffs by ordering some 40 textbooks removed from Alabama schools. This was an absurd decision, since Humanism properly defined is a non-theistic philosophy rejecting all belief in the supernatural and adopting as its supreme commitment the welfare and happiness of all humanity in this one and only life. The American Humanist Association and Humanists in general have never attempted to instill this viewpoint in American public schools.

The Hand decision not only sets a dangerous precedent for American education, but also is an act of far-reaching censorship that clearly violates the First Amendment of the Bill of Rights. However, it is being appealed by the Alabama Board of Education and in all probability will be reversed by a higher court.

Our analysis shows that the Moral Majority, the Liberty Federation and their allies, who insist they are the only true Christians, entirely neglect the civil liberties aspects of Jesus's life and the free speech meaning of the Crucifixion. Hypocrites all, they would have hounded Jesus to his death had they lived in his times.

Clifford Durr's provocative essay makes clear that civil libertarians throughout America and the world, regardless of their attitude towards religion, can claim Jesus as a dauntless hero in the great cause of free speech, ever in jeopardy over the ages. And thus Jesus carried on the far-famed tradition established by the foremost civil liberties martyr of philosophy, Socrates in ancient Greece.

> Corliss Lamont, Chairman
> National Emergency Civil Liberties Committee
> April, 1987

Trial by Terror 2,000 Years Ago

Jesus was undoubtedly a "troublemaker." Many of his associates were questionable characters; certainly they were of doubtful social standing. In defiance of the prevailing prejudice of his day, he had said pointedly that, on the test of behavior, a Samaritan might be just as good as a priest or a Levite. He had questioned the accepted belief that wealth and virtue necessarily go hand in hand. He had been outspoken and vigorous in his attacks upon certain established business interests. He had exposed the corruption of those in positions of power. Such language as the following was certainly regarded as "intemperate" by those at whom it was aimed: "hypocrites," "serpents," "generation of vipers," "whited sepulchers, which indeed appear beautiful outward, but are within full of dead men's bones and of all uncleanness," "blind guides which strain at a gnat and swallow a camel."

Hypocrisy in high places was a constant target: "All therefore whatsoever they bid you observe," he told his followers with reference to the Scribes and Pharisees, "that observe and do; but," he warned, "do not ye after their works: for they say and do not." The words stung because they hit their mark. He stripped the cloak of respectability and righteousness from those who "for pretense make long prayer," and left them exposed in their moral and spirtual nakedness: "Now they (had) no cloak for their sin."

Jesus's appeal was to the "malcontents," and he was effective in stirring them up and in gaining followers in ever increasing numbers. He effectively challanged the status quo. In other words, he was "subversive" in the truest sense of the term; as the chief priests put it, he was "perverting the nation" by his teaching. He was a "dangerous" influence, and he had to be stopped.

The Techniques of Suppression

A description of the tactics used to stop Jesus has a familiar ring. His speeches and even private conversations were to be used against him: "Then went the Pharisees and took counsel how they might entangle him in his talk." Secret agents and "confidential informants" were put to work: "And they watched him, and sent forth spies, which should feign themselves just men, that they might take hold of his words, that so they might deliver him unto the power and authority of the governor."

They questioned him on his loyalty to the government: "Tell us therefore, what thinkest thou? Is it lawful to give tribute unto Caesar, or not?" They inquired into his religious beliefs, the soundness of his views on marriage and the resurrection of the dead. They set a lawyer on him in an effort to entrap him in legal questions, for he had not spared that profession in his exposure of hypocrisy: "Woe unto you, lawyers! for ye have taken away the key of knowledge: ye entered not in yourselves, and them that were entering in ye hindered."

But Jesus's great intelligence was too much for his questioners. He confounded them with his answers. He "put the Sadducees to silence": "And no man was able to answer him a word, neither durst any man from that day forth ask him any more questions."

In the arena of public opinion his ideas were clearly winning the victory. Converts were rallying to his banner in ever increasing numbers. The Scribes and the Pharisees "feared the people," and hence were unwilling to trust them with ideas. Though "they hated him without cause," their hatred became an obsession. Unable to answer him, they decided to kill him. Argument having failed them, they took fear as their weapon: "If we let him thus alone," they said, "all men will believe on him; and the Romans shall come and take away both our place and nation." Jesus thus became a threat to *national security*. They now had a propaganda line with which public opinion could be effectively aroused.

Courage on the battlefield is commonplace, for there men face death with the approval of their fellows. The courage required to face the disapproval of society in defense of a cause is far rarer. "Disloyalty" whether to "place" or "nation" is an odious label, and none want to wear it. Those who wear it—whether justly or unjustly—are to be avoided, for the taint of guilt becomes attached by association.

Their victim was driven underground for a while and "Jesus walked no more openly among the Jews."

Hypocrisy in High Places

His followers were intimidated, but his ideas were not so easily destroyed. Even among the top officers of government, many still "believed on him": "But because of the Pharisees they did not confess him, lest they should be put out of the synagogues. For they loved the praise of men more than the praise of God."

The symbols of a great religion based on justice and humanity were prostituted to fan the flames of hatred. This man was guilty of "blasphemy" they said. The attack took on the zeal of a religious crusade. The threat of physical violence was added to the social and religious pressures.

Jesus fully understood what nature of men his enemies were. They were tolerant of dissent so long as that dissent was weak and ineffective. They paid reverence to the memory of dead reformers because those reformers were safely dead. But once their positions of power and authority were really threatened, they were ruthless. They would stop at nothing. He had the measure of their viciousness and their hypocrisy and told them so: "Ye build the tombs of the prophets, and garnish the sepulchers of the righteous, and say: 'If we had been in the days of our fathers, we would not have been partakers with them in the blood of the prophets.'"

But he reminded them: "Ye are the children of them which killed the prophets—" "Behold, I send unto you prophets, and wise men, and scribes; and some of them ye kill and crucify; and some of them ye scourge in your synagogues, and persecute them from city to city."

He frankly warned his followers of their danger: "They shall put you out of the synagogues; yea, the time cometh that whosoever killeth you will think that he doeth God's service."

And again: "Now the brother shall betray the brother to death, and the father, the son; and children shall rise up against their parents, and shall cause them to be put to death. And ye shall be hated of all men for my name's sake."

It was under these circumstances that Jesus made his decision to face trial. He would offer himself as a victim to the mob lest its mounting thirst for blood demand many victims.

He still had followers who were devoted and unafraid; so the arrest by the servants of Annas was made at night. The kiss of Judas was to no purpose. Jesus readily admitted his identity and chided the multitude who came to arrest him for their mob-given courage: "Are ye come out as against a thief with swords and staves for to take me? I sat daily with you teaching in the temple and ye laid no hold on me."*

The next day he was carried for trial before Caiaphas, the high priest who also, quite conveniently, happened to be Annas' son-in-law.

The Bill of Rights in an Old Setting

The first question concerned his "beliefs" and his "associations": "The high priest then asked Jesus of his disciples and of his doctrine."

Jesus was not one to betray his friends. He silently refused to expose his associates and immediately forced the trial into the issue of freedom

---

*Walter M. Chandler, in his fascinating and excellently documented *Trial of Jesus* (Empire Publishing Company, New York, 1908) gives the clue to the motive underlying the entire campaign against Jesus: "Now it is historically true that Annas and Caiaphas and their friends owned and controlled the stalls, booths, and bazaars connected with the Temple and from which flowed a most lucrative trade. The profits from the sale of lambs and doves, sold for sacrifice, alone were enormous. When Jesus threatened the destruction of their trade, he assaulted the interests of Annas and his associates in the Sanhedrin in a vital place. The driving of the cattle from the stalls was probably more effective in compassing the destruction of Christ than any miracle that he performed or any discourse that he delivered."

of speech: "I spake openly to the world, I ever taught in the synagogue, and in the temple, whither the Jews always may resort; and in secret have I said nothing." "Why askest thou me? Ask them which heard me, what I have said unto them; behold, they know what I said." He knew the law and stood on his right not to incriminate himself.

But this was not what the court wanted. The response to his statement was a blow from an officer who stood by, and the implied threat of an additional charge of contempt of court: "Answerest thou the high priest so?" Jesus's reply was a demand for the evidence against him: "If I have spoken evil, bear witness of that evil; but if well, why smitest thou me?"

But the evidence was not forthcoming. If he were in fact guilty of a crime, then Judas was his accomplice and the testimony of an accomplice was not legally admissible in the Sanhedrin Court: "Now the chief priests, and elders, and all the council sought false witnesses against Jesus; to put him to death, yet found they none." Finally two false witnesses were found who attempted to testify about a remark of Jesus that he could destroy the temple and rebuild it in three days, but even the testimony of these witnesses was in conflict. Moreover, it was irrelevant to any criminal charge that could be properly framed.

The chief priests were on the spot. Here was a dangerous man, and he had to be gotten rid of, but they had no evidence on which to convict him. Moreover, they had to think of the dignity of their court. The judicial forms at least had to be observed. The whole business began to look messy, and it would be better if someone else took over the dirty job.

So they took Jesus over to the hall of judgment where Pilate presided. But: "They themselves went not into the judgment hall, lest they should be defiled." Pilate, instead, came out to them and, trained judge that he was, demanded to be informed of the charges against the man he was to try: "What accusation bring ye against this man?" But here also the charges, like the evidence, were lacking.

Let the accused prove his innocence, the priests said in effect. By virtue of the arrest, the burden of proof was reversed, and it thereby became the task of the defendant to prove his innocence beyond all reasonable doubt. At least that was their theory: "If he were not a malefactor, we would not have delivered him up unto thee." But Pilate, the judge, refused to accept any such theory because it did violence to the most basic legal concept. He could not put a man on trial when it was not even charged that he had violated the law. He declined jurisdiction and threw the case back into the laps of the high priests. This man hadn't violated any Roman law, and he said: "Take ye him and judge him according to your law."

Here was complete frustration. The Jewish law was not equal to the occasion either, even if testimony sufficient to convict him could be manufactured. They reminded Pilate that: "It is not lawful for us to put any man to death." The situation at this point was getting quite embarrassing for Pilate as well as the chief priests. Public opinion had been whipped up to a high pitch, and Pilate, after all, was a politician. At this point fortune played into his hands.

Jesus Undergoes the Third Degree

Jesus was a Galilean and, as it happened, Herod, the Governor of Galilee, was in Jerusalem at that particular time. Here was a chance to please Herod by a nice gesture deferring to his jurisdiction and at the same time get rid of a case that was loaded with political dynamite. So Pilate waived jurisdiction and sent Jesus to Herod for trial.

Herod at first was pleased. He liked this token of Pilate's recognition. Moreover, he had heard quite a bit about the man Jesus and was curious to see what he was like. He hoped Jesus might even perform some miracle in his presence. But after fruitless questioning, to the accompaniment of the vehement accusations of the chief priests and scribes, Herod realized how Pilate was using him. So back the defendant was sent to Pilate's court.

Again Pilate demanded to know the charges. This time a chief priest whispered in his ear, and he asked: "Art thou King of the Jews?" Here was a definite charge of subversion, if not of treason. For Tiberius Caesar was in power, and anyone acting as a king in his realm challenged the sovereignty of Caesar. Jesus immediately understood the origin of the question. The charges clearly did not originate with the civil magistrate: "Jesus answered him, 'Sayest thou this thing of thyself, or did others tell it thee of me?'" Pilate admitted that he was prompted: "Am I a Jew? Thine own nation and the chief priests have delivered thee to me; what hast thou done?"

Jesus readily gave the answer that his interest was in spiritual and not temporal power: "My kingdom is not of this world; if my kingdom were of this world, then would my servants fight, that I should not be delivered to the Jews; but now is my kingdom not from hence." The answer made sense to Pilate, and he asked one further question to make the record entirely clear: "Art thou a king then?" To this Jesus answered that his only function and purpose was to "bear witness unto the truth." From this point on Pilate sought to turn his cross-examination into a philosophical discussion on the interesting question, "What is truth?" He was satisfied that there was no case and announced his verdict: "I find in him no fault at all."

Pilate suggested, as it was the custom to release one prisoner at the passover, that he release the defendant. But the priests and their followers were adamant. Jesus had ideas, and he was articulate about them. He was therefore, dangerous. So they demanded the release of Barabbas instead. Now as it happened Barabbas was no mere dabbler in ideas. He was a man of action. He had been arrested for attempting to overthrow the government by force and violence. He "had made insurrection" and "had committed murder in the insurrection."

By this time, public feeling had been worked up to an explosive pitch. There was no evidence on which Jesus could be convicted, but there were definite political dangers in releasing him. So Pilate followed the only course left open. He resorted to the third degree. The defendant was "scourged," and the soldiers "smote him with their hands." But even this treatment brought forth nothing in the way of evidence. Again Pilate reported to the high priests: "Behold I bring him forth to you, that ye may know I find no fault in him." The priests, however, were after blood. And the chant, "Crucify him! Crucify him!" was steadily mounting in intensity. But Pilate persisted in his finding of "Not guilty."

Expediency vs. Principle

At this point, the chief priests again changed their tactics. As messy as the job was, it was better for them to take over the trial than to have Jesus go scot free. They now thought of a charge under which they could assume jurisdiction. They announced to Pilate: "We have a law, and by our law he ought to die, because he made himself the Son of God." With this new development, Pilate's position became even more difficult. "He was the more afraid." Again he went into the judgment hall and questioned Jesus, warning him: "I have the power to crucify thee and have the power to release thee." But still Jesus remained steadfast in his refusal to "confess" his guilt of any crime: "And from thenceforth Pilate sought to release him."

Now the quarry was about to escape; so the chief priests played their last card. In order to set aside Pilate's judgment of acquittal, they proposed to try the judge himself. Pilate was threatened with a charge of "disloyalty."

The chief priests thus applied the last ounce of political pressure. Jesus, it is true, had explained that his interest lay in spiritual and not temporal affairs. But after all, he has said that he was a "king," and for one to proclaim his kingship in Caesar's realm was, according to their theory, treason to Caesar. Maybe Caesar would not be quite as ready as Pilate to accept Jesus's explanation. So the chief priests became the most vociferous exponents of patriotism and champions of Caesar. They proclaimed themselves more loyal to Caesar than Pilate, the Roman and Caesar's own appointee. "We have no king but Caesar" became their cry. Pilate, they implied, by releasing Jesus had demonstrated his "disloyalty." They threatened to go to Caesar with the story. "If thou let this man go," they said, "thou art not Caesar's friend; whosoever maketh himself a king speaketh against Caesar."

This last bit of pressure was too much. Pilate's job was at stake, and it was a good job. It carried with it power, prestige, and wealth. He might even find himself in the position of defendant in a "loyalty" case; so "When Pilate saw that he could prevail nothing, but that rather a tumult was made, he took water, and washed his hands before the multitude, saying, 'I am innocent of the blood of this just person: see ye to it.'" And he delivered Jesus up to be crucified.

Pilate, however, made one last obeisance to the integrity of the judicial process. He "wrote a title and put it on the cross. And the writing was: 'JESUS OF NAZARETH THE KING OF THE JEWS.'" But the chief priests were still not satisfied with the judgment of the court. Again they shifted their ground. This man, Jesus, was not really a king; he just said he was. And so they demanded of Pilate: "Write not, The King of the Jews; but that *he* said, 'I am King of the Jews.'" But Pilate had gone his limit. There was one line from which he would not retreat. He was a judge and respected the law. There was no provision of law under which a man could be crucified merely for what he had said. If he had to send a man to his death, the order of judgment, at least, would be clear that it was for his illegal deeds and not mere words; so: "Pilate answered, 'What I have written, I have written.'" A legal principle, at least, was saved from the mob.

Perhaps Pilate's judicial conscience was satisfied. Certainly the Scribes and the Pharisees were satisfied, for Jesus was dead and the great voice of protest was silenced—or so they thought.

But what did the suppression gain the suppressors? Perhaps the profits from their money-changing operations and from the sale of sacrificial animals continued a few years longer. Perhaps they succeeded in continuing, for a while, their political control over the people whom they so greatly "feared." But the ideas they sought to destroy still lived, and they have continued to live and spread because men have found them good.

Now, two thousand years later, we can see that the folly of the Scribes and Pharisees was even greater than their wickedness.

About the Author

Clifford J. Durr (1899–1975) was a brilliant lawyer with a long record of U.S. Government service that culminated with his appointment in 1941 by President Franklin D. Roosevelt as a Commissioner of the Federal Communications Commission. He resigned from this position in 1948 because he refused to administer the U.S. Government Loyalty Oath, which he considered unconstitutional. He later practiced law in his native city, Montgomery, Alabama, and was counsel in many important civil liberties and civil rights cases. Mr. Durr was a member and Deacon of the Presbyterian Church.

27
The Assurance of Free Choice (1987)

Contents

Freedom of Choice (From *The Humanist*, March-April, 1965)
Humanism and Free Choice (From *The American Rationalist*, July-August, 1962)
Free Choice and Responsibility (From *Freedom of Choice: A Symposium*, 1970)
Self-Determinism and Freedom of Choice (From *The Humanist*, May-June, 1974)
A Review of B. F. Skinner's *Beyond Freedom and Dignity* (From *Science and Society*, Summer, 1973)

Foreword

The five essays by me in this chapter discuss the important and much neglected philosophical and psychological issue of free choice and determinism, an issue that in Western thought goes back to the time of the ancient Greeks. These essays present the main reasons for asserting that all men and women possess true freedom of choice (or free will in the traditional phrase), that human beings are essentially free-wheeling and autonomous. This is the same position that I upheld in detail in my book *Freedom of Choice Affirmed* published in 1967.

Corliss Lamont
September, 1987

Freedom of Choice

When the fatalistic Mohammedan fighters in the motion picture *Lawrence of Arabia* wanted to persuade Colonel Lawrence of the impossibility of one of his proposed military ventures in World War I they said, "It is written." To which Lawrence's spirited answer was always, *"Nothing* is written." And the film in each case proceeds to show how he carried out the venture against immense odds.

Actually, Lawrence was not right, nor were the Arabs. The truth is that in human life there is a great deal that is inexorably determined ("written") and a great deal that springs from man's free choice ("free will" in traditional terminology). Both Lawrence and the Arabs made the mistake of considering these concepts, freedom of choice and determinism, to be mutually exclusive, as if there must be universal determinism *or* absolute freedom. Philosophers, too, have sometimes made the same error.

In modern times man has gained enormous control over Nature by discovering a multitude of scientific laws and then using them to his own advantage. Those laws represent determinism and are always the expression of if-then relations or sequences. *If* the temperature drops to 32 degrees Fahrenheit, *then* water freezes into ice. Fortunately, many human functions, such as breathing and the circulation of the blood, are automatic and deterministic. At the same time an individual functioning on the level of intellectual deliberation can exercise true freedom of choice in deciding between two or more genuine alternatives that confront him.

I want to emphasize the word "alternatives" because it expresses a key concept in the analysis of freedom of choice. It was the psychoanalyst and author Erich Fromm who suggested that Bertrand Russell, Britain's greatest philosopher of the twentieth century, was not a determinist as usually thought, but an "alternativist who sees that what is determined are certain limited and ascertainable alternatives." I wrote to Earl Russell in 1968, quoting Fromm's comment and added:

"Now this fits in precisely with my own viewpoint. Opposing extremes to which Sartre goes on this question, I claim that free choice is *always* limited by one's heredity, environment, economic circumstances and so on. Those are the deterministic elements in the picture. But beyond them, though established by them, are real alternatives among which a man can choose. That is where freedom of choice comes in.

"You have usually been classified as a determinist," I went on to say. "But If Fromm's remarks are correct, as well as my interpretation of them, you are by no means a total determinist and have been misunderstood."

Russell promptly replied: "I am in broad agreement with what you say about the free will question. Anything one says on this is sure to be wrong! It is difficult to find a form of words, and the difficulty is due to linguistic problems. There are no laws of nature that make the future certain. Any scientific investigator would always have to assume determinism as a working hypothesis, without complete belief or complete denial. *I cannot be described as a determinist,* and my views are closer to yours than to Sartre's." [My italics.—C.L. Aug. 16, 1968.]

Another outstanding philosopher commonly thought to have been a determinist is George Santayana. However, in *Dominations and Powers* (1951), the last of his books published while he was alive, Santayana comes around to a free choice position. He offers a rather unusual view of free will, but makes plain that he thinks it exists. He writes (pages 53-54):

"I think that intense scrutiny of immediate experience does yield an intuition of a truth; not at all, however, of the truth about the ground or origin of human decision, but about the *inadequacy* of the conscious arguments crowding and disputing in the mind to cause or justify the decision taken. With this comes also the intuition of a positive truth, that beneath that loud forum of sophistical pleadings there is a silent judge, the *self,* that decides according to its free will, contingently and inexplicably. For the close texture of events in nature is what it is by chance; yet what it is by chance determines, according to the occasion offered, what it shall do by nature.

"The affinities of this self are far more constant and certain than the passing passions or influences that may absorb conscious attention. Therefore the self can check its reasoning fancy; it can repel sensuous suggestion; it can seek dangerous adventures apparently without reason; it can recover its freedom, and reverse its habits and opinions. Moreover, this hidden self is, like every other center or kind of movement in nature, perfectly contingent in being groundlessly determinate; and to this profound characteristic of all existence self-consciousness bears witness in the conviction that a man is the author of his actions, and that his actions are free."

It is important to know that Bertrand Russell and George Santayana, two of the most brilliant minds in the history of philosophy, acknowledge the existence of the free choice in human beings.

Returning to my initial analysis of the interplay of human freedom and determinism, we can see that when a person wishes to go somewhere in his car, he relies on its built-in determinisms of self-starter, accelerator, steering wheel and brakes. But it is he, not the automobile, that makes the decision as to precisely what road he will take or what his destination is to be. This is an everyday example of how freedom utilizes determinism. In fact, successful human living is built upon this basic principle, which reaches its apex in a machine civilization like that of the United States. There is, then, in human existence a constant, interlocking pattern of *both* freedom and determinism.

Freedom of choice always operates within definite limits. It is conditioned by natural law, by heredity, by the past, by ingrained habit, by education, by the present environment, by economic circumstance and other factors. All humans are governed by the law of gravity and yet have very wide liberty of movement. To cite another familiar example, persons who play chess abide ordinarily by its established rules, which represent determinism; but within that broad framework a tremendous variety of moves are possible, and they represent freedom. The same principle holds true for all competitive games and sports.

The *if* of every if-then law points to the fact that chance or contingency is involved in the occurrence of any *if*. When such occurrence is initiated, by a human being or by a nonhuman force, certain specific consequences will necessarily follow. But Nature does not decree when and how any particular causal law will come into effect. As Professor Sterling P. Lamprecht states in his brilliant book *Nature and History:* "Necessity and contingency, so far from being unconnected ideas to be taken, one wholesale and the other retail, are supplementary ideas which belong together in the analysis of every separate event."

Contingency occurs when two independently initiated event-streams, with no common cause behind them, meet at a definite point in space and time. We must say that the more than four hundred persons killed by lightning annually in the United States are victims of chance in the form of very bad luck. To analyze an instance of contingency in more detail, let us look at the collision in midair over Chesapeake Bay on November 23, 1962, between a United Airlines Viscount and two whistling swans weighing some eight pounds each. When the bodies of the birds penetrated the tail mechanism of the plane, the pilot lost control and the Viscount plunged to earth. All seventeen aboard were killed.

It is my claim that no matter how far back into the past we are able to trace the event-stream represented by the Viscount and the event-stream represented by the swans, we shall find no relevant common cause that started both causal series on their respective ways so that they intersected on that November day. This was the first airplane accident involving whistling swans in the records of the Federal Aviation Agency.

If contingency really does exist as an ultimate and pervasive trait of the universe, then the thesis of universal necessity cannot be logically upheld and the hard-core determinist is proved wrong. His position is that the great cosmic Juggernaut rolls on inexorably and that each event and thing of the present down to its last detail, including his own argument and my answer, has been predetermined since the beginning of time. The existence of contingency undermines that position and opens the door for freedom of choice, without guaranteeing that it will come into being.

For only thinking creatures such as humans have freedom of choice. They possess this capacity because they usually do not need to react immediately to a challenge or a problem in a speedy stimulus-response manner. They are able instead to stand aside temporarily from the flux of events and to delay a decision while they reason concerning the advantages or disadvantages of the different alternatives that may be followed. It is well to remember that the word "intelligence" originates in the Latin *inter* (between) and *legere* (to choose). "Choosing" means making up one's mind.

In the intellectual process that leads to a decision, the individual ordinarily employs general concepts or "universals," as they are called in philosophy. As Professor Charles Hartshorne puts it, "our very power to form general conceptions (in a sense in which these are beyond the reach of other animals) is the same as our not being determined by irresistible impulse, habit or antecedent character, to but one mode of acting in a given case. . . . Freedom in the indeterministic sense is thus inherent in rational understanding as such, understanding through universals."

Suppose that you are living in a fairly large city and that you want to go with your wife on a Saturday night to a good motion picture. Going to the movies is, then, your general idea, and under it can be subsumed the various possibilities, the particular instances, listed in the leading newspaper or some magazine like New York's *Cue*. You talk the plan over carefully with your wife and finally select five pictures that you both agree would be worth seeing. Then you check on the time when each movie begins and how long it will take to get to each theater. Finally, you make your choice and take a bus to the theater in question.

I insist that a complex thought process such as I have just described is not mere play-acting for setting up an evening's entertainment that was predetermined prior even to one's general desire to see a movie. On the contrary, such a weighing of pros and cons is a serious exercise in deliberation that in itself all but implies freedom of choice. The determinist argument that even human thinking and its results are all decided in advance turns thought into an incomprehensible and superfluous appendage of Homo sapiens.

That argument also robs the concept of potentiality of its fundamental meaning. For "potentiality" means the presence of *plural* possibilities in Nature and in the lives of human beings. If universal and absolute determinism rules the world, then there is always and everywhere only one potentiality, namely, the potentiality of that which actually occurs. This doctrine runs counter to logic, common sense and human experience.

A potent reason for the widespread acceptance of the determinist thesis is a rather common misunderstanding of the operation of cause and effect. Many individuals look upon the present as merely the effect of preceding causes and forget that the present in its multitudinous forms is itself an active cause. It is the spearhead of all activity, the great forward thrust of universal being. In truth, the past, which is dead and gone, does not create the present; it is the present which creates the past. For the present alone exists, and the past has efficacy only as embodied in the substance or structure of some present event or object. As the dynamic present forges ahead, it leaves its past behind it, making a trail as it were, as a skier gliding downhill through the snow, or a boat producing a foamy wake.

Human beings, functioning as causes themselves, constitute the surging crest of an ongoing and unending wave of the present. And now we return to the theme of contingency. When man-as-cause acts upon some subject matter external to himself, there occurs, unless a regular pattern has been previously established, a conjunction between two separately initiated event-streams. This is why freedom of choice is inextricably linked with contingency. When I decide one morning to drive from New York City to Vermont for a weekend of skiing, I am the immediate cause-stimulus for the event-stream that is myself intersecting with the event-stream represented by my automobile.

In that situation true freedom of choice is possible for me owing to the open world of contingency, as compared with the closed world of omnipotent determinism. So it is that a free choice becomes a free cause. The human individual, a thinking, initiating, choosing agent, can be and frequently is the free cause of his actions. This knowledge, I believe, helps to build up the morale of a man and stimulates him to greater creativity. It also gives deeper meaning to human ethics, for awareness of freedom of choice brings home to every individual that he must take full responsibility for his actions.

Now at the end of my analysis I raise an issue that is usually mentioned at the start of discussions on freedom of choice: the very strong intuition native to most human beings that they are not slaves of fate, but are free to make the choices they do. This feeling is not to be considered conclusive, but only as a hint or hypothesis. It must be checked and double-checked against the available evidence. When this is done, I am convinced that the intuition of free choice emerges as an important truth buttressed by reason.

To summarize, we find eight main points in support of the case for freedom of choice. First, the central issue is not that of freedom *versus* determinism, since human beings constantly utilize the if-then deterministic laws of nature. Second, there is no absolute free choice, since it always functions within limits. Third, the existence of chance or contingency as an ultimate trait of Nature negates the thesis of universal determinism or necessity. Fourth, human thinking continually goes on in terms of general conceptions or universals under which many different particulars or potentialities may be considered; and the reality of the potentialities shows that no one line of action has been foreordained. Fifth, to take seriously the meaning of potentiality as signifying plural possibilities in itself controverts the determinist position. Sixth, the fact that only the present exists and that it creates the past make impossible the determining of present and future by the past. Seventh, freedom of choice encourages ethical behavior. And, eighth, most human beings possess a powerful intuition of free choice.

I must add a final observation. Philosopher William James was right when he said that free choice is a melioristic doctrine which "holds up improvement as at least possible; whereas determinism assures us that our whole notion of possibility is born of human ignorance, and that necessity and impossibility between them rule the destinies of the world." In other words, a person who believes in free choice and the natural fulfillment of basic human potentialities is likely to take a more optimistic view of the future than the hard-core determinist.

Humanism and Free Choice

Naturalistic Humanism, like all other philosophies, finds great difficulty in resolving the age-long issue of human freedom of choice versus determinism. I am referring to the question of whether a man, when he makes a definite decision between two or more significant alternatives, is free to do so at the moment of choosing or whether he is completely determined in his choice by his heredity, environment, economic circumstances, education, and indeed his whole history as an individual. While a person's choices are always conditioned by these factors and always limited in scope by the objective situation he faces, I hold that he does possess true freedom as I have defined it. Obviously, however, there is sharp disagreement among Humanists concerning this problem.

I use the phrase "freedom of choice" because the traditional term "free will" has become so closely associated with theological disputes and because in any case I doubt that a human being has a faculty that can be properly identified as "the will." In the West, Christian theologians and philosophers who have defended the existence of freedom of choice have in general relied upon a dualistic psychology in which the mind, soul, and "will," operating in and from a supernatural realm, can intervene in the neutral, this-earthly functioning of cause and effect. As a Humanist, I cannot utilize this convenient supernaturalist device, because I believe that mind and personality are activities of the body and are therefore inseparably connected with it in an altogether this-worldly union.

Our first task in this discussion is to examine the doctrine that absolute determinism prevails throughout the universe as a whole. If it does, then the great cosmic Juggernaut inexorably rolls on and all human actions, decisions and thoughts were totally predetermined five billion years ago just like all other earthly events. I stand with Aristotle, Epicurus, William

James and John Dewey in opposing the idea of a universal determinism and in insisting that Nature is everywhere permeated by objective chance, by contingent happenings that are by no means pre-determined by any past configuration of events. There are separate cause-effect streams in which strict determinism rules, but the intersection, the meeting of two or more independently initiated event-series is often a matter of pure chance. Behind such meetings there is no common, relevant cause to bind them together in the framework of determinism. Necessity (determinism, mechanism) and contingency (chance, tychism) are both fundamental traits of Nature, and neither can ever swallow up the other; in fact, they are polar categories that supplement each other as complementary counterparts.

Contingency is entirely consistent with the operations of science. For every scientific law takes the form of an if-then relation. *If* the temperature drops to 32 degrees Fahrenheit or below, *then* exposed water will freeze. *If* you heat water to 212° F, *then* you will be able to boil food for a good meal. But in neither case has Nature issued a command that at some particular point in time and space the *if* in the question will take place. The occurrence of a specific *if* is frequently due to chance or to human decision. Man's utilization of the limited *determinism* and predictability signified by scientific laws has been an enormous factor in his progress.

Professor Sterling P. Lamprecht clarifies the situation further: "Contingency is often regarded as an alternative to mechanism. In fact it is a correlative aspect of Nature's ways. In our world we find that forces, once initiated, work out to their inevitable consequences. But the initiation of forces is not itself decreed. The laws of Nature are statements of the mechanical phase of Nature. They state the uniformities of correlation and sequence which events manifest. The laws of Nature are not, however, dictates that compel procedure—they are not statutes or prescriptive enactments. The presence of contingency is not evident at a glance because it is not effectively exploited by inanimate agents. Inanimate agents react to the actual stimulus of the moment; they react, it may be said, to the superficial. Intelligent agents react to more than the actual stimulus; they react to the potentialities of the actual. And these potentialities are always plural . . . The alternative possibilities were present in Nature from the start even though they received no notable exploitation until intelligent creatures came to pass."

The plural potentialities of existence are of immense advantage to human beings and constantly make available new realms for them to conquer. But universal determinism drastically curtails our powers of achievement by limiting the play of potentiality to one potentiality, namely, the possibility of whatever actually happens. Thus all-embracing cosmic necessity connotes that through all time all things—atoms, rivers, life, men, planets, stars and galaxies—have had and will have only one possible line of development. And this theory as applied to human activity implies that when Shakespeare wrote his many plays and sonnets, his every line, word and punctuation mark had long before been pre-ordained in the whirling convulsions that marked the birth of the solar system.

Contingency, the "surgent spontaneity" (Professor Horace M. Kallen's phrase) that goes with it, and plural potentialities all help to open the way for human freedom of choice without guaranteeing it. In addition, we find another important aspect of Nature that enters into the picture.

In John Dewey's words, "Preferential action in the sense of behavior is a universal trait of all things, atoms and molecules as well as plants, animals, and man . . . We may say that a stone has its preferential selections set by a relatively fixed, a rigidly set, structure and that no anticipation of the results of acting one way or another enter into the matter. The reverse is true of human action. Insofar as a variable life-history and intelligent insight and foresight enters into it, choice signifies a capacity for deliberately changing preferences . . . The fact that all things show bias, preference or selectivity of reaction, while not itself freedom, is an indispensable condition of any human freedom."

Dewey's mention of intelligent foresight points to the fact that freedom of choice is inextricably bound up with man's capacity for thought. As stated earlier, the word *intelligence* originates from the Latin *inter* (between) and *legere* (to choose). Choosing means making up one's mind. The enterprise of thinking enables us to stand aside temporarily from the flux of existence, and to reflect about the various solutions possible for a problem and the probable consequences of such solutions. This delayed reaction sets the stage for a free and intelligent choice, and contrasts with immediate animal reaction to a situation in terms of reflex, instinctive, or habitual behavior.

In the intellectual process that leads to a decision, the individual almost always uses general concepts. According to Professor Charles Hartshorne, "our very power to form general conceptions (in a sense in which these are beyond the reach of other animals) is the same as our being not determined by irresistible impulse, habit, or antecedent character, to but one mode of acting in a given case. The openness of alternatives, the flexibility, of our response is the behavioristic aspect of our knowledge of the universal as that which can be indifferently instanced by this particular or by that. Such instancing, by its very meaning, must have wide ranges of freedom. Freedom in the indeterministic sense is thus inherent in rational understanding as such, understanding through universals."

Suppose that I wish to spend a month's vacation in travel. "Travel," then, is my general conception, and almost innumerable possibilities can be subsumed under it. I might go to Europe, to the Far East, to the Rocky Mountain area of the United States, or a hundred other places. My trip of course is limited by the amount of money I can spend for it. To make more explicit Professor Hartshorne's meaning, my ability to think of the general idea of "travel," to explore mentally many different alternative plans and finally pick out one to carry through—all this is not mere play-acting for the selection of an itinerary that was pre-determined prior even to my thought of traveling. It is a serious exercise in deliberation that in itself implies freedom of choice.

The determinists claim that the different solutions we envisage for a problem and the reasoning we perform regarding them are completely determined by past cause-effect sequences in our brain. In this philosophy, the greatest degree of freedom one can have is the capacity to act according to one's true character; to be altogether one's self and not subject to external coercion. As Professor Gardner Williams puts it, "Preference plus power contain the essence of freedom."

I am convinced that the determinists misunderstand the operation of cause and effect, conceiving the present as merely the effect of preceding causes and neglecting the fact that the present itself is an active cause and in truth the only cause. For the past as past has no efficacy; it is dead and gone. The present, including thinking, choosing, productive human individuals, is always the ongoing spearhead of activity in the world. All causation takes place in the instantaneous *now* and creates its own past, as a steamship leaves a trail of smoke behind it. There is indeed a cause for each human choice; it is the man himself choosing at the split-second moment of final decision. *You*, an active initiating agent working upon whatever subject matter is involved in the situation—*you* are the free cause of your own actions.

The comments of Professor Douglas Clyde Macintosh are much to the point: "In addition to whatever partially predetermining factors there may be, may not the conscious, purposing self of the moment of decision, of choice and action, be, within whatever limits, a creatively determining factor in the voluntary deed? Why should we suppose that it must be the character and thought of the self immediately preceding the action which is operative in it, rather than the strictly contemporaneous character and thought? If character changes at all—and it certainly does—why may it not change to some extent *in the decision,* and not simply before it or after it? May not partial self-transcendence be of the very nature of free decision, at least in every instance of momentous deliberate decision?"

There are many other points which I should like to discuss in this paper, but which considerations of space prevent me from doing. For example, there is the clear intuition every normal person experiences that he or she is a free agent at the moment of conscious choice, an intuition that is most important for the sense of moral responsibility. Common sense gives this deep inner feeling of freedom great weight.

Then we have significant philosophic, religious, and social implications stemming from the reality of freedom of choice. If my position is correct, we must discard as untrue all systems of religion and philosophy that are basically deterministic or fatalistic. Also erroneous are those theories of history, Marxist or otherwise, that are based on economic determinism or assert that some particular outcome for society is inevitable. For if individuals are genuinely free in the way I have indicated, it follows that groups, communities, nations, and civilizations—all of which are composed of human individuals—likewise in the large possess freedom of choice.

Free Choice and Responsibility

It is my thesis that a man who is convinced he possesses freedom of choice or free will has a greater sense of responsibility than a person who thinks that total determinism rules the universe and human life. Determinism in the classic sense means that the flow of history, including all human choices and actions, is completely predetermined from the beginning of time. He who believes that "whatever is, was to be" can try to escape moral responsibility for wrongdoing by claiming that he was compelled to act as he did because it was predestined by the iron laws of cause and effect.

But if free choice truly exists at the moment of choosing, men clearly have full moral responsibility in deciding between two or more genuine alternatives, and the deterministic alibi has no weight. The heart of our discussion, then, lies in the question of whether free choice or universal determinism represents the truth. I shall try to summarize briefly the main reasons that point to the existence of free will.

First, there is the immediate, powerful common-sense intuition shared by virtually all human beings that freedom of choice is real. This intuition seems as strong to me as the sensation of pleasure or pain; and the attempt of the determinists to explain the intuition away is as artificial as the Christian Scientist claim that pain is not real. The intuition of free choice does not, of course, in itself prove that such freedom exists, but that intuition is so strong that the burden of proof is on the determinists to show that it is based on an illusion.

Second, we can defuse the determinist argument by admitting and indeed insisting that a great deal of determinism exists in the world. Determinism in the form of if-then causal laws governs much of the human body's functioning and much of the universe as a whole. We can be glad that the autonomic system of breathing, digestion, circulation of the blood, and beating of the heart operate deterministically—until they get out of order. Determinism *versus* free choice is a false issue; what we always have is *relative* determinism and *relative* free choice. Free will is ever limited by the past and by the vast range of if-then laws. At the same time human beings utilize free choice to take advantage of those deterministic laws embodied in science and man-made machines. Most of us drive cars, but it is we and not the autos that decide when and where they are to go. Determinism wisely used and controlled—which is by no means always the case—can make us freer and happier.

Third, determinism is a relative thing not only because human free choice exists, but also because contingency or chance is an ultimate trait of the cosmos. Contingency is best seen in the intersection of mutually independent event-streams between which there was no previous causal connection. My favorite example here is the collision of the steamship *Titanic* with an iceberg off Newfoundland in the middle of the night on April 14, 1912. It was a terrible accident, with more than 1,500 persons lost. The drifting of the iceberg down from the north and the steaming of the *Titanic* west from England clearly represented two causal streams independent of each other.

Even if a team of scientific experts had been able, *per impossible*, to track back the two causal streams and ascertain that the catastrophe had been predestined from the moment the steamship left Southampton, that would not upset my thesis. For the space-time relation of the iceberg and the *Titanic*, as the ship started on its voyage, would have been itself a matter of contingency, since there was no relevant cause to account for that precise relation.

The pervasive presence of contingency in the world is also proved by the fact that all natural laws, as I have observed, take the form of if-then sequences or relations. The *if* factor is obviously conditional and demonstrates the continual co-existence of contingency with determinism. The actuality of contingency negates the idea of total and all-inclusive necessity operating throughout the universe. As regards human choice, contingency ensures that at the outset the alternatives one faces are indeterminate in relation to the act of choosing, which proceeds to make one of them determinate.

My fourth point is that the accepted meaning of potentiality, namely, that every object and event in the cosmos possesses plural possibilities of behavior, interaction and development, knocks out the determinist thesis. From the determinist viewpoint multiple potentialities are an illusion. If you want to take a vacation trip next summer, you will no doubt think over a number of possibilities before you make a final decision. Determinism logically implies that such deliberation is mere play-acting, because you were destined all the time to choose the trip you did choose. When we relate the causal pattern to potentiality, we find that causation as mediated through free choice can have its appropriate effect in the actualization of any one of various possibilities.

Fifth, the normal processes of human thought are tied in with potentiality as I have just described it and likewise tend to show that freedom of choice is real. Thinking constantly involves general conceptions, universals, or abstractions under which are classified many varying particulars. In the case that I discussed under my fourth point, "vacation travel" was the general conception and the different places that might be visited were the particulars, the alternatives, the potentialities, among which one could freely choose. Unless there is free choice, the function of human thought in solving these problems becomes superfluous and a mask of make-believe.

Sixth, it is clarifying for the problem of free choice to realize that only the present exists and that it is always some present activity that builds up the past, as a skier weaves a trail behind him in the snow as he weaves down a hill. Everything that exists—the whole vast aggregate of inanimate matter, the swarming profusion of earthly life, man in his every aspect—exists only as an event or events taking place at this instant moment which is now. The past is dead and gone; it is efficacious only as it is embodied in present structures and activities.

The activity of former presents establishes the foundations upon which the immediate present operates. What happened in the past creates both limitations and potentialities, always conditioning the present. But conditioning in this sense is not the same as determining; and each day sweeps onward under its own momentum, actualizing fresh patterns of existence, maintaining other patterns and destroying still others. Thus a man choosing and acting in the present is not wholly controlled by the past, but is part of the unending forward surge of cosmic power. He is an active, initiating agent, riding the wave of the present, as it were, and deliberating among open alternatives to reach decisions regarding the many different phases of his life.

My seventh point is that the doctrine of universal and eternal determinism is seen to be self-refuting when we work out its full implications in the cases of *reductio ad absurdum* implied. If our choices and actions today were all predestined yesterday, then they were equally predestined yesteryear, at the day of our birth and at the birth of our solar system and earth some five billion years ago. To take another instance, for determinism the so-called "irresistible impulse" that the law recognizes in assessing crimes by the insane must hold with equal force for the actions of the sane and virtuous. In the determinist philosophy the good man has an irresistible impulse to tell the truth, to be kind to animals, and to expose the graft in City Hall.

Eighth, in the novel dialect of determinism many words lose their normal meaning. I refer to such words as *refraining, forbearance, self-restraint*, and *regret*. If determinism turns out to be true, we shall have to scrap a great deal in existing dictionaries and do a vast amount of redefining. What meaning, for example, is to be assigned to *forbearance* when it is determined in advance that you are going to refuse that second Martini cocktail? You can truly forbear only when you refrain from doing something that it is possible for you to do. But under the determinist dispensation it is not possible for you to accept the second cocktail because fate has already dictated your "No." I am not saying that Nature necessarily conforms to our linguistic usages, but human language habits that have evolved over aeons of time cannot be neglected in the analysis of free choice and determinism.

Finally, I do not think that the term *moral responsibility* can retain its traditional meaning unless freedom of choice exists. From the viewpoint of ethics, law and criminal law, it is difficult to understand how a consistent determinist would have a sufficient sense of personal responsibility for the development of decent ethical standards. But the question remains whether there have ever been or can be any consistent determinists or whether free choice runs so deep in human nature as an innate characteristic that, as Jean-Paul Sartre suggests, "We are not free to cease being free."

Self-Determinism and Freedom of Choice

Professor Frederick Ferré of Dickinson College has written such an illuminating essay on the issue of free choice and determinism that I think it warrants special comment. Ferré ascribes to human beings the power of self-determinism, but it seems to me that his concept is essentially what I have elsewhere called freedom of choice or free will.*

Ferré defines philosophical determinism as "the view that all events are uniquely and regularly assured, in principle, by prior events—the earlier events standing as sufficient conditions for the later ones." Recognizing that a large proportion of human choices and actions are governed by prior cause-effect determinants, he suggests that in some human happenings "the sufficient condition is supplied by the conscious agent himself and that his exercise of this determination is not simply fixed by prior events." In such situations, a human being can make determinations, "not within a regress of caused causes but as an agent: a creative initiator of events within a limited and evanescent nexus of open possibilities."

Professor Ferré then proceeds to the decisive point in his argument: ". . . under these conditions, the person, not prior determining factors, would be the 'end of the line' for inquiries into the causes of consequent behaviors. Without such a stopping place, every event would be entitled to 'pass the buck' to its predecessors *ad infinitum*; self-determination provides a basis for saying (sometimes) 'the buck stops here,' and in this sense establishes,

---

**This review of "Self-Determinism"* (American Philosophy Quarterly, *July 1973) was published in* The Humanist, *May/June 1974.*

in a way impossible either for philosophical determinism or for simple indeterminism, the foundations of human responsibility."

When Ferré says that "every event would be entitled to 'pass the buck' to its predecessors *ad infinitum*," he is referring to the fact that if universal determinism were true, then our choices and actions of today were predestined not only yesterday, but a year ago, one hundred years ago and indeed from the moment the earth came into existence. Self-determinism makes this infinite regress irrational and irrelevant and at the same time undermines the thesis that all of a person's faults and mistakes can be ascribed to antecedent causes, such as the genes handed down to him by his parents, grandparents or great-grandparents. Thus, Ferré's concept of self-determinism knocks out the use of the theory of overall determinism as the great alibi for human weakness and misconduct.

Of course, as Ferré makes clear, cause-effect sequences in the long process of evolution have created living forms upon this earth, including human beings. But once a complex organism like man, with his unique power of thought, has been caused, there emerges the ability under some circumstances for that organism to break free from the strict control of prior causes and to exercise self-determination. Man can make choices among genuine alternatives and put them into effect through the conscious control of the organism's relevant structures and potencies. Such self-determinism is equivalent, in my opinion, to what is usually meant by freedom of choice.

A Review of B. F. Skinner's *Beyond Freedom and Dignity*

In his controversial book *Beyond Freedom and Dignity* (1941) Professor Emeritus B. F. Skinner of Harvard makes at the outset the enormous assumption that absolute determinism rules throughout the universe, the earth and human life. He goes on from there to outline how individuals and society would function on a purely deterministic basis. The author does not make the slightest effort to come to grips with the underlying question of freedom of choice and determinism, one of the most hotly and widely debated issues in history and at the present time.

It is Professor Skinner's thesis that every action, every thought, every emotion of every human being is completely determined by his genetic inheritance and the external environment. The logic of this position is that every sentence, word and punctuation mark in Skinner's own book were preordained in strict cause-effect sequence not only yesteryear, but at the time of the American Revolution and some five billion years ago when our planetary system was probably born. This is a *reductio ad absurdum* Skinner can't escape.

As the argument proceeds in *Beyond Freedom and Dignity*, the author hardly mentions the genetic factors and places overwhelming emphasis on how the outside environment determines and controls what men and women do. "A scientific analysis of behavior," states Skinner, "dispossesses autonomous man and turns the control he has been said to exert over to the environment" (p. 205); "a scientific analysis shifts the credit as well as the blame to the environment" (p. 21); "a scientific analysis shifts both the responsibility and the achievement to the environment" (p. 25); "abstract thinking is the product of a particular kind of environment, not of a cognitive faculty" (p. 189).

These statements by Skinner are one-sided and overlook the fact that the human individual and the external environment are always *interacting*. He talks as if man were an entirely passive creature, reacting automatically to outside pressures, whereas man is an active, initiating, and forceful being who often controls or alters the environment to a considerable extent. This point does not in itself disprove determinism, but it shows that Skinner has not really thought through the problems he discusses.

My quotations from *Beyond Freedom and Dignity* underline Skinner's repeated insistence that we ought not to praise persons for their achievements or blame them for wrongdoing, since all of their actions were predestined before they were born. According to Skinner nobody is responsible for what he does or does not do; the environment bears *all* the responsibility. Of course the environment bears much of the responsibility, but the implication of Skinner's position is that we ought not to condemn the war criminals in Washington who have been guilty of waging a cruel and immoral war of aggression against Vietnam that has included the wholesale shooting of peasants and terror bombings of civilian centers.

Skinner constantly makes the assertion that "scientific analysis" and science support his position that free choice does not exist and total determinism does. But as Professor Noam Chomsky conclusively demonstrated in *The New York Review of Books* (December 20, 1971), Skinner's "science" is of a most questionable variety. And Skinner himself bewails the fact (p. 19) that "almost all" the specialists in political science, law, economics, anthropology, sociology, psychotherapy, education, child care, and linguistics still believe in "autonomous man" (the author's phrase for a human being having free choice or free will). Skinner, then, refutes his own claim that science in general sustains his thesis.

In Skinner's deterministic Utopia the efficacy of the far-reaching controls he would establish depends on what he describes as "the predictability of human nature." Indeed, that alleged predictability is a major premise in his philosophy of determinism. Here, again, I must challenge him. The key organ in human choice is the thinking brain, which possesses 10^{11} (100 billion) neurons or nerve cells and 10^{14} synapses. A few minutes of intense thought may involve intricate interneuronic connections all but infinite in number. The sheer complexity of human thought—not to mention its internal privacy—must always prevent an outside observer from making a 100 percent prediction as to what an individual is going to think or choose. This complexity renders it impossible to prove that any human being is completely subject to determinism. And perhaps in the complexity of the brain with its cerebral cortex—through vast quantity giving rise to a new quality— lies the secret of free choice in humans.

Skinner keeps implying that the theory of "autonomous man" bestows on the individual almost absolute freedom of choice. This is a caricature concocted by the author to make his own theories seem more plausible. Free choice is always *relative*, and limited by one's genetic endowment, upbringing, education, knowledge, economic situation, and the environment in general. Human choice, then, is conditioned, but not determined, by a number of factors. An acceptable theory of free choice does not, as Skinner implies, rule out determinism (or necessity) in the world, but finds that determinism, as exemplified, for instance, in the if-then laws of science, coexists with chance (or contingency) and human freedom. We constantly utilize the determinism embodied in natural law and in a thousand and one mechanical devices. When I drive my car, I rely on its deterministic functioning, but it is I, not the automobile, that decides where to go.

If my analysis is correct, those who wish to build a better society (and Skinner is definitely among them) can adopt many of the author's suggestions for improving human behavior, without accepting his overall determinism. For instance, he believes the "reinforcers" (his special word for "rewards" or "incentives") are more effective for educating children and reeducating criminals than punitive measures. Most educators and sociologists agree with Skinner here.

Again, Skinner strikes an enlightened note when he speaks in favor of "the intentional design of a culture." What he clearly means is the purposeful planning of a society, with "*planned* diversification, in which the importance of variety is recognized" (p. 162). Much of his discussion in this connection is consistent with socialist planning. But while socialist planning entails general directives for economic production and distribution, Skinner's "design of a culture" goes to an impossible extreme by proposing that there be detailed rules for the behavior of every last person in the community.

It is true, as some critics have suggested, that Skinner's program could be easily utilized by a fascist state, but in my opinion it could be used by *any* kind of state that decides to institute for its own purposes propaganda and brainwashing to the nth degree.

Much as I disagree with *Beyond Freedom and Dignity*, I think the book is valuable for three reasons: First, as I have pointed out, many of Skinner's ideas for the improvement of present-day society are valid;

second, the book represents an interesting and stimulating *tour de force* by pursuing to a logical extreme the social implications of hard-core determinism; and, third, this volume, which has become something of a best seller, has evoked widespread and animated discussion concerning the significant issue of free choice and determinism.